Modern Proverbs
Quotes, Maxims and Words of Wisdom for the 21st Century

Compiled and Edited
by Chris Murphy

F

FAITHFUL BOOKS
Palo Alto, California

Modern Proverbs: Quotes, Maxims and Words of Wisdom for the 21st Century

Copyright © 2013 by Chris Murphy

Scripture quotations taken from the *King James Version* of the Bible.

Published by Faithful Books, Palo Alto, California.
For more information, visit faithfulbooks.com.

10 9 8 7 6 5 4 3 2 1

ISBN 13: 978-0-61588-478-3

ISBN 10: 0-61588-478-4

TO MIREYA

who stood by me during the brightest days and darkest nights of my life.

You inspire me with

a Hope, an Example and true Words of Wisdom.

I am eternally grateful.

You are a Virtuous Woman.

CONTENTS

O

P

ACKNOWLEDGMENTS

Each of us is the product of the experiences, education and wisdom that is instilled in us through those with whom we have acquiesced. Wisdom is not the status of knowing all things any more than intelligence is a measure of accumulated knowledge. Rather, it is simply the ability of an individual to differentiate between truth and lie.

It has been said that the wisest amongst us learns from the mistakes of others instead of making all of the mistakes himself. A truly wise person learns from the past while wisely applying such knowledge judiciously in the future.

Shakespeare once said, "*What is past is prologue.*" John Locke, the English sociopolitical philosopher who directly influenced many of the founding fathers of the United States, spoke of the idea of a *Tabula Rosa* or "*clean slate*" of which we all are given by God. It is a profound thought to consider that each day that God gives us is fresh and new. History is filled with the stories of men and women who took the fresh canvas of their lives and changed the course of history.

Leonard Ravenhill, the great English revivalist, once stated, "*The greatest thing that we learn from history is that we rarely learn from history.*" We are the product of things learned from history.

Our hearts and minds are imprinted with the fingerprints of those who managed to exert influence upon our lives. The words of our parents, siblings, teachers and friends have rightfully left a lasting impact upon our lives.

We are also helped by the advice, wisdom and wit of men and women who have gone before us. While we may never have met these individuals, the impact of their wisdom is just as real and just as lasting. This collection of wisdom is a result of the impact that they and others have had upon my own life.

I also believe that this compilation would not be complete without mentioning those who have directly or indirectly influenced its creation. Specifically, I would like to acknowledge a few of the individuals who have had such a lasting impact in my life:

My parents, **Ray and Rosemary Everett**, have made a perpetual impact upon my mind and heart. My father, a retired veteran of the US Navy, instilled a sense of curiosity and logic. My mother instilled a love of reading and the arts. Together, they challenged me to use all of my God-given talents and soar to my highest potential. When I stumbled, my dad's encouragement to "get up and try it again" has echoed throughout my life.

My wife, **Mireya**, has taught me how to speak up for truth – no matter how uncomfortable it may be.

My Grammy, **Florence Everett**, was a wise Pennsylvania Dutch woman who taught me the immense wisdom that comes from carefully removing weeds from a garden.

My siblings, **Mindy, Cindy and Kellony** have reminded me of how to outthink adversity.

My in-laws, **the Ayala family**, have demonstrated that faith, hard work and perseverance can cause an immigrant family of migrant farm workers to achieve great things.

Carol and Ruby Wommack told me the things that I needed to hear when I needed to hear them. They provoked me to find beauty and possibility in every circumstance.

My college professors – many who became dear friends, such as **Carl Saltarelli, Ed Rowley, Richard Hartwig, Matthew Price, Albert Ellis, Leslie Hunter, Cecilia Aros Hunter, J.D. Phaup, Bill Alnor, Mario Carranza** and **Thomas Hays** – taught me to engage myself in the search for truth. These wise teachers demonstrated the need to properly consider and scrutinize the past in order to correctly understand the present and future.

And finally…

Rick and JoNell Shaw have provided more wisdom than I can possibly detail. Rick has demonstrated that God truly loves a wise and cheerful giver. JoNell has provided the spiritual and gentle advice that could only come from a true friend of God. Words cannot suffice to explain what their words and example have meant to me. I am comforted by the knowledge that Heaven will not forget their kindness.

Chris Murphy
Palo Alto, California

INTRODUCTION

"Where no counsel is, the people fall: but in the multitude of counselors there is safety."

- Proverbs 11:14 (KJV)

Wisdom is one of the scarcest commodities on Earth. The Biblical book of Proverbs decries of its value exceeding that of gold or precious jewels. This concept has never been quite so true as it is today. We live in a world that is saturated by the media. We receive advice from the media at an alarming rate. Television, movies, radio, music, books, magazines, newspapers – and now the internet – fill our thoughts with counsel of questionable value. It is often difficult to sort through this advice and find real wisdom that can help us through various situations in our lives. So where do we find such treasure?

God, of course, is the Author of true wisdom for people of faith. He then bestows such wisdom as he sees fit. Many great men and women throughout history relied upon His guidance.

It must be noted that the purpose of this book is not to financially profit from the words of others. Rather, it is an attempt to glean and share wisdom and insight from men and women who have mostly gone before us. This is not a "copy and paste" effort. This is the product of years of collecting bits of insight and compiling it into one simple yet profound collection.

The words of wisdom found within this book have been collected from many sources. For the sake of time and necessity, these quotes have been gathered together under many different subject categories. These categories themselves are listed in alphabetical order. As the situation dictates, some of these quotes are contained under more than one subject heading.

Some might be compelled to point out that some of the quotes contained within this "book of wisdom" come from individuals of questionable character and virtue. For instance, there are several quotes from historically *evil* men, such as Adolf Hitler and Joseph Stalin, contained within these pages. The inclusion of their quotes is not meant to be seen as an embrace of their character or behavior, but rather to gain wisdom by noting the source of the malevolence that they have demonstrated. This is true in the Scriptures, as we learn from Cain's question in Genesis 4:9, "*Am I my brother's keeper?*"

Within each category, the quotations are given alphabetically by author (whenever possible). For each of the quotations, I have attempted to identify the oldest or original author of each particular quote.

Understandably, there are quotes that are derived from unknown or anonymous sources. These are marked accordingly. There are also quotes that have questionable origins or attributions. Every effort has been made to verify the authenticity. In addition, a faulty attribution doesn't make a truth any less powerful. After all, would the *Mona Lisa* (or *La Gioconda*) be any less impressive if it had been painted by an unnamed starving artist in Paris instead of Leonardo da Vinci?

There are bound to be quotes from individuals who are neither famous or infamous. If you read a quote or morsel of wisdom from someone that you have little knowledge of, I encourage you to engage is further research. Learn more about who they are, what they did and what made them "tick." The Internet is a valuable tool for finding such information and, in the end, you may learn a little more about what prompted such pearls of wisdom to originate from that individual.

If you would like to contact us, please do so! We are open-minded when it comes to any suggestion or criticism. Please use the information located on the publisher's website to contact us. Readers of future editions will be glad for it.

Whenever Scripture is used, it is taken from the King James Version (AV). An index is included in the back for entries that are derived from known sources.

Finally, it is my hope that the words found within this book will be helpful in all matters of life, understanding and faith. I hope that these words will encourage, rouse, challenge and incite. More than anything else, I desire that the words found within this book might offer hope during situations where all hope seems gone. As the old proverb goes, "*There is hope…*"

A

ABILITY

"Children in whom was no blemish, but well favoured, and skilful in all wisdom, and cunning in knowledge, and understanding science, and such as had ability in them to stand in the king's palace, and whom they might teach the learning and the tongue of the Chaldeans."
- Daniel 1:4

"And unto one he gave five talents, to another two, and to another one; to every man according to his several ability; and straightway took his journey."
- Matthew 25:15

"Then the disciples, every man according to his ability, determined to send relief unto the brethren which dwelt in Judaea."
- Acts 11:29

"If any man speak, let him speak as the oracles of God; if any man minister, let him do it as of the ability which God giveth: that God in all things may be glorified through Jesus Christ, to whom be praise and dominion forever and ever. Amen."
- I Peter 4:11

"For success, attitude is equally as important as ability."
- Harry Banks

"Ability is of little account without opportunity and determination."
- Napoleon Bonaparte

"It is not my ability, but my response to God's ability, that counts."
- Corrie ten Boom

"Do not pray for easy lives; pray to be stronger men. Do not pray for tasks equal to your powers; pray for powers equal to your tasks. Then the doing of your work shall be no miracle, but you yourself shall be a miracle. Every day you shall wonder at yourself, at the richness of life which has come to you by the grace of God."
- Phillip Brooks

"If Jesus ever commanded us to do something that He was unable to equip us to accomplish, He would be a liar. And if we make our own inability a stumbling block or an excuse not to be obedient, it means that we are telling God that there is something which He has not yet taken into account."
- Oswald Chambers

"It is not enough to have a good mind; the main thing is to use it well."
- Rene Descartes

"There isn't a person anywhere who isn't capable of doing more than he thinks he can."
- Henry Ford

"Whether you believe you can do a thing or not, you're right."
- Henry Ford

"The ability to think straight, some knowledge of the past, some vision of the future, some urges to fit that service into the well-being of the community - these are the most vital things that education must try to produce."
- Virginia Gildersleeve

"Ability is what you're capable of doing. Motivation determines what you do. Attitude determines how well you do it."
- Lou Holtz

"I have not yet begun to fight!"
- John Paul Jones

"Get your texts from God - your thoughts, your words, from God... It is not great talents God blesses so much as great likeness to Jesus. A holy minister is an awful weapon in the hand of God. A word spoken by you when your conscience is clear, and your heart full of God's Spirit, is worth ten thousand words spoken in unbelief and sin.""
- Robert Murray M'Cheyne

"God is far more concerned with your availability, rather than your ability."
- Carl Mendez

"Enduring setbacks while maintaining the ability to show others the way to go forward is a true test of leadership."
- Nitin Nohria

"The height of ability in the least able consists in knowing how to submit to the good leadership of others."
- François Rochefoucauld

"To know how to hide one's ability is a great and terrible skill."
- François Rochefoucauld

"If I were given the opportunity to present a gift to the next generation, it would be the ability for each individual to learn to laugh at himself."
- Charles M. Schultz

"I consider my ability to arouse enthusiasm among men the greatest asset I possess. "
- Charles M. Schultz

"Nothing so conclusively proves a man's ability to lead others as what he does from day to day to lead himself."
- Thomas Watson

"Ability may get you to the top, but it takes character to keep you there."
-   John Wooden

"You are the only person on earth who can use your ability."
-   Zig Zigler

"Success is the maximum utilization of the ability that you have."
-   Zig Zigler

"We rate ability in men by what they finish, not by what they attempt"
-   Unknown

"We are limited, not by our abilities, but by our vision."
-   Unknown

"What lies before us and what lies behind us are tiny matters to what lies within us."
-   Unknown

"It doesn't take an *extraordinary* person - just devotion to our *extraordinary* God - to live an *extraordinary* life."
-   Unknown

"God does not call the qualified; He qualifies the called."
-   Unknown

ABORTION

"And if men struggle with each other and strike a woman with child so that she has a miscarriage, yet there is no further injury, he shall surely be fined as the woman's husband may demand of him; and he shall pay as the judges decide. But if there is any further injury, then you shall appoint as a penalty life for life." -   Exodus 21:22-23

"Yet Thou art He who didst bring me forth from the womb; Thou didst make me trust when upon my mother's breasts. Upon Thee I was cast from birth; Thou hast been my God from my mother's womb."
-   Psalms 22:9-10

"Listen to Me, O islands, And pay attention, you peoples from afar. The LORD called Me from the womb; From the body of My mother He named Me."

- Isaiah 49:1

"For he will be great in the sight of the Lord, and he will drink no wine or liquor; and he will be filled with the Holy Spirit, while yet in his mother's womb."

- Luke 1:15

"The product, abortion, is skillfully marketed and sold to the woman at the crisis time in her life. She buys the product, finds it defective and wants to return it for a refund. But, it's too late."

- Carol Everett

"Republicans are against abortion until their unmarried daughters get pregnant; Democrats are for abortion until their daughter wants one."

- Grace McGarvie

"I've noticed that everybody that is for abortion has already been born."

- Ronald Reagan

"Make no mistake, abortion-on-demand is not a right granted by the Constitution. No serious scholar, including one disposed to agree with the Court's result, has argued that the framers of the Constitution intended to create such a right."

- Ronald Reagan

"The abortionist who reassembles the arms and legs of a tiny baby to make sure all its parts have been torn from its mother's body can hardly doubt whether it is a human being."

- Ronald Reagan

"As a nation today, we have not rejected the sanctity of human life. The American people have not had an opportunity to express their view on the sanctity of human life in the unborn. I am convinced that Americans do not want to play God with the value of human life. It is not for us to decide who is worthy to live and who is not. Even the Supreme Court's opinion in Roe v. Wade did not explicitly reject the traditional American idea of intrinsic worth and value in all human life; it simply dodged this issue."

- Ronald Reagan

"Doctors today know that unborn children can feel a touch within the womb and that they respond to pain."

- Ronald Reagan

"Abortion is inherently different from other medical procedures because no other procedure involves the purposeful termination of a potential life."

- Potter Stewart

"If we accept that a mother can kill even her own child, how can we tell other people to not kill each other? Any country that accepts abortion is not teaching its people to love, but to use any violence to get what they want."

- Mother Teresa

"Only half the patients who go into an abortion clinic come out alive."

- Unknown

"If it isn't a baby, then you aren't pregnant, so what are you aborting?"

- Unknown

ABUSE

"The greater the power, the more dangerous the abuse."

- Edmund Burke

"An injury is much sooner forgotten than an insult."

- Lord Chesterfield

"Abuse is the weapon of the vulgar."

- Samuel Griswold Goodrich

"The million little things that drop into your hands, The small opportunities each day brings, He leaves us free to use or abuse, And goes unchanging along His silent way."
- Helen Keller

"If the cruelties of slavery could not stop us, the opposition we now surely fail. . . . Because the goal of America is freedom, abused and scorned tho' we may be, our destiny is tied up with America's destiny."
- Martin Luther King, Jr.

"Liberty may be endangered by the abuse of liberty, but also by the abuse of power."
- James Madison

"More than 90 percent of all the prisoners in our American prisons have been abused as children."
- John Powell

ACCOMPLISMENT

"Because your own strength is unequal to the task, do not assume that it is beyond the powers of man; but if anything is within the powers and province of man, believe that it is within your own compass also."
- Marcus Aurelius Antoninus

"The bad news is time flies. The good news is you're the pilot."
- Michael Althsuler

"A young person, to achieve, must first get out of his mind any notion either of the ease or rapidity of success. Nothing ever just happens in this world."
- Edward William Bok

"'I can't do it' never yet accomplished anything; 'I will try' has performed wonders."
- George P. Burnham

"Start by doing what's necessary, then what's possible, and suddenly you are doing the impossible."
- Francis of Assisi

"It is hard for an empty bag to stand upright."
- Benjamin Franklin

"The man who does things makes many mistakes, but he never makes the biggest mistake of all - doing nothing."
- Benjamin Franklin

"Success without honor is an unseasoned dish; it will satisfy your hunger, but it won't taste good."
- Joe Paterno

"Competition is a by-product of productive work, not its goal. A creative man is motivated by the desire to achieve, not by the desire to beat others."
- Ayn Rand

"The height of your accomplishments will equal the depth of your convictions."
- William Scolavino

"Respect results with the least possible effort. Never substitute effort for accomplishment. Disassociate effort and reward."
- Fred Smith

"It is by what we ourselves have done, and not by what others have done for us, that we shall be remembered in after ages."
- Francis Wayland

ACCOUNTABILITY

"Good men prefer to be accountable."
- Michael Edwards

"The individual is not accountable to society for his actions in so far as these concern the interests of no person but himself."
- John Stuart Mill

"It is not only what we do, but also what we do not do, for which we are accountable."
- Moliere

"We must reject the idea that every time a law's broken, society is guilty rather than the lawbreaker. It is time to restore the American precept that each individual is accountable for his actions."
- Ronald Reagan

"My greatest thought is my accountability to God."
- Daniel Webster

"Accountability gives birth to responsibility."
- Unknown

ACTION

"The men who have done the most for God in this world have been early on their knees. He who fritters away the early morning, its opportunity and freshness, in other pursuits than seeking God will make poor headway seeking Him the rest of the day. If God is not first in our thoughts and efforts in the morning, He will be in the last place the remainder of the day."
- E. M. Bounds

"A man full of hope will be full of action."
- Thomas Brooks

"All that is necessary for the triumph of evil is that good men do nothing."
- Edmund Burke

"By gnawing through a dyke, even a rat may drown a nation."
- Edmund Burke

"Expect great things from God, attempt great things for God."
- William Carey

"The ones who want to achieve and win…must learn to motivate themselves."
- Mike Ditka

"The minute you settle for less than you deserve, you get even less than you settled for."
- Maureen Dowd

"Prayer is the only adequate way to multiply our efforts fast enough to reap the harvest God desires."
- Wesley L. Duewel

"We must not, in trying to think about how we can make a big difference, ignore the small daily differences we can make which, over time, add up to big differences that we often cannot foresee."
- Marion Wright Edelman

"Watch how much of our speech is aimed at justifying our actions. We find it almost impossible to act and allow the act to speak for it. No, we must explain it, justify it, and demonstrate the righteousness of it. Why do we feel this compulsion to set the record straight? Because of pride and fear, because our reputations are at stake."
- Richard Foster

"Well done is better than well said."
- Benjamin Franklin

"The man who does things makes many mistakes, but he never makes the biggest mistake of all - doing nothing."
- Benjamin Franklin

"He that lives upon hope will die fasting."
- Benjamin Franklin

"Entrance to Heaven is all about faith and grace. Rewards in Heaven are all about our works on earth."
- Josh Hunt

"There are risks and costs to a program of action, but they are far less than the long-range risks and costs of comfortable inaction."
- John F. Kennedy

"The only people who achieve much are those who want knowledge so badly that they seek it while the conditions are still favorable. For them, unfavorable conditions never come."
- C.S. Lewis

"We are saved by faith alone. However, faith that saves is never alone...it is always accompanied by works."
- Martin Luther

"Let me burn out for God."
- Henry Martyn

"Action without prayer is arrogance, prayer without action is hypocrisy."
- Jose Zayas

ADULTERY – See IMMORALITY

ADVERSITY

"If you're going through hell, don't stop! Keep going!"
- Winston Churchill

"Everyone has his own Atlantics to fly. Whatever you want very much to do, against the opposition of tradition, neighborhood opinion, and so-called 'common sense' – that is an Atlantic."
- Amelia Earhart

"Whether you think you can do a thing or not, you're right."
- Henry Ford

"The ultimate measure of a man is not where he stands in moments of comfort and convenience, but where he stands at times of challenge and controversy."

- Martin Luther King, Jr.

"Your enemy makes you wise."

- Italian saying

"There is no prosperity without adversity."

- Welsh proverb

"Never let adversity get you down – except onto your knees."

- Unknown

"Adversity doesn't build character; it reveals it."

- Unknown

ADVICE

"He that gives good advice, builds with one hand; he that gives good counsel and example, builds with both; but he that gives good admonition and bad example, builds with one hand and pulls down with the other."

- Sir Francis Bacon

"A leader must have the courage to act against an expert's advice."

- James Callaghan

"An ounce of prevention is worth a pound of cure."

- Benjamin Franklin

"Practical advice for life:

1. Never put off until tomorrow what you can do today.
2. Never trouble another for what you can do yourself.
3. Never spend your money before you have it.
4. Never buy what you do not want, because it is cheap; it will be dear to you.
5. Pride costs us more than hunger, thirst, and cold.

6. We never repent of having eaten too little.
7. Nothing is troublesome that we do willingly.
8. How much pain have cost us the evils which never have happened.
9. Take things always by their smooth handle.
10. When angry, count ten, before you speak; if very angry, an hundred."

      -    Thomas Jefferson

"We should be careful and discriminating in all the advice we give. We should be especially careful in giving advice that we would not think of following ourselves. Most of all, we ought to avoid giving counsel which we don't follow when it damages those who take us at our word."

      -    Adlai Stevenson

"I have found the best way to give advice to your children is to find out what they want and then advise them to do it."

      -    Harry Truman

"A word to the wise isn't necessary. It's the foolish ones who need the advice."

      -    Unknown

AGE

"Remember now thy Creator in the days of thy youth, while the evil days come not, nor the years draw nigh, when thou shalt say, I have no pleasure in them."

      -    Ecclesiastes 12:1

"He who would pass his declining years with honor and comfort, should, when young, consider that he may one day become old, and remember when he is old, that he has once been young."

      -    Joseph Addison

"Aging is mandatory. Maturity is optional."

      -    Chris Antonak

"Come, grow old with me – the best is yet to be!"
- Robert Browning

"If you're not a liberal at 20, you have no heart. If you're not a conservative by 40, you have no brain".
- Winston Churchill

"Cheerfulness and contentment are great beautifiers and are famous preservers of youthful looks."
- Charles Dickens

"It was the best of times, it was the worst of times; it was the age of wisdom, it was the age of foolishness; it was the epoch of belief, it was the epoch of incredulity; it was the season of Light, it was the season of Darkness; it was the spring of hope, it was the winter of despair; we had everything before us, we had nothing before us; we were all going directly to Heaven, we were all going the other way."
- Charles Dickens

"Whatever you may look like, marry a man your own age -- as your beauty fades, so will his eyesight."
- Phyllis Diller

"Anyone who stops learning is old, whether at 20 or 80. Anyone who keeps learning stays young. The greatest thing in life is to keep your mind young."
- Henry Ford

"There are three great friends: an old wife, an old dog, and ready money."
- Benjamin Franklin

"Life's tragedy is that we get old to soon and wise too late."
- Benjamin Franklin

"Beware of the young doctor and the old barber."
- Benjamin Franklin

"A diplomat is a man who always remembers a woman's birthday but never remembers her age."
- Robert Frost

"Nobody can be so amusingly arrogant as a young man who has just discovered an old idea and thinks it is his own."
- Sydney Harris

"To be 70 years young is sometimes far more cheerful and hopeful than to be 40 years old."
- Oliver Wendell Holmes

"Blessed are the young for they shall inherit the national debt."
- Herbert Hoover

"I don't feel old. I don't feel anything until noon. Then it's time for my nap."
- Bob Hope

"Forty is the old age of youth; fifty is the youth of old age."
- Victor Hugo

"The surprising thing about young fools is how many survive to become old fools."
- Doug Larson

"The day a person becomes a cynic is the day he loses his youth."
- Marvin Levy

"You are as young as your faith, as old as your doubt; as young as your self-confidence, as old as your fear; as young as your hope, as old as your despair."
- Douglas MacArthur

"You don't stop laughing because you grow old; You grow old because you stop laughing."
- Michael Pritchard

"Thomas Jefferson made a comment about the Presidency and age. He said that one should not worry about one's exact chronological age in reference to his ability to perform one's task. And ever since he told me that -- I stopped worrying."

- Ronald Reagan

"I want you to know that also I will not make age an issue of this campaign. I am not going to exploit, for political purposes, my opponent's youth and inexperience."

- Ronald Reagan

"Age is an issue of mind over matter. If you don't mind, it doesn't matter."

- Mark Twain

"Wrinkles should merely indicate where smiles have been."

- Mark Twain

"By the time a man realizes that maybe his father was right, he usually has a son who thinks he's wrong."

- Charles Wadsworth

"The deepest definition of youth is life as yet untouched by tragedy."

- Alfred North Whitehead

"Do you know that Old Age may come after you with equal grace, force, and fascination?"

- Walt Whitman

"A society grows great when old men plant trees whose shade they know they shall never sit in."

- Greek Proverb

"By the time a man is wise enough to watch his step, he's too old to go anywhere."

- Irish Proverb

"Growing old is nothing more than mind over matter; It doesn't matter even if you mind."
- Unknown

"Maybe it's true that life begins at fifty. But...everything else starts to wear out, fall out, or spread out."
- Unknown

"Old age isn't so bad if you consider the alternatives."
- Cato the Elder

ALCOHOL

"Wine is a mocker, strong drink is raging: and whosoever is deceived thereby is not wise."
- Proverbs 20:1

"All crimes on earth do not destroy so many of the human race, nor alienate so much property, as drunkenness."
- Sir Francis Bacon

"A hangover is your body's way of saying, 'Don't be an idiot!'"
- Dennis Miller

"We drink to one another's health, and spoil our own."
- Jerome K. Jerome

"The smaller the drink, the clearer the head."
- William Penn

"If drinking is interfering with your work, you're probably a heavy drinker. If work is interfering with your drinking, you're probably an alcoholic."
- Will Rogers

"When the wine goes in, strange things come out."
- Johann Friedrich von Schiller

"Drunkenness is nothing but voluntary madness."
- Senaca

"It takes 8,460 bolts to assemble an automobile, and one drunk driver to scatter it all over the road."
- Unknown

"If you must drink and drive, drink coffee."
- Unknown

ALTRUISM

"Pure religion and undefiled before God and the Father is this, To visit the fatherless and widows in their affliction, and to keep himself unspotted from the world."
- James 1:27

"The only right a Christian has is the right to give up his rights."
- Oswald Chambers

"He is no fool who gives what he cannot keep to gain what he cannot lose."
- Jim Elliot

"Every man must decide whether he will walk in the light of creative altruism or in the darkness of destructive selfishness."
- Martin Luther King, Jr.

"The old law of an eye for an eye leaves everybody blind."
- Martin Luther King, Jr.

"We cannot live for ourselves alone. Our lives are connected by a thousand invisible threads, and along these sympathetic fibers, our actions run as causes and return to us as results."
- Herman Melville

"Do what you can where you are with what you have."
- Theodore Roosevelt

"I have now concentrated all my prayers into one, and that one prayer is this, that I may die to self, and live wholly to him."
-     Charles H. Spurgeon

"If you give what you do not need, it isn't giving."
-     Teresa of Calcutta

"Kind words can be short and easy to speak, but their echoes are truly endless."
-     Teresa of Calcutta

"A sure way for one to lift himself up is by helping to lift someone else."
-     Booker T. Washington

"There is no limit to the amount of good people can do if they don't care who gets the credit."
-     Unknown

AMBITION

"Many of life's failures are people who did not realize how close they were to success when they gave up."
-     Thomas Edison

"A business that makes nothing but money is a poor kind of business."
-     Henry Ford

"Twenty years from now you will be more disappointed by the things you didn't do than the ones you did. So throw off the bowlines. Sail away from the safe harbor. Catch the trade winds in your sails. Explore. Dream. Discover."
-     Mark Twain

"When there is no wind, row."
-     Portuguese proverb

AMERICA

"I always consider the settlement of America with reverence and wonder, as the opening of a grand scene and design in providence, for the illumination of the ignorant and the emancipation of the slavish part of mankind all over the earth."
- John Adams

"I just want to say this. I want to say it gently but I want to say it firmly: There is a tendency for the world to say to America, "the big problems of the world are yours, you go and sort them out," and then to worry when America wants to sort them out."
- Tony Blair

"America has never been an empire. We may be the only great power in history that had the chance, and refused – preferring greatness to power and justice to glory."
- George W. Bush

"Only Americans can hurt America."
- Dwight D. Eisenhower

"America's greatest strength, and its greatest weakness, is our belief in second chances, our belief that we can always start over, that things can be made better."
- White Evans

"I have often looked at that picture behind the president without being able to tell whether it was a rising or a setting sun. Now at length I have the happiness to know that it is indeed a rising, not a setting sun."
- Benjamin Franklin,
Upon signing the
Declaration of Independence

"We dare not forget that we are the heirs of that first revolution."
- John F. Kennedy

"America - a great social and economic experiment, noble in motive and far-reaching in purpose."
- Herbert Hoover

"America will never be destroyed from the outside. If we falter and lose our freedoms, it will be because we destroyed ourselves."
- Abraham Lincoln

"We are a nation of communities...a brilliant diversity spread like stars, like a thousand points of light in a broad and peaceful sky."
- Peggy Noonan

"America is a rebellious nation. Our whole history is treason; our blood was attained before we were born; our creeds were infidelity to the mother church; our constitution treason to our fatherland. Thank God for that rebellion!"
- Theodore Parker

"America -- it's better than Europe. That's why we left."
- Brad Stine

"Europe was created by history. America was created by philosophy."
- Margaret Thatcher

"America is great because she is good. If America ceases to be good, America will cease to be great."
- Alexander de Tocqueville

"If there is anything in my thoughts or style to commend, the credit is due to my parents for instilling in me an early love of the Scriptures. If we abide by the principles taught in the Bible, our country will go on prospering and to prosper; but if we and our posterity neglect its instructions and authority, no man can tell how sudden a catastrophe may overwhelm us and bury all our glory in profound obscurity."
- Daniel Webster

"America lives in the heart of every man everywhere who wishes to find a region where he will be free to work out his destiny as he chooses."
- Woodrow Wilson

ANGER

"He that is soon angry dealeth foolishly..."
- Proverbs 14:17

"Be ye angry, and sin not: let not the sun go down upon your wrath."
- Ephesians 4:26

"Do not teach your children never to be angry; teach them how to be angry."
- Abbott Lyman

"How much more grievous are the consequences of anger than the causes of it."
- Marcus Antoninus Aurelius

"Anger makes dull men witty, but it keeps them poor."
- Sir Francis Bacon

"Speak when you are angry and you will make the best speech you will ever regret."
- Ambrose Bierce

"The honourable gentleman should not really generate more indignation than he can conveniently contain."
- Winston Churchill

"The world is a dangerous place. Not because of the people who are evil; but because of the people who don't do anything about it."
- Albert Einstein

"Anger is never without a reason, but seldom with a good one."
- Benjamin Franklin

"People who fly into a rage always make a bad landing."
-    Will Rogers

"No one can make you feel inferior without your consent."
-    Eleanor Roosevelt

"If you kick a stone in anger, you'll hurt your own foot."
-    Korean Proverb

"For every minute you are angry, you lose sixty seconds of happiness."
-    Unknown

"If you are patient in one moment of anger, you will escape a hundred days of sorrow."
-    Chinese Proverb

"The truth shall make you free, but first it shall make you angry."
-    English Proverb

ANIMALS

"I value my garden more for being full of blackbirds than of cherries, and very frankly give them fruit for their songs."
-    Joseph Addison

"I like pigs. Dogs look up to us. Cats look down on us. Pigs treat us as equals."
-    Winston Churchill

"Animals are such agreeable friends; they ask no questions, they pass no criticisms."
-    George Eliot

"No matter how much the cats fight, there always seem to be plenty of kittens."
-    Abraham Lincoln

"I love a dog. He does nothing for political reasons."
-   Will Rogers

"Animals have these advantages over man: they never hear the clock strike, they die without any idea of death, they have no theologians to instruct them, their last moments are not disturbed by unwelcome and unpleasant ceremonies, their funerals cost them nothing, and no one starts lawsuits over their wills."
-   Voltaire

"Don't approach a goat from the front, a horse from the back, or a fool from any side."
-   Yiddish Proverb

"One reason a dog can be such a comfort when you're feeling blue is that he doesn't try to find out why."
-   Unknown

"One reason a dog is such a lovable creature is his tail wags instead of his tongue."
-   Unknown

ANXIETY

"A merry heart doeth good like a medicine: but a broken spirit drieth the bones."
-   Proverbs 17:22

"Casting all your care upon him; for he careth for you."
-   I Peter 5:7

"Therefore I say unto you, Take no thought for your life, what ye shall eat, or what ye shall drink; nor yet for your body, what ye shall put on. Is not the life more than meat, and the body than raiment? ... Which of you by taking thought can add one cubit unto his stature?   And why take ye thought for raiment? Consider the lilies of the field, how they grow; they toil not, neither do they spin: And yet I say unto you, That even

Solomon in all his glory was not arrayed like one of these. Wherefore, if God so clothe the grass of the field, which today is, and tomorrow is cast into the oven, shall he not much more clothe you, O ye of little faith? … But seek ye first the kingdom of God, and his righteousness; and all these things shall be added unto you. Take therefore no thought for the morrow: for the morrow shall take thought for the things of itself. Sufficient unto the day is the evil thereof."
-     Matthew 6:25-34

"Worrying is carrying tomorrow's load with today's strength -- carrying two days at once. It is moving into tomorrow ahead of time. Worrying doesn't empty tomorrow of its sorrow, it empties today of its strength."
-     Corrie Ten Boom

"Any concern too small to be turned into a prayer is to small to be made into a burden."
-     Corrie ten Boom

"We have a lot of anxieties, and one cancels out another very often."
-     Winston Churchill

"If you see ten troubles coming down the road, you can be sure that nine will run into the ditch before they reach you."
-     Calvin Coolidge

"If things go wrong, don't go with them."
-     Ray Everett

"How much pain they have cost us, the evils which have never happened."
-     Thomas Jefferson

"Heavy thoughts bring on physical maladies; when the soul is oppressed so is the body."
-     Martin Luther

"Worry, doubt, fear and despair are the enemies which slowly bring us down to the ground and turn us to dust before we die."

- Douglas MacArthur

"We can easily manage if we will only take, each day, the burden appointed to it. But the load will be too heavy for us if we carry yesterday's burden over again today, and then add the burden of the morrow before we are required to bear it."

- John Newton

"I am an old man and have known a great many troubles, but most of them never happened."

- Mark Twain

"Drag your thoughts away from your troubles... by the ears, by the heels, or any other way you can manage it."

- Mark Twain

"Anxiety is the rust of life, destroying its brightness and weakening its power. A childlike and abiding trust in Providence is its best preventive and remedy."

- George Washington

"You can't change the past but you can ruin a perfectly good present by worrying about the future."

- Unknown

"Don't be afraid of tomorrow -- God is already there."

- Unknown

APOLOGY

"A stiff apology is a second insult. The injured party does not want to be compensated because he has been wronged; he wants to be healed because he has been hurt."

- G. K. Chesterton

"Apology is only egotism wrong side out."

- Oliver Wendell Holmes

"True remorse is never just regret over consequence; it is regret over motive."
- Mignon McLaughlin

"The best apology against false accusers is silence and sufferance, and honest deeds set against dishonest words."
- John Milton

"The best way to have the last word is to apologize."
- American Proverb

"An apology should never be ruined by interjecting an excuse."
- Unknown

APPEARANCE

"...He hath no form nor comeliness; and when we shall see him, there is no beauty that we should desire him. He is despised and rejected of men; a man of sorrows, and acquainted with grief: and we hid as it were our faces from him; he was despised, and we esteemed him not."
- Isaiah 53:2

"But the LORD said unto Samuel, Look not on his countenance, or on the height of his stature; because I have refused him: for the LORD seeth not as man seeth; for man looketh on the outward appearance, but the LORD looketh on the heart."
- I Samuel 16:7

"Your beauty should not come from outward adornment, such as braided hair and the wearing of gold jewelry and fine clothes. Instead, it should be that of your inner self, the unfading beauty of a gentle and quiet spirit, which is of great worth in God's sight."
- I Peter 3:3-4

"Appearances can be, and are often, deceiving."
- Aesop

"Clothes and manners do not make the man; but, when he is made, they greatly improve his appearance."
- Henry Ward Beecher

"Think not I am what I appear."
- Lord Byron

"When I see a bird that walks like a duck and swims like a duck and quacks like a duck, I call that bird a duck."
- Richard Cushing

"Don't judge men's wealth or godliness by their Sunday appearance."
- Benjamin Franklin

"The Lord prefers common looking people. That is why he made so many of them."
- Abraham Lincoln

"No one is so miserable as the poor person who strives to maintain the appearance of wealth."
- Charles Spurgeon

"The world is governed more by appearance than realities so that it is fully as necessary to seem to know something as to know it."
- Daniel Webster

"Cleanliness is indeed next to godliness."
- John Wesley

"Be not deceived with the first appearance of things, for show is not substance."
- English Proverb

"Never frown, because you never know when someone is falling in love with your smile."
- Unknown

"A smile is a relatively inexpensive way to improve you looks."
- Unknown

ARGUMENTS

"But though we, or an angel from heaven, preach any other gospel unto you than that which we have preached unto you, let him be accursed. As we said before, so say I now again, if any man preach any other gospel unto you than that ye have received, let him be accursed. For do I now persuade men, or God? or do I seek to please men? For if I yet pleased men, I should not be the servant of Christ. But I certify you, brethren, that the gospel which was preached of me is not after man."
- Galatians 1:8

"Argument is meant to reveal the truth, not to create it."
- Edward de Bono

"What counts is not necessarily the size of the dog in the fight-it's the size of the fight in the dog."
- Dwight Eisenhower

"Never [enter] into dispute or argument with another. I never yet saw an instance of one of two disputants convincing the other by argument. I have seen many on their getting warm, becoming rude and shooting one another."
- Thomas Jefferson

"If you examined a hundred people who had lost their faith in Christianity, I wonder how many of them would turn out to have reasoned out of it by honest argument? Do not most people simply drift away?"
- C. S. Lewis

"When I'm getting ready to reason with a man, I spend one-third of my time thinking about myself and what I am going to say -- and two-thirds thinking about him and what he is going to say."
- Abraham Lincoln

"The people to fear are not those who disagree with you, but those who disagree with you and are too cowardly to let you know."
- Jack L. Murphy

"That God cannot lie, is no advantage to your argument, because it is no proof that priests do not."
- Thomas Paine

"An ounce of wit is worth a pound of argument."
- Sydney Smith

"Argument is the worst sort of conversation."
- Jonathan Swift

"Anyone who conducts an argument by appealing to authority is not using his intelligence; he is just using his memory."
- Leonardo da Vinci

"The more arguments you win, the fewer friends you'll have."
- English Proverb

"The only fool bigger than the person who knows it all is the person who argues with him."
- Polish Proverb

"Arguing about religion is much easier than practicing it."
- Unknown

"More homes are destroyed by fusses than by funerals or fires."
- Amish Proverb

ART

"The heavens declare the glory of God; and the firmament sheweth the works of his hands."
- Psalm 19:1

"I must study politics and war that my sons may have liberty to study mathematics and philosophy. My sons ought to study mathematics and philosophy, geography, natural history, naval architecture, navigation, commerce and agriculture in order to give their children a right to study painting, poetry, music, architecture, statuary, tapestry, and porcelain."
- John Adams

"No form of Nature is inferior to Art; for the arts merely imitate natural forms."
- Marcus Antoninus Aurelius

"Every artist dips his brush in his own soul, and paints his own nature into his pictures."
- Henry Ward Beecher

"The music that really turns me on is either running toward God or away from God. Both recognize the pivot that God is at the center of the jaunt."
- Bono

"Without tradition, art is a flock of sheep without a shepherd. Without innovation, it is a corpse."
- Winston Churchill

"As for the degenerate artists, I forbid them to force their so-called experiences upon the public. If they do see fields blue, they are deranged, and should go to an asylum. If the only pretend to see them blue, they are criminals, and should go to prison. I will purge the nation of them."
- Adolph Hitler

"The true work of art is but a shadow of the divine perfection."
- Michelangelo

"A man paints with his brains and heart and not with his hands."
- Michelangelo

"All children are artists. The problem is how to remain an artist once he grows up."
- Pablo Picasso

"Nothing is more the child of art than a garden."
- Sir Walter Scott

"As my artist's statement explains, my work is utterly incomprehensible and is therefore full of deep significance."
- Bill Watterson

"God is the Master Artist. The entire Earth is His canvas."
- Unknown

ATHEISM

"The fool hath said in his heart there is no God."
- Psalm 14:1

"True atheism is found in a man's behavior rather than in the heart. It is in the lip rather than the heart of man."
- Sir Francis Bacon

"Nobody talks so constantly about God as those who insist that there is no God."
- Heywood Broun

"Shouldn't atheist have an equal obligation to explain pleasure in a world of randomness? Where does pleasure come from?"
- G. K. Chesterton

"There are no atheists in foxholes."
- William Cummings

"I, at any rate, am convinced that He (God) is not playing at dice."
- Albert Einstein

"Science, without religion, is lame. Religion, without science, is blind."
- 　Albert Einstein

"Most of us professing Christians, from liberals to fundamentalists remain practical atheist in most of our lives."
- 　Stanley Hauerwas

"The reason why many say they do not believe in God...they look at this collection of "saints" called the church and say that they cannot see anybody who looks much different from somebody who does not believe."
- 　Stanley Hauerwas

"An atheist is one who hopes the Lord will do nothing to disturb his disbelief."
- 　Franklin Jones

"A young man who wishes to remain a sound atheist cannot be too careful of his reading."
- 　C.S. Lewis

"You're an atheist? Can you prove it?"
- 　Jesse Morrell

"I understand the rationale behind your belief. But are you atheist enough to wager your entire Eternity upon such a belief?"
- 　Jack Murphy

"I might believe in the Redeemer if His followers looked more Redeemed."
- 　Fredrick Nietzsche

"The worst moment for the atheist is when he is really thankful and has nobody to thank."
- 　Dante Gabriel Rossetti

"Atheism is the death of hope, the suicide of the soul."
- Unknown

"During times of crisis, all atheists at least half-believe in God."
- Unknown

AUTHORITY

"He that is faithful in that which is least is faithful also in much: and he that is unjust in the least is unjust also in much."
- Luke 16:10

"Unthinking respect for authority is the greatest enemy of truth."
- Albert Einstein

"To punish me for my contempt for authority, fate made me an authority myself."
- Albert Einstein

"The goal of the pastor is not to get people to show up but to get people to grow up."
- John Maxwell

"Surround yourself with the best people you can find, delegate authority, and don't interfere."
- Ronald Reagan

"If we and our posterity reject religious instruction and authority, violate the rules of eternal justice, trifle with the injunctions of morality, and recklessly destroy the political constitution which holds us together, no man can tell how sudden a catastrophe may overwhelm us, that shall bury all our glory in profound obscurity."
- Daniel Webster

"Authority makes some people grow. Others just swell."
- Unknown

"Leave no authority existing that is not accountable and responsible to the people."

-   Thomas Jefferson

"The Church that is man-managed instead of God-governed is doomed to failure. A ministry that is college-trained but not Spirit-filled works no miracles."

-   Samuel Chadwick

"Nothing intoxicates some people like a sip of authority."

-   Unknown

B

BACKSLIDING

"For a just man falleth seven times, and riseth up again: but the wicked shall fall into mischief."
- Proverbs 24:6

"O LORD, though our iniquities testify against us, do thou *it* for thy name's sake: for our backslidings are many; we have sinned against thee."
- Jeremiah 14:7

"Nevertheless I have somewhat against thee, because thou hast left thy first love."
- Revelation 2:4

"See that backslider? He has tasted the waters of life. He has been greatly enlightened. Perhaps he has really known the Lord by true faith -- and then see, he turns away to beg the husks of earthly pleasure! He turns his back on the bleeding Lamb! Now, put together all the guilt of every Heathen soul that has gone to hell -- of every soul that has gone from a state of utter moral darkness, and your guilt, backsliding Christian, is greater than all theirs! Do you, therefore, say, may God then, have mercy on my soul? So say we all; but we must add if it be possible; for who can say that such guilt as yours can be forgiven! Can Christ pray for you as he prayed for his murderers, "Father, forgive them, for they know not what they do?" Can he plead in your behalf, that you knew not what you were doing? Awful! Awful! Where is the sounding line that shall measure the ocean-depth of your guilt?"
- Charles Finney

BEAUTY

"I will praise thee; for I am fearfully and wonderfully made: marvelous are thy works; and that my soul knoweth right well."
-     Psalm 139:14

"Charm is deceitful, and beauty is vain: but a woman that feareth the LORD, she shall be praised."
-     Proverbs 31:30

"Anything in any way beautiful derives its beauty from itself and asks nothing beyond itself. Praise is no part of it, for nothing is made worse or better by praise."
-     Marcus Antoninus Aurelius

"God is the Author of beauty. He indeed is the Divine Artist."
-     Albert Einstein

"The most beautiful thing we can experience is the mysterious. It is the source of all true art and all science. He to whom this emotion is a stranger, who can no longer pause to wonder and stand rapt in awe, is as good as dead: his eyes are closed."
-     Albert Einstein

"The absence of flaw in beauty is itself a flaw."
-     Havelock Ellis

"Beauty and folly are old companions."
-     Benjamin Franklin

"A man should hear a little music, read a little poetry, and see a fine picture every day of his life, in order that worldly cares may not obliterate the sense of the beautiful which God has implanted in the human soul."
-     Johann Wolfgang
      von Goethe

"The best and most beautiful things in the world cannot be seen or even touched - they must be felt with the heart."
- Helen Keller

"I look forward to an America which will not be afraid of grace and beauty."
- John F. Kennedy

"Beauty is only skin deep, but ugly goes clean to the bone."
- Dorothy Parker

"Beauty is in the eye of the beholder."
- Plato

"The future belongs to those who believe in the beauty of their dreams."
- Eleanor Roosevelt

"No object is so good that, in certain circumstances, some will consider it ugly."
- Oscar Wilde

"It is often beauty that captures your attention; but it is personality which captures your heart."
- Unknown

"Some people are born pretty. Beauty, however, is a work of the heart. It takes work to become beautiful."
- Unknown

"Character contributes to beauty. It fortifies a woman as her youth fades. A mode of conduct, a standard of courage, discipline, fortitude, and integrity can do a great deal to make a woman beautiful – long after her appearance fades."
- Unknown

BEHAVIOR – See ACTIONS; MANNERS

BELIEF – See FAITH

BETRAYAL

"A talebearer revealeth secrets: but he that is of a faithful spirit concealeth the matter."
-        Proverbs 11:13

"But Jesus said unto him, Judas, betrayest thou the Son of Man with a kiss?"
-        Luke 22:48

"Only a friend can betray a friend;
  A stranger has nothing to gain.
  And only a friend comes close enough
  To ever cause so much pain."
-        Michael Card

"They talk of a man betraying his country, his friends, his sweetheart. There must be a moral bond first. All a man can betray is his conscience."
-        Joseph Conrad

"One should rather die than be betrayed. There is no deceit in death. It delivers precisely what is has promised. Betrayal, though? Betrayal is the willful slaughter of hope."
-        Steven Deitz

"All our experience with history should teach us, when we look back, how badly human wisdom is betrayed when it relies on itself."
-        Martin Luther

"To betray, you must first belong."
-        Harold Philby

"To be deceived by our enemies or betrayed by our friends in insupportable; yet by ourselves we are often content to be so treated."
-        Duc de La Rochefoucauld

"No one can make you feel inferior without your consent."
- Eleanor Roosevelt

"Distrust is our only defense against betrayal. Yet it is a high price to pay for such security. It's price? Trust and love."
- Tennessee Williams

BIBLE

"Let us hear the conclusion of the whole matter: Fear God, and keep his commandments: for this is the whole duty of man."
- Ecclesiastes 12:13

"It is written…"
- Jesus in Matthew 4:4, 7, 10

"No one ever became, or can become truly eloquent without being a reader of the Bible, and an admirer of the purity and sublimity of its language."
- Fisher Ame

"Young man, my advice to you is that you cultivate an acquaintance with and firm belief in the Holy Scriptures, for this is your certain interest. I think Christ's system of morals and religion, as He left them with us, the best the world ever saw or is likely to see."
- Benjamin Franklin

"I have said and always will say that the studious perusal of the sacred volume will make better citizens, better fathers, and better husbands."
- Thomas Jefferson

"I believe the Bible is the best gift God has ever given to man. All the good from the Savior of the world is communicated through this book...All things desirable to men are contained in the Bible."
- Abraham Lincoln

"Don't try to bring the Word of God down to your level. Let it pull you up to its level."
- David MacDonald

"Too often we see the Bible through whatever lens we get from our culture."
- Brian McLaren

"This book (the Bible) will keep you from sin or sin will keep you from this book."
- D.L. Moody

"Out of 100 men, one will read the Bible, the other 99 will read the Christian."
- D.L. Moody

"Defend the Bible? I would just as soon defend a lion. Just turn the Bible loose. It will defend itself."
- Charles Spurgeon

"Having to carry the living water to others, we must go oftener to the well, and we must go with more capacious vessels than the general run of Christians. Look, then, to the vigor of your personal piety, and pray to be 'filled with all the fullness of God.'"
- Charles H. Spurgeon

"A man says to me, "Can you explain the seven trumpets of the Revelation?" No, but I can blow one in your ear, and warn you to escape from the wrath to come."
- C.H. Spurgeon

"It's not the parts of the Bible I don't know that worry me…it's the parts that I do."
- Mark Twain

"Some people read their Bible in Hebrew, some in Greek; I like to read mine in the Holy Ghost."
- Smith Wigglesworth

"It shall greatly help you to understand Scripture
if thou mark not only what is spoken or written
- but of whom
- and to whom
- with what words
- at what time
- where
- to what intent
- with what circumstances
- considering what goeth before
- and what followeth."

- John Wycliffe

"Throughout the Bible, God shows a marked preference for 'real' people over 'good' people."

- Phillip Yancey

"You may be the only "Bible" that this world ever reads."

- Unknown

BOLDNESS

"…but the righteous are as bold as a lion."

- Proverbs 28:1

"Let us therefore come boldly unto the throne of grace, that we may obtain mercy, and find grace to help in time of need."

- Hebrews 4:16

"Boldness is ever blind, for it sees not dangers and inconveniences whence it is bad in council though good in execution."

- Sir Francis Bacon

"Then indecision brings its own delays,
And days are lost lamenting o'er lost days.
Are you in earnest? Seize this very minute;
What you can do, or dream you can, begin it;
Boldness has genius, power and magic in it."
- Johann Wolfgang
von Goethe

"I am prejudiced in favor of him who, without impudence, can ask boldly. He has faith in humanity, and faith in himself. No one who is not accustomed to giving grandly can ask nobly and with boldness."
- Johann Kaspar Lavater

"The unforgivable crime is soft hitting. Do not hit at all if it can be avoided; but never hit softly."
- Theodore Roosevelt

"It is wonderful what strength of purpose and boldness and energy of will are roused by the assurance that we are doing our duty."
- Sir Walter Scott

"He was a bold man that first did eat an oyster. He was a bold man that did first milk a cow."
- Jonathan Swift

"Where necessity pinches, boldness is prudence."
- Unknown

"Boldness without restraint is just well-meaning disruption that typically lacks humility."
- Unknown

BOOKS

"Of making many books there is no end; and much study is a weariness of the flesh."
- Ecclesiastes 12:12

"Some books are to be tasted, others to be swallowed, and some few to be chewed and digested."
- Sir Francis Bacon

"Books are not made for furniture, but there is nothing else that so beautifully furnishes a house."
- Henry Ward Beecher

"After all manner of professors have done their best for us, the place we are to get knowledge is in books. The true university of these days is a collection of books."
- Albert Camus

"It is chiefly through books that we enjoy the intercourse with superior minds... In the best books, great men talk to us, give us their most previous thought, and pour their souls into ours. God be thanked for books."
- William Ellery Channing

"There is no frigate like a book
  To take us lands away."
- Emily Dickinson

"The test of literature is, I suppose, whether we ourselves live more intensely for the reading of it."
- Elizabeth Drew

"A book is more than 15 ounces of paper, glue and ink. It is a perspective by which empires can rise or fall."
- Edward Everett

"Wherever they burn books they will also, in the end, burn human beings."
- Heinrich Heine

"An intellectual without books is like a workman without tools."
- Thomas Jefferson

"Books tend to show men that those original thoughts of his aren't very new after all."

- Abraham Lincoln

"For books are more than books, they are the life
The very heart and core of ages past,
The reason why men lived and worked and died,
The essence and quintessence of their lives."

- Amy Lowell

"A classic is a book in which many people praise yet seldom read."

- Mark Twain

"A book is a gift that you can open again and again."

- Unknown

"Reading is plentiful; perception is rare."

- Unknown

BOREDOM

"No place is boring, if you've had a good night's sleep and have a pocket full of unexposed film."

- Robert Adams

"In order to live free and happily, you must sacrifice boredom. It is not always an easy sacrifice."

- Richard Bach

"I've got a great ambition to die of exhaustion rather than boredom."

- Thomas Carlyle

"Success is achieved by simply working past anxiety, boredom, discouragement and near-success."

- Thomas Edison

"Boredom: A condition of those suffering from a diseased purpose."
- Edward Everett

"The cure for boredom is curiosity. There is no cure for curiosity."
- Ellen Parr

"Boredom, after all, is a form of criticism."
- Wendell Phillips

"The world is condemned and Hell waits: How, then, is life boring?"
- Leonard Ravenhill

"A bore is a man who, when you ask him how he is, tells you."
- Bert Taylor

BRAVERY – See COURAGE

BROKENESS

"I am forgotten as a dead man out of mind: I am like a broken vessel."
- Psalm 31:12

"The LORD is nigh unto them that are of a broken heart; and saveth such as be of a contrite spirit."
- Psalm 34:18

"The sacrifices of God are a broken spirit: a broken and a contrite heart, O God, thou wilt not despise."
- Psalm 51:17

"The Spirit of the Lord GOD is upon me; because the LORD hath anointed me to preach good tidings unto the meek; he hath sent me to bind up the brokenhearted, to proclaim liberty to the captives, and the opening of the prison to them that are bound."
- Isaiah 61:1

"Introspection can easily become the tool of Satan, who is called the accuser. One of his chief weapons is discouragement. He knows that if he can make us discouraged and dispirited we will not fight the battle for holiness."
-      Jerry Bridges

"Never despair, but if you do, work on in despair."
-      Edmund Burke

"It is wonderful what God can do with a broken heart, if He gets all the pieces."
-      Samuel Chadwick

"We will never receive if we ask with an end in view; if we ask, not out of our poverty but out of our lust. A pauper does not ask from any other reason than the abject panging condition of his poverty, he is not ashamed to beg. - Blessed are the paupers in spirit."
-      Oswald Chambers

"God uses broken things. It takes broken soil to produce a crop, broken clouds to give rain, broken grain to give bread, broken bread to give strength. It is the broken alabaster box that gives forth perfume...it is Peter, weeping bitterly, who returns to greater power than ever."
-      Vance Havner

"Being broken is both God's work and ours. He brings His pressure to bear, but we have to make the choice...All day long the choice will be before us in a thousand ways."
-      Roy Hession

"God whispers to us in our pleasures, speaks to us in our conscious but shouts to us in our pains. Suffering is God's megaphone in a deaf world."
-      C.S. Lewis

"Contrary to what might be expected, I look back on experience that at the time seemed especially desolating and painful with particular satisfaction. Indeed, I can say with complete truthfulness that everything I have learned in my seventy-five years in this world, everything that has truly enhanced and enlightened my experience, has been through affliction and not through happiness, whether pursued or attained. In other words, if it were ever possible to eliminate affliction from our earthly existence by means of some drug or other medical mumbo jumbo...the result would make life too banal and trivial to be endurable. This, of course is what the cross signifies. And it is the Cross that has called me inexorably to Christ."

- Malcolm Muggeridge

"God uses people. God uses people to perform His work. He does not send angels. Angels weep over it, but God does not use angels to accomplish His purposes. He uses burdened broken-hearted weeping men and women."

- David Wilkerson

BURDENS

"Come unto me, all ye that labor and are heavy laden, and I will give you rest. Take my yoke upon you, and learn of me; for I am meek and lowly in heart: and ye shall find rest unto your souls. For my yoke is easy, and my burden is light."

- Matthew 11:28-30

"Bear ye one another's burdens, and so fulfill the law of Christ."

- Galatians 6:2

"No one is useless in the world who lightens the burden of someone else."

- Charles Dickens

"Americans, indeed all free men, remember that in the final choice a soldier's pack is not so heavy a burden as a prisoner's chains."

- Dwight Eisenhower

"Don't ask for a lighter burden. Rather ask for a stronger back."

- Edward Everett

"Hate is too great a burden to bear. It injures the hater more than it injures the hated."
- Coretta Scott King

"The will is a beast of burden. If God mounts it, it wishes and goes as God wills; if Satan mounts it, it wishes and goes as Satan wills; Nor can it choose its rider...the riders contend for its possession."
- Martin Luther

"We can easily manage if we will only take, each day, the burden appointed to it. But the load will be too heavy for us if we carry yesterday's burden over again today, and then add the burden of the morrow before we are required to bear it."
- John Newton

"From my many years experience I can unhesitatingly say that the cross bears those who bear the cross."
- Sadhu Sundar Singh

"Hope is like the sun, which, as we journey toward it, casts the shadow of our burden behind us."
- Samuel Smiles

"Fifty keys are a burden for one person. But they open doors for fifty people."
- Unknown

"Knowledge is a considerable burden."
- Unknown

"Let me walk three weeks in the footsteps of my enemy, carry the same burden, have the same trials as he, before I say one word to criticize."
- Unknown

"A burden, coupled with service and purpose, seems lighter."
- Unknown

BUSINESS

"Dishonest scales are an abomination to the Lord, But a just weight is His delight."
- Proverbs 11:1

"Wealth gotten by vanity shall be diminished: but he that gathereth by labor shall increase."
- Proverbs 13:11

"Seest thou a man diligent in his business? he shall stand before kings."
- Proverbs 22:29

"When one door closes another door opens; but we so often look so long and so regretfully upon the closed door, that we do not see the ones which open for us."
- Alexander Graham Bell

"Here is the prime condition of success: Concentrate your energy, thought and capital exclusively upon the business in which you are engaged. Having begun on one line, resolve to fight it out on that line, to lead in it, adopt every improvement, have the best machinery, and know the most about it."
- Andrew Carnegie

"I am certainly not one of those who need to be prodded. In fact, if anything, I am the prod."
- Winston Churchill

"If you don't drive your business, you will be driven out of business."
- B. C. Forbes

"Obstacles are those frightful things you see when you take your eyes off your goal."
- Henry Ford

"A business that makes nothing but money is a poor business. The man who will use his skill and constructive imagination to see how much he can give for a dollar, instead of how little he can give for a dollar, is bound to succeed."
- Henry Ford

"He that is of the opinion money will do everything may well be suspected of doing everything for money."
- Benjamin Franklin

"In this world nothing is certain but death and taxes."
- Benjamin Franklin

"If you owe the bank $100, that's your problem. If you owe the bank $100 million, that's the bank's problem."
- J. Paul Getty

"Lots of folks confuse bad management with destiny."
- Frank Hubbard

"Nearly all men can stand adversity, but if you want to test a man's character, give him power and authority."
- Abraham Lincoln

"Method goes far to prevent trouble in business: for it makes the task easy, hinders confusion, saves abundance of time, and instructs those that have business depending, both what to do and what to hope."
- William Penn

"An economist's guess is liable to be as good as anybody else's."
- Will Rogers

"Mental attitude is more important than mental capacity."
- Sir Walter Scott

"If all the economists were laid end to end, they'd never reach a conclusion."
- George Bernard Shaw

"Men who do things without being told draw the most wages."
-      Edwin Stuart

"And there is no trade or employment but the young man following it may become a hero."
-      Walt Whitman

C

CARE

"For every man shall bear his own burden."
- Galatians 6:5

"Casting all your care upon him; for he careth for you."
- I Peter 5:7

"I met a brother who, describing a friend of his, said he was like a man who had dropped a bottle and broken it; and put all the pieces in his bosom, where they were cutting him perpetually."
- Henry Ward Beecher

"Men do not avail themselves of the riches of God's grace. They love to nurse their cares, and seem as uneasy without some fret as an old friar would be without his hair girdle. They are commanded to cast their cares upon the Lord, but even when they attempt it, they do not fail to catch them up again, and think it meritorious to walk burdened."
- Henry Ward Beecher

"It is better to have a sore than a seared conscience."
- Thomas Brooks

"Second-hand cares, like second-hand clothes, come easily off and on."
- Charles Dickens

"Why art thou troubled and anxious about many things? One thing is needful--to love Him and to sit attentively at His feet."

- François Fénelon

"He that taketh his own cares upon himself loads himself in vain with an uneasy burden. I will cast all my cares on God; He hath bidden me; they cannot burden Him."

- Joseph Hall

"Light burdens, long borne, grow heavy."

- George Herbert

"Cast all your care on God; that anchor holds."

- Lord Alfred Tennyson

"Providence has given us hope and sleep as a compensation for the many cares of life."

- Voltaire

"Care to our coffin adds a nail, no doubt;
And every Grin, so merry, draws one out."

- John Wolcott

CARELESSNESS

""It is a very sad and dangerous thing to trifle and dally with...God, His word, our own souls, and eternity!"

- Thomas Brooks

"Whoever is careless with the truth in small matters cannot be trusted with important matters."

- Albert Einstein

"For the want of a nail the shoe was lost,
  For the want of a shoe the horse was lost,
    For the want of a horse the rider was lost,
      For the want of a rider the battle was lost,
        For the want of a battle the kingdom was lost--
          And all for the want of a horseshoe nail."
- Benjamin Franklin

"Carelessness does more harm than a want of knowledge."
- Benjamin Franklin

"The most pitiful thing I have seen in this life is men without Christ and have peace."
- Gary Kopfstein

"Men use care in purchasing a horse, and are neglectful in choosing friends."
- John Muir

"He who fights with monsters should be careful lest he thereby become a monster. And if thou gaze long into an abyss, the abyss will also gaze into thee."
- Friedrich Nietzsche

"Carelessness about our security is dangerous; carelessness about our freedom is also dangerous."
- Adlai Stevenson

CAUSE

"I would seek unto God, and unto God would I commit my cause:
  Which doeth great things and unsearchable; marvellous things without number: Who giveth rain upon the earth, and sendeth waters upon the fields: To set up on high those that be low; that those which mourn may be exalted to safety."
- Job 5:8-11

"It becomes extremely hard to disentangle our idea of the cause from the effect by which we know it."
- Edmund Burke

"The great chain of causes, which, linking one to another, even to the throne of God Himself, can never be unraveled by any industry of ours."
- Edmund Burke

"Cause and effect, means and ends, seed and fruit cannot be severed; for the effect already blooms in the cause, the end preexists in the means, the fruit in the seed."
- Ralph Waldo Emerson

"Is life so dear, or peace so sweet, as to be purchased at the price of chains or slavery? Forbid it, Almighty God! I know not what course others may take: but as for me, give me liberty, or give me death!"
- Patrick Henry

"A person may cause evil to others not only by his actions but by his inaction, and in either case he is justly accountable to them for the injury."
- John Stuart Mill

"To understand 'cause and effect' is vital in leadership, whether a father, a farmer, a president or a king."
- Jack Murphy

CERTAINTY

"If we begin with certainties, we shall end in doubts; but if we begin with doubts, and are patient in them, we shall end in certainties."
- Sir Francis Bacon

"Events are never absolute, their outcome depends entirely upon the individual. Misfortune is a stepping stone for a genius, a piscina for a Christian, a treasure for a man of parts, and an abyss for a weakling."
- Honore de Balzac

"Certainty is the mother of quiet and repose, and uncertainty the cause of variance and contentions."
- Lord Edward Coke

"The odds are six to five that the light in the end of the tunnel is the headlight of an oncoming train."
- Paul Dickson

"We can be absolutely certain only about things we do not understand."
- Eric Hoffer

"It is not certain that everything is uncertain."
- Blaise Pascal

"We do know of certain knowledge that he [Osama bin Laden] is either in Afghanistan, or in some other country, or dead."
- Donald Rumsfeld

"Do not feel certain of anything. The whole problem with the world is that fools and fanatics are always so certain of themselves, but wiser people so full of doubts."
- Bertrand Arthur Russell

CHANGE

"Jesus Christ the same yesterday, and today, and forever."
- Hebrews 13:8

"Time is a dressmaker specializing in alterations."
- Faith Baldwin

"When you are through changing, you are through."
- Bruce Barton

"Neither a wise man nor a brave man lies down on the tracks of history to wait for the train of the future to run over him."
- Dwight D. Eisenhower

"Change is inevitable - except from a vending machine."
- Robert C. Gallagher

"There is a certain relief in change, even though it be from bad to worse! As I have often found in travelling in a stagecoach, that it is often a comfort to shift one's position, and be bruised in a new place."
- Washington Irving

"God loves you just the way you are, but He refuses to leave you that way."
- Max Lucado

"There is good change and there is bad change. No one should ever embrace change for changes sake."
- John McCain

"I am not what I ought to be. I am not what I want to be. I am not what I hope to be. But still, I am not what I used to be. And by the grace of God, I am what I am."
- John Newton

"If you're in a bad situation, don't worry it'll change. If you're in a good situation, don't worry it'll change."
- John Simone

"You are the way you are because that's the way you want to be. If you really wanted to be any different, you would be in the process of changing right now."
- Fred Smith

"He who rejects change is the architect of decay. The only human institution which rejects progress is the cemetery."
- Harold Wilson

"If you want to make enemies, try to change something."
- Woodrow Wilson

"If nothing ever changed, there'd be no butterflies."
-    Unknown

CHARACTER

"All that is necessary for the triumph of evil is that good men do nothing."
-    Edmund Burke

"Integrity is the glue that holds our way of life together. We must constantly strive to keep our integrity intact. When wealth is lost, nothing is lost; when health is lost, something is lost; when character is lost, all is lost."
-    Billy Graham

"I have a dream that my four little children will one day live in a nation where they will not be judged by the color of their skin but by the content of their character."
-    Martin Luther King, Jr.

"The measure of a man's real character is what he would do if he would never be found out."
-    Thomas Macauley

"Every little action of the common day makes or unmakes character."
-    Gordon MacDonald

"Out of 100 men, one will read the Bible; the other 99 will read the Christian."
-    D.L. Moody

"Your character is essentially the sum of your habits; it is how you habitually act."
-    Rick Warren

"Adversity doesn't build character; it reveals it."
-    Unknown

"Your character is who you are when no one but God is watching you."
- Unknown

"The fundamental attribution error: We attribute other people's errors as character flaws. We attribute our own errors to our circumstances and our environment."
- Unknown

"Sow a thought reap an action. Sow an action reap a habit. Sow a habit and reap a character. Sow a character and reap a destiny."
- Unknown

CHILDREN

"I must study politics and war that my sons may have liberty to study mathematics and philosophy. My sons ought to study mathematics and philosophy, geography, natural history, naval architecture, navigation, commerce and agriculture in order to give their children a right to study painting, poetry, music, architecture, statuary, tapestry, and porcelain."
- John Adams

"Children have never been very good at listening to their elders, but they have never failed to imitate them."
- James Baldwin

"There's nothing sadder in this world than to awake Christmas morning and not be a child."
- Erma Bombeck

"It is very difficult and expensive to undo after you are married the things that your mother and father did to you while you were putting your first six birthdays behind you."
- U.S. Social Hygiene Study, 1928

"People who say they sleep like a baby usually don't have one."
- Leo Burke

"There are only two lasting bequests we can hope to give our children. One is roots; the other, wings."
- Hodding Carter

"How far you go in life depends on your being tender with the young, compassionate with the aged, sympathetic with the striving and tolerant of the weak and strong. Because someday in life you will have been all of these."
- George Washington Carver

"One generation plants the trees; another gets the shade."
- Chinese Proverb

"Human beings are the only creatures that allow their children to come back home."
- Bill Cosby

"If you as parents cut corners, your children will too. If you lie, they will too. If you spend all your money on yourselves and tithe no portion of it, your children won't either. And if parents snicker at racial and gender jokes, another generation will pass on the poison adults still have not had the courage to snuff out."
- Marian Wright Edelman

"The thing that impresses me the most about America is the way parents obey their children."
- King Edward VIII

"Parents can only give good advice or put them on the right paths, but the final forming of a person's character lies in their own hands."
- Anne Frank

"To nourish children and raise them against odds is in any time, any place, more valuable than to fix bolts in cars or design nuclear weapons."
- Marilyn French

"My son is my son till he have got him a wife,
But my daughter's my daughter all the days of her life."
- Thomas Fuller

"Bitter are the tears of a child: Sweeten them.
Deep are the thoughts of a child: Quiet them.
Sharp is the grief of a child: Take it from him.
Soft is the heart of a child: Do not harden it."
- Pamela Glenconner

"Children are our most valuable natural resource."
- Herbert Hoover

"You can learn many things from children. How much patience you have, for instance."
- Franklin P. Jones

"Having children makes you no more a parent than having a piano makes you a pianist."
- Michael Levine

"Level with your child by being honest. Nobody spots a phony quicker than a child."
- Mary McCracken

"If you bungle raising your children, I don't think whatever else you do well matters very much."
- Jacqueline Kennedy Onassis

"When I approach a child, he inspires in me two sentiments; tenderness for what he is, and respect for what he may become."
- Louis Pasteur

"All children are artists. The problem is how to remain an artist once he grows up."
- Pablo Picasso

"If thy daughter marry well, thou hast found a son; if not, thou hast lost a daughter."
- Francis Quarles

"No matter how old a mother is, she watches her middle-aged children for signs of improvement."
- Florida Scott-Maxwell

"It is a wise father that knows his own child."
- William Shakespeare

"Making the decision to have a child - it's momentous. It is to decide forever to have your heart go walking outside your body."
- Elizabeth Stone

"Children require guidance and sympathy far more than instruction."
- Anne Sullivan

"Adam and Eve had many advantages, but the principal one was that they escaped teething."
- Mark Twain

"When I was a boy of fourteen, my father was so ignorant I could hardly stand to have the old man around. But when I got to be twenty-one, I was astonished at how much the old man had learned in seven years."
- Mark Twain

"A three-year-old child is a being who gets almost as much fun out of a fifty-six dollar set of swings as it does out of finding a small green worm."
- Bill Vaughn

"People who get nostalgic about childhood were obviously never children."
- Bill Watterson

"Before I got married I had six theories about bringing up children; now I have six children and no theories."
— John Wilmot

"Give me the children until they are seven and anyone may have them afterward."

-     Francis Xavier

"Blessed indeed is the man who hears gentle voices call him father!"

-     English Proverb

"Anyone who uses the phrase 'easy as taking candy from a baby' has never tried taking candy from a baby."

-     Unknown

"Your children are not your children. They are investments on loan to you from God."

-     Unknown

CHRIST

"I know men and I tell you that Jesus Christ is no mere man. Between Him and every other person in the world there is no possible term of comparison. Alexander, Caesar, Charlemagne, and I have founded empires. But on what did we rest the creation of our genius? Upon force. Jesus Christ founded His empire upon love; and at this hour millions of men would die for Him."

-     Napoleon Bonaparte

"In answer to your inquiry, I consider that the chief dangers which confront the coming century will be religion without the Holy Ghost, Christianity without Christ, forgiveness without repentance, salvation without regeneration, politics without God, and heaven without hell."

-     William Booth

"If ever man was God, or God man, Jesus Christ was both."

-     Lord Byron

"The sages and heroes of history are receding from us, and history contracts the record of their deeds into a narrower and narrower page. But time has no power over the name and deeds and words of Jesus Christ."

- William Channing

"I like your Christ, I do not like your Christians. Your Christians are so unlike your Christ."

- Mahatma Gandhi

"God proved His love on the Cross. When Christ hung, and bled, and died, it was God saying to the world, "I love you.""

- Billy Graham

"All the world would be Christian if they were taught the pure Gospel of Christ!"

- Thomas Jefferson

"Enemy occupied territory--that is what the world is. Christianity is the story of how the rightful King has landed in disguise, and is calling us all to take part in a great campaign of sabotage."

- C.S. Lewis

"It is a masterpiece of the devil to make us believe that children cannot understand religion. Would Christ have made a child the standard of faith if He had known that it was not capable of understanding His words?"

- Dwight L. Moody

"The main thing is to keep the main thing the main thing - and the main thing is Christ."

- Clay Peck

"One could wish no easier death than that of Socrates, calmly discussing philosophy with his friends; one could fear nothing worse than that of Jesus, dying in torment, among the insults, the mockery, the curses of the whole nation. In the midst of these terrible sufferings, Jesus prays for his cruel murderers. Yes, if the life and death of Socrates are those of a philosopher, the life and death of Christ are those of a God."

- Jean Jacques Rousseau

"Jesus Christ did not come into this world to make bad people good, he came into this world to make dead people live."

- Lee Stroebel

"Faith, as Paul saw it, was a living, flaming thing leading to surrender and obedience to the commandments of Christ."

- A. W. Tozer

"If Christ were here now there is one thing he would not be - a Christian."

- Mark Twain

"How else but through a broken heart may Lord Christ enter in?"

- Oscar Wilde

"Nails did not hold Jesus to the cross. Love did."

- Unknown

"Only Christ could build a bridge to God with only two pieces of wood."

- Unknown

CHRISTIANITY

"The best argument for Christianity is Christians: their joy, their certainty, their completeness. But the strongest argument against Christianity is also Christians--when they are somber and joyless, when they are self-righteous and smug in complacent consecration, when they are narrow and repressive, then Christianity dies a thousand deaths."

- Joe Aldrich

"If you don't plan to live the Christian life totally committed to knowing your God and to walking in obedience to Him, then don't begin; for this is what Christianity is all about. It is a change of citizenship, a change of governments, a change of allegiance. If you have no intentions of letting Christ rule your life, then forget Christianity; it's not for you."
-    K. Authur

"Sheep that are well feed seldom wander off."
-    Wes Baker

"The Church that is man-managed instead of God-governed is doomed to failure. A ministry that is college-trained but not Spirit-filled works no miracles."
-    Samuel Chadwick

"The wildest dreams of their rabbis have been far exceeded. Has not Jesus conquered Europe and changed its name to Christendom? All countries that refuse the cross wither, and the time will come, when the vast communities and countless myriads of America and Australia, looking upon Europe as Europe now looks upon Greece, and wondering how so small a space could have achieved such great deeds, will find music in the songs of Zion and solace in the parables of Galilee."
-    Benjamin Disraeli

"'*For I tell you...no man can serve two masters...*' (Matt 6:24). In a day when believers seem to be trying to please both the world and the Lord (which is an impossible thing), when people are far more concerned about offending their friends than offending God, there is only one answer... '*Deny yourself, take up your cross and follow Him*' (Luke 9:23)."
-    Keith Green

"Going to Church doesn't make you a 'Christian' any more than going to McDonalds will make you a hamburger."
-    Keith Green

"It can not be emphasized too strongly or too often that this great nation was founded, not by religionists, but by Christians, not on religions, but on the gospel of Jesus Christ!"
- Patrick Henry

"One of the greatest dangers in the Christian life is losing interest in what is familiar."
- Brad Lambert

"I believe in Christianity as I believe that the sun has risen. Not only because I believe it, but because I see everything by it."
- C.S. Lewis

"The man…looking at him with a smile that only half concealed his contempt, inquired, "Now Mr. Morrison do you really expect that you will make an impression on the idolatry of the Chinese Empire?" "No sir," said Morrison, "but I expect that God will."
- Robert Morrison

"The long painful history of the church is the history of people ever and again tempted to choose power over love, control over the cross, being a leader over being led. Those who resisted this temptation to the end and thereby give us hope are the true saints."
- Henri Nouwen

"For many of us the great danger is not that we will renounce our faith. It is that we will become so distracted and rushed and preoccupied that we will settle for a mediocre version of it."
- John Ortberg

"It's a whole lot easier to WEAR a cross than to BEAR a cross!"
- Leonard Ravenhill

"Jehovah Witnesses don't believe in hell and neither do most Christians."
- Leonard Ravenhill

"The Sunday morning service shows how popular your church is. The evening services show how popular your pastor is. Your private prayer time shows you how popular God is!"
- Leonard Ravenhill

"The true man of God is heartsick, grieved at the worldliness of the Church...grieved at the toleration of sin in the Church, grieved at the prayerlessness in the Church. He is disturbed that the corporate prayer of the Church no longer pulls down the strongholds of the devil."
- Leonard Ravenhill

"This cheap, modern Christianity...offends nobody, requires no sacrifice, costs nothing, and is worth nothing!"
- J. C. Ryle

"Boundaries are like the banks of a river. Banks create depth and increase the momentum of the water as it flows. Rivers without banks are slow and shallow. Churches without boundaries in their vision statements try to please everyone and everything. The result is ministry that is 'a mile wide and an inch deep'"
- Wayne Schmidt

"From my many years experience I can unhesitatingly say that the cross bears those who bear the cross."
- Sadhu Sundar Singh

"Answering a student's question, 'Will the heathen who have not heard the Gospel be saved?' thus, 'It is more a question with me whether we who have the Gospel and fail to give it to those who have not, can be saved.'"
- C.H. Spurgeon

"One of the hardest jobs in ministry is keeping your own relationship with God where it needs to be."
- Harold Warner

"The call of the Cross, therefore, is to enter into this passion of Christ. We must have upon us the print of the nails."
- Gordon Watt

"The secret of Christianity is not asking Jesus into your heart; it is Jesus asking us into His."
- Unknown

"The world isn't reading the Bible; they're reading Christians like you. And if they don't like what they see in you, they're not going to want what you've got -- Jesus."
- Unknown

"New Testament Christianity must not hang out at headquarters. In times of war, we must get into the trenches."
- Unknown

CHURCH

"When the church and the world can jog comfortably along together, you can be sure something is wrong. The world has not compromised- its spirit is exactly the same as it ever was. If Christians were equally as faithful to the Lord, separated from the world, and living so that their lives were a reproof to all ungodliness, the world would hate them as much as it ever did. It is the church that has compromised, not the world."
- Catherine Booth

"Despite all the fancy buildings, sophisticated programs and highly visible presence, it is my contention that the church is almost a non-entity when it comes to shaping culture."
- Bob Briner

"We are playing church. We are so busy trying to be relevant to the world that we have become just like the world...AND the world is not impressed."
- Nancy Leigh DeMoss

"Suppose I was a lawyer, and should go into court and spread out my client's case, the issue is joined, and I make my statements, and tell what I expect to prove, and then call in my witnesses. My first witness takes his oath, and then rises up and contradicts me to my face. What good will all my pleading do? I might address the jury a month, and be as eloquent as Cicero, but so long as my witnesses contradicted me, all my pleading would do no good. Just so it is with a minister who is preaching in the midst of a cold, stupid, and God-dishonoring church. In vain does he hold up to view the great truths of religion, when every member of the church is ready to swear he lies."

-     Charles Finney

"Lastly--are not the Church in their present state, a standing, public, perpetual denial of the gospel? Do they not stand out before the world, as a living, unanswerable contradiction of the gospel; and do more to harden sinners and lead them into a spirit of caviling and infidelity, than all the efforts of professed infidels from the beginning of the world to the present day?"

-     Charles Finney

"A prayer-meeting is an index to the state of religion in a Church."

-     Charles Finney

"Playing marbles with diamonds, that's what we are doing in the church today."

-     Vance Havner

"Now if the church ever recovers the power to break up demonism in the community it will bring down the wrath of evil and the church may land in jail but she'll learn how to sing in prison, pray down an earth quake. Folks are asking 'will the church go underground?' Well she may develop more power underground then she's got above ground these days. We're not going to pray down earth quakes in committee meetings, sipping coffee and reading the minutes of the last meeting."

-     Vance Havner

"It is possible to evangelize the world in this generation, if the Church will but do her duty. The trouble is not with the heathen. A dead Church will prevent it, if it is prevented. Why should it not be accomplished? God will have all men to be saved and come unto the knowledge of the truth. The resources of the Church are boundless. Let the will of the Church be brought into line with the will of God, and nothing will be found to be impossible. May God grant it!"

- John Griffith

"The church is unique in that it is so able to cut across age boundaries and social-status boundaries. When one loves the Lord Jesus Christ and sincerely seeks to follow Him, then one quite by surprise comes upon a community that he did not know existed, a community that is experienced within the heart; and when this community is found, nothing is ever quite the same again."

- Gerald J. Jud

"The Church exists for nothing else but to draw men into Christ, to make them little Christs. If they are not doing that, all the cathedrals, clergy, missions, sermons, even the Bible itself, are simply a waste of time. God became Man for no other purpose."

- C.S. Lewis

"Where God builds a church the devil builds a chapel."

- Martin Luther

"Rather than growing bigger churches we should be concerned with growing bigger Christians."

- Rich Mullins

"I might believe in the Redeemer if His followers looked more Redeemed."

- Fredrick Nietzsche

"In the New Testament church it says they were all amazed - And now in our churches everybody wants to be amused."

- Leonard Ravenhill

"The Church used to be a lifeboat rescuing the perishing. Now she is a cruise ship recruiting the promising."
- Leonard Ravenhill

"What I have seen in the past 10 years of traveling- performing at a church one day and a casino the next- is that a lot of people in the church want to be entertained, and people in casinos want to be ministered to. That's hard to understand, but I see a *hunger* in the world that I don't see in the church."
- Ricky Skaggs

"The whole history of the Church is one long story of this tendency to settle down on this earth and to become conformed to this world, to find acceptance and popularity here and to eliminate the element of conflict and of pilgrimage. That is the trend and the tendency of everything. Therefore outwardly, as well as inwardly, pioneering is a costly thing."
- T. Austin Sparks

"The mark of a great church is not its seating capacity, but its capacity for unconditional love – even to those who are in the deepest pits of sin."
- Mike Stachura

"One hundred religious persons knit into a unity by careful organization does not constitute a church any more than eleven dead men make a football team. The first requisite is life, always.""
- A. W. Tozer

"We must not think of the Church as an anonymous body, a mystical religious abstraction. We Christians are the Church and whatever we do is what the Church is doing. The matter, therefore, is for each of us a personal one. Any forward step in the Church must begin with the individual."
- A.W. Tozer

"I look upon the entire world as my parish."
- John Wesley

"Elisha had more of the Holy Spirit, dead, than most Christians have of Him, alive."
- Steve Wilburn

"The Church is an organism that grows best in an alien society."
- C. Stacey Woods

"We manufacture atheists with mundane Christianity."
- Robert Wurtz

"The Church, like the believers that met at Solomon's Porch, is not confined by walls."
- Unknown

CLEANLINESS

"Have mercy upon me, O God, according to thy loving kindness: according unto the multitude of thy tender mercies blot out my transgressions. Wash me thoroughly from mine iniquity, and cleanse me from my sin...Purge me with hyssop, and I shall be clean: wash me, and I shall be whiter than snow...Create in me a clean heart, O God; and renew a right spirit within me."
- Psalm 51:1-2, 7, 10

"For cleanness of body was ever esteemed to proceed from a due reverence to God, to society, and to ourselves."
- Sir Francis Bacon

"Mrs. Joe was a very clean housekeeper, but had an exquisite art of making her cleanliness more uncomfortable and unacceptable than dirt itself."
- Charles Dickens

"Certainly this is a duty, not a sin. Cleanliness is indeed next to godliness."
- John Wesley

CLOTHING

"In like manner also, that women adorn themselves in modest apparel, with shamefacedness and sobriety; not with broided hair, or gold, or pearls, or costly array; But (which becometh women professing godliness) with good works."
- I Timothy 2:9-10

"Any man may be in good spirits and good temper when he's well dressed. There ain't much credit in that."
- Charles Dickens

"If most of us are ashamed of shabby clothes and shoddy furniture, let us be more ashamed of shabby ideas and shoddy philosophies.... It would be a sad situation if the wrapper were better than the meat wrapped inside it."
- Albert Einstein

"The vanity of loving fine clothes and new fashions, and valuing ourselves by them, is one of the most childish pieces of folly that can be."
- Sir Matthew Hale

"Dress is a table of your contents."
- Johann Kaspar Lavater

"Those who think that in order to dress well it is necessary to dress extravagantly or grandly make a great mistake. Nothing so well becomes true feminine beauty as simplicity."
- George Denison Prentice

"No man is esteemed for gay garments but by fools and women."
- Sir Walter Raleigh

"Beauty, like truth, never is so glorious as when it goes plainest."
- Lawrence Sterne

"Clothes make the man. Naked people have little or no influence on society."

- Mark Twain

"The finest clothing made is a person's skin, but, of course, society demands something more than this."

- Mark Twain

COMMITMENT – See DEDICATION

COMPASSION

"Compassion will cure more sins than condemnation."

- Henry Ward Beecher

"Compassion is an emotion of which we ought never to be ashamed. Graceful, particularly in youth, is the tear of sympathy, and the heart that melts at the tale of woe. We should not permit ease and indulgence to contract our affections, and wrap us up in a selfish enjoyment; but we should accustom ourselves to think of the distresses of human, life, of the solitary cottage; the dying parent, and the weeping orphan. Nor ought we ever to sport with pain and distress in any of our amusements, or treat even the meanest insect with wanton cruelty."

- Hugh Blair

"By compassion we make others' misery our own, and so, by relieving them, we relieve ourselves also."

- Sir Thomas Browne

"Man may dismiss compassion from his heart,
  But God will never."

- William Cowper

"Our task must be to free ourselves . . . by widening our circle of compassion to embrace all living creatures and the whole of nature and its beauty."

- Albert Einstein

"It is the crown of justice, and the glory, where it may kill with right, to save with pity."
- John Fletcher

"Poor naked wretches, wheresoe'er you are,
  That hide the pelting of this pitiless storm,
  How shall your houseless heads and unfed sides,
   Your loop'd and window'd raggedness, defend you
    From seasons such as these? Oh, I have ta'en
     Too little care of this! Take physic, pomp;
      Expose thyself to feel what wretches feel;
       That thou may'st shake the superflux to them,
        And show the heavens more just."
- William Shakespeare

"There never was any heart truly great and generous, that was not also tender and compassionate."
- Robert South

"The mark of a great church is not its seating capacity, but its capacity for unconditional love – even to those who are in the deepest pits of sin."
- Mike Stachura

"Some wish to live within a mile of the church building; I want to run a rescue shop within a yard of Hell."
- C.T. Studd

"You can't cut off a person's nose and then offer them a rose."
- Ravi Zacharias

"People do not care how much you know until they know how much you care."
- Unknown

COMPLAINTS

"All our murmurings are so many arrows shot at God Himself, and they will return upon our own hearts; they reach not Him, but they will hit us;

they hurt not Him, but they will wound us; therefore it is better to be mute than to murmur; it is dangerous to provoke a consuming fire."
- James Aughey

"We have first raised a dust and then complain we cannot see."
- George Berkeley

"It is a general error to suppose the loudest complainers for the public to be the most anxious for its welfare."
- Edmund Burke

"I will not be as those who spend the day in complaining of headache, and the night in drinking the wine that gives it."
- Johann Wolfgang von Goethe

"Every one must see daily instances of people who complain from a mere habit of complaining."
- Richard Graves

"To hear complaints with patience, even when complaints are vain, is one of the duties of friendship."
- Samuel Johnson

"It is better to light a candle than to curse the darkness."
- Eleanor Roosevelt

"Our murmuring is the devil's music."
- Thomas Watson

"Beating a dead horse will not get you to the market any sooner."
- English Proverb

"Some people complain that God placed thorns on roses, while others praise him for putting roses among thorns."
- Unknown

CONCENTRATION

"Beware lest you lose the substance by grasping at the shadow."
- Aesop

"Concentrate all your thoughts upon the work at hand. The sun's rays do not burn until brought to a focus."
- Alexander Graham Bell

"As the gardener, by severe pruning, forces the sap of the tree into one or two vigorous limbs, so should you stop off your miscellaneous activity and concentrate your force on one or a few points. For concentration is the secret of strength."
- Ralph Waldo Emerson

"The secret of concentration is elimination."
- Howard Hendricks

"The jack-of-all-trades seldom is good at any. Concentrate all of your efforts on one definite chief aim."
- Napoleon Hill

"If you chase two rabbits, both will escape."
- English Proverb

"A person who aims at nothing is sure to hit it."
- Unknown

CONDEMNATION

"For God sent not his Son into the world to condemn the world; but that the world through him might be saved. He that believeth on him is not condemned: but he that believeth not is condemned already, because he hath not believed in the name of the only begotten Son of God. 9And this is the condemnation, that light is come into the world, and men loved darkness rather than light, because their deeds were evil."
- John 3:17-19

"There is therefore now no condemnation to them which are in Christ Jesus, who walk not after the flesh, but after the Spirit. For the law of the Spirit of life in Christ Jesus hath made me free from the law of sin and death."
- Romans 8:1

"Others proclaim the infirmities of a great man with satisfaction and complacence, if they discover none of the like in themselves."
- Joseph Addison

"Compassion will cure more sins than condemnation."
- Henry Ward Beecher

"It is undoubtedly true, though it may seem paradoxical,--but, in general, those who are habitually employed in finding and displaying faults are unqualified for the work of reformation."
- Edmund Burke

"Censure is often useful, praise often deceitful."
- Charles Churchill

"The readiest and surest way to get rid of condemnation and censure, is to correct ourselves."
- Demosthenes

"Self-condemnation is Satan's lie to prevent sinners from repenting."
- Jan Greenley

"There are but three ways for a man to revenge himself of the censure of the world,--to despise it, to return the like, or to endeavor to live so as to avoid it; the first of these is usually pretended, the last is almost impossible, the universal practice is for the second."
- Jonathan Swift

"Invective may be a sharp weapon, but overuse blunts its edge. Even when the denunciation is just and true it is an error of art to indulge it too long."
- John Tyndall

CONSECRATION – See HOLINESS

CONVERSION

"God is not glorified in any transaction upon earth so much as in the conversion of a sinner."
- Archibald Alexander

"It is slow work to be born again."
- Henry Ward Beecher

"I had a conversion experience which was very real... There were no blinding lights, simply a quiet conviction I had found something."
- George Carey

"I wish there were more true conversion, and then there would not be so much backsliding, and, for fear of suffering, living at ease, when there are so few to contend for Christ and His cause."
- Donald Cargill

"Every man or woman who turns to Christ must bear in mind that they are breaking with their old master, and enlisting under a new leader. Conversion is a revolutionary process."

"But see that impenitent sinner. Convicted of his sin under the clear gospel light that shines all around him, he is driven to pray. He knows he ought to repent, and almost thinks he wants to, and will try. Yet still he clings to his sins, and will not give up his heart to God. Still he holds his heart in a state of impenitence. Now mark here; his sin in thus withholding his heart from God under so much light, involves greater guilt than all the abominations of the Heathen world. Put together the guilt of all those widows who immolate themselves on the funeral pile -- of those who hurl their children into the Ganges, or into the burning arms of Moloch -- all does not begin to approach the guilt of that convicted sinner's prayer who comes before God under the pressure of his conscience, and prays a heartless prayer, determined all the while to withhold his heart from God. Oh! why does this sinner thus tempt God, and thus abuse his love, and thus trample on his known authority? Oh! that moment of impenitence, while his prayers are forced by conscience from his burning lips, and yet he will not yield the controversy with his Maker -- that moment involves direr guilt than rests on all the Heathen world together! He knows more than they all, yet sins despite of all his knowledge. The many stripes belong to him -- the few to them."

- Charles Finney

"To pass from estrangement from God to be a son of God is the basic fact of conversion. That altered relationship with God gives you an altered relationship with yourself, with your brother man, with nature, with the universe."

- E. Stanley Jones

"A man to be converted has to give up his will, his ways, and his thoughts."

- Dwight L. Moody

"A revival does two things. First, it returns the Church from her backsliding and second, it causes the conversion of men and women; and it always includes the conviction of sin on the part of the Church. What a spell the devil seems to cast over the Church today!"

- Billy Sunday

"Conversion is a complete surrender to Jesus. It's a willingness to do what he wants you to do."

- Billy Sunday

"I am convinced that many evangelicals are not truly and soundly converted. Among the evangelicals it is entirely possible to come into membership, to ooze in by osmosis, to leak through the cells of the church and never know what it means to be born of the Spirit and washed in the blood. A great deal that passes for the deeper life is nothing more or less than basic Christianity. There is nothing deeper about it, and it is where we should have been from the start. We should have been happy, joyous, victorious Christians walking in the Holy Spirit and not fulfilling the lusts of the flesh. Instead we have been chasing each other around the perpetual mountain.

What we need is what the old Methodists called a sound conversion. There is a difference between conversion and a sound conversion. People who have never been soundly converted do not have the Spirit to enlighten them. When they read the Sermon on the Mount or the teaching passages of the epistles that tell them how to live or the doctrinal passages that tell how they can live, they are unaffected. The Spirit who wrote them is not witnessing in their hearts because they have not been born of the Spirit. That often happens."

– A.W. Tozer

COUNSEL

"Where no counsel is, the people fall: but in the multitude of counselors there is safety."

- Proverbs 11:14

"He that gives good advice, builds with one hand; he that gives good counsel and example, builds with both; but he that gives good admonition and bad example, builds with one hand and pulls down with the other."

- Sir Francis Bacon

"Don't speak too much when you counsel sir. Get to the point and pray. Let God do it!"

- Keith Daniel

"Good counsels observed are chains to grace, which neglected, prove halters to strange undutiful children."

- Thomas Fuller

"Three may keep counsel, if two are away."

- Johann Wolfgang von Goethe

"If honest of heart and uprightness before God were lacking or if I did not patiently wait on God for instruction, or if I preferred the counsel of my fellow-men to the declarations of the Word of God, I made great mistakes."

- George Muller

"Go not to the elves for counsel, for they will say both yes and no."
- J. R. R. Tolkien

COURAGE

"There shall not any man be able to stand before thee all the days of thy life: as I was with Moses, so I will be with thee: I will not fail thee, nor forsake thee. Be strong and of a good courage: for unto this people shalt thou divide for an inheritance the land, which I sware unto their fathers to give them. Only be thou strong and very courageous, that thou mayest observe to do according to all the law, which Moses my servant commanded thee: turn not from it to the right hand or to the left, that thou mayest prosper withersoever thou goest. This book of the law shall not depart out of thy mouth; but thou shalt meditate therein day and night, that thou mayest observe to do according to all that is written therein: for then thou shalt make thy way prosperous, and then thou shalt have good success. Have not I commanded thee? Be strong and of a good courage; be not afraid, neither be thou dismayed: for the LORD thy God is with thee whithersoever thou goest."
- Joshua 1:5-9

"But straightway Jesus spake upto them saying, Be of good cheer: it is I; be not afraid."
- Matthew 14:27

"Courage makes a man more than himself; for he is then himself plus his valor."
- William Alger

"It takes a lot of courage to show your dreams to someone else."
- Erma Bombeck

"Courage is the thing; all goes if courage goes."
- Sir J. M. Barrie

"A real spirit should neither court neglect, nor dread to bear it."
- Lord Byron

"He who loses wealth loses much; he who loses a friend loses more; but he that loses his courage loses all."

- Cervantes

"Courage is rightly esteemed the first of human qualities, because it is the quality which guarantees all others."

- Winston Churchill

"Upon this battle depends the survival of Christian civilisation. Upon it depends our own British life and the long continuity of our institutions and our Empire. The whole fury and might of the enemy must very soon be turned on us now. Hitler knows that he will have to break us in this island or lose the war. If we can stand up to him, all Europe may be free and the life of the world may move forward into broad, sunlit uplands. But if we fail, then the whole world, including the United States, including all that we have known and cared for, will sink into the abyss of a new Dark Age, made more sinister, and perhaps more protracted, by the lights of perverted science. Let us therefore brace ourselves to our duties, and so bear ourselves that, if the British Empire and its Commonwealth last for a thousand years, men will still say, '*This was their finest hour.*'"

- Winston Churchill

"This is the way to cultivate courage: First, by standing firm on some conscientious principle, some law of duty. Next, by being faithful to truth and right on small occasions and common events. Third, by trusting in God for help and power."

- James Clarke

"Never forget that no military leader has ever become great without audacity."

- Karl von Clausewitz

"Courage multiplies the chances of success by sometimes making opportunities, and always availing itself of them; and in this sense Fortune may be said to favor fools by those who, however prudent in their opinion, are deficient in valor and enterprise."

- Samuel Coleridge

"Heroes and winners aren't always the same people."
- Michael Farreli

"I have often been downcast, but never in despair; I regard our hiding as a dangerous adventure, romantic and interesting at the same time. In my diary I treat all the privations as amusing. I have made up my mind now to lead a different life from other girls and, later on, different from ordinary housewives. My start has been so very full of interest, and that is the sole reason why I have to laugh at the humorous side of the most dangerous moments."
- Anne Frank

"We only need a little courage and perseverance. Actually, we have enough of both in our earthly affairs, but none at all in the only thing that really matters (Luke 10:42)."
- Jeanne Guyon

"Security is mostly superstition. It does not exist in nature. Avoiding danger is no safer in the long run than outright exposure. The fearful are caught as often as the bold. Life is either a daring adventure, or nothing."
- Helen Keller

"Refusal to take risks makes for a life of mediocrity at best."
- Michael LeBoeuf

"That so few now dare to be eccentric, marks the chief danger of our time."
- John Stuart Mill

"Courage with knowledge is valor. Courage without knowledge is stupidity."
- Jack Murphy

"I love the man that can smile in trouble, that can gather strength from distress, and grow brave by reflections."
- Thomas Paine

"A pint of sweat, saves a gallon of blood."
- General George S. Patton

"The future doesn't belong to the faint hearted, it belongs to the brave."
- Ronald Reagan

CREATIVITY

"In the beginning, God created the Heavens and the Earth."
- Genesis 1:1

"I will praise thee; for I am fearfully and wonderfully made: marvelous are thy works; and that my soul knoweth right well. My substance was not hid from thee, when I was made in secret, and curiously wrought in the lowest parts of the earth."
- Psalm 139:14-15

"For we are his workmanship, created in Christ Jesus unto good works, which God hath before ordained that we should walk in them."
- Ephesians 2:10

"To have the sense of creative activity is the great happiness and the great proof of being alive."
- Matthew Arnold

"The secret to creativity is knowing how to hide your sources."
- Albert Einstein
"Creative minds have always been known to survive any kind of bad training."
- Anna Freud

"Every individual who is not creative has a negative, narrow, exclusive taste and succeeds in depriving creative being of its energy and life."
- Johann Wolfgang von Goethe

"From inaccessible mountain range by way of desert untrod by human foot to the ends of the unknown seas, the breath of the everlasting creative spirit is felt, rejoicing over every speck of dust that hearkens to it and lives."

- Johann Wolfgang von Goethe

"Creative people have to be fed from a divine source."

- Dag Hammarskjold

"Creativity is not the finding of a thing, but the making something out of it after it is found."

- James Russell Lowell

"Creativity is a divine attribute. God, in His infinite creativity, created all there is in six days."

- Jack Murphy

"Creativity is the power to connect the seemingly unconnected."

- W. S. Plumer

CRIME

"Because sentence against an evil work is not executed speedily, therefore the heart of the sons of men is fully set in them to do evil."

- Ecclesiastes 8:11

"He that is without sin among you, let him first cast a stone at her."

- John 8:7

"The contagion of crime is like that of the plague. Criminals collected together corrupt each other; they are worse than ever when at the termination of their punishment they re-enter society."

- Napoleon Bonaparte

"Crimes lead one into another; they who are capable of being forgers are capable of being incendiaries."

- Edmund Burke

"Responsibility prevents crimes."
- Edmund Burke

"If we were brought to trial for the crimes we have committed against ourselves, few would escape the gallows."
- Paul Eldridge

"No matter how you seem to fatten on a crime, that can never be good for the bee which is bad for the hive."
- Ralph Waldo Emerson

"A thief believes everybody steals."
- Edgar Watson Howe

"Organized crime constitutes nothing less than a guerrilla war against society."
- Lyndon B. Johnson

"We are easily shocked by crimes which appear at once in their full magnitude; but the gradual growth of our wickedness, endeared by interest and palliated by all the artifices of self-deceit, gives us time to form distinctions in our favor."
- Samuel Johnson

"We don't seem to be able to check crime, so why not legalize it and then tax it out of business."
- Will Rogers

"Most people fancy themselves innocent of those crimes of which they cannot be convicted. Yet he who profits by a crime commits it."
- Seneca

"Educate your children to self-control, to the habit of holding passion and prejudice and evil tendencies to an upright and reasoning will, and you have done much to abolish misery from their future lives and crimes to society."
- Daniel Webster

"The cure for crime is not found in the "electric chair." It is found in the "high chair."

>   -   American Proverb

CRITICISM

"He that wrestles with us strengthens our nerves and sharpens our skill. Our antagonist is our helper."

>   -   Edmund Burke

"Any fool can criticize, condemn, and complain but it takes character and self control to be understanding and forgiving."

>   -   Dale Carnegie

"Criticism may not be agreeable, but it is necessary. It fulfils the same function as pain in the human body. It calls attention to an unhealthy state of things."

>   -   Winston Churchill

"You know who critics are? They are the men who have failed in literature and art."

>   -   Benjamin Disraeli

"Never fear criticism when you're right; never ignore it when you're wrong."

>   -   Benjamin Franklin

"Any fool can criticize, condemn and complain and most fools do."

>   -   Benjamin Franklin

"He has a right to criticize, who has a heart to help."

>   -   Abraham Lincoln

"The strength of criticism lies only in the weakness of the thing criticized."

>   -   Henry Wadsworth Longfellow

"How many people would like to get up in a social prayer-meeting to say a few words for Christ, but there is such a cold spirit of criticism in the church that they dare not do it."
- Dwight L. Moody

"Reply to critics: I like the way I do it better than the way you don't."
- Will Rogers

"It is not the critic who counts; not the man who points out how the strong man stumbles, or where the doer of deeds could have done them better. The credit belongs to the man who is actually in the arena, whose face is marred by dust and sweat and blood, who strives valiantly; who errs and comes short again and again; because there is not effort without error and shortcomings; but who does actually strive to do the deed; who knows the great enthusiasm, the great devotion, who spends himself in a worthy cause, who at the best knows in the end the triumph of high achievement and who at the worst, if he fails, at least he fails while daring greatly. So that his place shall never be with those cold and timid souls who know neither victory nor defeat."
- Theodore Roosevelt

"The malignant deity Criticism dwelt on the top of a snowy mountain in Nova Zembla; Momus found her extended in her den upon the spoils of numberless volumes half devoured. At her right sat Ignorance, her father and husband, blind with age; at her left Pride, her mother, dressing her up in the scraps of paper herself had torn. There was Opinion, her sister, light of foot, hoodwinked and headstrong, yet giddy and perpetually turning. About her played her children, Noise and Impudence, Dullness and Vanity, Positiveness, Pedantry and Ill Manners."
- Jonathan Swift

"One mustn't criticize other people on grounds where he can't stand perpendicular himself."
- Mark Twain

"Flatter me, and I may not believe you. Criticize me, and I may not like you. Ignore me, and I may not forgive you. Encourage me, and I will not forget you. Love me and I may be forced to love you."

- William Arthur Ward

"Before you go and criticize the younger generation, just remember who raised them."

- American Proverb

"All of us could take a lesson from the weather. It pays no attention to criticism."

- Unknown

CRITICAL THINKING

"Test everything. Hold onto that which is good."

- I Thessalonians 5:21

"One must live the way one thinks or end up thinking the way one has lived."

- Paul Bourget

"The best thinking has been done in solitude. The worst has been done in turmoil."

- Thomas Edison

"I think and think for months and years. Ninety-nine times, the conclusion is false. The hundredth time I am right."

- Albert Einstein

"Small is the number of people who see with their eyes and think with their minds."

- Albert Einstein

"Thinking is the hardest work there is, which is probably the reason why so few engage in it."

- Henry Ford

"We must think anew -- and act anew."
- Abraham Lincoln

"Where all think alike, no one thinks very much."
- Walter Lippman

"No man thinks clearly when his fists are clenched."
- George Jean Nathan

"Most people would sooner die than think; in fact, they do so. Thinking you know when in fact you don't is a fatal mistake, to which we are all prone."
- Bertrude Arthur Russell

CROSS – See CHRIST; CHRISTIANITY

CRUELTY

"Cruelty and fear shake hands together."
- Honore de Balzac

"A good thing can't be cruel."
- Charles Dickens

"Cruelty, like every, other vice, requires no motive outside of itself; it only requires opportunity."
- George Eliot

"I would love to see the grimace he [Marquis de Cinq-Mars] is now making on the scaffold."
- King Louis XIII

"When cruelty is inflicted on innocent people, it discredits whatever cause."
- Ronald Reagan

"All cruelty springs from weakness."
- Seneca

"My doctrine is this, that if we see cruelty or wrong that we have the power to stop, and do nothing, we make ourselves sharers in the guilt."
-     Anna Sewell

CULTURE

"And Ruth said, Intreat me not to leave thee, or to return from following after thee: for whither thou goest, I will go; and where thou lodgest, I will lodge: thy people shall be my people, and thy God my God:"
-     Ruth 1:16

"Culture is to know the best that has been said and thought in the world."
-     Matthew Arnold

"Many Christians have what we might call a "cultural holiness". They adapt to the character and behavior pattern of Christians around them. As the Christian culture around them is more or less holy, so these Christians are more or less holy. But God has not called us to be like those around us. He has called us to be like himself. Holiness is nothing less than conformity to the character of God."
- Jerry Bridges

"Despite all the fancy buildings, sophisticated programs and highly visible presence, it is my contention that the church is almost a non-entity when it comes to shaping culture."
- Bob Briner

"The great law of culture is, Let each become all that he was created capable of being; expand, if possible, to his full growth; resisting all impediments, casting off all foreign, especially all noxious adhesions, and show himself at length in his own shape and stature be these what they may."
-     Thomas Carlyle

"The only worthy end of all learning, of all science, of all life, in fact, is that human beings should love one another better. Culture merely for culture's sake can never be anything but a sapless root, capable of producing at best a shriveled branch."

- John Walker Cross

"One ought every day at least to hear a little song, read a good poem, see a fine picture, and, if it were possible, to speak a few reasonable words."

- Johann Wolfgang von Goethe

"There are some races more cultured and advanced and ennobled by education than others; but there are no races nobler than others. All are equally destined for freedom."

- Alexander Humboldt

"Though men of delicate taste be rare, they are easily to be distinguished in society by the soundness of their understanding, their embrace of fine music and the superiority of their faculties above the rest of mankind."

- David Hume

"The prosperity of a country depends, not on the abundance of its revenues, nor on the strength of its fortifications, nor on the beauty of its public buildings; but it consists in the number of its cultivated citizens, in its men of education, enlightenment and character."

- Martin Luther

"Too often we see the Bible through whatever lens we get from our culture."

- Brian McLaren

"As the soil, however rich it may be, cannot be productive without culture, so the mind, without cultivation, can never produce good fruit."

- Seneca

"The test of the vitality of a religion is to be seen in its effect on the culture."

- Elton Trueblood

"Culture is an instrument wielded by professors to manufacture professors, who when their turn comes will manufacture professors."
- Simone Weil

CYNICISM

"The cynic is one who never sees a good quality in a man, and never fails to see a bad one. He is the human owl, vigilant in darkness and blind to light, mousing for vermin, and never seeing noble game. The cynic puts all human actions into two classes--openly bad and secretly bad. All virtue and generosity and disinterestedness are merely the appearance of good; but selfish at the bottom. He holds that no man does a good thing except for profit. The effect of his conversation upon your feelings is to chill and sear them; to send you away sour and morose. His criticisms and hints fall indiscriminately upon every lovely thing, like frost upon flowers."
- Henry Ward Beecher

"Indifference to all the actions and passions of mankind was not supposed to be such a distinguished quality at that time, I think. I have known it very fashionable indeed. I have seen it displayed with such success that I have encountered some fine ladies and gentlemen who might as well have been born caterpillars."
- Charles Dickens

"A cynic can chill and dishearten with a single word."
- Ralph Waldo Emerson

"The cynics are right nine times out of ten."
- Henry Louis Mencken

"Inside of every cynic, there lay a disheartened optimist."
- Jack Murphy

"The poorest way to face life is to face it with a sneer."
- Theodore Roosevelt

"The power of accurate observation is often called cynicism by those who don't have it."

- George Bernard Shaw

"A cynic is a man who knows the price of everything and the value of nothing."

- Oscar Wilde

D

DARKNESS

"In the beginning God created the heaven and the earth. And the earth was without form, and void; and darkness was upon the face of the deep. And the Spirit of God moved upon the face of the waters."
- Genesis 1:1-2

"Ye are the light of the world. A city that is set on an hill cannot be hid. Neither do men light a candle, and put it under a bushel, but on a candlestick; and it giveth light unto all that are in the house. Let your light so shine before men, that they may see your good works, and glorify your Father which is in heaven."
- Matthew 5:14-16

"When it is dark enough, men see the stars."
- Ralph Waldo Emerson

"It is always darkest just before the day dawneth."
- Thomas Fuller

"Darkness is only driven out with light, not more darkness."
- Martin Luther King, Jr.

"Yet from those flames
No light, but rather darkness visible."
- John Milton

"It is better to light a candle than to curse the darkness."
- Eleanor Roosevelt

"Even the smallest stars shine in the darkness."
- Danish Proverb

"It's always darkest before the dawn."
- English Proverb

DEATH

"Precious in the sight of the LORD is the death of his saints."
- Psalm 116:15

"O death, where is thy sting? O grave, where is thy victory?"
- I Corinthians 15:55

"Death is as near to the young as to the old; here is all the difference: death stands behind the young man's back, before the old man's face."
- Thomas Adams

"Call no man happy till he is dead."
- Aeschylus of Eleusis

"Life is pleasant. Death is peaceful. It's the transition that's troublesome."
- Isaac Asimov

"To a father, when his child dies, the future dies; to a child, when his parents die, the past dies."
- Berthold Auerbach

"Death to the Christian is the funeral of all his sorrows and evils, and the resurrection, of all his joys."
- James Aughey

"He that dies in an earnest pursuit is like one that is wounded in hot blood; who, for the time, scarce feels the hurt; and therefore a mind fixed and bent upon somewhat that is good doth avert the dolors of death; but above all, believe it, the sweetest canticle is, 'Lord, now lettest Thou Thy servant depart in peace.'"
- Sir Francis Bacon

"Death, so called, is a thing which makes men weep,
And yet a third of life is pass'd in sleep."
- Lord Byron

"A few feet under the ground reigns so profound a silence, and yet so much tumult on the surface!"
- Victor Hugo

"We begin to die as soon as we are born, and the end is linked to the beginning."
- Anicius Manilius

"Regardless of where you are or how you live, you are still just a few heartbeats from death."
- Leonard Ravenhill

"Is death the last sleep? No, it is the last final awakening."
- Sir Walter Scott

"...And when I am dying, how happy I'll be, if the lamp of my life has been burned out for Thee."
- Charles T. Studd

DECISIONS

"Multitudes, multitudes in the valley of decision: for the day of the Lord is near in the valley of decision."
- Joel 3:14

"I take one decisive and immediate step, and resign my all to the sufficiency of my Saviour."
- Thomas Chalmers

"I reverence the individual who understands distinctly what he wishes; who unweariedly advances, who knows the means conducive to his object, and can seize and use them."
- Johann Wolfgang von Goethe

"The way to develop decisiveness is to start right where you are, with the very next question you face."
- Napoleon Hill

"To be energetic and firm where principle demands it, and tolerant in all else, is not easy. It is not easy do abhor wickedness, and oppose it with every energy, and at the same time to have the meekness and gentleness of Christ, becoming all things to all men for the truth's sake. The energy of patience, the most godlike of all, is not easy."
- Mark Hopkins

"Most of us could summarize our lives around 5 or 6 defining moments-- moments that if we had chosen differently would have radically altered the trajectory of our lives."
- Erwin McManus

"Heaven never helps the man who will not act."
- William Shakespeare

"Decision is a vastly important thing with a convicted sinner. He must choose, or he must be lost. If he will not do it, he may expect the Divine Spirit to depart from him, and leave him to his own way."
- Ichabod Spencer

"Almost only counts in horseshoes, hand grenades and nuclear war."
- American Proverb

"Essentially there are 2 actions in life: performance and excuses. Make a decision as to which you will accept from yourself--and those you manage. People fail in direct proportion to their willingness to accept socially acceptable excuses for failure."

- Unknown

DEDICATION

On a tablet in a large church, this inscription was placed in memory of John Geddie: "When he landed in 1848, there were no Christians here; when he left in 1872, there were no heathen."

- Memorial to John Geddie, missionary in the South Seas

"In the confrontation between the stream and the rock, the stream always wins, not through strength but by perseverance."

- H. Jackson Brown

"All that is necessary for the triumph of evil is that good men do nothing."

- Edmund Burke

"Expect great things from God. Attempt great thing for God."

- William Carey

"Prayer, not works, is the acid test of devotion."

- Samuel Chadwick

"A vision without a task makes a visionary.
A task without a vision is drudgery.
A vision with a task makes a missionary."

- Samuel Chadwick

"We shall go on to the end, we shall fight in France, we shall fight on the seas and oceans, we shall fight with growing confidence and growing strength in the air, we shall defend our Island, whatever the cost may be, we shall fight on the beaches, we shall fight on the landing grounds, we shall fight in the fields and in the streets, we shall fight in the hills; we shall never surrender, and even if, which I do not for a moment believe, this Island or a large part of it were subjugated and starving, then our Empire beyond the seas, armed and guarded by the British Fleet, would carry on the struggle, until, in God's good time, the New World, with all its power and might, steps forth to the rescue and the liberation of the Old."

- Winston Churchill

"Everyone has his own Atlantics to fly. Whatever you want very much to do, against the opposition of tradition, neighborhood opinion, and so-called 'common sense' – that is an Atlantic."

- Amelia Earhart

"We must not, in trying to think about how we can make a big difference, ignore the small daily differences we can make which, over time, add up to big differences that we often cannot foresee."

- Marion Wright Edelman

"Many of life's failures are people who did not realize how close they were to success when they gave up."

- Thomas Edison

"Our greatest weakness lies in giving up. The most certain way to success is always to try just one more time."

- Thomas Edison

"Wherever you are, be all there. Live to the hilt of every situation you believe to be the will of God...Let not our longing slay the appetite of our living."

- Jim Elliot

"If we look carefully within ourselves, we shall find that there are certain limits beyond which we refuse to go in offering ourselves to God. We hover around these reservations, making believe not to see them, for fear of self-reproach. The more we shrink from giving up any such reserved point, the more certain it is that it needs to be given up. If we were not fast bound by it, we should not make so many efforts to persuade ourselves that we are free."

- François Fénelon

"Whether you think you can do a thing or not, you're right."

- Henry Ford

"Successful men are influenced by the desire for pleasing results. Failures are influenced by the desire for comfortable methods and are inclined to be satisfied with such results as can be obtained by doing things they like to do."

- Albert Gray

"Unless we have WITHIN us that which is ABOVE us, we will eventually yield to that which is AMONG us."

- William Gurnall

"It's amazing what can be accomplished if you don't worry about who gets the credit."

- Clarence W. Jones

"Most joyfully will I confirm with my blood that truth which I have written and preached."

- John Huss, as he was burned at the stake

"I submit to you that if a man has not discovered something that he will die for, he isn't fit to live."

- Martin Luther King, Jr.

"One of the greatest dangers in the Christian life is losing interest in what is familiar."

- Brad Lambert

"The quality of a person's life is in direct proportion to their commitment to excellence, regardless of their chosen field of endeavor."
- Vince Lombardi

"There is something infinitely better than doing a great thing for God, and the infinitely better thing is to be where God wants us to be, to do what God wants us to do, and to have no will apart from His."
- G. Campbell Morgan

"A pint of sweat, saves a gallon of blood."
- George S. Patton

"The difference between a successful person and others is not a lack of strength, not a lack of knowledge, but a lack of will."
- Norman Vincent Peale

"Nothing is too great and nothing is too small to commit into the hands of the Lord."
- A. W. Pink

"The men that have been the most heroic for God have had the greatest devotional lives."
- Leonard Ravenhill

"Keep me. Lord, from fainting
In this fierce fight,
When the foe is rising,
Clothe me with Thy might."
- Evan Roberts

"Far better is to dare mighty things, to win glorious triumphs, even though checkered by failure, than take rank with those poor spirits who neither enjoy much nor suffer much, because they live in the gray twilight that knows not victory nor defeat."
- Theodore Roosevelt

"My Lord was pleased to die for my sins; why should I not be glad to give up my poor life out of love for Him."

- Girolamo Savonarola

"Aspire to be something more than the mass of church members. Lift up your cry to God and beseech him to fire you with a nobler ambition than that which possesses the common Christian—that you may be found faithful unto God at the last, and may win many crowns for your Lord and Master, Christ."

- C.H. Spurgeon

"Devoting a little of yourself to everything means committing a great deal of yourself to nothing."

- Andy Stanley

"If Jesus Christ be God and died for me, then no sacrifice can be too great for me to make for Him."

- C.T. Studd

"The only fear I have is to fear to get out of the will of God. Outside of the will of God, there's nothing I want, and in the will of God there's nothing I fear, for God has sworn to keep me in His will. If I'm out of his will that's another matter. But if I'm in His will, He's sworn to keep me."

- A. W. Tozer

"Carpe Diem! Seize the day!"

- Latin Proverb

DEMOCRACY

"And the eye cannot say unto the hand, I have no need of thee: nor again the head to the feet, I have no need of you. Nay, much more those members of the body, which seem to be more feeble, are necessary: And those members of the body, which we think to be less honourable, upon these we bestow more abundant honour; and our uncomely parts have more abundant comeliness. For our comely parts have no need: but God hath tempered the body together, having given more abundant honour to that part which lacked. That there should be no schism in the

body; but that the members should have the same care one for another. And whether one member suffer, all the members suffer with it; or one member be honoured, all the members rejoice with it. Now ye are the body of Christ, and members in particular."
-    I Corinthians 12:21-27

"Democracy arose from men's thinking that if they were equal in any respect, they were equal absolutely."
-    Aristotle

"America's support for human rights and democracy is our noblest export to the world."
-    William Bennett

"To govern according to the sense, and agreeably to the interests of the people is a great and glorious object of government. This object cannot be obtained but through the medium of popular election, and popular election is a mighty evil."
-    Edmund Burke

"Many forms of Government have been tried, and will be tried in this world of sin and woe. No one pretends that democracy is perfect or all-wise. Indeed, it has been said that democracy is the worst form of government except all those other forms that have been tried from time to time."
-    Winston Churchill

"At the bottom of all the tributes paid to democracy is the little man, walking into the little booth, with a little pencil, making a little cross on a little bit of paper. . . ."
-    Winston Churchill

"Democracy is essentially anti-authoritarian--that is, it not only demands the right but imposes the responsibility of thinking for ourselves."
-    Bergen Evans

"Democracy which cannot defend itself has no right to exist."
-    Emil Franke

"In a democracy, dissent is an act of faith."
- William Fulbright

"A democracy is nothing more than mob rule, where fifty-one percent of the people may take away the rights of the other forty-nine."
- Thomas Jefferson

"I have no fear that the result of our experiment will be that men may be trusted to govern themselves without a master."
- Thomas Jefferson

"We are not afraid to entrust the American people with unpleasant facts, foreign ideas, alien philosophies, and competitive values. For a nation that is afraid to let its people judge the truth and falsehood in an open market is a nation that is afraid of its people."
- John F. Kennedy

"Democracy does not guarantee equality of conditions--it only guarantees equality of opportunity."
- Irving Krystol

"Democracy is the government of the people, by the people, for the people."
- Abraham Lincoln

"Democracy gives every man the right to be his own oppressor."
- James Lowell

"The cry of Hollywood liberals for 'more democracy' is actually a cry for continued capitalism without restraint."
- Jack Murphy

"Democracy means not 'I am as good as you are,' but 'You are as good as I am.'"
- Theodore Parker

"One has the right to be wrong in a democracy."
- Claude Pepper

"We must be the great arsenal of democracy."
- Franklin D. Roosevelt

"A great democracy must be progressive or it will soon cease to be a great democracy."
- Theodore Roosevelt

"Democracy is a device that insures we shall be governed no better than we deserve."
- George Bernard Shaw

"All the ills of democracy can be cured by more democracy."
- Alfred Smith

"Your little child is the only true democrat."
- Harriet Beecher Stowe

"Democratic nations must try to find ways to starve the terrorist and the hijacker of the oxygen of publicity on which they depend."
- Margaret Thatcher

"Democracy is the recurrent suspicion that more than half of the people are right more than half of the time."
- E. B. White

"Thunder on! Stride on! Democracy. Strike with vengeful strokes."
- Walt Whitman

"The world must be made safe for democracy."
- Woodrow Wilson

"I believe in Democracy because it releases the energies and potential of every human being."
- Woodrow Wilson

"Too many people expect wonders from democracy, when the most wonderful thing of all is just having it."
- Walter Winchell

DESPAIR – See BROKENESS

DIFFICULTY – See TRIALS & TRIBULATIONS

DISAPPOINTMENT

"And hope maketh not ashamed; because the love of God is shed abroad in our hearts by the Holy Ghost which is given unto us."
- Romans 5:5

"It is sometimes of God's mercy that men in the eager pursuit of worldly aggrandizement are baffled; for they are very like a train going down an inclined plane,--putting on the brake is not pleasant, but it keeps the car on the track."
- Henry Ward Beecher

"In the light of eternity we shall see that what we desired would have been fatal to us, and that what we would have avoided was essential to our well-being."
- Francois Fenelon

"We must accept finite disappointment, but never lose infinite hope."
- Martin Luther King, Jr.

"Welcome, Disappointment! Thy hand is cold and hard, but it is the hand of a friend. Thy voice is stern and harsh, but it is the voice of a friend. Oh, there is something sublime in calm endurance, something sublime in the resolute, fixed purpose of suffering without complaining, which makes disappointment oftentimes better than success!"
- Henry Longfellow

"Out of the same substances one stomach will extract nutriment, another poison; and so the same disappointments in life will chasten and refine one man's spirit, and embitter another's."
- William F. Matthews

"Disappointment is often the salt of life."
- Theodore Parker

"For Disappointments, that come not by our own Folly, they are the Trials or Corrections of Heaven: And it is our own Fault, if they prove not our Advantage. To repine at them does not mend the Matter: It is only to grumble at our Creator. But to see the Hand of God in them, with an humble submission to his Will, is the Way to turn our Water into Wine, and engage the greatest Love and Mercy on our side."
- William Penn

"Disappointment to a noble soul is what cold water is to burning metal; it strengthens, tempers, intensifies, but never destroys it."
- Eliza Tabor

"God always answers our prayers, but sometimes the answer is no."
- Irish Proverb

DISCIPLESHIP

"Sheep that are well feed seldom wander off."
- Wes Baker

"Christianity without discipleship is always Christianity without Christ."
- Dietrich Bonheoffer

"At the back of it there lies the central citadel of obstinacy: I will not give up my right to myself--the thing God intends you to give up if ever you are going to be a disciple of Jesus Christ."
- Oswald Chambers

"The only way a member should leave the church is either to transfer to a new church or to be buried in a casket."

- David Yonggi Cho

"Nothing disciplines the inordinate desires of the flesh like service, and nothing transforms the desires of the flesh like serving in hiddenness. The flesh whines against service but it screams against hidden service. It strains and pulls for honor and recognition."

- Richard Foster

"It is only by a total death to self we can be lost in God."

- Jeanne Guyon

"Those who teach by their doctrine must teach by their life, or else they pull down with one hand what they build up with the other."

- Matthew Henry

"The invitation is not, "Give Me thine head." The invitation is, "My Son, give Me thine heart."

- John G. Lake

"Until you have given up yourself to Him you will not have a real self..."

- C.S. Lewis

"God creates out of nothing. Therefore, until a man is nothing, God can make nothing out of him."

- Martin Luther

"The goal of the pastor is not to get people to show up but to get people to grow up."

- John Maxwell

"All we have—ourselves--to Him, and if that be all, that is enough."

- Watchman Nee

"Discipleship is anything that causes what is believed in the heart to have demonstrable consequences in our daily life."

- Eugene Peterson

"The Bible parable says that while men slept, the enemy sowed tares among the wheat. A boy who rises at 4:30 to deliver papers is considered a go-getter, but to urge our young people to rise at 5:30 to pray is considered fanaticism. We must once again wear the harness of discipline. There is no other way."

- Leonard Ravenhill

"Let no one imagine that he will lose anything of human dignity by this voluntary sell-out of his all to his God. He does not by this degrade himself as a man; rather he finds his right place of high honor as one made in the image of his Creator. His deep disgrace lay in his moral derangement, his unnatural usurpation of the place of God. His honor will be proved by restoring again that stolen throne. In exalting God over all, he finds his own highest honor upheld."

- A.W Tozer

DISCIPLINE

"I defy you to read the life of any saint that has ever adorned the life of the Church without seeing at once that the greatest characteristic in the life of that saint was discipline and order. Invariably it is the universal characteristic of all the outstanding men and women of God."

- William Booth

"Nothing disciplines the inordinate desires of the flesh like service, and nothing transforms the desires of the flesh like serving in secret. The flesh whines against service but it screams against hidden service. It strains and pulls for honor and recognition."

- Richard Foster

"Success is not a matter of mastering subtle, sophisticated theory, but rather of embracing common sense with uncommon levels of discipline and persistence."

- Patrick Lencioni

"We must all suffer from one of two pains in life: the pain of discipline or the pain of regret. The difference is discipline weighs ounces while regret weighs tons."

- Jim Rohn

"We need Divine help to preach aright to a congregation of one. If a thing is worth doing at all, it is worth doing well."

- Charles H. Spurgeon

"Discipline--the decision to do today what most people won't so I can have tomorrow what most people won't. Discipline is delayed gratification. The key to delayed gratification is advanced decision making."

– Unknown

"What we do upon some great occasion will probably depend on what we already are; and what we already are will be the result of previous years of self-discipline."

- Unknown

DIVISION – See UNITY

DOCTRINE

"Therefore leaving the principles of the doctrine of Christ, let us go on unto perfection; not laying again the foundation of repentance from dead works, and of faith toward God, Of the doctrine of baptisms, and of laying on of hands, and of resurrection of the dead, and of eternal judgment."

- Hebrews 6:1-2

"Doctrine is nothing but the skin of truth set up and stuffed."

- Henry Ward Beecher

"Go on your knees before God. Bring all your idols; bring self-will, and pride, and every evil lust before Him, and give them up. Devote yourself, heart and soul, to His will; and see if you do not "know of the doctrine."
- Henry Ward Beecher

"In religion as in politics it so happens that we have less charity for those who believe half our creed, than for those who deny the whole of it."
- Charles Colton

"'Twas God the word that spake it,
    He took the bread and brake it,
      And what the word did make it,
        That I believe and take it."
- Queen Elizabeth I

"It is an undoubted truth that every doctrine that comes from God, leads to God; and that which doth not tend to promote holiness is not of God."
- George Whitefield

DRINKING - See ALCOHOL

E

ECONOMICS

"The moment that government appears at market, the principles of the market will be subverted."
- Edmund Burke

"There can be no economy where there is no efficiency."
- Benjamin Disraeli

"If you know how to spend less than you get you have the philosopher's stone."
- Benjamin Franklin

"A penny saved is a penny earned."
- Benjamin Franklin

"As boys should be educated with temperance, so the first greatest lesson that should be taught them is to admire frugality. It is by the exercise of this virtue alone they can ever expect to be useful members of society."
- Oliver Goldsmith

"It is no small commendation to manage a little well. He is a good waggoner that can turn in a little room. To live well in abundance is the praise to the estate, is the praise not of the person. I will study more how to give a good account of my little, than how to make it more."
- Joseph Hall

"No man is rich whose expenditure exceeds his means; and no one is poor whose incomings exceed his outgoings."
- Thomas Halliburton

"He who is taught to live upon little owes more to his father's wisdom than he that has a great deal left him does to his father's care."
- William Penn

"To balance Fortune by a just expense,
 Join with Economy, Magnificence."
- Alexander Pope

"Depression is when you're out of work. A recession is when your neighbor's out of work. Recovery is when Carter's out of work."
- Ronald Reagan

"An economist's guess is liable to be as good as anybody else's."
- Will Rogers

"Too often in recent history liberal governments have been wrecked on rocks of loose fiscal policy."
- Franklin D. Roosevelt

"If all economists were laid end to end, they would not reach a conclusion."
- George Bernard Shaw

"Economy is half the battle of life; it is not so hard to earn money as to spend it well."
- Charles Spurgeon

"The truth is we are all caught in a great economic system which is heartless."
- Woodrow Wilson

EDUCATION

"Histories make men wise; poets, witty; the mathematics, subtile; natural philosophy, deep; morals, grave; logic and rhetoric, able to contend."
- Sir Francis Bacon

"A child cannot be taught by anyone who despises him, and a child cannot afford to be fooled."
- James Baldwin

"We know that the gifts which men have do not come from the schools. If a man is a plain, literal, factual man, you can make a great deal more of him in his own line by education than without education, just as you can make a great deal more of a potato if you cultivate it than if you do not; but no cultivation in this world will ever make an apple out of a potato."
- Henry Ward Beecher

"Ask me my three priorities for Government, and I tell you: education, education and education."
- Tony Blair

"Education makes a people easy to lead, but difficult to drive; easy to govern, but impossible to enslave."
- Lord Henry Brougham

"Education is the cheapest method of defense for a nation."
- Edmund Burke

"The essential difference between a good and a bad education is this, that the former draws on the child to learn by making it sweet to him, the latter drives the child to learn, by making it sour to him if he does not."
- Charles Buxton

"That there should one man die ignorant who had capacity for knowledge, this I call a tragedy."
- Thomas Carlyle

"Education is the key to unlock the golden door of freedom."
- George Washington Carver

"He is to be educated because he is a man, and not because he is to make shoes, nails, and pins."
- William Ellery Channing

"Do not ask if a man has been through college. Ask if a college has been through him; if he is a walking university."
- Edwin Hubbell Chapin

"What greater or better gift can we offer the republic than to teach and instruct our youth?"
- Marcus Tullius Cicero

"Upon the education of the people of this country the fate of this country depends."
- Benjamin Disraeli

"Education isn't play--and it can't be made to look like play. It is hard, hard work. But it can be made interesting work."
- Thomas Edison

"Education is what remains after one has forgotten what one has learned in school."
- Albert Einstein

"It is not so very important for a person to learn facts. For that he does not really need a college. He can learn them from books. The value of an education in a liberal arts college is not the learning of many facts but the training of the mind to think about something that cannot be learned from textbooks."
- Albert Einstein

"Education is a better safeguard of liberty than a standing army. If we retrench the wages of the schoolmaster, we must raise those of the recruiting sergeant."
- Edward Everett

"Genius without education is like silver in the mine."
- Benjamin Franklin

"Education is the ability to listen to almost anything without losing your temper."
- Robert Frost

"The most distinguished professional men bear witness, with an overwhelming authority, in favor of a course of education in which to train the mind shall be the first object, and to stock it, the second."
- William Gladstone

"Whenever the people are well informed, they can be trusted with their own government; that whenever things get so far wrong as to attract their notice, they may be relied on to set them to rights."
- Thomas Jefferson

"The highest result of education is tolerance."
- Helen Keller

"I attribute the little I know to my not having been ashamed to ask for information and to my rule of conversing with all descriptions of men on these topics that form their own peculiar professions and pursuits."
- John Locke

"A well-instructed people alone can be permanently a free people."
- James Madison

"To educate a man in mind and not in morals is to educate a menace to society."
- Theodore Roosevelt

"Education is either from nature, from man, or from things; the developing of our faculties and organs is the education of nature; that of man is the application we learn to make of this very developing; and that of things is the experience we acquire in regard to the different objects by which we are affected. All that we have not at our birth, and that we stand in need of at the years of maturity, is the gift of education."
- Jean Jacque Rousseau

"The greatest education is received at a mother's knee."
- Mark Twain

"Teachers, do not simply teach 'lessons.' Teach 'children.'"
- English Proverb

EGO

"One may understand the cosmos, but never the ego; the self is more distant than any star."
- G. K. Chesterton

"My father always wanted to be the corpse at every funeral, the bride at every wedding, and the baby at every christening."
- Alice Roosevelt Longworth

"Don't let that chip on your shoulder be your only reason for walking erect."
- James Thurber

"Ego: The fallacy whereby a goose thinks that he's a swan."
- Unknown

ELECTIONS

"Elections are won by men and women chiefly because most people vote against somebody rather than for somebody."
- Franklin Adams

"Where elections end, there slavery begins."
- John Adams

"Each candidate behaved well in the hope of being judged worthy of election. However, this system was disastrous when the city had become corrupt. For then it was not the most virtuous but the most powerful that stood for election, and the weak, even if virtuous, were too frightened to run for office."
- Niccolo Machiavelli

"Next Tuesday all of you will go to the polls, will stand there in the polling place and make a decision. I think when you make that decision, it might be well if you would ask yourself, are you better off than you were four years ago?"
- Ronald Reagan

"An election cannot give a country a firm sense of direction if it has two or more national parties which merely have different names but are as alike in their principles and aims as two peas in the same pod."
- Franklin D. Roosevelt

"The most successful politician is he who says what everybody is thinking most often and in the loudest voice."
- Theodore Roosevelt

"I will not accept if nominated, and will not serve if elected."
- William Sherman

"Fifty percent of people won't vote, and fifty percent don't read newspapers. I hope it's the same fifty percent."
- Gore Vidal

ENCOURAGEMENT

"David was greatly distressed because the men were talking of stoning him; each one was bitter in spirit because of his sons and daughters. But David found strength in the LORD his God."
- I Samuel 30:6

"One of the highest of human duties is the duty of encouragement...It is easy to laugh at men's ideals; it is easy to pour cold water on their enthusiasm; it is easy to discourage others. The world is full of discouragers. We have a Christian duty to encourage one another. Many a time a word of praise or thanks or appreciation or cheer has kept a man on his feet. Blessed is the man who speaks such a word."
- William Barclay

"The truest help we can render an afflicted man is not to take his burden from him, but to call out his best energy, that he may be able to bear the burden."
- Phillip Brooks

"Nine tenths of education is encouragement."
- Anatole France

"Correction does much, but encouragement does more. Encouragement after censure is as the sun after a shower."
- Johann Wolfgang von Goethe

"Faint not; the miles to heaven are but few and short."
- Samuel Rutherford

"I am not afraid of tomorrow, for I have seen yesterday and I love today."
- William White

"More hearts pine away in secret anguish for the want of kindness from those who should be their comforters than for any other calamity in life."
- Edward Young

"A word of encouragement during a failure is worth more than an hour of praise after success."
- English Proverb

"Encouragement is the butter on the bread of life."
- English Proverb

ENEMIES

"But I say unto you which hear, Love your enemies, do good to them which hate you, Bless them that curse you, and pray for them which despitefully use you. And unto him that smiteth thee on the one cheek offer also the other; and him that taketh away thy cloak forbid not to take thy coat also. Give to every man that asketh of thee; and of him that taketh away thy goods ask them not again. And as ye would that men should do to you, do ye also to them likewise.
 For if ye love them which love you, what thank have ye? for sinners also love those that love them. And if ye do good to them which do good to you, what thank have ye? for sinners also do even the same. And if ye lend to them of whom ye hope to receive, what thank have ye? for sinners also lend to sinners, to receive as much again. But love ye your enemies, and do good, and lend, hoping for nothing again; and your reward shall be great, and ye shall be the children of the Highest: for he is kind unto the unthankful and to the evil."

-   Luke 6:27-35

"Therefore if thine enemy hunger, feed him; if he thirst, give him drink: for in so doing thou shalt heap coals of fire on his head."

-   Romans 12:20

"A friend exaggerates a man's virtues; an enemy inflames his crimes."

-   Joseph Addison

"We often give our enemies the means for our own destruction."

-   Aesop

"It is easier to forgive an enemy than to forgive a friend."

-   William Blake

"Never interrupt your enemy when he is making a mistake."

-   Napoleon Bonaparte

"Yet is every man his greatest enemy, and, as it were, his own executioner."

-   Sir Thomas Browne

"You can judge of a man by his foes as well as by his friends."
- Joseph Conrad

"You have enemies? Good. That means you've stood up for something, sometime in your life."
- Winston Churchill

"Love your enemies, for they tell you your faults."
- Benjamin Franklin

"Love is the only force capable of transforming an enemy into friend."
- Martin Luther King, Jr.

"The surest way to get rid of an enemy is to make that enemy a friend."
- Abraham Lincoln

"If we could read the secret history of our enemies we should find in each man's life sorrow and suffering enough to disarm all hostility."
- Henry Wadsworth Longfellow

"The only thing more hurtful than the words of our enemies is but the silence of our friends."
- Martin Luther

"One enemy can do more hurt than ten friends can do good."
- Jonathan Swift

"If you want to make enemies, try to change something."
- Woodrow Wilson

"Friends come and go, but enemies accumulate."
- French Proverb

ENTERTAINMENT

"Of all the diversions of life, there is none so proper to fill up its empty spaces as the reading of useful and entertaining authors."
- Joseph Addison

"Television is the triumph of machine over the mind of the people."
- Fred Allen

"I remain just one thing, and one thing only and that is a clown. It places me on a far higher plane than any politician."
- Charlie Chaplin

"We don't make films primarily for children. We try to make them for the child in all of us."
- Walt Disney

"We dare not trust our wit for making our house pleasant to our friend, so we buy ice cream."
- Ralph Waldo Emerson

"Nobody climbs mountains for scientific reasons. Science is used to raise money for the expeditions, but you really climb for the hell of it."
- Sir Edmund Hillary

"If you watch a game, it's fun. If you play it, it's recreation. If you work at it, it's golf."
- Bob Hope

"No entertainment is so cheap as reading, nor any pleasure so lasting."
- Mary Wortley Montagu

"Over the course of a lifetime, most people will pay more to be entertained than to be educated."
- Jack Murphy

"The world is going to Hell. Since when did Christians have time to be entertained?"
- Leonard Ravenhill

"Too many pieces of music finish too long after the end."
- Igor Stravinsky

"Golf is a good walk, spoiled."
- Mark Twain

"Television is chewing gum for the eyes."
- Frank Lloyd Wright

EPITAPHS

"A tomb now suffices him for whom the whole world was not sufficient."
- Tomb of Alexander the Great

"Praised, wept,
  And honoured, by the muse he loved."
- Tomb of James Craggs

"The body of
  B. Franklin, Printer
  (Like the Cover of an Old Book
    Its Contents torn Out
  And Stript of its Lettering and Gilding)
  Lies Here, Food for Worms.
  But the Work shall not be Lost;
  For it will (as he Believ'd) Appear once More
  In a New and More Elegant Edition
  Revised and Corrected
  By the Author."
- Tomb of Benjamin Franklin

"Here lie together, waiting for the Messiah
  The little David and the great Goliath."
- Tomb of David Garrick

"Like a worn out type, he is returned to the Founder in the hope of being recast in a better and more perfect mold."
- Tomb of Peter Gedge

"Here lies
Jedediah Goodwin,
Auctioneer
Born 1828
Going!
Going!!
Gone!!!"
- Tomb of Jedediah Goodwin

"Beneath these green trees rising to the skies,
the planter of them, Isaac Greentree, lies;
The time shall come when these green trees shall fall,
And Isaac Greentree rise above them all."
- Tomb of Isaac Greentree

"Farewell, vain world, I've had enough of thee,
And Valies't not what thou Can'st say of me;
Thy Smiles I count not, nor thy frowns I fear,
My days are past, my head lies quiet here.
What faults you saw in me take Care to shun,
Look but at home, enough is to be done."
- Tomb of William Harvey

"Here was buried Thomas Jefferson, Author of the Declaration of Independence, of the statute of Virginia for Religious Freedom, and Father of the University of Virginia."
- Tomb of Thomas Jefferson

"Here lies one whose name was writ in water."
- Tomb of John Keats

"This work, newly revised and improved by its great Author, will reappear in a splendid day."

- Tomb of Oscar Meader

"Here lies the remains of James Pady, Brickmaker, in hope that his clay will be remoulded in a workmanlike manner, far superior to his former perishable materials."

- Tomb of James Pady

"Pease is not here,
  Only his pod
  He shelled out his Peas
  And went to his God."

- Tomb of Ezekiel Pease

"Are the things you're living for worth Christ dying for?"

- Tomb of Leonard Ravenhill

"Good Frend for Jesvs Sake Forbeare,
  To Digg the Dvst Encloased Heare.
  Blese be ye Man yt Spares Thes Stones.
  And Cvrst be he yt Moves my Bones."

- Tomb of
William Shakespeare

"Here lies an honest lawyer.
  And that is Strange."

- Tomb of Sir John Strange

"Here lies Du Vall; reader, if male thou art,
  Look to thy purse; if female, to thy heart."

- Tomb of Claude du Vall

"Looking into the portals of eternity
  Teaches that the Brotherhood of Man
  Is inspired by God's Word;
  Then all prejudice of race vanishes away."

- Tomb of
  George Washington

"If you would see his monument look around."

- Tomb of
  Sir Christopher Wren

"Harry Edsel Smith
  Born 1903 - Died 1942
  Looked up the elevator shaft
    to see if the car
    was on the way down.
  It was."

- Tomb near Albany,
  New York

"Gone, but not Forgiven."

- Tomb at Atlanta, Georgia

"Here lies Anne Mann; she lived an
  Old maid and died an old Mann."

- Tomb at Bath Abbey

"Here lies the body
  of John Round.
  Lost at sea
    and never found."

- Tomb at Belturbet, Ireland

"I would
  rather be here
  than in Texas."

- Tomb at Colorado Springs, Colorado

"Here lies a man named Zeke.
  Second fastest draw in Cripple Creek."
                              -       Tomb at Cripple Creek, Colorado

"He called
  Bill Smith
  A Liar"
                              -       Tomb at Cripple Creek, Colorado

"He was young
  He was fair
  But the Injuns
  Raised his hair"
                              -       Tomb at Denver, Colorado

"Full many a life he saved
  With his undaunted crew;
    He put his trust in Providence,
      And Cared Not How It Blew."
                              -       Tomb at Deal, England

"Here lies the body
  Of Margaret Bent
  She kicked up her heels
  And away she went."
                              -       Tomb at Dorsetshire, England

"Here lies
  Ezekiel Aikle
  Age 102
  Why do
  The Good
  Die Young?"
                              -       Tomb at East Dalhousie Cemetery,
                                      Nova Scotia

"Here I lie at the Chancel door;
   Here lie I because I am poor;
   The farther in the more you pay;
   Here I lie as warm as they."

>   -   Tomb at Kingsbridge, England

"See, I told you I was sick!"

>   -   Tomb at Littleton, Colorado

"Here lies Pa.
   Pa liked wimin.
   Ma caught Pa in with two swimmin.
   Here lies Pa."

>   -   Tomb at Raleigh,
>   North Carolina

"The children of Israel wanted bread
   And the Lord sent them manna;
   Old clerk Wallace wanted a wife,
   And the devil sent him Anna."

>   -   Tomb at Ribbesford, England

"Here lies
   Johnny Yeast.
   Pardon me
   For not rising."

>   -   Tomb at Ruidoso,
>   New Mexico

"Here lies old Rastus Sominy
   Died a-eating hominy
   In 1859 anno domini"

>   -   Tomb at Savannah, Georgia

"For the Lord Jesus Christ's sake,
  Do all the good you can,
   To all the people you can,
    In all the ways you can,
     As long as ever you can."

        -   Tomb in Shrewsbury, England

"Here lays Butch.
  We planted him raw.
  He was quick on the trigger
  But slow on the draw."

        -   Tomb at Silver City, Nevada

"This turf has drank a
  Widow's tear;
   Three of her husbands
    Slumber here."

        -   Tomb at Staffordshire, England

"Here lies
  an Atheist
  All dressed up
  And no place to go."

        -   Tomb at Thurmont, Maryland

"Here lies Lester Moore.
  Four slugs
  From a forty-four.
  No Les
  No More."

        -   Tomb in Tombstone, Arizona

"Bill Blake
  Was hanged by mistake."

        -   Tomb in Tombstone, Arizona

"Sacred to the memory of
My husband
John Barnes
Who died January 3, 1803.
His comely young widow, aged 23,
    has many qualifications of a good wife,
        and yearns to be comforted."
                            -    Tomb at Mount Negro, Vermont

"Here lies the body
    of Jonathan Blake.
Stepped on the gas
Instead of the brake."
                            -    Tomb at Uniontown, Pennsylvania

"You who come my grave to view,
    A moment stop and think,
        That I am in eternity,
            And you are on the brink."
                            -    Tomb in Yorkshire, England

"Underneath this crust
    Lies the mouldering dust
        Of Eleanor Batchelor Stoven,
            Well versed in the arts
                Of pies, custards and tarts,
                    And the lucrative trade of the oven.
                    When she lived long enough,
                        She made her last puff,
                            A puff by her husband much praised,
                                And now she doth lie
                                And make a dirt pie,
                                    In hopes that her crust may be raised."
                            -    Tomb of a Cook, in Yorkshire, England

EQUALITY

"And it shall come to pass afterward, that I will pour out my spirit upon all flesh; and your sons and your daughters shall prophesy, your old men shall dream dreams, your young men shall see visions: And also upon the servants and upon the handmaids in those days will I pour out my spirit."
-     Joel 2:28-29

"For ye are all the children of God by faith in Christ Jesus. For as many of you as have been baptized into Christ have put on Christ. There is neither Jew nor Greek, there is neither bond nor free, there is neither male nor female: for ye are all one in Christ Jesus. And if ye be Christ's, then are ye Abraham's seed, and heirs according to the promise."
-     Galatians 3:26-29

"When we leave this world, and are laid in the earth, the prince walks as narrow a path as the day-laborer."
-     Cervantes

"Whatever difference there may appear to be in men's fortunes, there is still a certain compensation of good and ill in all, that makes them equal."
-     Peter Charron

"As soon the dust of a wretch whom thou wouldest not, as of a prince whom thou couldest not look upon, will trouble thine eyes if the wind blow it thither; and when a whirlwind hath blown the dust of the churchyard into the church, and the man sweeps out the dust of the church into the churchyard, who will undertake to sift those dusts again, and to pronounce, "This is the patrician, this is the noble flower, and this the yeoman, this the plebeian bran?"
-     John Donne

"We hold these truths to be self-evident, that all men are created equal, that they are endowed by their Creator with certain unalienable Rights, that among these are Life, Liberty and the pursuit of Happiness."
-     Declaration of Independence

"Before God we are equally wise and equally foolish."
- Albert Einstein

"Legislation to apply the principle of equal pay for equal work without discrimination because of sex is a matter of simple justice."
- Dwight Eisenhower

"Spoons and skimmers you can be indistinguishably together; but vases and statues require each a pedestal for itself."
- Ralph Waldo Emerson

"There are some races more cultured and advanced and ennobled by education than others; but there are no races nobler than others. All are equally destined for freedom."
- Alexander Humboldt

"I have supposed the black man, in his present state, might not be in body and mind equal to the white man; but it would be hazardous to affirm that, equally cultivated for a few generations, he would not become so."
- Thomas Jefferson

"So far is it from being true that men are naturally equal, that no two people can be half an hour together but one shall acquire an evident superiority over the other."
- Samuel Johnson

"Well, I don't know what will happen now. We've got some difficult days ahead. But it doesn't matter with me now. Because I've been to the mountaintop. And I don't mind. Like anybody, I would like to live a long life. Longevity has its place. But I'm not concerned about that now. I just want to do God's will. And He's allowed me to go up to the mountain. And I've looked over. And I've seen the promised land. I may not get there with you. But I want you to know tonight, that we, as a people, will get to the promised land. And I'm happy, tonight. I'm not worried about anything. I'm not fearing any man. Mine eyes have seen the glory of the coming of the Lord."
- Martin Luther King, Jr.

"I have a dream that my four little children will one day live in a nation where they will not be judged by the color of their skin but by the content of their character."
-     Martin Luther King, Jr.

"Fourscore and seven years ago our fathers brought forth on this continent a new nation, conceived in liberty, and dedicated to the proposition that all men are created equal. Now we are engaged in a great civil war, testing whether that nation, or any nation so conceived and so dedicated, can long endure. We are met on a great battlefield of that war. We have come to dedicate a portion of that field, as a final resting-place for those who here gave their lives that that nation might live. It is altogether fitting and proper that we should do this. But, in a larger sense, we cannot dedicate--we cannot consecrate--we cannot hallow--this ground. The brave men, living and dead, who struggled here, have consecrated it, far above our poor power to add or detract. The world will little note, nor long remember, what we say here, but it can never forget what they did here. It is for us the living, rather, to be dedicated here to the unfinished work which they who fought here have thus far so nobly advanced. It is rather for us to be here dedicated to the great task remaining before us,--that from these honored dead we take increased devotion to that cause for which they gave the last full measure of devotion--that we here highly resolve that these dead shall not have died in vain--that this nation, under God, shall have a new birth of freedom-- and that government of the people, by the people, for the people, shall not perish from the earth."
-     Abraham Lincoln,
      The Gettysburg Address

"Some must follow, and some command, though all are made of clay!"
-     Henry Wadsworth Longfellow

"All animals are equal but some animals are more equal than others."
-     George Orwell,
      in *Animal Farm*

"Woman, once made equal to man, becomes his superior."
-     Socrates

"The majestic equality of laws forbids the rich as well as the poor to sleep under bridges, to beg in the streets and to steal bread."
- Jacque Anatole Thibault

"Equality is a slogan based on envy. It signifies in the heart of every republican: 'Nobody is going to occupy a place higher than I.'"
- Alexis de Tocqueville

"Mortals are equal; it is only their strength, talents or mask that differs."
- Voltaire

ERROR

"Behold, he put no trust in his servants; and his angels he charged with folly: How much less in them that dwell in houses of clay, whose foundation is in the dust, which are crushed before the moth?"
- Job 4:18-19

"Jesus answered and said unto them, Ye do err, not knowing the scriptures, nor the power of God."
- Matthew 22:29

"Prove all things; hold fast that which is good."
- I Thessalonians 5:21

"An error is the more dangerous in proportion to the degree of truth which it contains."
- Henri-Frederic Amiel

"Error soon passes away unless upheld by restraint on thought. History tells us (and the lesson is invaluable) that the physical force which has put down free inquiry has been the main bulwark of the superstitions and illusions of past ages."
- William Ellery Channing

"To err is human, but to persevere in error is only the act of a fool."
- Cicero

"Truth is a good dog; but beware of barking too close to the heels of an error, lest you get your brains kicked out."
-      Samuel Taylor Coleridge

"Consciousness of error is, to a certain extent, a consciousness of understanding; and correction of error is the plainest proof of energy and mastery."
-      Walter Savage Landor

"To err is human; to forgive is divine."
-      Alexander Pope

"To err is human, but it feels divine!"
-      Mae West

ETERNITY

"Remember the former things of old: for I am God, and there is none else; I am God, and there is none like me, Declaring the end from the beginning, and from ancient times the things that are not yet done, saying, My counsel shall stand, and I will do all my pleasure."
-      Isaiah 46:9-10

"I love to live on the brink of eternity."
-      David Brainerd

"Fear not death; for the sooner we die, the longer shall we be immortal."
-      Benjamin Franklin

"Eat well, stay fit, die anyway."
-      Benjamin Franklin

"When the Author walks on stage, the play is over."
-      C. S. Lewis

"If you read history you will find out that the Christians who did most for the present world were precisely those who thought most of the next."
-    C.S. Lewis

"I must keep alive in myself the desire for my true country, which I shall not find till after death; I must never let it get snowed under or turned aside; I must make it the main object of life to press on to that other country and to help others to do the same."
-    C.S. Lewis

"Learn to hold loosely all that is not eternal."
-    A.M. Royden

"To make the best use of your life, you must never forget two truths. 1st: Compared with eternity, life is extremely brief. 2nd: Earth is only a temporary residence."
-    Rick Warren

"Eternity to the godly is a day that has no sunset; eternity to the wicked is a night that has no sunrise."
-    Thomas Watson

"I judge all things only by the price they shall gain in eternity."
-    John Wesley

"One life to live
  And soon it will be past.
  Only things done for God
  Will ever truly last.

And When I am dying,
  How happy I'll be,
  If the lamp of my life
  Has been burned out for Thee."
-    Unknown

"At any point in all of eternity, we can say 'this is just the beginning'."
-    Unknown

EVANGELISM

On a tablet in a large church, this inscription was placed in memory of John Geddie: "When he landed in 1848, there were no Christians here; when he left in 1872, there were no heathen."
- Memorial to John Geddie, missionary in the South Seas

"No sort of defense is needed for preaching outdoors, but it would take a very strong argument to prove that a man who has never preached beyond the walls of his meetinghouse has done his duty. A defense is required for services within buildings rather than for worship outside of them."
- William Booth

"Making heaven on earth is our business."
- William Booth

"Can we go too fast in saving souls? If anyone still wants a reply, let him ask the lost souls in Hell."
- William Booth

"No Man can do a great and enduring work of God, who is not a man of prayer, and no man can be a man of prayer who does not give much time to praying."
- E. M. Bounds

"Instead of preaching the good news that sinners can be made righteous in Christ and escape the wrath to come, the gospel has degenerated into the pretext that we can be happy in Christ and escape the hassles of life."
- Ray Comfort

"Preach abroad....It is the cooping yourselves up in rooms that has dampened the work of God, which never was and never will be carried out to any purpose without going into the highways and hedges and compelling men and women to come in."
- Jonathon Edwards

"He is no fool who gives what he cannot keep to gain what he cannot lose."

- Jim Elliot

"Christian people, are you figuring round and round to get a little property, yet neglecting souls? Beware lest you ruin souls that can never live again! Do you say -- I thought they knew it all? They reply to you, "I did not suppose you believed a word of it yourselves. You did not act as if you did. Are you going to heaven? Well, I am going down to hell! There is no help for me now. You will sometimes think of me then, as you shall see the smoke of my woe rising up darkly athwart the glorious heavens. After I have been there a long, long time, you will sometimes think that I, who once lived by your side, am there. O remember, you cannot pray for me then; but you will remember that once you might have warned and might have saved me."

- Charles G. Finney

"Solid, lasting missionary work is done on our knees."

- J.O. Fraser

"The primary qualification for a missionary is not love for souls, as we so often hear, but love for Christ."

- Vance Havner

"Do not think me mad. It is not to make money that I believe a Christian should live. The noblest thing a man can do is, just humbly to receive, and then go amongst others and give."

- David Livingstone

"Ferdinand Foch said, 'The most powerful weapon on earth is the human soul on fire!' All the crafting in the world can't save a message that has no passion in it. If you can't get excited about a subject, don't preach on it."

- John Maxwell

"What are we here for, to have a good time with Christians or to save sinners?"

- Malla Moe

"I have seen, at different times, the smoke of a thousand villages - villages whose people are without Christ, without God, and without hope in the world."

- Robert Moffat

"Let methods be changed, therefore, if necessary, that prayer may be given its true place. Let there be days set apart for intercession; let the original purpose of the monthly concert of prayer for missions be given a larger place; let missionary prayer cycles be used by families and by individual Christians; let the best literature on prayer be circulated among the members of the Church; let special sermons on the Subject of intercession be preached. By these and by all other practical means a larger, deeper, wider spirit of prayer should be cultivated in the churches."

- John R. Mott

"The man…looking at him with a smile that only half concealed his contempt, inquired, 'Now Mr. Morrison do you really expect that you will make an impression on the idolatry of the Chinese Empire?' 'No sir,' said Morrison, 'but I expect that God will.'"

- Robert Morrison

"If I might be the means of saving one soul I should prefer it to all the riches and honor in the world."

- Asahel Nettleton

"Today Christians spend more money on dog food then missions"

- Leonard Ravenhill

"Could a mariner sit idle if he heard the drowning cry? Could a doctor sit in comfort and just let his patients die? Could a fireman sit idle, let men burn and give no hand? Can you sit at ease in Zion with the world around you DAMNED?"

- Leonard Ravenhill

"The command has been to "go," but we have stayed - in body, gifts, prayer and influence. He has asked us to be witnesses unto the uttermost parts of the earth….But 99% of Christians have kept puttering around in the homeland."

- Robert Savage

"We talk of the second coming, but half the world has never heard of the first."

- Oswald J. Smith

"A man says to me, "Can you explain the seven trumpets of the Revelation?" No, but I can blow one in your ear, and warn you to escape from the wrath to come."

- Charles Spurgeon

"If sinners be damned, at least let them leap to Hell over our bodies. If they will perish, let them perish with our arms about their knees. Let no one go there unwarned and unprayed for."

- Charles Spurgeon

"If sinners be damned, at least let them leap to Hell over our bodies. If they will perish, let them perish with our arms about their knees. Let no one GO there UNWARNED and UNPRAYED for."

- Charles Spurgeon

"If you have no wish to bring others to heaven, you are not going there yourself."

- Charles Spurgeon

"His authority on earth allows us to dare to go to all the nations. His authority in heaven gives us our only hope of success. And His presence with us leaves us no other choice."

- John R. W. Stott

"Some wish to live within a mile of the church building; I want to run a rescue shop within a yard of Hell."

- C.T. Studd

"Let us not glide through this world and then slip quietly into heaven, without having blown the trumpet loud and long for our Redeemer, Jesus Christ. Let us see to it that the devil will hold a thanksgiving service in hell, when he gets the news of our departure from the field of battle."
-     C. T. Studd

"Are we not told to seek first the Kingdom of God
--- not the means to advance it --- and that 'all these things' shall be added to us? Such promises are surely sufficient."
-     J. Hudson Taylor

"I feel now, that Arabia could easily be evangelized within the next thirty years if it were not for the wicked selfishness of Christians."
-     Samuel M. Zwemer

"When the Lord reveals His will to us and we obey, our mission will be a success regardless of the results."
- Chinese house church leaders

"One day a lady criticized D. L. Moody for his methods of evangelism in attempting to win people to the Lord. Moody's reply was 'I agree with you. I don't like the way I do it either. Tell me, how do you do it?' The lady replied, 'I don't do it.' Brother Moody responded, 'I like my way of doing it better than your way of not doing it.'"
- Unknown

EVIL

"And out of the ground made the LORD God to grow every tree that is pleasant to the sight, and good for food; the tree of life also in the midst of the garden, and the tree of knowledge of good and evil."
-     Genesis 2:9

"Woe unto them that call evil good, and good evil; that put darkness for light, and light for darkness; they put bitter for sweet, and sweet for bitter!"
-     Isaiah 5:20

"And lead us not into temptation, but deliver us from evil."
- Matthew 6:13

"For the good that I would I do not: but the evil which I would not, that I do."
- Romans 7:19

"Be not overcome of evil, but overcome evil with good."
- Romans 12:21

"The cardinal method with faults is to overgrow them and choke them out with virtues."
- John Bascom

"The only thing necessary for the triumph of evil is for good men to do nothing."
- Edmund Burke

"States like these, and their terrorist allies, constitute an axis of evil, arming to threaten the peace of the world. By seeking weapons of mass destruction, these regimes pose a grave and growing danger. They could provide these arms to terrorists, giving them the means to match their hatred. They could attack our allies or attempt to blackmail the United States. In any of these cases, the price of indifference would be catastrophic."
- George W. Bush

"The evil that is in the world almost always comes of ignorance, and good intentions may do as much harm as malevolence if they lack understanding."
- Albert Camus

"Even in evil, that dark cloud which hangs over the creation, we discern rays of light and hope, and gradually come to see in suffering and temptation proofs and instruments of the sublimest purposes of wisdom and love."
- William Ellery Channing

"Preventives of evil are far better than remedies; cheaper and easier of application, and surer in result."
- Tryon Edwards

"It is easier to denature plutonium than to denature the evil spirit of man."
- Albert Einstein

"Choose the lesser of the two evils."
- Desiderius Gerhard Erasmus

"He who does evil so that good may come is like a man paying a toll to the devil in order to obtain entrance into Heaven."
- A. W. and J. C. Hare

"Eager souls, mystics and revolutionaries, may propose to refashion the world in accordance with their dreams; but evil remains, and so long as it lurks in the secret places of the heart, utopia is only the shadow of a dream."
- Nathaniel Hawthorne

"There is evil in every human heart, which may remain latent, perhaps, through the whole of life; but circumstances may rouse it to activity."
- Nathaniel Hawthorne

"With every exertion, the best of men can do but a moderate amount of good; but it seems in the power of the most contemptible individual to do incalculable mischief."
- Washington Irving

"Philosophy triumphs easily over past and future evils, but present evils triumph over philosophy."
- François Rochefoucauld

"The dread of evil is a much more forcible principle of human actions than the prospect of good."
- John Locke

"An evil life is a kind of death."
- Ovid

"To do evil that good may come of it is for bunglers in politics as well as mortals."
- William Penn

"Evils destroy themselves, or they destroy us."
- Jean Jacque Rousseau

"The evil that men do lives after them;
 The good is oft interred with their bones."
- William Shakespeare

"It is easy--terribly easy--to shake a man's faith in himself. To take advantage of that to break a man's spirit is devil's work."
- George Bernard Shaw

EVOLUTION

"And God said, Let us make man in our image, after our likeness: and let them have dominion over the fish of the sea, and over the fowl of the air, and over the cattle, and over all the earth, and over every creeping thing that creepeth upon the earth. So God created man in his own image, in the image of God created he him; male and female created he them. And God blessed them, and God said unto them, Be fruitful, and multiply, and replenish the earth, and subdue it: and have dominion over the fish of the sea, and over the fowl of the air, and over every living thing that moveth upon the earth."
- Genesis 1:26-28

"In the beginning was the Word, and the Word was with God, and the Word was God. The same was in the beginning with God. All things were made by him; and without him was not any thing made that was made. In him was life; and the life was the light of men."
- John 1:1-4

"All the ills from which America suffers can be traced to the teaching of evolution."

- William Jennings Bryan

"I have called this principle, by which, each slight variation, if useful, is preserved, by the term of Natural Selection."

- Charles Darwin, 1859,
  from *Origin of the Species*

"With respect to the theological view of the question: This is always painful to me. I am bewildered. I had no intention to write atheistically, but I own that I cannot see as plainly as others do, and as I should wish to do, evidence of design and beneficence on all sides of us. There seems to me too much misery in the world. I cannot persuade myself that a beneficent and omnipotent God would have designedly created the Ichneumonidae with the express intention of their feeding within the living bodies of caterpillars or that a cat should play with mice... On the other hand, I cannot anyhow be contented to view this wonderful universe, and especially the nature of man, and to conclude that everything is the result of brute force. I am inclined to look at everything as resulting from designed laws, with the details, whether good or bad, left to the working out of what we may call chance."

- Charles Darwin, 1860

"The question is of course wholly distinct from that higher one, whether there exists a Creator and Ruler of the universe; and this has been answered in the affirmative by some of the highest intellects that have ever existed.

- Charles Darwin, 1871,
  from *The Decent of Man*

"The question concerning the existence of God at the time of conception for my theory because of the extreme difficulty or rather impossibility of conceiving this immense and wonderful universe, including man with his capacity of looking far backwards and far into futurity, as the result of blind chance or necessity. When thus reflecting I feel compelled to look to a First Cause having an intelligent mind in some degree analogous to that of man; and I deserve to be called a Theist."

- Charles Darwin, 1876,
from his *Autobiography*

"I was a young man with uninformed ideas. I threw out queries, suggestions, wondering all the time over everything; and to my astonishment the ideas took like wildfire. People made a religion of them."

- Charles Darwin, 1876,
from his *Autobiography*

"To suppose that the eye with all its inimitable contrivances for adjusting the focus to different distances, for admitting different amounts of light, and for the correction of spherical and chromatic aberration, could have been formed by natural selections, seems, I confess, absurd in the highest degree."

- Charles Darwin, 1876,
from his *Autobiography*

"I am not the least afraid to die."

- Charles Darwin
on his deathbed

"It is amazing that Darwin has concluded that 'Nature' is the ultimate designer for this Universe. 'Nature' just happens to be another historic name for God."

- Jack Murphy

"There are many holes in the theory of evolution. The lack of fossil evidence is not the least of these. If evolution is true, then why are there so many gaps in fossil records? In fact, the validity of this theory rests itself upon these gaps. Why do single-celled organisms still remain? If man descended from apes, why didn't the apes follow suit?"

-   Jack Murphy

"[Evolution] has in recent years been challenged in the world of science and is not yet believed in the scientific community to be as infallible as it once was believed. But if it was going to be taught in the schools, then I think that also the biblical theory of creation, which is not a theory but the biblical story of creation, should also be taught."

-   Ronald Reagan

"Since evolution became fashionable, the glorification of Man has taken a new form."

-   Bertrand Russell

"While the rest of the species is descended from apes, redheads are descended from cats."

-   Mark Twain

EXPERIENCE

"Though I might also have confidence in the flesh. If any other man thinketh that he hath whereof he might trust in the flesh, I more: Circumcised the eighth day, of the stock of Israel, of the tribe of Benjamin, an Hebrew of the Hebrews; as touching the law, a Pharisee; Concerning zeal, persecuting the church; touching the righteousness which is in the law, blameless. But what things were gain to me, those I counted loss for Christ. Yea doubtless, and I count all things but loss for the excellency of the knowledge of Christ Jesus my Lord: for whom I have suffered the loss of all things, and do count them but dung, that I may win Christ, And be found in him, not having mine own righteousness, which is of the law, but that which is through the faith of Christ, the righteousness which is of God by faith: That I may know him, and the power of his resurrection, and the fellowship of his sufferings, being made conformable unto his death; If by any means I might attain unto the resurrection of the dead."

- Philippians 3:4-11

"God sends experience to paint men's portraits."

- Henry Ward Beecher

"Too high an appreciation of our own talents is the chief cause why experience preaches to us all in vain."

- Charles Colton

"Great men never require experience."

- Benjamin Disraeli

"Experience is the common schoolhouse of fools and ill men. Men of wit and honesty be otherwise instructed."

- Desiderius Eramus

"Experience is a keen knife that hurts while it extracts the cataract that blinds."

- J. de Finod

"Experience keeps a dear school, but fools will learn in no other, and scarcely in that; for it is true, we may give advice, but we cannot give conduct. Remember this; they that will not be counseled cannot be helped. If you do not hear reason she will rap you over your knuckles."

- Benjamin Franklin

"Experience is no more transferable in morals than in art."

- James Froude

"I have but one lamp by which my feet are guided, and that is the lamp of experience."

- Patrick Henry

"Good judgment comes from experience; but often, experience comes from bad judgment."

- Thomas Jefferson

"Experience is the only teacher of fools."
-     Titus Livy

"One thorn of experience is worth a whole wilderness of warning."
-     James Lowell

"Whoever said, 'The man with an experience is never at the mercy of a man with an argument' has obviously never argued with God in prayer."
-     Jack Murphy

"Experience speaks, but seldom a man listens."
-     John Newton

"The value of experience is not in seeing much, but in seeing wisely."
-     Sir William Osler

"Good judgment comes from experience, and a lot of that comes from bad judgment."
-     Will Rogers

"Those who cannot remember the past are condemned to repeat it."
-     George Santayana

"Experience is a jewel, and it had need be so, for it is often purchased at an infinite rate."
-     William Shakespeare

"I shall the effect of this good lesson keep
  As watchman to my heart, but, good my brother,
    Do not as some ungracious pastors do,
      Show me the steep and thorny way to heaven,
        Whiles like a puffed and reckless libertine
          Himself the primrose path of dalliance treads
      And recks not his own rede."
-     William Shakespeare

"Each succeeding day is the scholar of that which preceded."
- Syrus

"Experience is the name everyone gives to their mistakes."
- Oscar Wilde

"Learn from the mistakes of others instead of making them all yourself."
- American Proverb

F

FACTS

"Facts are to the mind what food is to the body."
- Edmund Burke

"If the facts don't fit the theory, change the facts."
- Albert Einstein

"Facts are counterrevolutionary."
- Eric Hoffer

"One fact is better than one hundred analogies."
- D. L. Moody

"I believe in general in a dualism between facts and the ideas of those facts in human heads."
- George Santayana

"When facts were weak, his native cheek brought him serenely through."
- C. H. Spurgeon

"Never face facts; if you do you'll never get up in the morning."
- Mark Twain

"It is as fatal as it is cowardly to blink facts because they are not to our taste or liking."
- John Tyndall

"From principles is derived probability; but truth, or certainty, is obtained only from facts."
- Booker T. Washington

FAILURE

"For a just man falleth seven times, and riseth up again."
- Proverbs 24:16

"After crosses and losses, men grow humbler and wiser."
- Benjamin Franklin

"You will make all kinds of mistakes, but as long as you are generous and true, and also fierce, you cannot hurt the world or even seriously distress her."
- Sir Winston Churchill

"Many of life's failures are people who did not realize how close they were to success when they gave up."
- Thomas Edison

"Its how you deal with failure that determines how you achieve success."
- David Feherty

"It is a silly fish that is caught twice with the same bait."
- Thomas Fuller

"Successful men are influenced by the desire for pleasing results. Failures are influenced by the desire for comfortable methods and are inclined to be satisfied with such results as can be obtained by doing things they like to do."
- Albert Gray

"It is not the critic who counts, not the man who points out how the strong man stumbles, or where the doer of deeds could have done them better. The credit belongs to the man in the arena, whose face is marred by dust and sweat and blood, who strives valiantly...who knows the great enthusiasms, the great devotions, who spends himself in a worthy cause, who at the best know in the end the triumph of high achievement, and who at the worst, if he fails, at least fails while daring greatly, so that his place shall never be with those cold and timid souls who have never known neither victory nor defeat."

-   Theodore Roosevelt

"It is a mistake to suppose that men succeed through success; they much oftener succeed through failures. Precept, study, advice, and example could never have taught them so well as failure has done."

-   Samuel Smiles

"God wisely designed the human body so that we neither pat our own backs nor kick ourselves to easily."

-   Unknown

FAITH

"Upon a life I did not live, upon a death I did not die; another's life, another's death, I stake my whole eternity."

-   Horatius Bonar

"The greatest need we have is not to *do* things, but to *believe* things."

-   Oswald Chambers

"Life without Jesus is like a donut...because there is a hole in the middle of your heart."

-   Robert C. Evans

"The prayer of faith is the only power in the universe to which the Great Jehovah yields. Prayer is the sovereign remedy."

-   Robert Hall

"Let us have faith that right makes might, and in that faith, let us, to the end, dare to do our duty as we understand it."

-   Abraham Lincoln

"We are saved by faith alone. However, faith that saves is never alone...it is always accompanied by works."
- Martin Luther

"Craving clarity, we attempt to eliminate the risk of trusting God."
- Brennan Manning

"You are leaving port under sealed orders and in a troubled period. You cannot know whither you are going or what you are to do. But why not take the Pilot on board who knows the nature of your sealed orders from the outset, and who will shape your entire voyage accordingly? He knows the shoals and the sandbanks, the rocks and the reefs, He will steer you safely into that celestial harbor where your anchor will be cast for eternity. Let His almighty nail-pierced hands hold the wheel, and you will be safe."
- Peter Marshall

"Some say that faith is the gift of God. So is the air, but you have to breathe it; so is bread, but you have to eat it. Some are wanting some miraculous kind of feeling. That is not faith. 'Faith cometh by hearing and hearing by the Word of God' (Rom. 10:17). That is whence faith comes. It is not for me to sit down and wait for faith to come stealing over me with a strong sensation, but is for me to take God at His Word."
- D. L. Moody

"Our Faith must be tested. God builds no ships but what He sends to sea."
- D.L. Moody

"We have a God who delights in impossibilities."
- Andrew Murray

"For many of us the great danger is not that we will renounce our faith. It is that we will become so distracted and rushed and preoccupied that we will settle for a mediocre version of it."
- John Ortberg

"Men love to trust God (as they profess) for what they have in their hands, in possession, or what lies in an easy view; place their desires afar off, carry their accomplishment behind the clouds out of their sight, interpose difficulties and perplexities -- their hearts are instantly sick. They cannot wait for God; they do not trust Him, nor ever did. Would you have the presence of God with you? Learn to wait quietly for the salvation you expect from Him."

- John Owen

"One of these days some simple soul will pick up the Book of God, read it, and believe it. Then the rest of us will be embarrassed."

- Leonard Ravenhill

"Trust, but Verify."

- Damon Runyon

"God never fails those who trust Him."

- Alexander Simpson

"Never indulge, at the close of an action, in any self-reflective acts of any kind, whether of self-congratulation or of self-despair. Forget the things that are behind, the moment they are past, leaving them with God. This quote has been of unspeakable value to me. When the temptation comes, as it mostly does to every worker after the performance of any service, to indulge in these reflections, either of one sort or the other, I turn from them at once and positively refuse to think about my work at all, leaving it with the Lord to overrule the mistakes, and to bless it as he chooses. I believe there would be far fewer "blue Mondays" for ministers of the Gospel if they would adopt this plan."

- Hannah Whitall Smith

"While carnal men say *seeing is believing,* we assure them that to us *believing is seeing.*"

- C.H. Spurgeon

"It is no sin to doubt some things but it may be fatal to believe everything."

- A.W. Tozer

"Let us with caution indulge the supposition that morality can be maintained without religion. Reason and experience both forbid us to expect that national morality can prevail in exclusion of religious principle."
- George Washington

"Where reason cannot wade there faith may swim."
- Thomas Watson

"Fear looks – but faith jumps."
- Smith Wigglesworth

"What lies before us and what lies behind us are tiny matters to what lies within us."
- Unknown

"It has been said that faith is blind. This is not true. Faith simply believes in what your physical eyes cannot see."
- Unknown

FAITHFULNESS

"But the fruit of the Spirit is love, joy, peace, longsuffering, gentleness, goodness, faith, Meekness, temperance: against such there is no law."
- Galatians 5:22-23

"Fear none of those things which thou shalt suffer: behold, the devil shall cast some of you into prison, that ye may be tried; and ye shall have tribulation ten days: be thou faithful unto death, and I will give thee a crown of life."
- Revelation 2:10

"When you read, consider that it is God's Word which you read; and that his faithfulness is pledged to fulfill both its promises and threatenings."
- Adam Clarke

"The greatest ability is dependability."
-    Bob Jones

"At times one remains faithful to a cause only because its opponents do not cease to be insipid."
-    Friedrich Nietzsche

"Those who are faithless know the pleasures of lust; it is the faithful who know love's tragedies."
-    Oscar Wilde

FALSE TEACHING

"When a prophet speaketh in the name of the LORD, if the thing follow not, nor come to pass, that is the thing which the LORD hath not spoken, but the prophet hath spoken it presumptuously: thou shalt not be afraid of him."
-    Deuteronomy 18:22

"For the time will come when they will not endure sound doctrine; but after their own lusts shall they heap to themselves teachers, having itching ears;   And they shall turn away their ears from the truth, and shall be turned unto fables."
-    II Timothy 4:3-4

"All that one gains by falsehood is, not to be believed when he speaks the truth."
-    Aristotle

"Round dealing is the honor of man's nature; and a mixture of falsehood is like alloy in gold and silver, which may make the metal work the better, but it destroys its worth."
-    Sir Francis Bacon

"Let falsehood be a stranger to thy lips;
  Shame on the policy that first began
    To tamper with the heart to hide its thoughts!
    And doubly shame on that inglorious tongue,
      That sold its honesty and told a lie."
                    -   William Harvard

"Wisdom and truth, the offspring of the sky, are eternal; while cunning and deception, the meteors of the earth, after glittering for a moment, must pass away."
                    -   Robert Hall

"There is a set of harmless liars, frequently to be met with in company, who deal much in the marvellous. Their usual intention is to please and entertain; but as men are most delighted with what they conceive to be the truth, these people mistake the means of pleasing, and incur universal blame."
                    -   David Hume

"There is nothing more dangerous than a man who believes his false doctrine. Dependent upon the measure of that belief, a man could conquer and evangelize the world in the name of a lie."
                    -   Jack Murphy

"He who tells a lie is not sensible how great a task he undertakes; for he must be forced to invent twenty more to maintain that one."
                    -   Alexander Pope

"To lapse in fulness is sorer than to lie for need; and falsehood is worse in kings than beggars, in clergy than congregation."
                    -   William Shakespeare

"Although the Devil be the father of lies, he seems, like other great inventors, to have lost much of his reputation by the continual improvements that have been made upon him."
                    -   Jonathan Swift

FALSE WITNESS

"Thou shalt not bear false witness against thy neighbor."
- Exodus 20:16

"Speak not evil one of another, brethren. He that speaketh evil of his brother, and judgeth his brother, speaketh evil of the law, and judgeth the law: but if thou judge the law, thou art not a doer of the law but a judge."
- James 4:11

"I hate the man who builds his name
  On ruins of another's fame."
- John Gay

"There would not be so many open mouths if there were not so many open ears."
- Joseph Hall

"There is nothing wrong with the command of God to 'stone the false prophet!' The problem is that the church has discerned wrongly and stoned the true prophet! That is why there are no more true prophets in our days, because as soon as they begin their ministry, we rub them out. This is the reason that so many false prophets are running around, not just because it's the end of the age but because we have disobeyed God, His command, and killed off His prophets! We are like Herod, who in the midst of John the Baptist's ministry, chose a wrong time to listen to his conscience instead of the Holy Spirit!"
- G.A. Jarquin

"Many preachers bare false witness against God in every sermon that they preach and in every action of their lives."
- Jack Murphy

"Believe nothing against another, but on good authority; nor report what may hurt another, unless it be a greater hurt to another to conceal it."
- William Penn

"Those men who carry about and who listen to accusations, should all be hanged, if so it could be at my decision--the carriers by their tongues, the listeners by their ears."
- Titus Plautus

"To vilify a great man is the readiest way in which a little man can himself attain greatness."
- Edgar Allen Poe

"If any speak ill of thee, flee home to thy own conscience, and examine thy heart: if thou be guilty, it is a just correction; if not guilty, it is a fair instruction: make use of both; so shalt thou distil honey out of gall, and out of an open enemy create a secret friend."
- Francis Quarles

"What is slander? What is gossip? It is a supposed truth. A verdict of "guilty" pronounced in the absence of the accused, with closed doors, without defense or appeal, by an interested and prejudiced judge."
- Joseph Roux

"Oh! many a shaft, at random sent,
  Finds mark the archer little meant;
    And many a word, at random spoken,
      May soothe or wound a heart that's broken."
- Sir Walter Scott

"The worthiest people are the most injured by slander, as is the best fruit which the birds have been pecking at."
- Jonathan Swift

"Malice, in its false witness, promotes its tale with so cunning a confusion; so mingles truths with falsehoods, surmises with certainties, causes of no moment with matters capital, that the accused can absolutely neither grant nor deny, plead innocence nor confess guilt."
- Sir Philip Sydney

FAME

"So the LORD was with Joshua; and his fame was noised throughout all the country."
-     Joshua 6:27

"And when the queen of Sheba heard of the fame of Solomon concerning the name of the LORD, she came to prove him with hard questions."
-     I Kings 10:1

"And the fame of David went out into all lands; and the LORD brought the fear of him upon all nations."
-     I Chronicles 14:17

"What a wretched thing is all fame! A renown of the highest sort endures, say, for two thousand years. And then? Why, then, a fathomless eternity swallows it. Work for eternity; not the meagre rhetorical eternity of the periodical critics, but for the real eternity wherein dwelleth the Divine."
-     Thomas Carlyle

"When you can do the common things of life in an uncommon way, you will command the attention of the world."
-     George Washington Carver

"After I'm dead I'd rather have people ask why I have no monument than why I have one."
-     Cato the Elder

"Write your name in kindness, love and mercy on the hearts of the thousands you come in contact with year by year, and you will never be forgotten."
-     Thomas Chalmers

"Your fame is as the grass, whose hue comes and goes, and His might withers it by whose power it sprang from the lap of the earth."
-     Dante

"If my theory of relativity is proven successful, Germany will claim me as a German and France will declare that I am a citizen of the world. Should my theory prove untrue, France will say I am a German and Germany will declare that I am a Jew."
- Albert Einstein

"With fame I become more and more stupid, which of course is a very common phenomenon."
- Albert Einstein

"Fame is proof that people are gullible."
- Ralph Waldo Emerson

"An earthly immortality belongs to a great and good character. History embalms it; it lives in its moral influence, in its authority, in its example, in the memory of the words and deeds in which it was manifested; and as every age adds to the illustrations of its efficacy, it may chance to be the best understood by a remote posterity."
- Edward Everett

"Fame sometimes hath created something of nothing."
- Thomas Fuller

"Fame is the echo of actions, resounding them to the world, save that the echo repeats only the last part, but fame relates all, and often more than all."
- Thomas Fuller

"An enduring fame is one stamped by the judgment of the future -- that future which dispels illusions, and smashes idols into dust."
- William Gladstone

"He that would have his virtues published is not the servant of virtue, but glory."
- Ben Johnson

"If fame is only to come after death, I am in no hurry for it."
- Marcus Valerius Martial

"Before this time to-morrow I shall have gained a peerage, or Westminister Abbey."

- Lord Horatio Nelsen

"What is fame? a fancied life in others' breath. Grant me honest fame — or none at all!"

- Alexander Pope

"The fame of great men ought always to be estimated by the means used to acquire it."

- François Rochefoucauld

"Never throughout history has a man who lived a life of ease left a name worth remembering."

- Theodore Roosevelt

"Fame is but the breath of the people, and that often unwholesome."

- Jean-Jacque Rousseau

"It is better to die with a good name than to live with a bad."

- American Proverb

FAMILY

"But if any provide not for his own, and especially for those of his own house, he hath denied the faith, and is worse than an infidel."

- I Timothy 5:8

"In intimate family life, there comes a moment when children, willingly or no, become the judges of their parents."

- Honore de Balzac

"The family: We were a strange little band of characters trudging through life sharing diseases and toothpaste, coveting one another's desserts, hiding shampoo, borrowing money, locking each other out of our rooms, inflicting pain and kissing to heal it in the same instant, loving, laughing, defending, and trying to figure out the common thread that bound us all together."
- Erma Bombeck

"Family: A social unit where the father is concerned with parking space, the children with outer space, and the mother with closet space."
- Evan Esar

"Family quarrels are bitter things. They don't go by any rules. They're not like aches or wounds; they're more like splits in the skin that won't heal because there's not enough material."
- F. Scott Fitzgerald

"A man can't make a place for himself in the sun if he keeps taking refuge under the family tree."
- Helen Keller

"If you are fortunate enough to have a job, do it with all your heart. But remember that although it is a vital part of your life, it is only a part, and although you may rise to great heights, somebody else will one day take your place at the work bench or at the boardroom table. Nobody will ever take your place as the father of the child you are now cradling in your arms. You may well work for the best part of half a century, but the time you have been given to pass on the things that matter to your child is so very limited. There will be many demands on your time, and you will not always be able to give your children the time they ask. But so far as is possible, count the days. Try not to miss one of them."
- Rob Parsons

"God only allows us so many opportunities with our children to read a story, go fishing, play catch, and say our prayers together. Try not to miss one of them. The office can wait. It will still be there after the children are gone."
- Rob Parsons

"When our relatives are at home, we have to think of all their good points or it would be impossible to endure them."
- George Bernard Shaw

"The family: That dear octopus from whose tentacles we never quite escape, nor, in our inmost hearts, ever quite wish to."
- Dodie Smith

"The best test of a sanctified man is to ask his family about him."
- C.T. Studd

"Families are like fudge - mostly sweet with a few nuts."
- American Proverb

"You can choose your friends, but you can't choose your family."
- American Proverb

"Blood is thicker than water."
- American Proverb

"The family that prays together, stays together."
- American Proverb

"No success at work can make up for failure at home."
- English Proverb

"An ounce of blood is worth more than a pound of friendship."
- Spanish Proverb

FAVOR

"And Jesus increased in wisdom and stature, and in favour with God and man."
- Luke 2:52

"The esteem of wise and good men is the greatest of all temporal encouragements to virtue; and it is a mark of an abandoned spirit to have no regard to it."
- Edmund Burke

"Many men and many women enjoy popular esteem, not because they are known, but because they are not."
- Sebastian de Chamfort

"By virtue, integrity, perseverance and true modesty it is possible for all men to win the esteem of their fellow beings."
- Charles Douglas

"You can and you can't,
 You shall and you shan't
 You will and you won't
 And you will be damned if you do
 And you will be damned if you don't."
- Lorenzo Dow

"Prefer not the esteem of men to the approbation of God."
- John Jortin

"You have to accept whatever comes and the only important thing is that you meet it with courage and with the best that you have to give."
- Eleanor Roosevelt

"We acquire the love of people who, being in our proximity, are presumed to know us; and we receive reputation or celebrity, from such as are not personally acquainted with us. Merit secures to us the regard of our honest neighbors, and good fortune that of the public. Esteem is the harvest of a whole life spent in usefulness; but reputation is often bestowed upon a chance action, and depends most on success."
- George Augustus Sala

"God helps us seek popularity where it counts – at the court of God!"
- S. R. Zepp

FEAR

"The fear of the Lord is the beginning of wisdom: a good understanding have all they that do his commandments: his praise endureth for ever."
- Psalm 61:10

"Fear thou not; for I am with thee: be not dismayed; for I am thy God: I will strengthen thee; yea, I will help thee; yea, I will uphold thee with the right hand of my righteousness."
- Isaiah 41:10

"But now thus saith the LORD that created thee, O Jacob, and he that formed thee, O Israel, Fear not: for I have redeemed thee, I have called thee by thy name; thou art mine. When thou passest through the waters, I will be with thee; and through the rivers, they shall not overflow thee: when thou walkest through the fire, thou shalt not be burned; neither shall the flame kindle upon thee."
- Isaiah 43:1-2

"But straightway Jesus spake unto them, saying, Be of good cheer; it is I; be not afraid."
- Matthew 14:27

"For God has not given us a spirit of fear; but of power, and of love, and of a sound mind."
- II Timothy 1:7

"What can that man fear who takes care to please a Being that is able to crush all his adversaries?"
- Joseph Addison

"To suffering there is a limit; to fearing, none."
- Sir Francis Bacon

"Noble hearts are neither jealous nor afraid because jealousy spells doubt and fear spells pettiness."
- Honore de Balzac

"God planted fear in the soul as truly as He planted hope or courage. Fear is a kind of bell, or gong, which rings the mind into quick life and avoidance upon the approach of danger. It is the soul's signal for rallying."
- Henry Ward Beecher

"Never be afraid to trust an unknown future to a known God."
- Corrie Ten Boom

"He has but one great fear that fears to do wrong."
- Christian Nestell Bovee

"No passion so effectually robs the mind of all its powers of acting and reasoning as fear."
- Edmund Burke

"We often pretend to fear what we really despise, and more often to despise what we really fear."
- Charles Coulton

"Fear makes us remember our humanity."
- Benjamin Disraeli

"Do the thing you fear, and the death of fear is certain."
- Ralph Waldo Emerson

"We fear men so much, because we fear God so little. One fear cures another. When man's terror scares you, turn your thoughts to the wrath of God."
- William Gurnall

"Let us never negotiate out of fear, but let us never fear to negotiate."
- John F. Kennedy

"Live in Christ and the flesh need not fear death."
- John Knox

"I more fear what is within me than what comes from without."
- Martin Luther

"If I could hear Christ praying for me in the next room, I would not fear a million enemies. Yet distance makes no difference. He is praying for me"
- Robert Murray M'Cheyne

"Fear is faithlessness."
- George MacDonald

"Controlled fear is a healthy thing. Emerson said, 'Do the thing you fear, and the death of fear is certain.' That is – unless your parachute doesn't open. Then your death is certain. Thus, a fear of jumping into lava is not necessarily a bad thing."
- Jack Murphy

"Why do we fear death? Is it not greater than life? Remember he who asked, 'O Death, where is thy victory? Where, O Death, is thy sting? Because of Christ, we have overcome death. We need fear it no longer."
- Jack Murphy

"There is a virtuous fear which is the effect of faith; and there is a vicious fear, which is the product of doubt. The former leads to hope, as relying on God, in whom we believe; the latter inclines to despair, as not relying on God, in whom we do not believe. Persons of the one character fear to lose God; persons of the other character fear to find Him."
- Blaise Pascal

"We have nothing to fear but fear itself!"
- Franklin D. Roosevelt

"We have the truth and we need not be afraid to say so."
- J.C. Ryle

"Slavery to fear is the worst of slaveries."
- George Bernard Shaw

"Nothing so demoralizes the forces of the soul as fear. Only as we realize the presence of the Lord does fear give place to faith."
- Sarah Frances Smiley

"I don't fear heights. I don't even have a fear of falling. I fear the pain that arises from broken limbs after hitting the ground at a great amount of speed."
-     Mark Twain

"It is only the fear of God that can deliver us from the fear of man."
-     John Witherspoon

"Don't begin climbing if you are afraid of falling."
-     English Proverb

"Don't be afraid of tomorrow -- God is already there."
-     Unknown

FIGHTING

"For the weapons of our warfare are not carnal, but mighty through God to the pulling down of strong holds; Casting down imaginations, and every high thing that exalteth itself against the knowledge of God, and bringing into captivity every thought to the obedience of Christ; And having in a readiness to revenge all disobedience, when your obedience is fulfilled."
-     II Corinthians 10:4-6

"Fight the good fight of faith, lay hold on eternal life, whereunto thou art also called, and hast professed a good profession before many witnesses."
-     I Timothy 6:12

"You must not fight too often with one enemy, or you will teach him all your art of war."
-     Napoleon Bonaparte

"Pacifists proudly parade their beliefs as citizens of free societies. There are no pacifists living under tyranny. While they may still whisper their beliefs, they secretly long for tyranny's demise."
-     Albert Einstein

"Canada's peace is merely the suckling weaned from the breast of the Monroe Doctrine. Naturally, it is a nation filled with pacifists who point a finger of hypocrisy at America."
- Jack Murphy

"The pacifist is as surely a traitor to his country and to humanity as is the most brutal wrongdoer."
- Theodore Roosevelt

"I learned long ago, never to wrestle with a pig, you get dirty; and besides, the pig likes it."
- George Bernard Shaw

FOOD

"He causeth the grass to grow for the cattle, and herb for the service of man: that he may bring forth food out of the earth; And wine that maketh glad the heart of man, and oil to make his face to shine, and bread which strengtheneth man's heart."
- Psalm 54:14-15

"On the morrow, as they went on their journey, and drew nigh unto the city, Peter went up upon the housetop to pray about the sixth hour: And he became very hungry, and would have eaten: but while they made ready, he fell into a trance, And saw heaven opened, and a certain vessel descending upon him, as it had been a great sheet knit at the four corners, and let down to the earth: Wherein were all manner of fourfooted beasts of the earth, and wild beasts, and creeping things, and fowls of the air. And there came a voice to him, Rise, Peter; kill, and eat. But Peter said, Not so, Lord; for I have never eaten any thing that is common or unclean. And the voice spake unto him again the second time, What God hath cleansed, that call not thou common."
- Acts 10:9-15

"I would like to find a stew that will give me heartburn immediately, instead of at three o'clock in the morning."
- John Barrymore

"Edible, adj.: Good to eat, and wholesome to digest, as a worm to a toad, a toad to a snake, a snake to a pig, a pig to a man, and a man to a worm."
-    Ambrose Bierce

"The poets have been mysteriously silent on the subject of cheese."
-    G.K. Chesterton

"The bagel, an unsweetened doughnut with rigor mortis."
-    Beatrice and Ira Freeman

"There is one thing more exasperating than a wife who can cook and won't, and that's a wife who can't cook and will."
-    Robert Frost

"Great eaters and great sleepers are incapable of anything else that is great."
-    King Henry IV

"No man in the world has more courage than the man who can stop after eating one peanut."
-    Channing Pollock

"A bagel is a donut with the pleasures of sin removed."
-    George Rosenbaum

"Nothing would be more tiresome than eating and drinking if God had not made them a pleasure as well as a necessity."
-    Voltaire

"We live in a world where lemonade is now made from artificial flavor and furniture polish is made from real lemons!"
-    American Proverb

"Those who forget the pasta are condemned to reheat it."
-    American Proverb

"A dime will get you onto the subway, but beans and garlic will get you a seat."
-    American Proverb

"The way to a man's heart is through his stomach."
-    American Proverb

"The appetite rules the mind."
-    Spanish Proverb

FOOLISHNESS

"It is as sport to a fool to do mischief: but a man of understanding hath wisdom."
-    Proverbs 10:23

"It would be easier to endow a fool with intellect than to persuade him that he had none."
-    Jacques Babinet

"Fools gain greater advantages through their weakness than intelligent men through their strength. We watch a great man struggling against fate and we do not lift a finger to help him. But we patronize a grocer who is headed for bankruptcy."
-    Honore de Balzac

"A fool may now and then be right by chance."
-    William Cowper

"The fool wonders, the wise man asks."
-    Benjamin Disraeli

"Talk sense to a fool and he calls you foolish."
-    Euripides

"Fools need advice most, but wise men only are the better for it."
-    Benjamin Franklin

"The learned fool writes his nonsense in better language than the unlearned, but it is still nonsense."
- Benjamin Franklin

"Of all thieves, fools are the worst; they rob you of time and temper."
- Johann Wolfgang von Goethe

"The greatest fool is he who thinks he is not one and all others are."
- Baltasar Gracian

"Surely he is not a fool that hath unwise thoughts, but he that utters them."
- Joseph Hall

"None but a fool is always right."
- Augustus William Hare

"Never attribute to malice that which can be adequately explained by stupidity."
- Robert A. Heinlein
"Hanlon's Razor"

"None is a fool always, everyone sometimes."
- George Herbert

"Fools learn nothing from wise men, but wise men learn much from fools."
- Johann Kaspar Lavater

"Some old men, by continually praising the time of their youth, would almost persuade us that there were no fools in those days; but unluckily they are left themselves for examples."
- Alexander Pope

"Old fools are more foolish than young ones."
- François Rochefoucauld

"You pity a man who is lame or blind, but you never pity him for being a fool, which is often a much greater misfortune."
- Sydney Smith

"It is better to be quiet and thought a fool than to open your mouth and remove all doubt."
- American Proverb

"In the land of the blind, the one-eyed man is king. In a land of fools, he is king with just a little common sense."
- English Proverb

"Who is more foolish, the fool or the one who argues with him?"
- Hebrew Proverb

FORGIVENESS

"And forgive us our debts, as we forgive our debtors."
- Matthew 6:12

"For if ye forgive men their trespasses, your heavenly Father will also forgive you: But if ye forgive not men their trespasses, neither will your Father forgive your trespasses."
- Matthew 6:14-15

"I can forgive, but I cannot forget," is only another way of saying "I will not forgive." A forgiveness ought to be like a cancelled note, torn in two and burned up, so that it never can be shown against the man."
- Henry Ward Beecher

"The gospel comes to the sinner at once with nothing short of complete forgiveness as the starting-point of all his efforts to be holy. It does not say, "Go and sin no more, and I will not condemn thee." It says at once, "Neither do I condemn thee: go and sin no more."
- Horatius Bonar

"It is necessary to repent for years in order to efface a fault in the eyes of men; a single tear suffices with God."

- Francois August Rene de Chateaubriand

"Alas! if my best Friend, who laid down His life for me, were to remember all the instances in which I have neglected Him, and to plead them against me in judgment, where should I hide my guilty head in the day of recompense? I will pray, therefore, for blessings on my friends, even though they cease to be so, and upon my enemies, though they continue such."

- William Cowper

"It is easier to forgive an enemy than a friend."

- Dorothee DeLuzy

"May I tell you why it seems to me a good thing for us to remember wrong that has been done us? That we may forgive it."

- Charles Dickens

"We should always forgive,--the penitent for their sake, the impenitent for our own."

- Marie von
Ebner-Eschenbach

"Yes, we ought to forgive our enemies, but not until they are hanged."

- Heinrich Heine

"It is vain for you to expect, it is impudent for you to ask of God forgiveness on your own behalf, if you refuse to exercise this forgiving temper with respect to others."

- Benjamin Hoadley

"If we can still love those who have made us suffer, we love them all the more."

- Anna Brownell Jameson

"Forgive your enemies, but never forget their names."

- John F. Kennedy

"He who has not forgiven an enemy has never yet tasted one of the most sublime enjoyments of life."
- Johann Kaspar Lavater

"God's way of forgiving is thorough and hearty,--both to forgive and to forget; and if thine be not so, thou hast no portion of His."
- Robert Leighton

"Bear and forbear."
- Ovid

"To err is human, to forgive, divine."
- Alexander Pope

"Behold affronts and indignities, which the world thinks it right never to pardon, which the Son of God endures with a divine meekness! Let us cast at the feet of Jesus that false honor, that quick sense of affronts, which exaggerates everything, and pardons nothing, and, above all, that devilish determination in resenting injuries."
- Pasquier Quesnel

"When thou forgivest,--the man who has pierced thy heart stands to thee in the relation of the sea-worm that perforates the shell of the mussel which straightway closes the wound with a pearl."
- Jean Paul Richter

"We may forgive those who bore us, we cannot forgive those whom we bore."
- François Rochefoucauld

"Forgive others often, yourself never."
- Syrus

""To return evil for good is devilish; to return good for good is human; but to return good for evil is godlike."
- Richard Whateley

"Always forgive your enemies; nothing annoys them so much."
- Oscar Wilde

"Heaven is filled with repentant sinners, whereas their victims were not granted admission due to their hateful pride."
- German Proverb

"The cross is the cost of my forgiveness."
- Unknown

FORNICATION – See IMMORALITY

FREEDOM – See LIBERTY

FREE SPEECH

"Congress shall make no law respecting an establishment of religion, or prohibiting the free exercise thereof; or abridging the freedom of speech, or of the press; or of the people peaceably to assemble, and to petition the Government for a redress of grievances."
- 1ˢᵗ Amendment to the United States Constitution

"There is tonic in the things that men do not love to hear; and there is damnation in the things that wicked men love to hear. Free speech is to a great people what winds are to oceans and malarial regions, which waft away the elements of disease, and bring new elements of health. And where free speech is stopped miasma is bred, and death comes fast."
- Henry Ward Beecher

"Restriction of free thought and free speech is the most dangerous of all subversions. It is the one un-American act that could most easily defeat us."
- William Orville Douglas

"We are not afraid to entrust the American people with unpleasant facts, foreign ideas, alien philosophies, and competitive values. For a nation that is afraid to let its people judge the truth and falsehood in an open market is afraid of its people."

- John F. Kennedy

"Free speech is too dangerous to a democracy to be permitted."

- Henry Louis Mencken

"Free speech is intended to protect the controversial and even outrageous word; and not just comforting platitudes too mundane to need protection."

- Colin Powell

"If the fires of freedom and civil liberties burn low in other lands, they must be made brighter in our own. If in other lands the press and books and literature of all kinds are censored, we must redouble our efforts here to keep them free."

- Franklin D. Roosevelt

"Free speech, exercised both individually and through a free press, is a necessity in any country where people are themselves free."

- Theodore Roosevelt

"There is no more fundamental axiom of American freedom than the familiar statement: In a free country we punish men for crimes they commit but never for the opinions they have."

- Harry S. Truman

FRIENDSHIP

"A man that hath friends must show himself friendly; and there is a friend that sticketh closer than a brother."

- Proverbs 18:24

"Greater love hath no man than this, that a man lay down his life for his friends."
- John 15:13

"All my friends are but one, but He is all sufficient."
- William Carey

"He that lieth down with dogs, shall rise up with Fleas."
- Benjamin Franklin

"Be slow in choosing a friend, slower in changing."
- Benjamin Franklin

"I desire so to conduct the affairs of this administration that if at the end, when I come to lay down the reins of power, I have lost every other friend on earth, I shall at least have one friend left, and that friend shall be down inside of me."
- Abraham Lincoln

"You must constantly ask yourself these questions: Who am I around? What are they doing to me? What have they got me reading? What have they got me saying? Where do they have me going? What do they have me thinking? And most important, what do they have me becoming? Then ask yourself the big question: Is that okay?"
- Jim Rohn

"Associate yourself with men of good quality if you esteem your own reputation. It is better be alone than in bad company."
- George Washington

"I no doubt deserved my enemies, but I don't believe I deserved my friends."
- Walt Whitman

"A friend in need is a friend indeed."
- English Proverb

"Show me who your friends are, and I'll show you who you are."
-    Spanish Proverb

FUN

"While the work or play is on, it is a lot of fun if while you are doing one you don't constantly feel that you ought to be doing the other."
-    Franklin Pierce Adams

"People rarely succeed unless they have fun in what they are doing."
-    Dale Carnegie

"To a young heart everything is fun."
-    Charles Dickens

"It is a happy talent to know how to play."
-    Ralph Waldo Emerson

"To love what you do and feel that it matters - how could anything be more fun?"
-    Katherine Graham

"Spinnin' a rope is fun, if your neck ain't in it."
-    Will Rogers

"Fun is sugar-coated physics."
-    Henry Wheeler Shaw

"I have done my fiddling so long under Vesuvius that I have almost forgotten to play, and can only wait for the eruption and think it long of coming. Literally no man has more wholly outlived life than I. And still it is good fun."
-    Robert Louis Stevenson

FUTURE

"For I know the thoughts that I think toward you, saith the LORD, thoughts of peace, and not of evil, to give you an expected end."
- Jeremiah 29:11

"When they therefore were come together, they asked of him, saying, Lord, wilt thou at this time restore again the kingdom to Israel? And he said unto them, It is not for you to know the times or the seasons, which the Father hath put in his own power."
- Acts 1:6-7

"That what will come, and must come, shall come well."
- Sir Edwin Arnold

"God will not suffer man to have the knowledge of things to come; for if he had prescience of his prosperity, he would be careless; and, understanding of his adversity, he would be senseless."
- Augustine of Hippo

"It is the "where I am" that makes heaven. The life after death might become through its very endlessness a burden to our spirits, if it were not to be filled with the infinite variety and freshness of God's love. Some have shrunk from its very infinitude, because they have not realized what God's love can make of it. Human love helps us to understand this. When we have come to love any one with all our power of affection, then there is no monotony or weariness in the days and hours we spend with them."
- Maltbie Davenport Babcock

"While a man is stringing a harp, he tries the strings, not for music, but for construction. When it is finished it shall be played for melodies. God is fashioning the human heart for future joy. He only sounds a string here and there to see how far His work has progressed."
- Henry Ward Beecher

"The future ain't what it used to be."
- Yogi Berra

"Never be afraid to trust an unknown future to a known God."
- Corrie ten Boom

"Do not fear for the future of our Faith. The end of the Book cannot change."
- John Bunyan

"You can never plan the future by the past."
- Edmund Burke

"It is a mistake to try to look too far ahead. The chain of destiny can only be grasped one link at a time."
- Winston Churchill

"The best way to predict the future is to create it."
- Peter Drucker

"Don't worry about the future--it comes soon enough."
- Albert Einstein

"What lies behind us and what lies before us are tiny matters compared to what lies within us."
- Ralph Waldo Emerson

"Tis easy to see, hard to foresee."
- Benjamin Franklin

"I have often looked at that picture behind the president without being able to tell whether it was a rising or a setting sun. Now at length I have the happiness to know that it is indeed a rising, not a setting sun."
- Benjamin Franklin,
Upon signing the
Declaration of Independence

"I like the dreams of the future better than the history of the past."
- Thomas Jefferson

"There was a wise man in the East whose constant prayer was that he might see to-day with the eyes of tomorrow."
- Alfred Mercier

"Today is the past of the future. Today is tomorrow's history."
- Jack Murphy

"We are lead to the belief of a future state, not only by the weaknesses, by the hopes and fears of human nature, but by the noblest and best principles which belong to it,--by the love of virtue, and by the abhorrence of vice and injustice."
- Adam Smith

"The best preparation for tomorrow is today."
- American Proverb

"Sorrow looks back; Fear looks forward; Faith looks up."
- Irish Proverb

"Don't worry about tomorrow. God is already there!"
- Unknown

G

GAMBLING

"Wealth gotten by vanity shall be diminished: but he that gathereth by labour shall increase."
- Proverbs 13:11

"Let him that stole, steal no more; but rather let him labor, working with his hands the thing which is good, that he may have to give to him that needeth."
- Ephesians 4:28

"My advice: Keep flax from fire, youth from gambling."
- Benjamin Franklin

"Gambling corrupts our dispositions, and teaches us the habit of hostility against mankind."
- Thomas Jefferson

"Gambling is a disease of barbarians superficially civilized."
- Dean Inge

"In gambling the many must lose in order that the few may win."
- George Bernard Shaw

"Gambling is the child of avarice, the brother of iniquity, and the father of mischief."
- George Washington

GENTLENESS

"Come unto me, all ye that labour and are heavy laden, and I will give you rest. Take my yoke upon you, and learn of me; for I am meek and lowly in heart: and ye shall find rest unto your souls. For my yoke is easy, and my burden is light."
-     Matthew 11:28-30

"But the fruit of the Spirit is love, joy, peace, longsuffering, gentleness, goodness, faith, Meekness, temperance: against such there is no law."
-     Galatians 5:22-23

"The best and simplest cosmetic for women is constant gentleness and sympathy for the noblest interests of her fellow-creatures. This preserves and gives to her features an indelibly gay, fresh, and agreeable expression. If women would but realize that harshness makes them ugly, it would prove the best means of conversion."
-     Berthold Auerbach

"Gentleness is far more successful in all its enterprises than violence; indeed, violence generally frustrates its own purpose, while gentleness scarcely ever fails."
-     John Locke

"Better make penitents by gentleness than hypocrites by severity."
-     Francis de Salas

GIFTS

"God has given me special gifts and resources to help me become the person He intends for me to be. That is His gift to me. I must choose daily to manage these gifts and resources for His glory and not my own. That is my gift to Him."
-     Corrie ten Boom

"I owe everything to the gift of Pentecost. For fifty days the facts of the Gospel were complete, but no conversions were recorded. Pentecost registered three thousand souls. It is by fire that a holy passion is kindled in the soul whereby we live the life of God. The soul's safety is in its heat. Truth without enthusiasm, morality without emotion, ritual without soul, make for a Church without power...Destitute of the Fire of God, nothing else counts; possessing Fire, nothing else matters."
- Samuel Chadwick

"More than 2 billion people who do not know Jesus head toward hell to perish for eternity, while the church laughs its way to hysteria, claiming this is the sign of the last days' outpouring of the Holy Spirit. My brothers and sisters this is not Christianity."
- K.P. Yohannan

"The cost of your sins is more than you can pay. The gift of your God is more than you can imagine."
- Unknown

GIVING

"But when thou doest alms, let not thy left hand know what thy right hand doeth: That thine alms may be in secret: and thy Father which seeth in secret himself shall reward thee openly."
- Matthew 6:3-4

"Every man according as he purposeth in his heart, so let him give; not grudgingly, or of necessity: for God loveth a cheerful giver."
- II Corinthians 9:7

"We make a living by what we get; we make a life by what we give."
- Winston Churchill

"He is no fool who gives what he cannot keep to gain what he cannot lose."
- Jim Elliot

"To pity distress it but human; to relieve it is Godlike."
- Horace Mann

"Earn all you can, save all you can, and then give all you can."
- C.H. Spurgeon

"Behold I do not give lectures or a little charity, When I give I give myself."
- Walt Whitman

"A grasping hand is never full. A giving hand is always full."
- Irish Proverb

GOD

"In the beginning, God…"
- Genesis 1:1

"In the beginning was the Word, and the Word was with God, and the Word was God. The same was in the beginning with God. All things were made by him; and without him was not any thing made that was made. In him was life; and the life was the light of men. And the light shineth in darkness; and the darkness comprehended it not."
- John 1:1-5

"Then Paul stood in the midst of Mars' hill, and said, Ye men of Athens, I perceive that in all things ye are too superstitious. For as I passed by, and beheld your devotions, I found an altar with this inscription, TO THE UNKNOWN GOD. Whom therefore ye ignorantly worship, him declare I unto you."
- Acts 17:22-23

"He that loveth not knoweth not God; for God is love."
- I John 4:8

"They that deny a God destroy man's nobility; for certainly man is of kin to the beasts by his body; and, if he be not of kin to God by his spirit, his is a base and ignoble creature."
- Sir Francis Bacon

"Let us think less of men and more of God. Naught but God can satisfy the soul."
- Philip James Bailey

"God wishes to exhaust all means of kindness before His hand takes hold on justice."
- Henry Ward Beecher

"To be struck with His power, it is only necessary to open our eyes."
- Edmund Burke

"His eye is upon every hour of my existence."
- Thomas Chalmers

"The root of all sin is the suspicion that God is not good."
- Oswald Chambers

"Once a nation abolishes God, the government becomes the God."
- G.K. Chesterton

"The more I know of astronomy, the more I believe in God."
- Herber Doust Curtis

"I want to know all Gods thoughts; all the rest are just details."
- Albert Einstein

"Quantum mechanics is very impressive. But an inner voice tells me that it is not yet the real thing. The theory yields a lot, but it hardly brings us any closer to the secret of the Old One. In any case I am convinced that He doesn't play dice."
- Albert Einstein

"God is our true Friend, who always gives us the counsel and comfort we need. Our danger lies in resisting Him; so it is essential that we acquire the habit of hearkening to His voice, or keeping silence within, and listening so as to lose nothing of what He says to us. We know well enough how to keep outward silence, and to hush our spoken words, but we know little of interior silence. It consists in hushing our idle, restless, wandering imagination, in quieting the promptings of our worldly minds, and in suppressing the crowd of unprofitable thoughts which excite and disturb the soul."

- François Fénelon

"The discovery of God lies in the daily and the ordinary, not in the spectacular and the heroic. If we cannot find God in the routines of home and shop, then we will not find Him at all."

- Richard J. Foster

"God governs in the affairs of men; and if a sparrow cannot fall to the ground without His notice, neither can a kingdom rise without His aid."

- Benjamin Franklin

"I do not feel obliged to believe that the same God who has endowed us with sense, reason, and intellect has intended us to forgo their use."

- Galileo Galilei

"Some men treat the God of their fathers as they treat their father's friend. They do not deny him; by no means: they only deny themselves to him, when he is good enough to call upon them."

- A. W. and J. C. Hare

"Nothing reveals character more than self-sacrifice. So the highest knowledge we have of God is through the gift of His Son."

- William Harris

"In all God's providences, it is good to compare His word and His works together; for we shall find a beautiful harmony between them, and that they mutually illustrate each other."

- Matthew Henry

"God is the tangential point between zero and infinity."
- Alfred Jarry

"God governs the world, and we have only to do our duty wisely, and leave the issue to Him."
- John Jay

"The wisdom of the Lord is infinite as are also His glory and His power. Ye heavens, sing His praises; sun, moon, and planets, glorify Him in your ineffable language! Praise Him, celestial harmonies, and all ye who can comprehend them! And thou, my soul, praise thy Creator! It is by Him and in Him that all exist."
- Johannes Kepler

"It is more important to know that we are on God's side."
- Abraham Lincoln
  when asked whether he believed that God
  was on the side of the Union

"The slender capacity of man's heart cannot comprehend, much less utter, that unsearchable depth and burning zeal of God's love towards us."
- Martin Luther

"If you were to spend a month feeding on the precious promises of God, you would not be going about with your heads hanging down like bulrushes, complaining how poor you are; but you would lift up your heads with confidence, and proclaim the riches of His grace because you could not help it."
- Dwight L. Moody

"God in his wisdom made the fly and then chose not to tell us why."
- Ogden Nash

"We are not to consider the world as a body of God: He is an uniform being, devoid of organs, members, or parts; and they are His creatures, subordinate to Him, and subservient to His will."
- Sir Isaac Newton

"God is dead. God remains dead. And we have killed him. How shall we comfort ourselves, the murderers of all murderers? What was holiest and mightiest of all that the world has yet owned has bled to death under our knives: who will wipe this blood off us? What water is there for us to clean ourselves? What festivals of atonement, what sacred games shall we have to invent? Is not the greatness of this deed too great for us? Must we ourselves not become gods simply to appear worthy of it?"

- Frederich Nietzsche

"One plus God is a majority."

- Wendell Phillips

"There never was a man of solid understanding, whose apprehensions are sober, and by a pensive inspection advised, but that he hath found by an irresistible necessity one true God and everlasting being."

- Sir Walter Raleigh

"God's patience is infinite. Men, like small kettles, boil quickly with wrath at the least wrong. Not so God. If God were as wrathful, the world would have been a heap of ruins long ago."

- Sadhu Sundar Singh

"Our God is so wonderfully good, and lovely, and blessed in every way that the mere fact of belonging to Him is enough for an untellable fullness of joy!"

- Hannah Whitall Smith

"There is nothing little in God."

- C.H. Spurgeon

"Each one of us is God's special work of art. Through us, He teaches and inspires, delights, and encourages, informs and uplifts all those who view our lives. God, the master artist, is most concerned about expressing Himself - His thoughts and His intentions - through what He paints in our character... [He] wants to paint a beautiful portrait of His Son in and through your life. A painting like no other in all of time."

- Joni Eareckson Tada

196

"I have found that there are three stages in every great work of God: first, it is impossible, then it is difficult, then it is done."
- J. Hudson Taylor

"The Lord came not to destroy, but to save. Everything is save which we commit to Him and nothing is really save which is not so committed."
- A.W. Tozer

"It is impossible to rightly govern a nation without God and the Bible."
- George Washington

"You do well to wish to learn our arts and our ways of life and above all, the religion of Jesus Christ. These will make you a greater and happier people than you are. Congress will do everything they can to assist you in this wise intention."
- George Washington
to the Delaware Indian Chiefs

"I believe the promises of God enough to venture an eternity on them."
- Isaac Watts

"Tell me how it is that in this room there are three candles and but one light, and I will explain to you the mode of the Divine existence."
- John Wesley

"Some people complain that God placed thorns on roses, while others praise him for putting roses among thorns."
- Unknown

GODLINESS – See HOLINESS

GOOD

"Know, man hath all which nature hath, but more, and in that more lie all his hopes of good."
- Matthew Arnold

"Because indeed there was never law, or sect, or opinion, did so much magnify goodness, as the Christian religion doth."
- Sir Francis Bacon

"No good deed goes unpunished."
- Clare Booth Luce

"Goodness thinks no ill where no ill seems."
- John Milton

"We cannot be certain that a thing is right because it is old, for Satan is old, and sin is old, and death is old, and hell is old; yet none of these things are right and desirable on that account."
- C.H. Spurgeon

"The good is the enemy of the best."
- Voltaire

"Real goodness does not attach itself merely to this life; it points to another world."
- Daniel Webster

"Whatever makes men good Christians, makes them good citizens."
- Daniel Webster

"Do all the good you can, in all the ways you can, to all the souls you can, in every place you can, at all the times you can, with all the zeal you can, as long as ever you can."
- John Wesley

"The best portion of a good man's life is his little, nameless, unremembered acts of kindness and of love."
- William Wordsworth

GOSSIP

"He that covereth a transgression seeketh love: but he that repeateth a matter separateth very friends." - Proverbs 17:9

"Then said I, Woe is me! for I am undone; because I am a man of unclean lips, and I dwell in the midst of a people of unclean lips: for mine eyes have seen the King, the LORD of hosts."
- Isaiah 6:5

"And withal they learn to be idle, wandering about from house to house; and not only idle, but tattlers also and busybodies, speaking things which they ought not."
- I Timothy 5:13

"In order for three people to keep a secret, two must be dead."
- Benjamin Franklin

"Gossip is a sort of smoke that comes from the dirty tobacco-pipes of those who diffuse it; it proves nothing but the bad taste of the smoker."
- George Eliot

"What people say behind your back is your standing amongst the fools near where you live."
- Edgar Watson Howe

"Whoever gossips to you will probably gossip about you."
- Don Leavell

"Much of our gossip is erroneously 'sanctified.' This 'sanctified gossip' will often begin with the word, 'Please pray for...'"
- Jack Murphy

"Not only is the world informed of everything about you, but of a great deal more."
- William Thackeray

"Notice, we never pray for folks we gossip about, and we never gossip about the folk for whom we pray! For prayer is a great deterrent."
- Leonard Ravenhill

"What good does it do to speak in tongues on Sunday if you have been using your tongue during the week to curse and gossip?"
- Leonard Ravenhill

"There is only one thing in the world worse than being talked about, and that is not being talked about."
- Oscar Wilde

"Gossip is the art of saying nothing in a way that leaves practically nothing unsaid."
- Walter Winchell

GOVERNMENT

"Blessed is the nation whose God is the LORD; and the people whom he hath chosen for his own inheritance."
- Psalm 33:12

"Let every soul be subject unto the higher powers. For there is no power but of God: the powers that be are ordained of God. Whosoever therefore resisteth the power, resisteth the ordinance of God: and they that resist shall receive to themselves damnation."
- Romans 13:1-2

"Honour all men. Love the brotherhood. Fear God. Honour the king."
- I Peter 2:17

"The worst thing in the world, next to anarchy, is government."
- Henry Ward Beecher

"Governments last only as long as the undertaxed can defend themselves against the overtaxed."
- Bernard Berenson

"The people of the United States very deliberately framed their government with the view of remaining the masters of it, and not of being mastered by it; and they are not yet willing to abdicate in favor of any, even the most audacious conspirator against their sovereignty."
- John Bigelow

"Well, will anybody deny now that the Government at Washington, as regards its own people, is the strongest government in the world at this hour? And for this simple reason, that it is based on the will, and the good will, of an instructed people."
- John Bright

"Your representative owes you, not his industry only, but his judgment; and he betrays, instead of serving you, if he sacrifices it to your opinion."
- Edmund Burke

"And having looked to Government for bread, on the very first scarcity they will turn and bite the hand that fed them."
- Edmund Burke

"A power has arisen up in the Government greater than the people themselves, consisting of many and various and powerful interests, combined into one mass, and held together by the cohesive power of the vast surplus in the banks."
- John Calhoun

"It seems to me a great truth that human things cannot stand on selfishness, mechanical utilities, economies and law courts; that if there be not a religious element in the relations of men, such relations are miserable, and doomed to ruin."
- Thomas Carlyle

"Many forms of Government have been tried, and will be tried in this world of sin and woe. No one pretends that democracy is perfect or all-wise. Indeed, it has been said that democracy is the worst form of government except all those other forms that have been tried from time to time."
- Winston Churchill

"The United States invariably does the right thing, after having exhausted every other alternative."
- Winston Churchill

"I contend that for a nation to try to tax itself
into prosperity is like a man standing in a
bucket and trying to lift himself up by the handle."
- Winston Churchill

"A monarchy is like a man-of-war--bad shots between wind and water hurt it exceedingly; there is danger of capsizing. But democracy is a raft. You cannot easily overturn it. It is a wet place, but it is a pretty safe one."
- Joseph Cook

"You campaign in poetry. You govern in prose."
- Mario Cuomo

"It may be true that you can't fool all the people all the time, but you can fool enough of them to rule a large country."
- Will Durant

"The proper function of a government is to make it easy for people to do good, and difficult for them to do evil."
- William Gladstone

"Which is the best government? That which teaches self-government."
- Johann Wolfgang von Goethe

"How fortunate for governments that the people they administer don't think."
- Adolph Hitler

"A government big enough to give you everything
you want, is strong enough to take everything you
have."
- Thomas Jefferson

"A republican government is slow to move, yet when once in motion, its momentum becomes irresistible."
-     Thomas Jefferson

"The course of history shows that as a government grows, liberty decreases. That government is best which governs the least, because its people discipline themselves. That government is the strongest of which every man feels himself a part."
-     Thomas Jefferson

"When the people fear the government you have tyranny...when the government fears the people you have liberty."
-     Thomas Jefferson

"A house divided against itself cannot stand--I believe this government cannot endure permanently half-slave and half-free."
-     Abraham Lincoln

"The world will little note, nor long remember what we say here, but it can never forget what they did here. It is for us the living, rather, to be dedicated here to the unfinished work which they who fought here have thus far so nobly advanced. It is rather for us to be here dedicated to the great task remaining before us -- that from these honored dead we take increased devotion to that cause for which they gave the last full measure of devotion -- that we here highly resolve that these dead shall not have died in vain -- that this nation, under God, shall have a new birth of freedom -- and that government of the people, by the people, for the people, shall not perish from the earth."
-     Abraham Lincoln
       from the *Gettysburg Address*

"It is best to be both feared and loved, however, if one cannot be both it is better to be feared than loved."
-     Niccolo Machiavelli

"The government of the Union, then, is emphatically and truly a government of the people. In form and in substance it emanates from them. Its powers are granted by them, and are to be exercised directly on them and for their benefit."
- Chief Justice John Marshall
  in *McCulloch v. Maryland*

"Big Brother is watching you."
- George Orwell
  from *Animal Farm*

"Government is the problem – not the solution."
- Ronald Reagan

"A troubled and afflicted mankind looks to us, pleading for us to keep our rendezvous with destiny; that we will uphold the principles of self-reliance, self-discipline, morality, and, above all, responsible liberty for every individual that we will become that shining city on a hill."
- Ronald Reagan

"I have left orders to be awakened at any time in case of national emergency, even if I'm in a cabinet meeting."
- Ronald Reagan

"I don't make jokes. I just watch the government and report the facts."
- Will Rogers

"This country has come to feel the same when Congress is in session as when the baby gets hold of a hammer."
- Will Rogers

"A hated government does not last long."
- Seneca

"A government which robs Peter to pay Paul can always depend on the support of Paul."
- George Bernard Shaw

"Those who cast the votes decide nothing. Those who count the votes decide everything."
- Josef Stalin

"In America, anybody can be president. That's one of the risks you take."
- Adlai Stevenson

"All government without the consent of the governed is slavery."
- Jonathan Swift

"Any woman who understands the problems of running a home will be nearer to understanding the problems of running a country."
- Margaret Thatcher

"The Athenians govern the Greeks; I govern the Athenians; you, my wife, govern me; your son governs you."
- Themistocles

"I've still got a lot to learn about Washington. Thursday, I accidentally spent some of my own money."
- Fred Thompson

"No man's life, liberty, or property is safe while the legislature is in session."
- Mark Twain

"The art of government is to make two-thirds of a nation pay all it possibly can pay for the benefit of the other third."
- Voltaire

"It is the duty of all Nations to acknowledge the providence of Almighty God, to obey His will, to be grateful for His benefits, and humbly to implore His protection and favor."
- George Washington

"Let us raise a standard to which the wise and honest can repair; the rest is in the hands of God."
- George Washington

"The people's government made for the people, made by the people, and answerable to the people."
- Daniel Webster

"Government is created to protect the poor from the lust of the rich, and to protect the rich from the lust of the poor."
- Unknown

GRACE

"Where sin doth abound, grace doth much more abound."
- Romans 5:20

"For if we sin willfully after that we have received the knowledge of the truth, there remaineth no more sacrifice for sins, but a certain fearful looking for of judgment and fiery indignation, which shall devour the adversaries. He that despised Moses' law died without mercy under two or three witnesses: Of how much sorer punishment, suppose ye, shall he be thought worthy, who hath trodden under foot the Son of God, and hath counted the blood of the covenant, "wherewith he was sanctified, an unholy thing, and hath done despite unto the Spirit of grace?"
- Hebrews 10:26-29

"Any concept of grace that makes us feel more comfortable sinning is not biblical grace. God's grace never encourages us to live in sin, on the contrary, it empowers us to say no to sin and yes to truth."
- Randy Alcorn

"Cheap grace replaces truth with tolerance, lowering the bar so everyone can jump over it and we can all feel good about ourselves."
- Randy Alcorn

"Cheap grace is the deadly enemy of our church. We are fighting today for costly grace."
- Dietrich Bonhoeffer

"Grace in the soul is heaven in that soul."
- Matthew Henry

"Grace is given to heal the spiritually sick, not to decorate spiritual heroes."
- Martin Luther

"My faith isn't in the idea that I'm more moral than anybody else. My faith is in the idea that God and His love are greater than whatever sins any of us commit."
- Rich Mullins

"Grace Abuse or cheap grace: Why be good if you know in advance you will be forgiven? This is the wrong question, the right question is...Why Love? Do you ask your wife, *'How far can I go with other women'*?"
- Phillip Yancey

"The proof of spiritual maturity is not how pure you are but awareness of your impurity. That very awareness opens the door to grace."
- Phillip Yancey

GREATNESS

"And Jesus came to Capernaum: and being in the house he asked them, 'What was it that ye disputed among yourselves by the way?' But they held their peace: for by the way they had disputed among themselves, who should be the greatest. And he sat down, and called the twelve, and saith unto them, 'If any man desire to be first, the same shall be last of all, and servant of all.'"
- Mark 9:33-35

"It is true greatness to realize the frailty of man in one ear and the security of God in the other."
- Sir Francis Bacon

"Greatness lies, not in being strong, but in the right using of strength."
- Henry Ward Beecher

"Great things are done when men and mountains meet."
- William Blake

"Great men are meteors, consuming themselves to light the world."
- Napoleon Bonaparte

"No man has come to true greatness who has not felt in some degree that his life belongs to his race, and that what God gives him, He gives him for mankind."
- Philips Brooks

"Great men are never sufficiently shown but in struggles."
- Edmund Burke

"The price of greatness is responsibility."
- Winston Churchill

"A great man is one who affects the mind of his generation."
- Benjamin Disraeli

"Those who do things that truly count do not usually stop to count them."
- Benjamin Franklin

"There is no king who has not had a slave among his ancestors, and no slave who has not had a king among his."
- Helen Keller

"The tomb is the pedestal of greatness. It make the distinction between the greatness of Christ and the greatness of the king."
- Walter Landor

"Be great and you will be lonely."
- Mark Twain

"A great city is that which has the greatest men and women."
- Walt Whitman

"Some men were great because they were destined to be; most men were great because they were determined to be."

-   American Proverb

"Not all good men were knights, but all knights were good men."

-   Unknown

"I would much rather have men ask why there is no statue of me than why there is one."

-   Cato the Elder

H

HAPPINESS

"Without strong affection, and humanity of heart, and gratitude to that Being whose code is mercy, and whose great attribute is benevolence to all things that breathe, true happiness can never be attained."
- Charles Dickens

"Happiness is relative."
- Albert Einstein

"We all live with the objective of being happy; our lives are all different and yet the same."
- Anne Frank

"Happiness is a butterfly, which, when pursued, is just beyond your grasp, but which, if you will sit down quietly, may alight upon you."
- Nathaniel Hawthorne

"Your success and happiness lie in you. . . . Resolve to keep happy, and your joy and you shall form an invincible host against difficulties."
- Helen Keller

"Most folks are about as happy as they make up their minds to be."
- Abraham Lincoln

"All men seek happiness. This is without exception. Whatever different means they employ, they all tend to this end. The will never takes the least step but to this object. This is the motive of every action of every man, even those who hang themselves."
- Blaise Pascal

"Happiness is not a goal; it is a by-product."
- Eleanor Roosevelt

"My life has no purpose, no direction, no aim, no meaning, and yet I'm happy. I can't figure it out. What am I doing right?"
- Charles Schulz

"God's goal is not to make sure you're happy. Life is not about your being comfortable, happy, successful and pain free. It is about becoming the man God has called you to be. Life is not about you. It's about God. He doesn't exist to make us happy. We exist to bring Him glory."
- Chuck Swindoll

"Most fools are happy."
- English Proverb

"Blessed be the man who is happy in the midst of trouble. Woe to the man who is happy because of trouble."
- Irish Proverb

HATE

"He that loveth not knoweth not God; for God is love."
- I John 4:8

"Were one to ask me in which direction I think man strongest, I should say, his capacity to hate."
- Henry Ward Beecher

"Hatred is like fire -- it makes even light rubbish deadly."
- George Eliot

"Some men hate because they believe that it makes the heart grow strong through callous. Hate does make the heart grow as strong and lifeless as a rock sinking to the bottoms of the abyss."
- Jack Murphy

"Men often hate each other because they fear each other; they fear each other because they don't know each other; they don't know each other because they can not communicate; they can not communicate because they are separated."
- Martin Luther King, Jr.

"We have just enough religion to make us hate, but not enough to make us love one another."
- Jonathan Swift

"I will permit no man to narrow and degrade my soul by making me hate him."
- Booker T. Washington

"It is better to be hated for who you are, than to be loved for someone you are not."
- Irish Proverb

"Hate is weakest when it is justified."
- Italian Proverb

HEALING & HEALTH

"The cure for anything is saltwater--sweat, tears, or the sea."
- Isaac Dinesen

"The world is a dangerous place to live, not because of the people who are evil, but because of the people who don't do anything about it."
- Albert Einstein

"Do I believe in the gift of healing? Yes. But why do television faith healers force people to come to them? They will be forced to give an account for claiming such a gift but failing to demonstrate it in the hospitals and battlefields."

- Jack Murphy

"Be careful about reading health books. You may die of a misprint."

- Mark Twain

"Christ heals with more ease than any other. Christ makes the devil go out with a word (Mark 9:25). Nay, he can cure with a look: Christ's look melted Peter into repentance; it was a healing look. If Christ doth but cast a look upon the soul he can recover it. Therefore David prays to have a look from God, 'Look Thou upon me, and be merciful unto me' (Psalm 119:132)."

- Thomas Watson

HEAVEN & HELL

"What sin is so sweet or profitable, that is
worth burning in hell for—or worth being shut
out of heaven for?"

- Thomas Brooks

"God sees us in secret, therefore, let us seek his face in secret. Though heaven be God's palace, yet it is not his prison."

- Thomas Brooks

"There is a way to Hell even from the gates of Heaven."

- John Bunyan

"When I pastored a country church, a farmer didn't like the sermons I preached on hell. He said, "Preach about the meek and lowly Jesus." I said, "That's where I got my information about hell.""

- Vance Havner

"Indeed the safest road to Hell is the gradual one--the gentle slope, soft underfoot, without sudden turnings, without milestones, without signposts."

- C.S. Lewis

"Jehovah Witnesses don't believe in hell and neither do most Christians."
- Leonard Ravenhill

"When asked during a phone interview: 'Say you were asked, Leonard, to speak for the annual convention of the National Religious Broadcasters, and the Lord directed you to accept that invitation, what message might you bring to that group?' Ravenhill replied: 'I believe I'd preach on hell.'"
- Leonard Ravenhill

"Would that God would make hell so read to us that we cannot rest; heaven so real that we must have men there."
- J. Hudson Taylor

"Once a poor soul entered the school of prayer after his arrival in hell. He asked for relief from his agony; it was refused. He asked that a beggar warn his brothers; he was turned down. He was praying to Abraham, a man; he could not locate God. He dared not ask to get out; he plainly knew that he was beyond all hope. Prayerless on earth, unanswered in hell, he suffers on as the man who tried to learn to pray too late."
- Cameron V. Thompson

"Wide is the gate that leads to death, yet people today still eagerly jump over each other with much haste to get there. If Hell had no door, the men of this world would dig for a million years to get in. The world works harder for their damnation than most Christians do to work out their salvation."
- Unknown

HEROES – See COURAGE

HISTORY

"History is a pact between the dead, the living, and the yet unborn."
- Edmund Burke

"History will be kind to me, for I intend to write it."
- Winston Churchill

"The further back I look, the further forward I can see."
- Winston Churchill

"I know of no other way of judging the future but by the past."
- Patrick Henry

"The greatest thing that we learn from history is that we seldom learn from history."
- Leonard Ravenhill

"Yesterday is history. Tomorrow is a mystery. Today is a gift...that's why it's called the present."
- Unknown

"History is written by the victors."
- Unknown

"Those who cannot remember the past are condemned to repeat it."
- Unknown

HOLIDAYS

"The second day of July, 1776, will be the most memorable epoch in the history of America. I am apt to believe that it will be celebrated by succeeding generations as the great anniversary festival. It ought to be commemorated as the day of deliverance, by solemn acts of devotion to God Almighty. It ought to be solemnized with pomp and parade, with shows, games, sports, guns, bells, bonfires, and illuminations, from one end of the continent to the other, from this time forward forevermore."
- John Quincy Adams

"There's nothing sadder in this world than to awake Christmas morning and not be a child."
- Erma Bombeck

"Christmas is not a time nor a season, but a state of mind. To cherish peace and goodwill, to be plenteous in mercy, is to have the real spirit of Christmas."
- Calvin Coolidge

"I will honor Christmas in my heart, and try to keep it all the year."
- Ebenezer Scrooge
in Charles Dickens'
A Christmas Carol

"It is Christmas in the heart that puts Christmas in the air."
- W. T. Ellis

"A goose never voted for an early Christmas."
- Irish Proverb

"Some businessmen are saying this could be the greatest Christmas ever. I always thought that the first one was."
- Unknown

HOLINESS

"Farewell, vain world; my soul can bid Adieu. My Savior taught me to abandon you. Your charms may gratify a sensual mind. But cannot please a soul for God Designed."
- David Brainerd

"Introspection can easily become the tool of Satan, who is called the accuser. One of his chief weapons is discouragement. He knows that if he can make us discouraged and dispirited we will not fight the battle for holiness."
- Jerry Bridges

"A baptism of holiness, a demonstration of godly living is the crying need of our day."
- Duncan Campbell

"People do not drift toward Holiness. Apart from grace-driven effort, people do not gravitate toward godliness, prayer, obedience to Scripture, faith, and delight in the Lord. We drift toward compromise and call it tolerance; we drift toward disobedience and call it freedom; we drift toward superstition and call it faith. We cherish the indiscipline of lost self-control and call it relaxation; we slouch toward prayerlessness and delude ourselves into thinking we have escaped legalism; we slide toward godlessness and convince ourselves we have been liberated."
- D.A. Carson

"I knew Jesus, and He was very precious to my soul; but I found something within me that would not keep sweet and patient and kind. I did what I could to keep it down, but it was there. I besought Jesus to do something for me, and when I gave Him my will, He came to my heart and took out all that would not be patient, all that would that would be kind, and then He shut the door."
- George Fox

"If they had a social gospel in the days of the prodigal son, somebody would have given him a bed and a sandwich and he never would have gone home."
- Vance Havner

"I bet you there will be people in Hell saying, 'I thought there was no condemnation for those in Christ Jesus.'"
- G.A. Jarquin

"With complete consecration comes perfect peace."
- Watchman Nee

"We must assess our thoughts and beliefs and reckon whether they are moving us closer to conformity to Christ or farther away from it."
- John Ortberg

"Let my heart be broken with the things that break the heart of God."
- Bob Pierce

"The greatest wisdom on this earth is holiness."
- W.S. Plumer

"There's only one proof of the Holy Ghost in your life and that's a holy life."
- Leonard Ravenhill

"No confined holiness—that is superstition; universal holiness—that is Christianity; not the bowls upon the altar holy—that is Judaism; but the bells upon the horses holy—that is true living godliness and vital Christianity."
- C.H. Spurgeon

"An unholy church! It is useless to the world, and of no esteem among men. It is an abomination, hell's laughter, heaven's abhorrence. The worst evils which have ever come upon the world have been brought upon her by an unholy church."
- C.H. Spurgeon

"In every generation the number of the righteous is small. Be sure you are among them."
- A. W. Tozer

"A whole new generation of Christians has come up believing that it is possible to 'accept' Christ without forsaking the world."
- A. W. Tozer

"Holiness is not to love Jesus and do whatever you want. Holiness is to love God and do what He wants."
- C. Peter Wagner

"It is an undoubted truth that every doctrine that comes from God, leads to God; and that which doth not tend to promote holiness is not of God."
- George Whitefield

"Holiness is an impossibility -- without the help of the Holy Spirit."
- Unknown

"All real growth in the spiritual life,
all victory over temptation,
all confidence and peace in the presence of difficulties and dangers,
all repose of spirit in times
of great disappointment or loss,
all habitual communion with God
- depends upon the practice of secret prayer."

- Unknown

HOME – See FAMILY

HONESTY

"Jesus saw Nathanael coming to him, and saith of him, Behold an Israelite indeed, in whom is no guile!"
- John 1:47

"Wherefore putting away lying, speak every man truth with his neighbour: for we are members one of another."
- Ephesians 4:25

"No one can earn a million dollars honestly."
- William Jennings Bryan

"An honest man's word is as good as his bond."
- Cervantes

"The best measure of a man's honesty isn't his income tax return. It's the zero adjust on his bathroom scale."
- Arthur Clarke

"Every honest man will suppose honest acts to flow from honest principles, and the rogues may rail without intermission."
- Thomas Jefferson

"I have always wanted to deal with everyone I meet candidly and honestly. If I have made any assertion not warranted by facts, and it is pointed out to me, I will withdraw it cheerfully."
- Abraham Lincoln

"It is easy to 'lose weight' by adjusting the accuracy of your scale. However, your pants still won't fit."
- Jack Murphy

"An honest man's the noblest work of God."
- Alexander Pope

"To make your children capable of honesty is the beginning of education."
- John Ruskin

"Honesty is the best policy – but it is not the norm."
- George Bernard Shaw

"I hope I shall always possess firmness and virtue enough to maintain what I consider the most enviable of all titles, the character of an 'Honest Man.'"
- George Washington

HOPE

"Hope deferred maketh the heart sick: but when the desire cometh, it is a tree of life."
- Proverbs 13:12

"Who against hope believed in hope, that he might become the father of many nations; according to that which was spoken, So shall thy seed be."
- Romans 4:18

"A man full of hope will be full of action."
- Thomas Brooks

"He that lives upon hope will die fasting."
-   Benjamin Franklin

"When our hopes break, let our patience hold."
-   Thomas Fuller

"In all things it is better to hope than to despair."
-   Johann Wolfgang von Goethe

"As long as the sun shines, as long as Christ lives, there is hope."
-   Jack Murphy

"In reality, false hope is the worst of all evils, because it prolongs man's torments."
-   Frederick Nietzsche

"We here in America, hold in our hands the hope of the world, the fate of the coming years; and shame and disgrace will be ours if in our eyes the light of high resolve is dimmed, if we trail in the dust the golden hopes of men."
-   Theodore Roosevelt

"Hope is like the sun, which, as we journey toward it, casts the shadow of our burden behind us."
-   Samuel Smiles

"Each one of us is God's special work of art. Through us, He teaches and inspires, delights, and encourages, informs and uplifts all those who view our lives. God, the master artist, is most concerned about expressing Himself - His thoughts and His intentions - through what He paints in our character... [He] wants to paint a beautiful portrait of His Son in and through your life. A painting like no other in all of time."
-   Joni Eareckson Tada

"Hope is the struggle against unbelief."
-   American Proverb

"Hope is the physician of each misery."
- Irish Proverb

"A life without Christ is a hopeless end. A life with Christ is an endless hope."
- Unknown

HUMILITY

"If I appear to be great in their eyes, the Lord is most graciously helping me to see how absolutely nothing I am without Him and helping me to keep little in my own eyes. He does use me. But I'm so concerned that He uses me and that it is not of me the work is done. The ax cannot boast of the trees it has cut down. It could do nothing but for the woodsman. He made it, he sharpened it, he used it. The moment he throws it aside it becomes only old iron. Oh, that I may never lose sight of this. The spiritual leader of today is in all probability one who yesterday expressed his humility by working gladly and faithfully in second place."
- Samuel Logan Brengle

"You will develop more in the next 2 months by taking a sincere interest in 2 people than spending the next 2 years trying to get people interested in you."
- Dale Carnegie

"Nothing disciplines the inordinate desires of the flesh like service, and nothing transforms the desires of the flesh like serving in secret. The flesh whines against service but it screams against hidden service. It strains and pulls for honor and recognition."
- Richard Foster

"After crosses and losses, men grow humbler and wiser."
- Benjamin Franklin

"It's amazing what can be accomplished if you don't worry about who gets the credit."
- Clarence W. Jones

"Humility is a key to the Kingdom."
- Art Katz

"God's choice acquaintances are humble men."
- Robert Leighton

"Moses spent 40 years thinking he was somebody; 40 years learning he was nobody; and 40 years discovering what God can do with a nobody."
- D.L. Moody

"We'd like to be humble...but what if no one notices?"
- John Ortberg

"Never indulge, at the close of an action, in any self-reflective acts of any kind, whether of self-congratulation or of self-despair. Forget the things that are behind, the moment they are past, leaving them with God. This quote has been of unspeakable value to me. When the temptation comes, as it mostly does to every worker after the performance of any service, to indulge in these reflections, either of one sort or the other, I turn from them at once and positively refuse to think about my work at all, leaving it with the Lord to overrule the mistakes, and to bless it as he chooses. I believe there would be far fewer "blue Mondays" for ministers of the Gospel if they would adopt this plan."
- Hannah Whitall Smith

"You can accomplish anything in life, provided that you don't mind who gets the credit."
- Harry Truman

"Small men never think they're small; great men never think they're great."
- Unknown

"Humility -- not thinking less of yourself but thinking of yourself less."
- Unknown

HUMOR

"A person without a sense of humor is like a wagon without springs. It's jolted by every pebble on the road."
- Henry Ward Beecher

"A keen sense of humor helps us to overlook the unbecoming, understand the unconventional, tolerated the unpleasant, overcome the unexpected, and outlast the unbearable."
- Billy Graham

"Above all things, and at all times, practice yourself in good humor."
- Thomas Jefferson

"Everything is funny as long as it is happening to somebody else."
- Will Rogers

"Sometimes I lie awake at night, and ask, 'Where have I gone wrong?' Then a voice says to me, 'This is going to take more than one night.'"
- Charles Schulz

"What an ornament and safeguard is humor! Far better than wit for a poet and writer. It is a genius itself, and so defends from the insanities."
- Sir Walter Scott

"My way of joking is to tell the truth. It is the funniest joke in the world."
- George Bernard Shaw

"Humor is tragedy plus time."
- Mark Twain

"It is a curious fact that people are never so trivial as when they take themselves seriously."
- Oscar Wilde

HURT – See BROKENESS

HYPOCRISY

"Thou hypocrite, first cast out the beam out of thine own eye; and then shalt thou see clearly to cast out the mote out of thy brother's eye."
-     Matthew 7:5

"Woe unto you, scribes and Pharisees, hypocrites! for ye compass sea and land to make one proselyte, and when he is made, ye make him twofold more the child of hell than yourselves."
-     Matthew 23:15

"So then because thou art lukewarm, and neither cold nor hot, I will spue thee out of my mouth."
-     Revelation 3:16

"A bad man is worse when he pretends to be a saint."
-     Sir Francis Bacon

"Many Christians are unthinkably horrified when a real sinner is suddenly discovered among the righteous. So we remain alone with our sin, living in lies and hypocrisy...He who is alone with his sins is utterly alone."
-     Dietrich Bonhoeffer

"Saint abroad, and a devil at home."
-     John Bunyan

"Hypocrisy can afford to be magnificent in its promises, for never intending to go beyond promise, it costs nothing."
-     Edmund Burke

"If Satan ever laughs, it must be at hypocrites; they are the greatest dupes he has."
-     Charles Colton

"Clean your finger before you point at my spots."
-     Benjamin Franklin

"A hypocrite is in himself both the archer and the mark, in all actions shooting at his own praise or profit."
- Thomas Fuller

"No man, for any considerable period, can wear one face to himself, and another to the multitude, without finally getting bewildered as to which may be the true."
- Nathaniel Hawthorne

"Most people have seen worse things in private than they pretend to be shocked at in public."
- Edgar Watson Howe

"The hypocrite reminds me of the man who murdered both his parents, and then when sentence was about to be pronounced pleaded for mercy on the grounds that he was an orphan."
- Abraham Lincoln

"In some sense we are all hypocrites in transition."
- Erwin McManus

"Whoever is a hypocrite in his religion mocks God, presenting to Him the outside and reserving the inward for his enemy."
- Jeremy Taylor

"Jesus reserved his hardest words for the hidden sins of hypocrisy, pride, greed and legalism."
- Philip Yancey

I

IDOLATRY

"Thou shalt have no other gods before me. Thou shalt not make unto thee any graven image, or any likeness of any thing that is in heaven above, or that is in the earth beneath, or that is in the water under the earth. Thou shalt not bow down thyself to them, nor serve them: for I the LORD thy God am a jealous God, visiting the iniquity of the fathers upon the children unto the third and fourth generation of them that hate me."

- Exodus 20:3-5

"Make no man your idol; for the best man must have faults, and his faults will usually become yours in addition to your own. This is as true in art as in morals."

- Washington Allston

"Man's mind is like a store of idolatry and superstition; so much so that if a man believes his own mind it is certain that he will forsake God and forge some idol in his own brain."

- John Calvin

"This idol gold can boast of two peculiarities: it is worshipped in all climates without a single temple, and by all classes without a single hypocrite."

- Charles Caleb Colton

"God will put up with a great many things in the human heart, but there is one thing that He will not put up with in it--a second place. He who offers God a second place, offers Him no place."
- John Ruskin

"'Tis mad idolatry,
  To make the service greater than the god."
- William Shakespeare

"The savage bows down to idols of wood and stone, the civilized man to idols of flesh and blood."
- George Bernard Shaw

"Idolatry is certainly the first-born of folly, the great and leading paradox; nay, the very abridgment and sum total of all absurdities."
- Robert South

"Philosophers and common heathen believed one God, to whom all things were referred; but under this God they worshipped many inferior and subservient gods."
- Benjamin Stillingfleet

IGNORANCE

"And the times of this ignorance God winked at; but now commandeth all men every where to repent."
- Acts 17:30

"I do not pretend to know what many ignorant men are sure of."
- Clarence Darrow

"Ignorance never settles a question."
- Benjamin Disraeli

"They most assume, who know the least."
- John Gay

"Ignorant men raise questions that wise men answered a thousand years ago."
- Johann Wolfgang von Goethe

"Where ignorance is bliss,
'Tis folly to be wise."
- Thomas Gray

"A man is never astonished or ashamed that he don't know what another does, but he is surprised at the gross ignorance of the other in not knowing what he does."
- Thomas Halliburton

"Far more crucial than what we know or do not know is what we do not want to know."
- Eric Hoffer

"Ignorance is preferable to error; and he is less remote from truth who believes nothing, than he who believes what is wrong."
- Thomas Jefferson

"An ignorant person is one who doesn't know what you have just found out."
- Will Rogers

"If I am wise, it is because I know nothing except of my ignorance."
- Socrates

"A wise man in the company of those who are ignorant has been compared by the sages to a beautiful girl in the company of blind men."
- Persian Proverb

IMAGINATION

"These six things doth the LORD hate: yea, seven are an abomination unto him: A proud look, a lying tongue, and hands that shed innocent blood, An heart that deviseth wicked imaginations, feet that be swift in running to mischief, A false witness that speaketh lies, and he that soweth discord among brethren."

> - Proverbs 6:16-19

"The level of our success is limited only by our imagination and no act of kindness, however small, is ever wasted."

> - Aesop

"Imagination was given to man to compensate him for what he is not; a sense of humor to console him for what he is."

> - Sir Francis Bacon

"The soul without imagination is what an observatory would be without a telescope."

> - Henry Ward Beecher

"I am enough of an artist to draw freely upon my imagination. Imagination is more important than knowledge. Knowledge is limited. Imagination encircles the world."

> - Albert Einstein

"Logic will get you from A to B. Imagination will take you everywhere else."

> - Albert Einstein

"It is the divine attribute of the imagination, that it is irrepressible, unconfinable; that when the real world is shut out, it can create a world for itself, and with a necromantic power can conjure up glorious shapes and forms, and brilliant visions to make solitude populous, and irradiate the gloom of a dungeon."

> - Washington Irving

"The world of reality has its limits, the world of imagination is boundless."

> - Jean Jacques Rosseau

"Imagination is the beginning of creation. You imagine what you desire;
you will what you imagine; and at last you create what you will."
- George Bernard Shaw

"A vile imagination, once indulged, gets the key of our minds, and can get
in again very easily, whether we will or no, and can so return as to bring
seven other spirits with it more wicked than itself; and what may follow
no one knows."
- Charles Spurgeon

"Imagination is only intelligence having fun."
- Mark Twain

IMMIGRATION

""For whither thou goest, I will follow; and where thou lodgest, I will
lodge: Thy people shall be my people, and thy God shall be my God:."
- Ruth 1:16

"The laws should be rigidly enforced which prohibit the immigration of a
servile class to compete with American labor, with no intention of
acquiring citizenship, and bringing with them and retaining habits and
customs repugnant to our civilization."
- Grover Cleveland

"No matter what other nations may say about the United States,
immigration is still the sincerest form of flattery."
- Clayton Cramer

"Give me your tired, your poor, your huddled masses, yearning to breathe
free, the wretched refuse of your teeming shores - send these, the
homeless,
tempest-tost to me; I lift my lamp beside the golden door."
- Emma Lazarus

"For an American citizen to vote as a German-American, an Irish-American, or an English-American, is to be a traitor to American institutions; and those hyphenated Americans who terrorize American politicians by threats of the foreign vote are engaged in treason to the American Republic."

- Theodore Roosevelt

"If you should turn back from this land to Europe the foreign ministers of the Gospel, and the foreign attorneys, and the foreign merchants, and the foreign philanthropists, what a robbery of our pulpits, our court rooms, our storehouses, and our beneficent institutions, and what a putting back of every monetary, merciful, moral, and religious interest of the land! This commingling here of all nationalities under the blessing of God will produce in seventy-five or one hundred years the most magnificent style of man and woman the world ever saw. They will have the wit of one race, the eloquence of another race, the kindness of another, the generosity of another, the aesthetic taste of another, the high moral character of another, and when that man and woman step forth, their brain and nerve and muscle an intertwining of the fibers of all nationalities, nothing but the new electric photographic apparatus, that can see clear through body and mind and soul, can take of them an adequate picture."

- Thomas DeWitt Talmage

"If America builds a hundred foot wall, Mexico will manufacture a 101 foot ladder."

- Mexican Proverb

IMMORALITY

"Now the works of the flesh are manifest, which are these; Adultery, fornication, uncleanness, lasciviousness, Idolatry, witchcraft, hatred, variance, emulations, wrath, strife, seditions, heresies, Envyings, murders, drunkenness, revellings, and such like: of the which I tell you before, as I have also told you in time past, that they which do such things shall not inherit the kingdom of God. "

- Galatians 5:19-21

"We need to weep over the immorality in our homes. We have to weep and wail that we have broken covenant with God."
- Nancy Leigh DeMoss

"No stronger case can be shown for prohibiting anything which is regarded as a personal immorality, than is made out for suppressing these practices in the eyes of those who regard them as impieties; and unless we are willing to adopt the logic of persecutors, and to say that we may persecute others because we are right, and that they must not persecute us because they are wrong, we must beware of admitting a principle of which we should resent as a gross injustice the application to ourselves."
- John Stuart Mill

"We cannot buy our security, our freedom from the threat of the bomb by committing an immorality so great as saying to a billion human beings now in slavery behind the Iron Curtain, 'Give up your dreams of freedom because to save our own skin, we are willing to make a deal with your slave-masters.'"
- Ronald Reagan

"New morality is too often the old immorality condoned."
- Hartley Shawcross

"Freedom's enemies are waste, lethargy, indifference, immorality, and the insidious attitude of something for nothing."
- William Arthur Ward

INDEPENDENCE

"When in the Course of human events, it becomes necessary for one people to dissolve the political bands which have connected them with another, and to assume among the powers of the earth, the separate and equal station to which the Laws of Nature and of Nature's God entitle them, a decent respect to the opinions of mankind requires that they should declare the causes which impel them to the separation."
- Thomas Jefferson
Declaration of Independence

"I never thrust my nose into other men's porridge. It is no bread and butter of mine: Every man for himself and God for us all."
- Cervantes

"All we ask is to be let alone."
- Jefferson Davis

"The king is the least independent man in his dominions; the beggar the most so."
- A. W. and J. C. Hare

"The whole trouble is that we won't let God help us."
- George MacDonald

"Let fortune do her worst, whatever she makes us lose, so long as she never makes us lose our honesty and our independence."
- Alexander Pope

"Independence now: and Independence forever."
- Daniel Webster
  Eulogy for Adams and Jefferson

"Tis better to sit alone on a pumpkin, and have it all to yourself, than to be crowded on a velvet cushion."
- Irish Proverb

INDIVIDUALITY

"Nature made him, and then broke the mold."
- Ludovico Ariosto

"No bird soars too high if he soars with his own wings."
- William Blake

"Not nations, not armies, have advanced the race; but here and there, in the course of ages, an individual has stood up and cast his shadow over the world."

- Edwin Hubbell Chapin

"We move too much in platoons; we march by sections; we do not live in our vital individuality enough; we are slaves to fashion, in mind and in heart, if not to our passions and appetites."

- Edwin Hubbell Chapin

"Individuality is the aim of political liberty."

- James Fenimore Cooper

"An institution is the lengthened shadow of one man; as, monachism of the Hermit Anthony, the Reformation of Luther, Quakerism of Fox, Methodism of Wesley, abolition of Clarkson. Scipio, Milton called "the height of Rome;" and all history resolves itself easily into the biography of a few stout and earnest persons. Let a man, then, know his worth, and keep things under his feet."

- Ralph Waldo Emerson

"Every individual nature has its own beauty. One is struck in every company, at every fireside, with the riches of nature, when he hears so many new tones, all musical, sees in each person original manners, which have a proper and peculiar charm, and reads new expressions of face. He perceives that nature has laid for each the foundations of a divine building, if the soul will build thereon."

- Ralph Waldo Emerson

"We fancy men are individuals; so are pumpkins."

- Ralph Waldo Emerson

"Human faculties are common, but that which converges these faculties into my identity separates me from every other man. That other man cannot think my thoughts, he cannot speak my words, he cannot do my works. He cannot have my sins, I cannot have his virtues."

- Henry Giles

"Individuals, not stations, ornament society."
- William Ewart Gladstone

"Thou art in the end what thou art. Put on wigs with millions of curls, set thy foot upon ell-high rocks. Thou abidest ever--what thou art."
- Johann Wolfgang von Goethe

"God gave every man individuality of constitution, and a chance for achieving individuality of character. He puts special instruments into every man's hands by which to make himself and achieve his mission."
- Josiah Gilbert Holland

"If individuality has no play, society does not advance; if individuality breaks out of all bounds, society perishes."
- Thomas Henry Huxley

"But society has now fairly got the better of individuality; and the danger which threatens human nature is not the excess, but the deficiency, of personal impulses and preferences."
- John Stuart Mill

"The worth of a state, in the long run, is the worth of the individuals composing it."
- John Stuart Mill

"Experience serves to prove that the worth and strength of a state depend far less upon the form of its institutions than upon the character of its men; for the nation is only the aggregate of individual conditions, and civilization itself is but a question of personal, improvement."
- Samuel Smiles

"Let us shun everything, which might tend to efface the primitive lineaments of our individuality. Let us reflect that each one of us is a thought of God."
- Anne Sophie Swetchine

INTEGRITY see CHARACTER

INTELLIGENCE

"I come from the Town of Stupidity; it lieth about four degrees beyond the City of Destruction."
- John Bunyan

"Genius is one percent inspiration and 99 percent perspiration."
- Thomas Edison

"We should take care not to make the intellect our god; it has, of course, powerful muscles, but no personality. "
- Albert Einstein

"Intellectuals solve problems. Geniuses prevent them."
- Albert Einstein

"There are no stupid questions, but there are LOT of inquisitive idiots."
- Albert Einstein

"You do not really understand something unless you can explain it to your grandmother."
- Albert Einstein

"The intelligent have a right over the ignorant; namely, the right of instructing them."
- Ralph Waldo Emerson

"Unless one is a genius, it is best to aim at being intelligible."
- Anthony Hope

"God multiplies intelligence, which communicates itself, like fire, *ad infinitum*. Light a thousand torches at one touch, the flame remains always the same."
- Joseph Joubert

"You don't need to know all the answers. No one is smart enough to ask you all the questions."
- Will Rogers

"There are too many stupid people in the world. I'm not saying we should kill them all or anything. Just take the warning labels off of everything and let the problem solve itself."

- Will Rogers

"Great minds discuss ideas;
Average minds discuss events;
Small minds discuss people."

- Eleanor Roosevelt

"Knowing a great deal is not the same as being smart; intelligence is not information alone but also judgment, the manner in which information is collected and used."

- Carl Sagan

"One man that has a mind and knows it can always beat ten men who haven't and don't."

- George Bernard Shaw

"It is no proof of a man's understanding to be able to confirm whatever he pleases; but to be able to discern that what is true is true, and that what is false is false, this is the mark and character of intelligence."

- Emanuel Swedenborg

"I must have a prodigious quantity of mind; it takes me as much as a week sometimes to make it up."

- Mark Twain

"Common sense is not so common."

- Voltaire

"Every breeze wafts intelligence from country to country, every wave rolls it, all give it forth, and all in turn receive it. There is a vast commerce of ideas, there are marts and exchanges for intellectual discoveries, and a wonderful fellowship of those individual intelligences which make up the mind and opinion of the age."

- Daniel Webster

"We should not only use the brains we have, but all that we can borrow."
-   Woodrow Wilson

"Never tell someone how to do something. Tell them what to do and they will surprise you with their ingenuity."
-   George Patton

"If you don't stand for something, you will fall for anything!"
-   American Proverb

"If at first you don't succeed, try again. But before you do think about why you're trying, and whether or not it's really worth the effort."
-   American Proverb

"For you to insult me, I must first value your opinion."
-   Italian Proverb

"Common sense is what tells us the earth is flat."
-   Spanish Proverb

"Intelligence: The ability to make finer distinctions on a subject."
-   Unknown

"A genius is someone who asks dumb questions that nobody else would ask, an idiot asks the smart questions that have already been answered."
-   Unknown

J

JEALOUSY

"Charity suffereth long, and is kind; charity envieth not; charity vaunteth not itself, is not puffed up, Doth not behave itself unseemly, seeketh not her own, is not easily provoked, thinketh no evil; Rejoiceth not in iniquity, but rejoiceth in the truth; Beareth all things, believeth all things, hopeth all things, endureth all things. Charity never faileth."
- I Corinthians 13:4-8

"Envy is the most stupid of vices, for there is no single advantage to be gained from it."
- Honore de Balzac

"Love looks through a telescope; envy, through a microscope."
- Josh Billings

"Jealousy sees things always with magnifying glasses which make little things large. It turns dwarfs into giants and suspicions into truths."
- Cervantes

"Envy is the art of counting the other fellow's blessings instead of your own."
- Harold Coffin

"It is not love that is blind, but jealousy."
- Lawrence Durrell

"Jealousy is never satisfied even when the truth be known."
- George Eliot

"The words of a jealous man are like constant cries of a baby that cannot be comforted."
- Jack Murphy

"In jealousy there is more self-love than love."
- François Rochefoucauld

"The jealous are troublesome to others, but a torment to themselves."
- William Penn

"Jealousy is not love, but self-love."
- François Rochefoucauld

"Jealousy is always born with love, yet is quick to make an end of it."
- François Rochefoucauld

"Jealousy is a cancer that infects those around us."
- Mark Twain

"Jealous rants stab the back with daggers of doubt and self-doubt. Run from the man or woman of jealousy!"
- English Proverb

"Jealousy is a poison that slowly kills our lovers."
- Irish Proverb

"Jealousy and love are mortal enemies."
- Russian Proverb

"Jealousy is mental purgatory that feels like eternal Hell."
- Spanish Proverb

JOBS

"Whatsoever thy hand findeth to do, do it with thy might; for there is no work, nor device, nor knowledge, nor wisdom, in the grave, whither thou goest."
- Ecclesiastes 9:10

"I hold every man a debtor to his profession; from the which as men of course do seek to receive countenance and profit, so ought they of duty to endeavor themselves, by way of amends, to be a help and ornament thereunto."
- Sir Francis Bacon

"Can you find a man who loves the occupation that provides him with a livelihood? Professions are like marriages; we end by feeling only their inconveniences."
- Honore de Balzac

"The highest excellence is seldom attained in more than one vocation. The roads leading to distinction in separate pursuits diverge, and the nearer we approach the one, the farther we recede from the other."
- Christian Nestell Bovee

"When we have learned to offer up every duty connected with our situation in life as a sacrifice to God, a settled employment becomes just a settled habit of prayer."
- Thomas Erskine

"All professions are conspiracies against laziness."
- George Bernard Shaw

"It is observed at sea that men are never so much disposed to grumble and mutiny as when least employed. Hence an old captain, when there was nothing else to do, would issue the order to 'scour the anchor.'"
- Samuel Smiles

"Some people let their work get to them before they get to it."
- American Proverb

242

"Be not a jack of all trades, but a master of one."
- Chinese Proverb

JOURNALISM

"Journalism is literature in a hurry."
- Matthew Arnold

"A journalist is a grumbler, a censurer, a giver of advice, a regent of sovereigns, a tutor of nations. Four hostile newspapers are more to be feared than a thousand bayonets."
- Napoleon Bonaparte

"The Press has become the invisible but loudest member of each President's cabinet meeting."
- Dick Cheney

"Journalism largely consists in saying "Lord Jones is dead" to people who never knew Lord Jones was alive."
- G.K. Chesterton

"The man who reads nothing at all is better educated than the man who reads nothing but newspapers."
- Thomas Jefferson

"If one morning I walked on top of the water across the Potomac River, the headline that afternoon would read: 'President Can't Swim.'"
- Lyndon B. Johnson

"The mission of the modern press is to spread culture while destroying the attention span."
- Karl Kraus

"The pen is mightier than the sword."
- Edward George Lytton

"No news is good news – except for the *Washington Post*."
- Jack Murphy

"You can tell the political leanings of the media by their willingness to publish dirt on one politician and their ability to keep such dirt a secret regarding another."

> -   Jack Murphy

"If you don't read the newspaper, you are uninformed. If you do read the newspaper, you are misinformed."

> -   Will Rogers

"An editor is one who separates the wheat from the chaff and prints the chaff."

> -   Adlai Stevenson

"Get your facts first, and then you can distort 'em as much as you please."

> -   Mark Twain

"I always turn to the sports section first. The sports section records people's accomplishments; the front page nothing but man's failures."

> -   Earl Warren

JOY

"Then he said unto them, Go your way, eat the fat, and drink the sweet, and send portions unto them for whom nothing is prepared: for this day is holy unto our LORD: neither be ye sorry; for the joy of the LORD is your strength."

> -   Nehemiah 8:10

"Rejoice in the Lord always: and again I say, Rejoice."

> -   Philippians 4:4

"Looking unto Jesus the author and finisher of our faith; who for the joy that was set before him endured the cross, despising the shame, and is set down at the right hand of the throne of God."

> -   Hebrews 12:2

"Whom having not seen, ye love; in whom, though now ye see him not, yet believing, ye rejoice with joy unspeakable and full of glory."
- I Peter 1:8

"There is not one blade of grass, there is no color in this world that is not intended to make us rejoice."
- John Calvin

"Joy is the best of wine."
- George Eliot

"For every minute you are angry you lose sixty seconds of happiness."
- Ralph Waldo Emerson

"Most joyfully will I confirm with my blood that truth which I have written and preached."
- John Huss, as he was burned at the stake

"We could never learn to be brave and patient if there were only joy in the world."
- Helen Keller

"Joy is the holy fire that keeps our purpose warm and our intelligence aglow."
- Helen Keller

"I can say that I never knew what joy was like until I gave up pursuing happiness, or cared to live until I chose to die. For these two discoveries I am beholden to Jesus."
- Malcolm Muggeridge

"Grief can take care of itself, but to get the full value of joy you must have somebody to divide it with."
- Mark Twain

"Joy is the will which labors, which overcomes obstacles, which knows triumph."
- William Butler Yeats

JUDGMENT

"Probably in the Day of Judgment it will be found that nothing is ever done by the truth, used ever so zealously, unless there is a spirit of prayer somewhere in connection with the presentation of truth."
- Charles G. Finney

"All roads lead to the judgment seat of Christ."
- Keith Green

"I have a dream that my four little children will one day live in a nation where they will not be judged by the color of their skin but by the content of their character."
- Martin Luther King, Jr.

"How much energy do we modern Christians put into condemning sexual sins compared to avoiding the judgmental, Pharisaical attitude of those with rocks in their hands? Who killed Jesus, adulterers or Pharisees?"
- Brian McLaren

"Anything that is not settled while you are on earth will have to be settled at the Judgment Seat of Christ."
- Zac Poonen

"The attitude of the average Christian today is to 'relax and be raptured.' But He is coming... and when God gets angry you've no idea what it is. Like a thousand volcanoes exploding. He has appointed a day in which He is going to judge the world and the poor blind world doesn't know much about it and the poor blind church doesn't think much about it now."
- Leonard Ravenhill

"My greatest thought is my accountability to God."
- Daniel Webster

"I judge all things only by the price they shall gain in eternity."
- John Wesley

"Christ died to save this lost world; he did not come to destroy, maim or pour out wrath."
- David Wilkerson

JUSTICE

"He hath shewed thee, O man, what is good; and what doth the LORD require of thee, but to do justly, and to love mercy, and to walk humbly with thy God?"
- Micah 6:8

"It is better that ten guilty persons escape, than that one innocent suffer."
- Sir William Blackstone

"Bad laws are the worst form of tyranny."
- Edmund Burke

"Peace and justice are two sides of the same coin."
- Dwight Eisenhower

"Capital punishment is as fundamentally wrong as a cure for crime as charity is wrong as a cure for poverty."
- Henry Ford

"Justice delayed, is justice denied."
- William Gladstone

"Injustice anywhere is a threat to justice everywhere."
- Martin Luther King, Jr.

"I have always found that mercy bears richer fruits than strict justice."
- Abraham Lincoln

"A jury consists of twelve persons chosen to decide who has the better lawyer."

- Robert Frost

"This is a court of law, young man, not a court of justice."

- Oliver Wendell Holmes

"Laws are like cobwebs, which may catch small flies, but let wasps and hornets break through."

- Jonathan Swift

"It is the spirit and not the form of law that keeps justice alive."

- Earl Warren

"God has never, in the history of mankind, allowed his name to go long offended."

- David Wilkerson

"Corn can't expect justice from a court composed of chickens."

- African Proverb

"Good lawyers know the law; great lawyers know the judge."

- Spanish Proverb

K

KINDNESS

"And beside this, giving all diligence, add to your faith virtue; and to virtue knowledge; And to knowledge temperance; and to temperance patience; and to patience godliness; And to godliness brotherly kindness; and to brotherly kindness charity."
- II Peter 1:5-7

"No act of kindness, no matter how small, is ever wasted."
- Aesop

"Those who bring sunshine to the lives of others cannot keep it from themselves."
- Sir J. M. Barrie

"Kindness is a language the dumb can speak and the deaf can hear and understand."
- Christian Nestell Bovee

"Have you had a kindness shown?
Pass it on;
'Twas not given for thee alone,
Pass it on;
Let it travel down the years,
Let it wipe another's tears,
'Til in Heaven the deed appears -
Pass it on."
- Henry Burton

"How far you go in life depends on your being tender with the young, compassionate with the aged, sympathetic with the striving and tolerant of the weak and strong. Because someday in your life you will have been all of these."

- George Washington Carver

"By swallowing evil words unsaid, no one has ever harmed his stomach."

- Winston Churchill

"The greatest good you can do for another is not just to share your riches but to reveal to him his own."

- Benjamin Disraeli

"You cannot do a kindness too soon, for you never know when it will be too late."

- Ralph Waldo Emerson

"Kindness has converted more sinners than either zeal, eloquence, or learning."

- Frederick William Faber

"I soothe my conscience now with the thought that it is better for hard words to be on paper than that Mummy should carry them in her heart."

- Anne Frank

"Treat everyone with politeness, even those who are rude to you -- not because they are kind, but because you are."

- Benjamin Franklin

"I expect to pass through life but once. If therefore, there be any kindness I can show, or any good thing I can do to any fellow being, let me do it now, and not defer or neglect it, as I shall not pass this way again."

- William Penn

"A good character is the best tombstone. Those who loved you and were helped by you will remember you when forget-me-nots have withered. Carve your name on hearts, not on marble."
-    Charles H. Spurgeon

"Kindness is the language which the deaf can hear and the blind can see."
-    Mark Twain

"One man cannot hold another man down in the ditch without remaining down in the ditch with him."
-    Booker T. Washington

"People don't care how much you know until they know how much you care."
-    American Proverb

"Kindness, like a boomerang, always returns."
-    Australian Proverb

"The kindest word in all the world is the unkind word, unsaid."
-    Irish Proverb

"It's nice to be important, but it's more important to be nice."
-    Unknown

KNOWLEDGE

"For in much wisdom is much grief: and he that increaseth knowledge increaseth sorrow."
-    Ecclesiastes 1:18

"My people are destroyed from lack of knowledge."
-    Hosea 4:6

"Yea doubtless, and I count all things but loss for the excellency of the knowledge of Christ Jesus my Lord: for whom I have suffered the loss of all things, and do count them but dung, that I may win Christ."
-    Philippians 3:8

"Real knowledge, like every thing else of the highest value, is not to be obtained easily. It must be worked for,--studied for,--thought for,--and, more than all, it must be prayed for."

- Thomas Arnold

"A woman, especially if she have the misfortune of knowing anything, should conceal it as well as she can."

- Jane Austen

"Knowledge is power."

- Sir Francis Bacon

"Growth is not more knowledge or increase of years: It is more of Him and less of me. He increases as I decrease. This is what it means to be a disciple."

- Chip Brogden

"I know too much to be conservative or liberal."

- David Brinkley

"Men are four:
   He who knows not and knows not he knows not, he is a fool -- shun him;
   He who knows not and knows he knows not, he is simple – teach him;
   He who knows and knows not he knows, he is asleep -- wake him;
   He who knows and knows he knows, he is wise -- follow him!"

- Lady Burton

"The tree of knowledge is not that of life."

- Lord George Byron
from *Manfred*

"Next to knowing when to seize an opportunity, the most important thing in life is to know when to forgo an advantage."

- Benjamin Disraeli

"A man should keep his little brain attic stocked with all the furniture that he is likely to use, and the rest he can put away in the lumber-room of his library, where he can get it if he wants it."
-     Sir Arthur Conan Doyle

"Lock yourself in a room; throw the key away; do something! Seek God and be found of Him. That is His promise: "If you will seek for Me with all your heart and all your soul, you shall be found of Me" (Deut. 4:29). When you do obtain that knowledge, maintain it, or else you will lose it."
-     Art Katz

"The advancement and diffusion of knowledge is the only guardian of true liberty."
-     James Madison

"Knowing God without knowing our wretchedness leads to pride. Knowing our wretchedness without knowing God leads to despair. Knowing Christ gives the balance."
-     Blaise Pascal

"The more one knows God, the greater one desires to know Him. Knowledge is commonly the measure of love. The deeper and more extensive our knowledge, the greater is our love."
-     Brother Lawrence

"Constant kindness can accomplish much. As the sun makes the ice melt, kindness causes misunderstandings, mistrust, and hostility to evaporate."
-     Albert Schweitzer

"Knowledge is like money,--the more a man gets, the more he craves."
-     Henry Wheeler Shaw

"Let no knowledge satisfy but that which lifts above the world, which weans from the world, which makes the world a footstool."
-     Charles H. Spurgeon

"If we value the pursuit of knowledge, we must be free to follow wherever that search may lead us. The free mind is not a barking dog, to be tethered on a ten-foot chain."

-    Adlai Stevenson

"The Word written is not only a rule of knowledge, but a rule of obedience; it is not only to mend our sight, but to mend our pace. Reading without practice will be but a torch to light men to hell."

-    Thomas Watson

L

LANGUAGE

"We have too many high sounding words and too few actions that correspond with them."
- Abigail Adams

"No one means all he says, and yet very few say all they mean, for words are slippery and thought is viscous."
- Henry Brooks Adams

"To God I speak Spanish, to women Italian, to men French, and to my horse--German."
- King Charles V

"The word "good" has many meanings. For example, if a man were to shoot his grandmother at a range of five hundred yards, I should call him a good shot, but not necessarily a good man."
- G.K. Chesterton

"Language is the armory of the human mind, and at once contains the trophies of its past, and the weapons of its future conquests."
- Samuel Taylor Coleridge

"Euphemisms are unpleasant truths wearing diplomatic cologne."
- Quentin Crisp

"Use what language you will, you can never say anything to others but what you are."

- Ralph Waldo Emerson

"A man who is ignorant of foreign languages is also ignorant of his own language."

- Johann Wolfgang von Goethe

"Languages are the barometers of national thought and character."

- A. W. and J. C. Hare

"Language is the blood of the soul into which thoughts run and out of which they grow."

- Oliver Wendell Holmes

"Language is the dress of thought."

- Samuel Johnson

"We should have a great fewer disputes in the world if words were taken for what they are, the signs of our ideas only, and not for things themselves."

- John Locke

"Only in America do people park their cars on the driveway and drive their cars on the parkway. "

- Jack Murphy

"But if thought corrupts language, language can also corrupt thought."

- George Orwell

"If you can speak three languages, you're trilingual. If you can speak two languages, you're bilingual. If you can speak only one language, you're an American."

- Will Rogers

"Great Britain and the United States are nations separated by a common language."

- George Bernard Shaw

"Language is the means of getting an idea from one brain into another without surgery. "

-   Mark Twain

"Language, as well as the faculty of speech, was the immediate gift of God."

-   Noah Webster

LAST WORDS

"Thomas Jefferson still lives."

-   John Adams,
    unaware that Jefferson died a few hours
    earlier, on July 4, 1826,
    the 50th Anniversary of the Signing of the
    Declaration of Independence

"This is the last of earth! I am content."

-   John Quincy Adams

"See how a Christian dies!"

-   Joseph Addison

"Friends applaud, the comedy is over."

-   Ludwig von Beethoven

"I don't feel good."

-   Luther Burbank

"I have been dying for twenty years, now I am going to live."

-   James Drummond Burns

"I realize that patriotism is not enough. I must have no hatred toward any one."

-   Edith Louisa Cavell,
    shortly before being shot by the Germans

"I'm checking for loopholes."

- W. C. Fields,
  when asked why he was reading the Bible

"And now, in keeping with Channel 40's policy of always bringing you the latest in blood and guts, in living color, you're about to see another first -- an attempted suicide."

- Christine Chubbock,
  just before shooting herself on national television

"All my earthly possessions for but a moment of time."

- Queen Elizabeth I (attributed)

"I've never felt better."

- Douglas Fairbanks, Sr.

"It is very beautiful over there."

- Benjamin Franklin

"The mountain is passed; now we shall get on better."

- Frederick the Great

"Why fear death? It is the most beautiful adventure in life."

- Charles Frohman

"Tortured for the Republic."

- James Abram Garfield

"I have spent my life laboriously doing nothing."

- Hugo Grotius

"I only regret that I have but one life to lose for my country."

- Nathan Hale

"My work is done; I have nothing left to do but to go to my Father."

- Selina Hastings

"God will pardon me. It is his trade."
- Heinrich Heine

"Now I am about to take my last voyage, a great leap in the dark."
- Thomas Hobbes

"Let us cross over the River, and rest under the shade of the Trees."
- Thomas "Stonewall" Jackson

"Is it the fourth yet?"
- Thomas Jefferson

"I wonder why he shot me?"
- Huey P. Long

"Thank God, I have done my duty."
- Lord Horatio Nelson

"Why yes – a bulletproof vest!"
- James Rodges,
on his final request before the firing squad

"I go to see the sun for the last time."
- Jean-Jacques Rousseau

"Don't let it end like this. Tell them I said something."
- Francisco "Pancho" Villa

"It is today, my dear, that I take a perilous leap."
- Voltaire

"Ah, well, then I suppose I shall have to die beyond my means."
- Oscar Wilde

"Tell them I've had a wonderful life."
- Ludwig Wittgenstein

LAUGHTER

"And Sarah said, God hath made me to laugh, so that all that hear will laugh with me."
-    Genesis 21:6

"Even in laughter the heart is sorrowful; and the end of that mirth is heaviness."
-    Proverbs 14:13

"For as the crackling of thorns under a pot, so is the laughter of the fool: this also is vanity."
-    Ecclesiastes 7:6

"If we may believe our logicians, man is distinguished from all other creatures by the faculty of laughter."
-    Joseph Addison

"To provoke laughter without joining in it greatly heightens the effect."
-    Honore de Balzac

"Many men will let you abuse them if only you will make them laugh."
-    Henry Ward Beecher

"If you lose the power to laugh, you lose the power to think."
-    Clarence Darrow

"It is a fair, even-handed, noble adjustment of things, that while there is infection in disease and sorrow, there is nothing in the world so irresistibly contagious as laughter and good-humor."
-    Charles Dickens

"Men show their character in nothing more clearly than by what they think laughable."
-    Johann Wolfgang von Goethe

"One laugh is worth a hundred groans."
-    Charles Lamb

"Beware of him who hates the laugh of a child."
-     Johann Kaspar Lavatar

"Laughter can be a weapon. It can defeat personal depression or feelings of sorrow. It can also, when uttered aloud, harm the dreams of another."
-     Jack Murphy

"The wrinkles of love are far more valuable than those caused by laughter or worry."
-     Jack Murphy

"Nothing is more valuable than honest laughter."
-     Sir Walter Scott

"Men are contented to be laughed at for their wit, but not for their folly."
-     Jonathan Swift

"Laughter is not at all a bad beginning for a friendship, and it is by far the best ending for one."
-     Oscar Wilde

"He laughs best who laughs last."
-     English Proverb

LAW

"The law of the LORD is perfect, converting the soul: the testimony of the LORD is sure, making wise the simple."
-     Psalm 19:7

"Now, O king, establish the decree, and sign the writing, that it be not changed, according to the law of the Medes and Persians, which altereth not."
-     Daniel 6:8

"They say unto him, Caesar's. Then saith he unto them, Render therefore unto Caesar the things which are Caesar's; and unto God the things that are God's."

- Matthew 22:21

"Law is merely the expression of the will of the strongest for the time being, and therefore laws have no fixity, but shift from generation to generation."

- Henry Brooks Adams

"At his best man is the noblest of all animals; separated from law and justice he is the worst."

- Aristotle

"A law is valuable not because it is law, but because there is right in it."

- Henry Ward Beecher

"The law is a gun, which if it misses a pigeon always kills a crow; if it does not strike the guilty, it hits some one else. As every crime creates a law, so in turn every law creates a crime."

- Edward Bulwer Lytton

"There is but one law for all; namely, that law which governs all law,--the law of our Creator, the law of humanity, justice, equity; the law of nature and of nations."

- Edmund Burke

"I sometimes wish that people would put a little more emphasis upon the observance of the law than they do upon its enforcement."

- Calvin Coolidge

"Laws alone cannot secure freedom of expression; in order that every man present his views without penalty there must be spirit of tolerance in the entire population."

- Albert Einstein

"The law sends us to Christ to be justified, and Christ sends us to the law to be regulated."
-      John Flavel

"Where there is Hunger, Law is not regarded; and where Law is not regarded, there will be Hunger."
-      Benjamin Franklin

"The English laws punish vice; the Chinese laws do more, they reward virtue."
-      Oliver Goldsmith

"It will be of little avail to the people that the laws are made by men of their own choice if the laws be so voluminous that they cannot be read, or so incoherent that they cannot be understood."
-      Alexander Hamilton

"Of law there can be no less acknowledged than that her seat is the bosom of God, her voice the harmony of the world; all things do her homage, the very least as feeling her care; and the greatest as not exempted from leer power; both angels and men, and creatures of what condition soever, though each in different sort and manner, yet all with uniform consent admiring her as the mother of their peace and joy."
-      Richard Hooker

"How does one determine whether a law is just or unjust? A just law is a man-made code that squares with the moral law or the law of God. An unjust law is a code that is out of harmony with the moral law. To put it in terms of St. Thomas Aquinas: An unjust law is a human law that is not rooted in eternal law and natural law. Any law that uplifts the human personality is just. Any law that degrades human personality is unjust. All segregation statutes are unjust because segregation distorts the soul and damages the personality. It gives the segregator a false sense of superiority and the segregated a false sense of inferiority."
-      Martin Luther King, Jr.

"Let every man remember that to violate the law is to trample on the blood of his father, and to tear that charter of his own and his children's liberty."
- Abraham Lincoln

"The law discovers the disease. The gospel gives the remedy."
- Martin Luther

"Because just as good morals, if they are to be maintained, have need of the laws, so the laws, if they are to be observed, have need of good morals."
- Niccolo Machiavelli

"Laws can discover sin, but not remove it."
- John Milton

"I do not believe the United States is well served by a policy that says it is OK to be immoral in any way."
- General Peter Pace

"Good people do not need laws to tell them to act responsibly, while bad people will find a way around the laws."
- Plato

"No man is above the law and no man is below it; nor do we ask any man's permission when we ask him to obey it."
- Theodore Roosevelt

"He who decides a case without hearing the other side, though he decide justly, cannot be considered just."
- Seneca

"There is a higher law than the Constitution."
- William Henry Seward

"It is a very easy thing to devise good laws; the difficulty is to make them effective. The great mistake is that of looking upon men as virtuous, or thinking that they can be made so by laws; and consequently the greatest

art of a politician is to render vices serviceable to the cause of virtue."
- 　Henry St. John

"Laws are like cobwebs, which may catch small flies, but let wasps and hornets break through."
- 　Jonathan Swift

"Laws made by common consent must not be trampled on by individuals."
- 　George Washington

"Our nation is being led astray by ungodly judges, mayors and governors, who are given to change, defying the Constitution and substituting their own wicked agendas."
- 　David Wilkerson

LAZINESS

"Go to the ant, thou sluggard; consider her ways, and be wise: Which having no guide, overseer, or ruler, Provideth her meat in the summer, and gathereth her food in the harvest. How long wilt thou sleep, O sluggard? when wilt thou arise out of thy sleep? Yet a little sleep, a little slumber, a little folding of the hands to sleep: So shall thy poverty come as one that travelleth, and thy want as an armed man."
- 　Proverbs 6:6-11

"The time will come when winter will ask you what you were doing all summer. "
- 　Henry Clay

"The lazy man aims at nothing, and generally hits it."
- 　James Ellis

"Every man is as lazy as he dares to be."
- 　Ralph Waldo Emerson
"'Could have' is the enemy of the 'did'."
- 　Ray Everett

"Laziness may appear attractive, but work gives satisfaction."
- Anne Frank

"Laziness travels so slowly that poverty soon overtakes him."
- Benjamin Franklin

"Early to bed, early to rise makes one healthy, wealthy and wise."
- Benjamin Franklin

"We have a system that increasingly taxes work and subsidizes non-work."
- Milton Friedman

"By too much sitting still, the body becomes unhealthy; and soon the mind."
- Henry Wadsworth Longfellow

"Laziness is like premature rigor mortis."
- Jack Murphy

"Laziness is a good deal like money,--the more a man has of it, the more he seems to want."
- Henry Wheeler Shaw

LEADERSHIP

"A helpful indicator of the type of leader you are comes from the observations and comments of those who know you best. None of us has the ability to objectively assess who we are or how we perform. If you doubt this, sit in on a dozen or so job interviews or employee performance reviews. The disconnect between self-perception and reality is frequently alarming."
- George Barna

"The art of leadership is saying no, not yes. It is very easy to say yes."
- Tony Blair

"No man will make a great leader who wants to do it all himself, or to get all the credit for doing it."
-    Andrew Carnegie

"The price of leadership is to simply do the thing you believe has to be done at the time it must be done."
-    Lyndon B. Johnson

"The final test of a leader is that he leaves behind him in other men the conviction and the will to carry on."
-    Walter Lippman

"Leadership is the capacity and will to rally men and women to common purpose, and having the character which inspires confidence."
-    George S. Patton

"We herd sheep, we drive cattle, we lead people. Lead me, follow me or get out of my way."
-    George Patton

"Leadership involves getting others to willingly move in a new direction in which they're not naturally inclined to move on their own."
-    Harry Truman

"I learned that a great leader is a man who has the ability to get other people to do what they don't want to do and like it."
-    Harry Truman

"If you're not the lead dog, the view never changes."
-    Alaskan Proverb

"Great leaders lead with questions rather than statements."
-    Unknown

"A good leader knows the way, shows the way, and goes the way."
-    Unknown

LIBERALISM

"The liberals can understand everything but people who don't understand them."

- Lenny Bruce

"The business of Progressives is to go on making mistakes. The business of Conservatives is to prevent mistakes from being corrected."

- G. K. Chesterton

"If you're not a liberal at 20, you have no heart. If you're not a conservative by 40, you have no brain".

- Winston Churchill

"A liberal is a man too broadminded to take his own side in a quarrel."

- Robert Frost

"There are two kinds of fools: one says, "This is old, therefore it is good"; the other says, "This is new, therefore it is better."

- William Inge

"The trouble with our liberal friends is not that they are ignorant, but that they know so much that isn't so."

- Ronald Reagan

"I can remember way back when a liberal was generous with his own money."

- Will Rogers

"If a conservative is a liberal who's been mugged, a liberal is a conservative who's been arrested."

- Thomas Wolfe

LIBERTY

"…where the Spirit of the Lord is, there is liberty."

- II Corinthians 3:17

"The true danger is when liberty is nibbled away, for expedients, and by parts."

-    Edmund Burke

"We shall go on to the end, we shall fight in France, we shall fight on the seas and oceans, we shall fight with growing confidence and growing strength in the air, we shall defend our Island, whatever the cost may be, we shall fight on the beaches, we shall fight on the landing grounds, we shall fight in the fields and in the streets, we shall fight in the hills; we shall never surrender, and even if, which I do not for a moment believe, this Island or a large part of it were subjugated and starving, then our Empire beyond the seas, armed and guarded by the British Fleet, would carry on the struggle, until, in God's good time, the New World, with all its power and might, steps forth to the rescue and the liberation of the Old."

-    Winston Churchill

"Upon this battle depends the survival of Christian civilisation. Upon it depends our own British life and the long continuity of our institutions and our Empire. The whole fury and might of the enemy must very soon be turned on us now. Hitler knows that he will have to break us in this island or lose the war. If we can stand up to him, all Europe may be free and the life of the world may move forward into broad, sunlit uplands. But if we fail, then the whole world, including the United States, including all that we have known and cared for, will sink into the abyss of a new Dark Age, made more sinister, and perhaps more protracted, by the lights of perverted science. Let us therefore brace ourselves to our duties, and so bear ourselves that, if the British Empire and its Commonwealth last for a thousand years, men will still say, *'This was their finest hour.'*"

-    Winston Churchill

"From Stettin in the Baltic to Trieste in the Adriatic an *iron curtain* has descended across the Continent."

-    Winston Churchill

"The cost of liberty is far less than the price of repression."

-    W.E.B. DuBois

"They that can give up essential liberty to obtain a little temporary safety deserve neither liberty nor safety."
- Benjamin Franklin

"Sell not virtue to purchase wealth, nor liberty to purchase power."
- Benjamin Franklin

"The millions of people, armed in the holy cause of liberty, and in such a country as that which we possess, are invincible by any force which our enemy can send against us. Besides, sir, we shall not fight our battles alone. There is a just God who presides over the destinies of nations, and who will raise up friends to fight our battles for us. The battle, sir, is not to the strong alone; it is to the vigilant, the active, the brave."
- Patrick Henry

"Is life so dear, or peace so sweet, as to be purchased at the price of chains or slavery? Forbid it, Almighty God! I know not what course others may take: but as for me, give me liberty, or give me death!"
- Patrick Henry

"I would rather be exposed to the inconveniences attending too much liberty than those attending too small a degree of it."
- Thomas Jefferson

"Our liberty depends on the freedom of the press and that cannot be limited without being lost."
- Thomas Jefferson

"No free man shall ever be debarred the use of arms."
- Thomas Jefferson

"The God who gave us life, gave us liberty at the same time."
- Thomas Jefferson

"Let us not wallow in the valley of despair. I say to you today, my friends, that in spite of the difficulties and frustrations of the moment, I still have a dream… I have a dream that one day this nation will rise up and live out the true meaning of its creed: "We hold these truths to be self-evident:

that all men are created equal." I have a dream that one day on the red hills of Georgia the sons of former slaves and the sons of former slaveowners will be able to sit down together at a table of brotherhood.... I have a dream that my four little children will one day live in a nation where they will not be judged by the color of their skin but by the content of their character. I have a dream today."

> -   Martin Luther King, Jr.

"Freedom is not the right to do what we want, but what we ought."

> -   Abraham Lincoln

"God is not willing to do everything, and thus take away our free will and that share of glory which belongs to us."

> -   Niccolo Machiavelli

"If all mankind minus one, were of one opinion, and one person were of the contrary opinion, mankind would be no more justified in silencing that one person, than he, if he had the power, would be justified in silencing mankind."

> -   John Stuart Mill

"That the only purpose for which power can be rightfully exercised over any member of a civilized community, against his will, is to prevent harm to others."

> -   John Stuart Mill

"None can love freedom heartily, but good men: the rest love not freedom, but license."

> -   John Milton

"Freedom is never more than one generation away from extinction. We didn't pass it on to our children in the bloodstream. It must be fought for, protected, and handed on for them to do the same, or one day we will spend our sunset years telling our children what it was once like in the United States when men were free."

> -   Ronald Reagan

"If you analyze it I believe the very heart and soul of conservatism is libertarianism. I think conservatism is really a misnomer just as liberalism is a misnomer for the liberals -- if we were back in the days of the Revolution, so-called conservatives today would be the Liberals and the liberals would be the Tories. The basis of conservatism is a desire for less government interference or less centralized authority or more individual freedom and this is a pretty general description also of what libertarianism is. Now, I can't say that I will agree with all the things that the present group who call themselves Libertarians in the sense of a party say, because I think that like in any political movement there are shades, and there are libertarians who are almost over at the point of wanting no government at all or anarchy."

- Ronald Reagan

"O liberty! O liberty! What crimes are committed in thy name!"
- Jeanne-Marie Roland

"My definition of a free society is a society where it is safe to be unpopular."
- Adlai Stevenson

LIES

"There are a terrible lot of lies going around the world, and the worst of it is half of them are true."
- Winston Churchill

"The great masses of the people will more easily fall victim to a big lie than to a small one."
- Adolf Hitler

"'Will you walk into my parlor?'
    Said the spider to the fly:
  "Tis the prettiest parlour
    That ever you did spy.'"
- Mary Howitt

272

"You can fool some of the people all of the time, and all of the people some of the time, but you cannot fool all of the people all of the time."
- Abraham Lincoln

"People do not believe lies because they have to, but because they want to."
- Malcolm Muggeridge

LIFE

"For what is your life?..."
- James 4:14

"The world can be divided into 3 parts: those who make things happen, those who watch things happen and those who don't know what's happening."
- Bill Bright

"Our lives are to be indisputable evidence of the resurrection of Jesus Christ."
- Carter Conlon

"Resolve never to do anything which you would be afraid to do if it were the last hour of your life."
- Jonathan Edwards

"He is no fool who gives what he cannot keep to gain what he cannot lose."
- Jim Elliot

"If you would not be forgotten
  As soon as you are dead and rotten,
  Either write things worthy reading,
  Or do things worth the writing."
- Benjamin Franklin

"Eat well, stay fit, die anyway."
- Benjamin Franklin

"In three words I can sum up everything I've learned about life: it goes on."
- Robert Frost

"It ought to be the business of everyday to prepare for our final day."
- Matthew Henry

"Life is a succession of lessons which must be lived to be understood."
- Helen Keller

"Life is either a daring adventure or nothing at all."
- Helen Keller

"Let us think often that our only business in this life is to please God. Perhaps all besides is but folly and vanity."
- Brother Lawrence

"When the most important things in our life happen, we quite often don't know, at the moment, what is going on."
- C.S. Lewis

"Most of us could summarize our lives around 5 or 6 defining moments-- moments that if we had chosen differently would have radically altered the trajectory of our lives."
- Erwin McManus

"Live your life in a way that you wouldn't mind living over again."
- Jack Murphy

"Is what you're living for worth Christ dying for?"
- Epitaph of Leonard Ravenhill

"Just because your days are numbered, it doesn't mean that they count. Live your life so that it counts."
- Emmanuel Ayala

"One life to live
And soon it will be past.
Only things done for God
Will ever truly last.

And When I am dying,
How happy I'll be,
If the lamp of my life
Has been burned out for Thee."
- Unknown

"God's goal is not to make sure you're happy. Life is not about your being comfortable, happy, successful and pain free. It is about becoming the man God has called you to be. Life is not about you. It's about God. He doesn't exist to make us happy. We exist to bring Him glory."
- Chuck Swindoll

"Life is 10% what happens to me and 90% how I choose to respond to it."
- Chuck Swindoll

"To make the best use of your life, you must never forget two truths. 1st: Compared with eternity, life is extremely brief. 2nd: Earth is only a temporary residence."
- Rick Warren

"The call of the Cross, therefore, is to enter into this passion of Christ. We must have upon us the print of the nails."
- Gordon Watt

"When a man is born, he cries and the world rejoices. Live your life in a way so that when you die, the world will cry and you will rejoice."
- Cherokee Proverb

"Though no one can go back and make a brand new start, anyone can start from now and make a brand new ending"
- Unknown

"Work like you don't need the money, love like you've never been hurt, and dance like no one is watching!"
- Unknown

"The world isn't reading the Bible; they're reading Christians like you. And if they don't like what they see in you, they're not going to want what you've got."
- Unknown

"Having a full life is not necessarily a long life."
- Unknown

"Life is not a journey to the grave with the intention of arriving safely in a pretty & well preserved body, but rather to skid in broadside, thoroughly used up, totally worn out and loudly proclaiming...'*Wow! What a ride!*'"
- Unknown

"Sow a thought, reap an action. Sow an action, reap a habit. Sow a habit and reap a character. Sow a character and reap a destiny."
- Unknown

"Many people lose their health to make money and then lose their money to restore health. By thinking anxiously about the future, they forget the present, such that they live neither for the present, nor the future. They live as if they will never die, and they die as if they never lived."
- Unknown

LONELINESS

"All my friends are but one, but He is all sufficient."
- William Carey

"What loneliness is more lonely than distrust?"
- T. S. Eliot

"Never marry someone who you can live with. Marry someone who you can't live without."
- Ray Everett

"Pray that your loneliness may spur you into finding something to live for, great enough to die for."
-    Dag Hammarskjold

"Man finds nothing so intolerable as to be in a state of complete rest, without passions, without occupation, without diversion, without effort. Then he feels his nullity, loneliness, inadequacy, dependence, helplessness, emptiness."
-    Blaise Pascal

"So together…but dying of loneliness."
-    Albert Schweitzer

"The biggest disease today is not leprosy or tuberculosis, but rather the feeling of being unwanted, uncared for and deserted by everybody."
-    Teresa of Calcutta

"It is easy to love the people far away. It is not always easy to love those close to us. It is easier to give a cup of rice to relieve hunger than to relieve the loneliness and pain of someone unloved in our own home. Bring love into your home for this is where our love for each other must start."
-    Mother Teresa

LOVE

"Greater love hath no man than this, that a man lay down his life for his friends."
-    John 15:13

"That Christ may dwell in your hearts by faith; that ye, being rooted and grounded in love, May be able to comprehend with all saints what is the breadth, and length, and depth, and height; And to know the love of Christ, which passeth knowledge, that ye might be filled with all the fullness of God."
-    Ephesians 3:17-19

"Behold, what manner of love the Father hath bestowed upon us, that we should be called the sons of God: therefore the world knoweth us not, because it knew him not."

- I John 3:1

"Beloved, let us love one another: for love is of God; and every one that loveth is born of God, and knoweth God. He that loveth not knoweth not God; for God is love."

- I John 4:7-8

"To love means loving the unlovable. To forgive means pardoning the unpardonable. Faith means believing the unbelievable. Hope means hoping when everything seems hopeless."

- Gilbert K. Chesterton

"A few hours ago I discharged my last duty as King and Emperor, and now that I have been succeeded by my brother, the Duke of York, my first words must be to declare my allegiance to him. This I do with all my heart. You all know the reasons which have impelled me to renounce the throne. But I want you to understand that in making up my mind I did not forget the country or the empire, which, as Prince of Wales and lately as King, I have for twenty-five years tried to serve. But you must believe me when I tell you that I have found it impossible to carry the heavy burden of responsibility and to discharge my duties as King as I would wish to do without the help and support of the woman I love."

- King Edward VIII
  upon abdicating his throne in order to marry
  American Wallis Simpson

"Love is the foundation of all obedience. Without it morality degenerates into mere casuistry. Love is the foundation of all knowledge. Without it religion degenerates into a chattering about Moses and doctrines and theories; a thing that will neither kill nor make alive, that never gave life to a single soul or blessing to a single heart, and never put strength into any hand in the conflict and strife of daily life."

- Alexander Maclaren

"Our love to God is measured by our everyday fellowship with others and the love it displays."

- Andrew Murray

"There is nothing I am less good at than love. I am far better in competition than in love. I am far better at responding to my instincts and ambitions to get ahead and make my mark than I am at figuring out how to love another. I am schooled and trained in acquisitive skills, in getting my own way. And yet I decide, every day, to set aside what I can do best and attempt what I do very clumsily—open myself to the frustrations and failures of loving, daring to believe that failing in love is better than succeeding in pride."

- Eugene Peterson

"In the essentials -- unity, in the non-essentials -- freedom, in all things -- love."

- John Wesley

"In short, Jesus moved the emphasis from God's holiness (exclusive) to God's mercy (inclusive). Instead of the message 'no undesirables allowed' he proclaimed, 'In God's kingdom there are no undesirables.'"

- Philip Yancey

"Kids will go where there is excitement. They will stay where there is love."

- Unknown

LOVE (EMOTIONAL) – See Romance

LUST

"Love not the world, neither the things that are in the world. If any man love the world, the love of the Father is not in him. For all that is in the world, the lust of the flesh, and the lust of the eyes, and the pride of life, is not of the Father, but is of the world. And the world passeth away, and the lust thereof: but he that doeth the will of God abideth for ever."

- I John 2:15-17

"The most violent appetites in all creatures are lust and hunger; the first is a perpetual call upon them to propagate their kind, the latter to preserve themselves."

- Joseph Addison

"So long as lust (whether of the world or flesh) smells sweet in our nostrils, so long we are loathesome to God."

- Charles Coultan

"It is easier to suppress the first desire than to satisfy all that follows it."

- Benjamin Franklin

"Servile inclinations, and gross love,
  The guilty bent of vicious appetite;
    At first a sin, a horror ev'n in bliss,
      Deprave the senses and lay waste the man;
        Passions irregular, and next a loathing,
          Quickly succeed to dash the wild."

- William Harvard

"Nature is content with little; grace with less; but lust with nothing."

- Matthew Henry

"The flesh endures the storms of the present alone; the mind, those of the past and future as well as the present. Gluttony is a lust of the mind."

- Thomas Hobbes

"Lust is simply this natural world's substitute for love. It is a means to an end in which the soul grows lonely. Only one person is needed for lust. It takes two in order to achieve true love."

- Jack Murphy

"Love grows. Lust wastes. It wastes by enjoyment. One springs from an Union of souls, and the other from an Union of selfish hunger and sense."

- William Penn

"It wasn't God's lust for this world that caused Him to give His Son. It was His love -- this unselfish desire to see the world redeemed."
- Leonard Ravenhill

"Lust is an enemy to the purse, a foe to the person, a canker to the mind, a corrosive to the conscience, a weakness of the wit, a besotter of the senses, and finally, a mortal bane to all the body."
- Caius Plinius Secundus

"There are two tragedies in life. One is not to get your heart's desire. The other is to get it."
- George Bernard Shaw

"Lust is a captivity of the reason and an enraging of the passions. It hinders business and distracts counsel. It sins against the body and weakens the soul."
- Jeremy Taylor

"A moment of pleasure is a powerful and terrible thing. It can ruin reputations, arrest inhibitions, feed gossips, produce babies, derail futures and destroy dreams – all for a moment of pleasure."
- English Proverb

LYING

"I believed, therefore have I spoken: I was greatly afflicted: I said in my haste, All men are liars."
- Psalm 66:11

"Wherefore putting away lying, speak every man truth with his neighbour: for we are members one of another."
- Ephesians 4:25

"Even when liars tell the truth, they are never believed. The liar will lie once, twice, and then perish when he tells the truth."
- Aesop,
in *The Boy Who Cried Wolf*

"A lie is a very short wick in a very small lamp. The oil of reputation is very soon sucked up and gone. And just as soon as a man is known to lie, he is like a two-foot pump in a hundred-foot well. He cannot touch bottom at all."

- Henry Ward Beecher

"Popular opinion is the greatest lie in the world."

- Thomas Carlyle

"History is written by the victors."

- Winston Churchill, attributed

"A liar is not believed even though he tell the truth."

- Marcus Tullius Cicero

"It is not right or manly to lie even about Satan."

- James Garfield

"Our opinions are not our own, but in the power of sympathy. If a person tells us a palpable falsehood, we not only dare not contradict him, but we dare hardly disbelieve him to his face. A lie boldly uttered has the effect of truth for the instant."

- William Hazlitt

"Make the lie big, make it simple, keep saying it, and eventually they will believe it."

- Adolph Hitler

"If I were two-faced, would I be wearing this one?"

- Abraham Lincoln,
  when accused of lying during a debate

"Satan doesn't care if you *speak* a lie or if you *sing* a lie – as long as you lie. Our worship services are filled with lies and half truths uttered by those singing about God's love while inwardly hating men, women, children and even the song. Churches are filled with preachers who preach about the 'love of God' who secretly despise someone in the congregation. This is the worst kind of lie, for it is joins lying with music and hypocrisy."

- Jack Murphy

"'Who controls the past,' ran the Party slogan, 'controls the future: who controls the present controls the past.'"

- George Orwell,
in *1984*

"The worst and most effective lies are those mingled with truth."

- Will Rogers

"That a lie which is completely a lie may be met and fought with outright -- but a lie which is part a truth is a harder matter to fight."

- Lord Alfred Tennyson

"Christians don't tell lies -- they just go to church and sing them."

- A.W. Tozer

"How can you tell when a lawyer is lying? When his lips are moving."

- American Proverb,
also directed toward politicians and tax collectors

"You can fool some of the people some of the time, but you can't fool all of the people all of the time."

- Unknown

M

MARRIAGE

"It is not good that the man should be alone. Bone of my bone, and flesh of my flesh."
- Genesis 2:18, 23

"A prudent wife is from the Lord."
- Proverbs 19:14

"What therefore God hath joined together let not man put asunder."
- Matthew 19:6

"A man finds himself seven years older the day after his marriage."
- Sir Francis Bacon

"A woman must be a genius to create a good husband!"
- Honore de Balzac

"Marriage is a lottery in which men stake their liberty, and women their happiness."
- Madame de Rieux

"There is a French saying: 'Love is often the dawn of marriage, and marriage is often the sunset of love.'"
- J. De Finod

"Keep your eyes wide open before marriage, half shut afterwards."
- Benjamin Franklin

"Where there is a marriage without love, there will be love without marriage."

- Benjamin Franklin

"One good Husband is worth two good Wives; for the scarcer things are, the more they're valued."

- Benjamin Franklin

"Keep thy eyes wide open before marriage; and half shut afterward."

- Thomas Fuller

"Men are not from Mars. Women are not from Venus. They are both from Earth. Until husbands and wives stop treating their spouse like an 'alien' and begin respecting the validity of an opposing opinion, then problems in a marriage will continue. A marriage can only be strengthened by an ability to stop, look, listen and consider the needs of a spouse."

- Jack Murphy

"If thou wouldst marry wisely, marry thine equal. An unequal yoke is a heavy burden to bear."

- Ovid

"Marriages are made in Heaven."

- Lord Alfred Tennyson

"Marriages decided on Earth rather than Heaven feel like Hell."

- Unknown

"Men marry because they are tired, women because they are curious: both are disappointed."

- Oscar Wilde

"Marriage is a romance novel in which the hero often dies in the first chapter. Aim to be a hero that remains until the end."

- Unknown

"No man has ever been shot while doing dishes."
- American Proverb

"A deaf husband and a blind wife are always a happy couple."
- Danish Proverb

"To marry once is a duty, twice a folly, thrice is madness."
- Dutch Proverb

"Weeping bride, laughing wife; laughing bride, weeping wife."
- German Proverb

"A marriage union creates one soul in two bodies."
- Greek Proverb

"It is better for a woman to marry a man who loves her than a man she loves."
- Italian Proverb

"The woman cries before the wedding; the man afterward."
- Polish Proverb

MATERIALISM

"Most Christians define materialism as a lifestyle that is one or two steps above their own."
- Tom Drake

"It is the eyes of other people that ruin us. If all but myself were blind, I should want neither a fine house nor fine furniture."
- Benjamin Franklin

"Once you have made the World an end, and faith a means, you have almost won your man, and it makes very little difference what kind of worldly end he is pursuing."
— Demon Screwtape to Wormwood,
from C.S. Lewis' *The Screwtape Letters*

"More people are sidetracked by serving materialism than by anything else."

- Rick Warren

"Government is created to protect the poor from the lust of the rich, and to protect the rich from the lust of the poor."

- Unknown

MEDIA -- See JOURNALISM

MEMORY

"And God said, 'I will look upon it, that I may remember the everlasting covenant between God and every living creature of all flesh that is upon the earth.'"

- Genesis 9:16

"**1**Remember now thy Creator in the days of thy youth, while the evil days come not, nor the years draw nigh, when thou shalt say, I have no pleasure in them."

- Ecclesiastes 12:1

"Remember the former things of old: for I am God, and there is none else; I am God, and there is none like me, declaring the end from the beginning, and from ancient times the things that are not yet done, saying, My counsel shall stand, and I will do all my pleasure."

- Isaiah 46:9-10

"Remember my bonds."

- Colossians 4:18, regarding Paul's chains

"Nevertheless I have somewhat against thee, because thou hast left thy first love. Remember therefore from whence thou art fallen, and repent, and do the first works; or else I will come unto thee quickly, and will remove thy candlestick out of his place, except thou repent."

- Revelation 2:4-5

"God gave us memories that we might have roses in December."
- J. M. Barrie

"The very first thing an executive must have is a fine memory. Of course it does not follow that a man with a fine memory is necessarily a fine executive. But if he has the memory he has the first qualification, and if he has not the memory nothing else matters."
- Thomas Edison

"Have you ever noticed how the sins of David are recorded in the 11ᵗʰ chapter of Second Samuel, but was strangely omitted hundreds of years later when recorded in the 20ᵗʰ chapter of First Chronicles? The entire ordeal of David's sins, including their aftermath, was not recorded. I believe that this was not the act of selective history, but of God's ability to forgive and forget. David's heartfelt repentance in Psalm 51 caused God to 'remember his sins no more.'"
- Jack Murphy

"Tomorrow's actions are next week's memories."
- Jack Murphy

"We do not remember days; we remember moments."
- Cesare Pavese

"Things that were hard to bear are often sweet to remember."
- Seneca

"The surest way to incite a patriot is by rewriting history or altering the memory. If you repeat something often enough, by shear repetition, a nation will believe it to be true."
- Josef Stalin

"Memories are not mental pacifists. They serve to either haunt us or delight us."
- Mark Twain

"Memory... is the diary that we all carry about with us."
- Oscar Wilde

"Time heals all wounds."
-   American Proverb

"You can rewrite history but you cannot remove memories."
-   English Proverb

"The man with a clear conscience probably has a poor memory."
-   Spanish Proverb

MEN

"When I was a child, I spake as a child, I understood as a child, I thought as a child: but when I became a man, I put away childish things."
-   I Corinthians 13:11

"Women are one of the Almighty's enigmas to prove to men that He knows more than they do."
-   Ellen Glasgow

"Boys will be boys, and so will a lot of middle-aged men."
-   Frank Hubbard

"The rule in the women's colleges was that after 7 p.m. all men were beasts. Up until 7 p.m. they were all angels, and the girls simply had to learn to live with that routine and practice love in the afternoon."
-   Harry G. Johnson

"If you can keep your head when all about you
Are losing theirs and blaming it on you,
If you can trust yourself when all men doubt you
But make allowance for their doubting too,
If you can wait and not be tired by waiting,
Or being lied about, don't deal in lies,
Or being hated, don't give way to hating,
And yet don't look too good, nor talk too wise:

If you can dream--and not make dreams your master,
If you can think--and not make thoughts your aim;

If you can meet with Triumph and Disaster
And treat those two impostors just the same;
If you can bear to hear the truth you've spoken
Twisted by knaves to make a trap for fools,
Or watch the things you gave your life to, broken,
And stoop and build 'em up with worn-out tools:

If you can make one heap of all your winnings
And risk it all on one turn of pitch-and-toss,
And lose, and start again at your beginnings
And never breath a word about your loss;
If you can force your heart and nerve and sinew
To serve your turn long after they are gone,
And so hold on when there is nothing in you
Except the Will which says to them: "Hold on!"

If you can talk with crowds and keep your virtue,
Or walk with kings--nor lose the common touch,
If neither foes nor loving friends can hurt you;
If all men count with you, but none too much,
If you can fill the unforgiving minute
With sixty seconds' worth of distance run,
Yours is the Earth and everything that's in it,
And--which is more--you'll be a Man, my son!"
- Rudyard Kipling

"Women's Liberation is just a lot of foolishness. It's the men who are discriminated against. They can't bear children. And no one's likely to try and do anything about that."
- Golda Meir

"Ironically, war makes women appreciate men. Even a lousy husband is appreciated on the battlefield."
- George S. Patton

"Never trust a husband too far, Nor a bachelor too near."
- Helen Rowland

"The more I see of men, the more I like dogs."
-    Madame de Staël

"If you want anything said, ask a man. If you want something done, ask a woman."
-    Margaret Thatcher

"All women become like their mothers. That is their tragedy. No man does. That's his."
-    Oscar Wilde

"A man who marries his mistress often leaves a vacancy sign for that position."
-    Oscar Wilde

"Men are like fish. Neither would get into trouble if they kept their mouths shut."
-    American Proverb

"Rules for girls: Never trust a stranger; All men are strange."
-    American Proverb

"A man who does great things is considered noble. A woman who does great things is considered a feminist who doesn't realize her place."
-    English Proverb

"No man is worth your tears, but once you find one that is, he won't make you cry/"
-    English Proverb

"No man stands so straight as when he stoops to help a boy."
-    Knights' Proverb

"Macho doesn't prove mucho."
-    Spanish Proverb

"If men can run the world, why can't they stop wearing neckties? How intelligent is it to start the day by tying a little noose around your neck?"
- Unknown

"Why are men attracted to the thrill of the chase?' They are like dogs that chase cars. Both are happy until they catch one."
- Unknown

"There are much easier things in life than finding a good man. Nailing Jell-O to a tree, for instance."
- Unknown

MERCY

"He hath shewed thee, O man, what is good; and what doth the LORD require of thee, but to do justly, and to love mercy, and to walk humbly with thy God?"
- Micah 6:8

"The glory of Christianity is to conquer by forgiveness."
- William Blake

"Nothing humbles and breaks the heart of a sinner like mercy and love. Souls that converse much with sin and wrath, may be much terrified; but souls that converse much with grace and mercy, will be much humbled."
- Thomas Brooks

"Among the attributes of God, although they are all equal, mercy shines to men with even more brilliancy than justice."
- Cervantes

"If this world were not mingled with His mercy, this wretched world could not subsist one hour."
- Sir William D'Avenant

"Good Heaven, whose darling attribute we find is boundless grace, and mercy to mankind, abhors the cruel."
- John Dryden

292

"We often hand folks over to God's mercy, and show none ourselves."
- George Eliot

"Mercy allows you to continue on in sin; grace empowers you to overcome it."
- Jacquelyn K. Heasley

"I tremble for my country when I reflect that God is just; that his justice cannot sleep forever."
- Thomas Jefferson

"Mercy, detached from Justice, grows unmerciful."
- C. S. Lewis

"Nearly all men can stand adversity, but if you want to test a man's character, give him power. Does he love the dispensation of rough justice or mercy?"
- Abraham Lincoln

"I have always found that mercy bears richer fruits than strict justice."
- Abraham Lincoln

"I tell you, brethren, if His mercies, love and judgments do not convert you, God has no other arrows in His quiver."
- Robert Murray M'Cheyne

"The pure, mere love of God is that alone from which sinners are justly to expect that no sin will pass unpunished, but that His love will visit them with every calamity and distress that can help to break and purify the bestial heart of man and awaken in him true repentance and conversion to God. It is love alone in the holy Deity that will allow no peace to the wicked, nor ever cease its judgments till every sinner is forced to confess that it is good for him that he has been in trouble, and thankfully own that not the wrath but the love of God has plucked out that right eye, cut off that right band, which he ought to have done but would not do for himself and his own salvation. This is the mercy of the Almighty."
- William Law

"Kinds hearts are here; yet would the tenderest one
Have limits to its mercy; God has none."
- Adelaide Anne Procter

"We may imitate the Deity in all His attributes; but mercy is the only one in which we can pretend to equal Him. We cannot, indeed, give like God; but surely we may forgive like Him."
- Lawrence Sterne

"The sun is the eye of the world; and he is indifferent to the negro or the cold Russian; to them that dwell under the line; and them that stand near the tropics,--the scalded Indian, or the poor boy that shakes at the foot of the Riphean hills; so is the mercy of God."
- Jeremy Taylor

"The vague and tenuous hope that God is too kind to punish the ungodly has become a deadly opiate for the consciences of millions. The availability of God's mercy is great, but it doesn't overcome our free will."
- A. W. Tozer

"Lenity will operate with greater force, in some instances, than rigor. It is therefore my first wish to have my whole conduct distinguished by it."
- George Washington

METHODS

"Irregularity and want of method are only supportable in men of great learning or genius, who are often too full to be exact, and therefore choose to throw down their pearls in heaps before the reader rather than be at the pains of stringing them."
- Joseph Addison

"What the Church needs to-day is not more machinery or better, not new organizations or more and novel methods, but men whom the Holy Ghost can use-men of prayer, men mighty in prayer. The Holy Ghost does not flow through methods, but through men. He does not come on machinery, but on men. He does not anoint plans, but men-men of prayer."

-    E.M. Bounds

"Make the most of time, it flies away so fast; yet method will teach you to win time."

-    Johann Wolfgang von Goethe

"Reason is the slow and torturous method by which those who do not know the truth discover it."

-    Blaise Pascal

"Method is the arithmetic of success."

-    Henry Wheeler Shaw

"Method is essential, and enables a larger amount of work to be got through with satisfaction. 'Method,' said Cecil (afterward Lord Burleigh), 'is like packing things in a box; a good packer will get in half as much again as a bad one.' Cecil's dispatch of business was extraordinary; his maxim being, 'The shortest way to do many things is to do only one thing at once.'"

-    Samuel Smiles

"The six step scientific method:
      1. State a problem
      2. Observe
      3. Form a hypothesis
      4. Experiment repeatedly
      5. Collect data
      6. Draw conclusion"

-    Unknown

MIDDLE AGE – See AGE

MILITARY

"Blessed be the LORD my strength which teacheth my hands to war, and my fingers to fight."
- Psalm 144:1

"Thou therefore endure hardness, as a good soldier of Jesus Christ."
- II Timothy 2:3

"It is an interesting and glorious thing to fight and die for the pacifists who exercise their American right to proclaim that fighting and dying for God and country is a sin. Yet it is still worth fighting and dying for."
- Dwight D. Eisenhower

"Airplanes are interesting toys but of no military value."
- Marshall Ferdinand Foch, in 1911

"The journey of a thousand miles begins with one step, and then there is a whole lot of walking."
- George S. Patton

"Lead me, follow me, or get out of my way."
- George S. Patton

"May God have mercy upon my enemies, because I won't."
- George S. Patton

"Over the years, the United States has sent many of its fine young men and women into great peril to fight for freedom beyond our borders. The only amount of land we have ever asked for in return is enough to bury those that did not return."
- Colin Powell,
when asked whether or not the United State's plans for Iraq were just an example of empire building by George Bush

"It's God's job to judge and to forgive. It's our job to set up the meeting."
- Norman Schwarzkopf

"Any soldier worth his salt should be anti-war. And yet there are things still worth fighting for."

- Norman Schwarzkopf

"You can always tell an old soldier by the inside of his holsters and cartridge boxes. The young men carry pistols and cartridges; the old ones, grub."

- George Bernard Shaw

"It may be laid down as a primary position, and the basis of our system, that every Citizen who enjoys the protection of a Free Government owes not only a proportion of his property, but even of his personal services to the defense of it."

- George Washington

"To be prepared for war is one of the most effective means of preserving peace."

- George Washington

"This We'll Defend!"

- Army Motto

"Orders to hold on:
 1. This position will be held, and the section will remain here until relieved.
 2. The enemy cannot be allowed to interfere with this programme.
 3. If the section cannot remain here alive,
 it will remain here dead, but in any case it will remain here.
 4. Should any man, through shell shock or other cause, attempt to surrender,
 he will remain here dead.
 5. Should all guns be blown out, the section will use Mills grenades and other novelties.
 6. Finally, the position as stated, will be held."

- Australian Military Order during WWI

"For King and Country!"

- British Revolutionary War Cry, contrasted with America's "For God and Country!"

"Kill them all. God will know His own."

- Latin Proverb

"Kill'em all, and let God sort'em out."

- Marine Proverb

"Semper Fidelis!"

- Marine Motto, translated to mean "Always Faithful!"

"Honor, Courage, Commitment."

- Navy Core Values

"Non Sibi Sed Patriae!"

- Navy Proverb, translated to mean "Not for self, but for country!"

MIND – See THOUGHTS

MINISTRY – See PREACHERS

MIRACLES

"Thou art the God that doest wonders: thou hast declared thy strength among the people."

- Psalm 77:14

"Miracles are not contrary to nature, but only contrary to what we know about nature and what we know about the nature of God."

- Augustine

"Every believer is God's miracle."

- Philip James Bailey

"Thou water turn'st to wine, fair friend of life; Thy foe, to cross the sweet arts of Thy reign, Distils from thence the tears of wrath and strife, And so he yearns to turn wine to water back again."
- Richard Crashaw

"There are only two ways to live your life. One is as though nothing is a miracle. The other is as though everything is a miracle."
- Albert Einstein

"The invariable mark of wisdom is to see the miraculous in the common."
- Ralph Waldo Emerson

"The discovery of God lies in the daily and the ordinary, not in the spectacular and the heroic. If we cannot find God in the routines of home and shop, then we will not find Him at all."
- Richard J. Foster

"Miracles? My dear man, just look at the world around you. Look at the sun, moon and stars. Feel the wind. Look at the order of the Universe and the laws in which all things fall into place. I tell you that this is all the miraculous work of God."
- Benjamin Franklin

"For the truly faithful, no miracle is necessary. For those who doubt, no miracle is sufficient."
- Nancy Gibbs

"We can only appreciate the miracle of a sunrise if we have waited in the darkness."
- Helen Keller

"Miracles are a retelling in small letters of the very same story which is written across the whole world in letters too large for some of us to see."
- C. S. Lewis

"Faith as a mustard seed can move mountains – but faith as a mountain can move the world!"
- Jack Murphy

"Don't believe in miracles -- depend on them."
- Lawrence J. Peter

"When I look to my guiltiness, I see that my salvation is one of our Saviour's greatest miracles, either in heaven or earth."
- Samuel Rutherford

"The miracle is not that we do this work, but that we are happy to do it."
- Teresa of Calcutta

"Seeing, hearing, feeling, are miracles."
- Walt Whitman

"How quickly we forget God's great deliverances in our lives. How easily we take for granted the miracles he performed in our past."
- David Wilkerson

MISSIONS – See EVANGELISM

MOCKERY – See PERSECUTION

MODESTY

"True modesty avoids everything that is criminal; false modesty everything that is unfashionable."
- Joseph Addison

"You little know what you have done, when you have first broke the bounds of modesty; you have set open the door of your fancy to the devil, so that he can, almost at his pleasure ever after, represent the same sinful pleasure to you anew."
- Richard Baxter

"The gravest events dawn with no more noise than the morning star makes in rising. All great developments complete themselves in the world and modestly wait in silence, praising themselves never, and announcing themselves not at all. We must be sensitive, and sensible, if we would see

the beginnings and endings of great things. That is our part."
- Henry Ward Beecher

"No padlocks, bolts, or bars can secure a maiden so well as her own reserve."
- Cervantes

"The woman and the soldier who do not defend the first pass will never defend the last."
- Henry Fielding

"Meekness is like the modesty of a beautiful woman. It is hiding all that is within behind the noble covering of selflessness."
- Jack Murphy

"Modesty once extinguished knows not how to return."
- Seneca

"As blushing will sometimes make a whore pass for a virtuous woman, so modesty may make a fool seem a man of sense."
- Jonathan Swift

"A woman's perpetual modesty will forever enhance the discovery of the wedding night and the unveiled treaure of the marriage."
- English Proverb

MONEY

"Then one of the twelve, called Judas Iscariot, went unto the chief priests, And said unto them, What will ye give me, and I will deliver him unto you? And they covenanted with him for thirty pieces of silver. And from that time he sought opportunity to betray him."
- Matthew 26:14-16

"For the love of money is the root of all evil: which while some coveted after, they have erred from the faith, and pierced themselves through with many sorrows."
- I Timothy 6:10

"In God We Trust."

- US National Motto, inscribed upon currency

"Money is a good servant but a bad master."

- Sir Francis Bacon

"A nickel ain't worth a dime anymore."

- Yogi Berra

"If you make money your god, it will plague you like the devil."

- Henry Fielding

"A penny saved is a penny earned."

- Benjamin Franklin

"Money never made a man happy yet, nor will it. There is nothing in its nature to produce happiness. The more a man has, the more he wants. Instead of its filling a vacuum, it makes one. If it satisfies one want, it doubles and trebles that want another way. That was a true proverb of the wise man, rely upon it: "Better is little with the fear of the Lord, than great treasure, and trouble therewith."

- Benjamin Franklin

"A man is usually more careful with his money than he is with his principles."

- Edgar Watson Howe

"Never spend your money before you have it."

- Thomas Jefferson

"Character is money; and according as the man earns or spends the money, money in turn becomes character. As money is the most evident power in the world's uses, so the use that he makes of money is often all that the world knows about a man."

- Edward George Lytton

"'*Your money or your life.*' We know what to do when a burglar makes this demand of us, but not when God does."
-     Mignon McLaughlin

"Greed is a cancer to which money is an aspirin."
-     Jack Murphy

"An excellent way to test our values is to observe what we do when we don't have anything to do, how we spend our leisure time and how we spend our extra money."
-     Eugene Peterson

"'Health and Wealth' are just another name for 'Feel Good' and 'Greed.'"
-     Leonard Ravenhill

"Plenty of people despise money, but few know how to give it away."
-     Francis Rochefoucauld

"The real measure of your wealth is how much you'd be worth if you lost all your money."
-     Will Rogers

"Those who believe that money can do anything will usually do anything for money."
-     George Savile

"Money will buy a pretty good dog, but it won't buy the wag of his tail."
-     Henry Wheeler Shaw

"You find no difficulty in trusting the Lord with the management of the universe and all the outward creation, and can your case be any more difficult than these, that you need to be anxious about His management of it?"
-     Hannah Whitall Smith

"More people are sidetracked by serving materialism than by anything else."
-     Rick Warren

"But there are those who are conscious before God that they are rich. And, doubtless, some among you are of the number. You have more of the goods of this world than is needful either for yourself or your family. Let each consider for himself. Do your riches increase? Do not you understand that plain expression? Have you not more money, or more of money's worth, than you had ten or twenty years ago, or at this time last year?"

- John Wesley

"When I have money, I get rid of it quickly, lest it find a way into my heart."

- John Wesley

"You can tell how little God values riches by how much of it He pours out on the wicked!"

- David Wilkerson

"Money can't buy you happiness, but it can at least pay the bills."

- American Proverb

"Are you so poor that you can't even pay attention?"

- American Proverb

"Money can't buy you happiness."

- English Proverb

"Always borrow money from a pessimist; he doesn't expect to be paid back."

- Spanish Proverb

"If you want to feel rich, just count all the things you have that money can't buy."

- Unknown

"If you think nobody cares if you're alive, try missing a couple of car payments."

- Unknown

MUSIC

"Whereupon are the foundations thereof fastened? or who laid the cornerstone thereof;
  When the morning stars sang together, and all the sons of God shouted for joy?"
-     Job 38:6-7

"Let us come before his presence with thanksgiving, and make a joyful noise unto him with psalms."
-     Psalm 95:2

"Speaking to yourselves in psalms and hymns and spiritual songs, singing and making melody in your heart to the Lord."
-     Ephesians 5:19

"Music can noble hints impart,
  Engender fury, kindle love,
  With unsuspected eloquence can move,
  And manage all the man with secret art."
-     Joseph Addison

"Music washes away from the soul the dust of everyday life."
-     Berthold Auerbach

"God gave us music so that we might be able to pray without having to use words."
-     Johann Sebastian Bach, attributed

"The discovery of song and the creation of musical instruments both owed their origin to a human impulse which lies much deeper than conscious intention: the need for rhythm in life...the need is a deep one, transcending thought, and disregarded at our peril."
-     Richard Baker

"Music cleanses the understanding; inspires it, and lifts it into a realm which it would not reach if it were left to itself."
- Henry Ward Beecher

"Music is the mediator between the spiritual and the sensual life."
- Ludwig van Beethoven

"Music is the wine which inspires one to new generative processes, and I am Bacchus who presses out this glorious wine for mankind and makes them spiritually drunken."
- Ludwig van Beethoven

"Opera is where a guy gets stabbed in the back, and instead of dying, he sings."
- Robert Benchley

"Its language is a language which the soul alone understands, but which the soul can never translate."
- Arnold Bennett

"There is no truer truth obtainable
By Man than comes of music."
- Robert Browning

"There's music in the sighing of a reed;
 There's music in the gushing of a rill;
 There's music in all things, if men had ears:
 Their earth is but an echo of the spheres."
- Lord Byron

"There is no greater love song to proclaim than the once for all sacrifice of Jesus Christ our Lord at Calvary, but yet others feel content to sing about the chaff of this world. What the New Testament church wrestled with the least is what our industry craves the most – money. How dare we think we can play politics with God, with His truth and with His church. We can't negotiate with sin no matter what kind of capital is at stake--and that really is the issue here."
- Steve Camp

"Music is well said to be the speech of angels."
- Thomas Carlyle

"All deep things are song. It seems somehow the very central essence of us, song; as if all the rest were but wrappages and hulls!"
- Thomas Carlyle

"He who sings scares away his woes."
- Cervantes

"Music has charms to soothe the savage beast, to soften rocks, or bend a knotted oak."
- William Congreve

"There is in souls a sympathy with sounds:
And as the mind is pitch'd the ear is pleased
With melting airs, or martial, brisk or grave;
Some chord in unison with what we hear
Is touch'd within us, and the heart replies."
- William Cowper

"Music is an outburst of the soul."
- Frederick Delius

"Were it not for music, we might in these days say, the Beautiful is dead."
- Benjamin Disraeli

"What passion cannot music raise and quell!"
- John Dryden

"You are the music while the music lasts."
- T.S. Eliot

"When I have no words left to pray, I play."
- Keith Green

"The only music minister to whom the Lord will say, "Well done, thy good and faithful servant," is the one whose life proves what their lyrics are saying, and to whom music is the least important part of their life. Glorifying the only worthy One has to be a minister's most important goal!"
- Keith Green

"When words leave off, music begins."
- Heinrich Heine

"The Irish gave the bagpipes to the Scots as a joke, but the Scots haven't got the joke yet."
- Oliver Herford

"Take a music bath once or twice a week for a few seasons. You will find it is to the soul what a water bath is to the body."
- Oliver Wendell Holmes

"Alas for those that never sing,
But die with all their music in them!"
- Oliver Wendell Holmes

"Country music is three chords and the truth."
- Harlan Howard

"Music expresses that which cannot be said and on which it is impossible to be silent."
- Victor Hugo

"A song has a few rights the same as ordinary citizens... if it happens to feel like flying where humans cannot fly... to scale mountains that are not there, who shall stop it?"
- Charles Ives

"Music is emotion – like love and hurt – in search of words."
- Sidney Lanier

"You can't possibly hear the last movement of Beethoven's Seventh and go slow."

- Oscar Levant,
  to a police officer after being pulled over for speeding

"Music's the medicine of the mind."

- John A. Logan

"Music is the universal language of mankind."

- Henry Wadsworth Longfellow

"Music, once birthed to the soul, becomes a sort of spirit, and never dies."

- Edward George Lytton

"If the music is pleasant, it is well with the land."

- Mencius

"There is nothing in the world so much like prayer as music is."

- William P. Merrill

"I heard your heart cry out in the music."

- Jack Murphy

"The best way to get lost is to plunge yourself into a melody. Through it, you can pour out your soul as if the world around you has faded into the bliss of unfathomable expression."

- Jack Murphy

"Music is a language set to the emotions and rhythm of the heart."

- Jack Murphy

"Music touches that inner emotion that cannot be otherwise be expressed with words."

- Jack Murphy

"Music rots when it gets too far from the dance. Poetry atrophies when it gets too far from music."
-    Ezra Pound

"When I pray, I cry to the Lord in English. When I run out of words, I cry out to the Lord in Welsh. And when I run out of words in the languages of men and of angels, I sing out of a melody of worship. And when all words and music is gone, I wait in silence."
-    Leonard Ravenhill

"If I were to begin life again, I would devote it to music. It is the only cheap and unpunished rapture upon earth."
-    Sydney Smith

"A painter paints pictures on canvas. But musicians paint their pictures on silence."
-    Leopold Stokowski

"The city is built
   To music, therefore never built at all,
     And therefore built forever."
-    Lord Alfred Tennyson

"Music that gentler on the spirit lies,
   Than tired eyelids upon tired eyes."
-    Lord Alfred Tennyson

"Why spend money on psychotherapy when you can listen to Bach's Mass in B Minor?"
-    American Proverb

"Music is what feelings sound like."
-    Chinese Proverb

"You can tell the condition of a people by the music that they produce."
-    Chinese Proverb

"Music allows the illiterate to become poets."
- English Proverb

"If a composer could say what he had to say in words he would not bother trying to say it in music."
- German Proverb

"Music is the medicine of the breaking heart."
- Spanish Proverb

"A bad opera is just setting a drama to music. A good opera attempts to illustrate the soul behind a story through the medium of music."
- Unknown

"Bach gave us God's Word. Mozart gave us God's laughter. Beethoven gave us God's fire. God gave us music, that we might pray without words."
- Unknown

N

NAMES

"A good name is rather to be chosen than great riches, and loving favour rather than silver and gold."
- Proverbs 22:1

"And the Gentiles shall see thy righteousness, and all kings thy glory: and thou shalt be called by a new name, which the mouth of the LORD shall name."
- Isaiah 62:2

"Wherefore God also hath highly exalted him, and given him a name which is above every name: That at the name of Jesus every knee should bow, of things in heaven, and things in earth, and things under the earth; And that every tongue should confess that Jesus Christ is Lord, to the glory of God the Father."
- Philippians 2:9-11

"A good name on Earth will last as long as the Judgment. A good name in Heaven will last as long as Eternity."
- John Bunyan

"Once you are dead and departed, and others hear a reference to your name, will it bring a smile, a frown or a laugh?"
- Benjamin Franklin

"How many legs does a dog have if you call the tail a leg? Four. Calling a tail a leg doesn't make it a leg."
- Abraham Lincoln

"It is quite as easy to give our children musical and pleasing names as those that are harsh and difficult; and it will be found by the owners, when they have grown to knowledge, that there is much in a name."
- John Locke

"You have the opportunity to turn your child's name into a blessing or a curse. It can be a testament or prophecy of greatness. Why name your son or daughter with an ordinary name when you can make it extraordinary? Nothing sets the tone for a life than a great name! Ask Jacob, Peter, Saul or Solomon."
- Jack Murphy

"Some preachers spend more time contemplating a name for the sermon, and some authors a name for their book, than they contemplate the name of their child."
- Jack Murphy

"Live your life so that your name is known for good and not evil. But remember that a mark of great evil (imaginary or not) will often blot out all of the good you may have done. Hitler is not known for being a fair painter or even a good son. Rather, he is infamous for his great evils. Likewise, do such great good that it would overwrite all of your supposed vices."
- Jack Murphy

"Even if you have soiled your name, there is still time to change. You can do something great that will cause those who hear your name to remember the good that was done."
- Jack Murphy

"It's better to die with a good name than to live with a bad one."
- George S. Patton

"Those who choose to name their sons after themselves can be quite vain. Unless you have done something great, or choose to do something greater, why perform such a lasting injustice to your boy? No, give that kid either an example to aim for, or a clean slate to make something new."

- Will Rogers

"What's in a name? That which we call a rose by any other name would smell as sweet."

- William Shakespeare

"The purpose of a middle name is so that children will know when they are really in trouble."

- Mark Twain

"A person with a bad name is already half hanged."

- Edwin Percy Whipple

"A young man went to the judge asking to change his name. The judge asked, 'Why? What's your name?' The man replied, 'John Dirt.' The judge immediately understood and agreed. He asked, 'Well, then, what do you want to change your name to?' The young man replied, 'Bob.' The moral of the story is: Whether his name was John or Bob, it was still 'Dirt!'"

- Bill Wilson

"A good name, like good will, is attained by many actions and may be lost by one."

- American Proverb

"Mr. Smith, if you want to set your child apart, do not name him John."

- English Proverb

"After times of trouble, either change your name or change the perception of your name."

- Spanish Proverb

NATURE

"Hearken unto this, O Job: stand still, and consider the wondrous works of God."
-    Job 37:14

"O LORD, our Lord, how excellent is thy name in all the earth! who hast set thy glory above the heavens."
-    Psalm 8:1

"When in the Course of human events it becomes necessary for one people to dissolve the political bands which have connected them with another and to assume among the powers of the earth, the separate and equal station to which the Laws of Nature and of Nature's God entitle them, a decent respect to the opinions of mankind requires that they should declare the causes which impel them to the separation."
-    Declaration of Independence

"A careful observation of Nature will disclose pleasantries of superb irony. It has, for instance, placed toads close to flowers and thorns next to roses."
-    Honore de Balzac

"All things in the natural world symbolize God, yet none of them speak of Him but in broken and imperfect words."
-    Henry Ward Beecher

"I love to think of nature as an unlimited broadcasting station, through which God speaks to us every hour, if we will only tune in."
-    George Washington Carver

"Nature is but a name for an effect, whose cause is God."
-    William Cowper

"The best remedy for those who are afraid, lonely or unhappy is to go outside, somewhere where they can be quiet, alone with the heavens, nature and God. Because only then does one feel that all is as it should be and that God wishes to see people happy, amidst the simple beauty of nature."

- Anne Frank

"The sun, with all those planets revolving around it and dependent on it, can still ripen a bunch of grapes as if it had nothing else in the universe to do. "

- Galileo Galilei

"There is not a sprig of grass that shoots uninteresting to me."

- Thomas Jefferson

"To me a lush carpet of pine needles or spongy grass is more welcome than the most luxurious Persian rug."

- Helen Keller

"God writes the gospel not in the Bible alone, but on trees and flowers and clouds and stars."

- Martin Luther

"How can you not behold the flowers, trees and stars and not behold the wonders of God? He is the creator of nature."

- Sir Isaac Newton

"Nature is a book of laws, of which Christ is the Author."

- Sir Isaac Newton

"Deviance is a crime against nature."

- Ronald Reagan

"One does not truly appreciate nature until they are old and shut in from its beauty."

- Theodore Roosevelt

NEGLECT

"Woe unto you, scribes and Pharisees, hypocrites! for ye pay tithe of mint and anise and cummin, and have omitted the weightier matters of the law, judgment, mercy, and faith: these ought ye to have done, and not to leave the other undone."

- Matthew 23:23

"Then the twelve called the multitude of the disciples unto them, and said, It is not reason that we should leave the word of God, and serve tables."

- Acts 6:2

"How shall we escape, if we neglect so great salvation; which at the first began to be spoken by the Lord, and was confirmed unto us by them that heard him."

- Hebrews 2:3

"Oh brother, pray; in spite of Satan, pray; spend hours in prayer; rather neglect friends than not pray; rather fast, and lose breakfast, dinner, tea, and supper - and sleep too - than not pray. And we must not talk about prayer, we must pray in right earnest. The Lord is near. He comes softly while the virgins slumber."

- Andrew Bonar

"A little neglect may breed great mischief. For want of a nail the shoe was lost; for want of a shoe the horse was lost; and for want of a horse the rider was lost, being overtaken and slain by the enemy; all for want of a little care about a horse-shoe nail."

- Benjamin Franklin

"The best ground untilled, soonest runs out into rank weeds. A man of knowledge that is negligent or uncorrected, cannot but grow wild and godless."

- Joseph Hall

"It is one of the ironies of the ministry that the very man who works in God's name is often hardest put to find time for God. The parents of Jesus lost Him at church, and they were not the last ones to lose Him there."

- Vance Havner

"He that thinks he can afford to be negligent is not far from being poor."
- Samuel Johnson

"I expect to pass through life but once. If therefore, there be any kindness I can show, or any good thing I can do to any fellow being, let me do it now, and not defer or neglect it, as I shall not pass this way again."
- William Penn

"Praying men stop sinning and sinning men stop praying."
- Leonard Ravenhill

"In persons grafted in a serious trust,
  Negligence is a crime."
- William Shakespeare

"Nothing can be more hurtful to the service, than the neglect of discipline; for that discipline, more than numbers, gives one army the superiority over another."
- George Washington

NEED

"For I was an hungred, and ye gave me meat: I was thirsty, and ye gave me drink: I was a stranger, and ye took me in: Naked, and ye clothed me: I was sick, and ye visited me: I was in prison, and ye came unto me. Then shall the righteous answer him, saying, Lord, when saw we thee an hungred, and fed thee? or thirsty, and gave thee drink? When saw we thee a stranger, and took thee in? or naked, and clothed thee? Or when saw we thee sick, or in prison, and came unto thee? And the King shall answer and say unto them, Verily I say unto you, Inasmuch as ye have done it unto one of the least of these my brethren, ye have done it unto me." - Matthew 25:35-40

"Because thou sayest, I am rich, and increased with goods, and have need of nothing; and knowest not that thou art wretched, and miserable, and poor, and blind, and naked."
- 　　Revelation 3:17

"Necessity is often the spur to genius."
- 　　Honore de Balzac

"A baptism of holiness, a demonstration of godly living is the crying need of our day."
- 　　Duncan Campbell

"A great many people do not pray because they do not feel any sense of need. The sign that the Holy Spirit is in us is that we realize that we are empty, not that we are full. We have a sense of absolute need. We come across people who try us, circumstances that are difficult, conditions that are perplexing, and all these things awaken a dumb sense of need, which is a sign that the Holy Spirit is there. If we are ever free from the sense of need, it is not because the Holy Spirit has satisfied us, but because we have been satisfied with as much as we have. 'A man's reach should exceed his grasp.' A sense of need is one of the greatest benedictions because it keeps our life rightly related to Jesus Christ."
- 　　Oswald Chambers

"Revival comes from heaven when heroic souls enter the conflict determined to win or die-or if need be, to win and die! "The kingdom of heaven suffereth violence, and the violent take it by force."
- 　　Charles Finney

"Immature love says: 'I love you because I need you.' Mature love says: 'I need you because I love you.'"
- 　　Erich Fromm

"Great necessity elevates man, petty necessity casts him down."
- 　　Johann Wolfgang von Goethe

"One of our troubles is we are not willing to humble ourselves. We are not willing to give up our opinions as to how things should be done. We want a revival to come just in our way. You never saw two revivals come just alike. We must let them come in God's way. People are ashamed to admit they need a revival. If you are not willing to take the shame on yourself, you then let it remain on Jesus Christ. You must bear the reproach of your sinful state of indifference, or the cause of our Master must bear it."

- Mordecai Ham

"None can believe how powerful prayer is, and what it is able to effect, but those who have learned it by experience. It is a great matter when in extreme need to take hold on prayer. I know whenever I have prayed earnestly that I have been amply heard, and have obtained more than I prayed for. God indeed sometimes delayed, but at last He came."

- Martin Luther

"A heart ready to melt at the sight of human suffering and need is necessary to successful soul-winning...Where there is no real soul-burden for sinners, there will be no revival. The early Church travailed in pain for the souls of dying men."

- J. W. Mahood

"There is need of a great revival of spiritual life, of truly fervent devotion to our Lord Jesus, of entire consecration to His service. It is only in a church in which this spirit of revival has at least begun, that there is any hope of radical change in the relation of the majority of our Christian people to mission work."

- Andrew Murray

"The feeling of need and not the force of habit will make thee a sincere suppliant."

- Evan Roberts

"The evangelization of the world in this generation depends first of all upon a revival of prayer. Deeper than the need for men; deeper, far, than the need for money; aye, deep down at the bottom of our spiritless life is the need for the forgotten secret of prevailing, world-wide prayer."

-    Robert E. Speer

"A prayerless man is proud and independent, and any church that neglects corporate prayer is sadly no better. Only God's humble and needy children take the time to pray. Everyone else is just going through the motions and naively trusting in their own strength!"

-    David Smithers

"We need a Heaven-sent revival,
a burning fire from on high,
  A purifying passion and a forsaking
of our stubborn pride.
  We need a vision of eternity,
of Hell and the Judgement Day,
  A fervent love for our Savior,
that will gladly serve and obey.
  We need a Pentecostal purging
and a breaking deep within,
  A vision of God Almighty
and a river of tears for our nations sin.
  We need a Heaven-sent revival,
a burning fire set ablaze.
  Yet, we'll never see such glory,
until the Church begins to pray."

-    David Smithers

"The church's concern for and identification with the poor are sure signs of its faithfulness to the Kingdom and are often signs of fundamental renewal."

-    Howard A. Snyder

"We need a baptism of clear seeing. We desperately need seers who can see through the mist--Christian leaders with prophetic vision. Unless they come soon it will be too late for this generation. And if they do come we will no doubt crucify a few of them in the name of our worldly orthodoxy."

- A. W. Tozer

"Do people need a fish or a lesson in fishing?"

- Mark Twain

"You have nothing to do but to save souls. Therefore spend and be spent in this work. And go not only to those that need you, but to those that need you most...It is not your business to preach so many times, and to take care of this or that society; but to save as many souls as you can; to bring as many sinners as you possibly can to repentance."

- John Wesley

"Tell me, is your ministry a burning and shining light, or a smoking wick, slowly dying out to ashes? ...It is a strange custom that we should supply a minister with a glass of water; if only we could supply him with a bonfire in the pulpit, a spiritual bonfire. We need the dynamic of a flaming ministry that will set the Church on fire."

- Samuel Zwemer

"Those who deserve love the least need it the most."

- American Proverb

"Work like you don't need the money, love like you've never been hurt, and dance like no one is watching!"

- Unknown

NEWS

"He shall not be afraid of evil tidings: his heart is fixed, trusting in the LORD."

- Psalm 112:7

"As cold waters to a thirsty soul, so is good news from a far country."
-     Proverbs 25:25

"The Spirit of the Lord GOD is upon me; because the LORD hath anointed me to preach good tidings unto the meek; he hath sent me to bind up the brokenhearted, to proclaim liberty to the captives, and the opening of the prison to them that are bound; To proclaim the acceptable year of the LORD, and the day of vengeance of our God; to comfort all that mourn; To appoint unto them that mourn in Zion, to give unto them beauty for ashes, the oil of joy for mourning, the garment of praise for the spirit of heaviness; that they might be called trees of righteousness, the planting of the LORD, that he might be glorified."
-     Isaiah 61:1-4

"The press, important as is its office, is but the servant of the human intellect, and its ministry is for good or for evil, according to the character of those who direct it. The press is a mill which grinds all that is put into its hopper. Fill the hopper with poisoned grain, and it will grind it to meal, but there is death in the bread."
-     William Cullen Bryant

"It's not the world that's gotten so much worse, but the news coverage that's gotten so much better."
-     G. K. Chesterton

"Newspapers often overthrow one tyrant only to establish a tyranny of their own."
-     James Cooper

"Calamity sells papers. If there be no calamity, make one up. A newspaper without a calamity is a tragedy!"
-     William Randolph Hearst

"It is good news, worthy of all acceptation, and yet not too good to be true."
-     Matthew Henry, commenting on
      I Timothy 1:15

"For evil news rides post, while good news baits."
- John Milton

"The average newspaper contains about the same amount of words as the entire New Testament. American Christians often read the newspaper seven days a week for 52 weeks a year. Yet most Christians have never read the New Testament all the way through. Their excuse? 'It is so important,' they proclaim, 'I want to digest it properly.' I'll tell you what: Read it once all the way through and you'll realize whether or not you have a digestion problem or spiritual anorexia."
- Jack Murphy

"I hope we never live to see the day when a thing is as bad as some of our newspapers make it."
- Will Rogers

"Newspapers are unable, seemingly to discriminate between a bicycle accident and the collapse of civilization."
- George Bernard Shaw

"The news of my death is greatly exaggerated."
- Mark Twain

"Hate the message, but don't kill the messenger."
- American Proverb

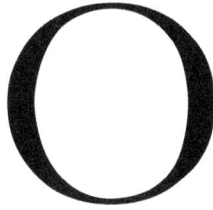

O

OBEDIENCE

"…to obey is better than sacrifice."
- I Samuel 15:22

"Whatever He says to you, do it."
- Mary, in John 4:14

"They cannot serve two masters God and the world. You know men will condemn you, if you be true to God: if, therefore, you must have the favor of men, you must take it alone without God's favor. A man-pleaser cannot be true to God, because he is a servant to the enemies of his service; the wind of a man's mouth will drive him about as the chaff, from any duty, and to any sin. How servile a person is a man-pleaser! How many masters hath he, and how mean ones! It perverteth the course of your hearts and lives, and turneth all from God to this unprofitable way."
- Richard Baxter

"Obedience is the crown and honor of all virtue."
- Martin Luther

"Obedience is the only validation of your salvation. It is the only possible indication that you recognize the Lordship of Jesus Christ."
- John MacArthur

"It is simply absurd to say you believe, or even want to believe, in Him, if you do not do anything He tells you."
- George Macdonald

"In obeying the Lord wholly, we rejoice in heart fully. With complete consecration comes perfect peace."
- Watchman Nee

"Nothing shall be lost that is done for God or in obedience to Him."
- John Owen

"The question isn't 'Were you challenged?' The question is 'Were you changed?'"
- Leonard Ravenhill

"Do you realize this? That if you were to somehow purpose to, from this day on, perfectly please God and succeed in doing it, that that perfect obedience, from this moment, would not acquire in the remainder of your life, enough merit to atone for one past sin, because God exacts and God demands perfect obedience and there's no merit for giving him the minimal requirement."
- Paris Reidhead

"I have said that there is nothing in the world or the Church, except its disobedience, to render the evangelization of the world in this generation an impossibility..."
- Robert E. Speer

OLD AGE – See AGE

OPINION

"And Elijah came unto all the people, and said, How long halt ye between two opinions? if the Lord be God, follow him: but if Baal, then follow him. And the people answered him not a word."
- I Kings 18:21

"But whom say ye that I am?"
- Jesus, in Matthew 16:15

"Nevertheless among the chief rulers also many believed on him; but because of the Pharisees they did not confess him, lest they should be put out of the synagogue."
-    John 12:42

"I could never divide myself from any man upon the difference of an opinion, or be angry with his judgment for not agreeing in that from which within a few days I might dissent myself."
-    Sir Thomas Browne

"The world is governed much more by opinion than by laws. It is not the judgment of courts, but the moral judgment of individuals and masses of men, which is the chief wall of defense around property and life. With the progress of society, this power of opinion is taking the place of arms."
-    William Ellery Channing

"Opinion is the blind goddess of fools."
-    George Chapman

"People seem not to see that their opinion of the world is also a confession of character."
-    Ralph Waldo Emerson

"The only sin which we never forgive in each other is difference of opinion."
-    Ralph Waldo Emerson

"The press commands to persuade opinion. Opinion is power."
-    Thomas Jefferson

"Popular opinions, on subjects not palpable to sense, are often true, but seldom or never the whole truth."
-    John Stuart Mill

"Opinion based upon rumor or bias is dangerous."
-    Jack Murphy

"An opinion need not be orthodox to be based upon truth. The greatest inventions of mankind were caused by those unorthodox opinions."
- Jack Murphy

"No man was ever burned at the stake for his opinion. He was burned for knowing the difference between his opinion and the truth."
- Leonard Ravenhill

"Broad-minded is just another way of saying a fellow's too lazy to form an opinion."
- Will Rogers

"There are as many opinions as there are experts."
- Franklin D. Roosevelt

"Opinions should be formed with great caution, and changed with greater."
- Henry Wheeler Shaw

"Don't let your opinions get in the way of the facts. Most people permit the opposite."
- American Proverb

OPPORTUNITY

"Making the most of every opportunity, because the days are evil."
- Ephesians 5:16

"Be wise in the way you act toward outsiders; make the most of every opportunity."
- Colossians 4:5

"So I counsel younger widows to marry, to have children, to manage their homes and to give the enemy no opportunity for slander."
- I Timothy 5:14

"A wise man will make more opportunities than he finds."
- Sir Francis Bacon

"The men who have done the most for God in this world have been early on their knees. He who fritters away the early morning, its opportunity and freshness, in other pursuits than seeking God will make poor headway seeking Him the rest of the day. If God is not first in our thoughts and efforts in the morning, He will be in the last place the remainder of the day."

- E. M. Bounds

"A word spoken in season, at the right moment; is the mother of ages."

- Thomas Carlyle

"Not only strike while the iron is hot, but make it hot by striking."

- Oliver Cromwell

"The secret of success in life is for a man to be ready for his opportunity when it comes."

- Benjamin Disraeli

"Opportunity is missed by most people because it is dressed in overalls and looks like work."

- Thomas Edison

"When written in Chinese, the word 'crisis' is composed of two characters. One represents danger and the other represents opportunity."

- John F. Kennedy

"No man can claim in Judgment that they had no opportunity!"

- Leonard Ravenhill

"I was seldom able to see an opportunity until it had ceased to be one."

- Mark Twain

"Opportunities are never lost; someone will take the one you miss."

- English Proverb

"Four things come not back: the spoken word, the spent arrow, time past, the neglected opportunity."

- Irish Proverb

OPTIMISM vs. PESSIMISM

"And David was greatly distressed; for the people spake of stoning him, because the soul of all the people was grieved, every man for his sons and for his daughters: but David encouraged himself in the LORD his God."
- I Samuel 30:6

"Finally, brethren, whatsoever things are true, whatsoever things are honest, whatsoever things are just, whatsoever things are pure, whatsoever things are lovely, whatsoever things are of good report; if there be any virtue, and if there be any praise, think on these things."
- Philippians 4:8

"The optimist proclaims that we live in the best of all possible worlds, and the pessimist fears this is true."
- James Cabell

"A pessimist sees the difficulty in every opportunity; an optimist sees the opportunity in every difficulty."
- Winston Churchill

"Optimism is not an excuse to neglect reason. Most of the great disasters came from optimistic engineers and scientists."
- Albert Einstein

"Pessimism results from an optimist losing faith. Cynicism results from a pessimist losing patience. Optimism results from cynicism proven biased."
- Edward Everett

"I'm a pessimist because of intelligence, but an optimist because of will."
- Antonio Gramsci

"The optimist sees the rose and not its thorns; the pessimist stares at the thorns, and doesn't recognize the rose. A realist recognizes the beauty of the roses and remains careful of the thorns."
- Jack Murphy

"Optimism is looking out a gray window and noticing the wonders of nature – the sky, the wonderful rain, or the purity of the snowflake. Pessimism is looking out the same window and only noticing that it needs to be cleaned."
- Jack Murphy

"Optimistic soldiers are more quickly killed than pessimists."
- Napoleon Bonaparte

"In times of sadness, weakness or disaster, people need your optimism and not your pessimism."
- Ronald Reagan

"In the long run the pessimist may be proved right, but the optimist has a better time on the trip."
- Daniel J. Riordan

"An optimist sees a gray sky but ventures outside anyway, hoping and expecting the sun to come out. A pessimist stays inside expecting the rain. A realist simply carries an umbrella, come what may."
- Will Rogers

"A pessimist is one who makes difficulties of his opportunities and an optimist is one who makes opportunities of his difficulties."
- Harry Truman

"It's easy being an optimist when you're wealthy and healthy."
- Mark Twain

"There is no sadder sight than a young pessimist."
- Mark Twain

"An optimist stays up until midnight to see the new year in. A pessimist stays up to make sure the old year leaves."
- Bill Vaughan

"Pessimist: One who, when he has the choice between two evils, chooses both."
- Oscar Wilde

"I'm an optimist, but an optimist who carries a raincoat."
- Harold Wilson

"Many pessimists move from expecting the worst to hoping for the worst."
- Woodrow Wilson

"Always borrow money from a pessimist, he doesn't expect to be paid back. "
- English Proverb

ORGANIZATION

"In those days was Hezekiah sick unto death. And Isaiah the prophet the son of Amoz came unto him, and said unto him. Thus saith the Lord, Set thine house in order: for thou shalt die, and not live."
- Isaiah 38:1

"Let all things be done decently and in order."
- I Corinthians 14:40

"Irregularity and want of method are only supportable in men of great learning or genius, who are often too full to be exact, and therefore they choose to throw down their pearls in heaps before the reader, rather than be at the pains of stringing them."
- Joseph Addison

"Intelligent people, when assembled into an organization, will tend toward collective stupidity."
- Karl Albrecht, in
Albrecht's Law

"Fretfulness of temper will generally characterize those who are negligent of order."

-     Hugh Blair

"Do you know what amazes me more than anything else? The impotence of force to organize anything."

-     Napoleon Bonaparte

"Good order is the foundation of all good things."

-     Edmund Burke

"And have we now forgotten that powerful Friend? Or do we imagine we no longer need His assistance? I have lived a long time; and the longer I live, the more convincing proofs I see of this truth: that God governs in the affairs of men. And if a sparrow cannot fall to the ground without His notice, is it probable that an empire can rise without His aid? We have been assured, Sir, in the Sacred Writings, that 'except the Lord build the House, they labor in vain that build it.' I firmly believe this; and I also believe that, without His concurring aid, we shall succeed in this political building no better than the builders of Babel."

-     Benjamin Franklin

"One of the many reasons for the bewildering and tragic character of human existence is the fact that social organization is at once necessary and fatal. Men are forever creating such organizations for their own convenience and forever finding themselves the victims of their home-made monsters."

-     Aldous Huxley

"Hope and confidence should not be placed in the extent and perfection of organizations, nor in the experience which has been accumulated and the agencies and methods which have been devised in a long century of missions, nor in the unusual strength of the missionary body, nor in the multitude who have been gathered from every nation and race and faith into the native Church, nor in the wonderful resources and facilities of the home Church, nor in far-sighted and comprehensive plans, nor in enthusiastic forward movements and inspiring watchwords. It is easy to magnify human personality and agencies. Prayer recognizes that God is

the source of life and light and energy."
- John R. Mott

"The complex laws of nature work in perfect order, yet the Church of God cannot reach a consensus on even the simplest of matters!"
- Jack Murphy

"A 'disorganized organization' is an oxymoron. It is as ridiculous as an ornate choir where each member sings completely different tunes in different keys."
- Jack Murphy

"We should not organize something, and then ask God to bless. We should organize only on behalf of what God has already called and ordained. If we do this, we don't have to worry about asking and receiving a blessing. We will already have it."
- Leonard Ravenhill

"Nothing bothers the inhabitants of a disorganized organization more than order. And nothing is more profitable."
- Will Rogers

"The moral of Babel was not to spurn organization; but 'twas to spurn organization without God's guidance."
- George Washington

P

PACIFISM

"Blessed be the LORD my strength which teacheth my hands to war, and my fingers to fight."

-   Psalm 144:1

"To every thing there is a season, and a time to every purpose under the heaven: A time to be born, and a time to die; a time to plant, and a time to pluck up that which is planted; A time to kill, and a time to heal; a time to break down, and a time to build up; A time to weep, and a time to laugh; a time to mourn, and a time to dance; A time to cast away stones, and a time to gather stones together; a time to embrace, and a time to refrain from embracing; A time to get, and a time to lose; a time to keep, and a time to cast away; A time to rend, and a time to sew; a time to keep silence, and a time to speak; A time to love, and a time to hate; a time of war, and a time of peace."

-   Ecclesiastes 3:1-8

"But I say unto you, Love your enemies, bless them that curse you, do good to them that hate you, and pray for them which despitefully use you, and persecute you; That ye may be the children of your Father which is in heaven: for he maketh his sun to rise on the evil and on the good, and sendeth rain on the just and on the unjust."

-   Matthew 5:44-45

"But if any provide not for his own, and especially for those of his own house, he hath denied the faith, and is worse than an infidel."

-   I Timothy 5:8

"Thou therefore endure hardness, as a good soldier of Jesus Christ. No man that warreth entangleth himself with the affairs of this life; that he may please him who hath chosen him to be a soldier."
- II Timothy 2:3-4

"Appeasers believe that if you keep on throwing steaks to a tiger, the tiger will become a vegetarian."
- Heyward Campbell Broun

"All that is necessary for the triumph of evil is that good men do nothing."
- Edmund Burke

"[Pacifists are] the last and least excusable on the list of the enemies of society. They preach that if you see a man flogging a woman to death you must not hit him. I would much sooner let a leper come near a little boy than a man who preached such a thing."
- G. K. Chesterton

"The era of procrastination, of half-measures, of soothing and soothing and baffling expedients, of delays, is coming to a close. In its place we are entering a period of consequences."
- Winston Churchill

"My conviction of pacifism does not extend to watching my family chained, beaten, tortured or killed."
- Edward Everett

"…even the pacifists in Auschwitz cheered for the approaching Allies."
- Dwight D. Eisenhower

"It is in vain, sir, to extenuate the matter. Gentlemen may cry, Peace, Peace-- but there is no peace. The war is actually begun! The next gale that sweeps from the north will bring to our ears the clash of resounding arms! Our brethren are already in the field! Why stand we here idle? What is it that gentlemen wish? What would they have? Is life so dear, or peace so sweet, as to be purchased at the price of chains and slavery? Forbid it,

Almighty God! I know not what course others may take; but as for me, give me liberty or give me death!"

- Patrick Henry

"True pacifism is not unrealistic submission to an evil power. ...It is rather a courageous confrontation with evil by the power of love, in the faith that it is better to be the recipient of violence than the inflictor of it, since the latter only multiplies the existence of violence and bitterness in the universe, while the former may develop a sense of shame in the opponent, and thereby bring about a transformation and change of heart."

- Martin Luther King, Jr.

"Many good men died for the right of a pacifist to do nothing."

- Douglas MacArthur

"The price paid for intellectual pacification is the sacrifice of the entire moral courage of the human mind."

- John Stuart Mill

"Most pacifists resist nothing except those who disagree with their philosophy. They preach against resistance, violence and political entanglement. Yet at the first sign of disagreement, many will fiercely resist disagreement to their philosophy by loudly politicking those around them."

- Jack Murphy

"Pacifism is objectively pro-fascist. This is elementary common sense. If you hamper the war effort of one side, you automatically help out that of the other. Nor is there any real way of remaining outside such a war as the present one. In practice, 'he that is not with me is against me."

- George Orwell

"Pacifism is a difficult position to hold during times of war. During the First War, there were few pacifists left in Europe. Yet after the war, they quickly returned. This incited Hitler and his Nazis to succeed in easy and rapid aggression. During the Second War, these pacifists once more disappeared. I wonder: Will they return again?"

- George S. Patton

"And the idea that you could appease them [terrorists] by stopping doing what we're doing…it's kind of like feeding an alligator, hoping it eats you last."

- Donald Rumsfeld

"Violent conquerors pray that the world be filled with pacifists."

- Mark Twain

"If we desire to secure peace, one of the most powerful instruments of our rising prosperity, it must be known that we are at all times ready for war."

- George Washington

"I find it odd that some preachers of pacifism still believe in the 'Lord of hosts.' They believe in the armies of the Bible and of Heaven, but feel that there are no such types and shadows on Earth."

- Woodrow Wilson

"So spiritually minded yet of no earthly good."

- Unknown

PAIN

"Looking unto Jesus the author and finisher of our faith; who for the joy that was set before him endured the cross, despising the shame, and is set down at the right hand of the throne of God."

- Hebrews 12:2

"There is no greater pain than to remember, in our present grief, past happiness."

- Dante,
  in *The Divine Comedy*

"Mental pain is more easily borne than physical; and if I had my choice between a bad conscience and a bad tooth, I should choose the former."

- Heinrich Heine

"So great was the extremity of Job's pain and anguish, that he did not only sigh but roar."

-     Matthew Henry

"God, who foresaw your tribulation, has specially armed you to go through it, not without pain but without stain."

-     C. S. Lewis

"God has scattered several degrees of pleasure and pain in all the things that environ and affect us, and blended them together in almost all our thoughts."

-     John Locke

"To give one's daughter away in marriage is to experience both inexpressible joy and pain at the same time."

-     Jack Murphy

"More men die from painful thoughts of 'could have' and 'should have' than from bullets and spears."

-     Will Rogers

"Pain is the root of development and maturity."

-     Mark Twain

"Pain is weakness leaving your body."

-     U.S. Marine Corp,
    Boot Camp Motto

PARENTING – See CHILDREN

PASSION

"But if they cannot contain, let them marry: for it is better to marry than to burn."

-     I Corinthians 7:9

"For the grace of God that bringeth salvation hath appeared to all men, Teaching us that, denying ungodliness and worldly lusts, we should live soberly, righteously, and godly, in this present world; Looking for that blessed hope, and the glorious appearing of the great God and our Saviour Jesus Christ; Who gave himself for us, that he might redeem us from all iniquity, and purify unto himself a peculiar people, zealous of good works."

- Titus 2:11-14

"One loving heart sets another on fire."
- Augustine

"Passion will move men beyond themselves, beyond their shortcomings, beyond their failures."
- Joe Campbell

"God will manifest himself in direct proportion to our PASSION for Him."
- Jim Cymbala

"If the spirit of prayer departs, it is a sure indication of a backslidden heart, for while the first love of a Christian continues he is sure to be drawn by the Holy Spirit to wrestle much in prayer. To pray as a duty and as if obliging God by our prayer, is quite ridiculous, and is certain indication of a backslidden heart."
- Charles G. Finney

"The end of passion is the beginning of repentance."
- Benjamin Franklin

"If passion drives you, let reason hold the reins."
- Benjamin Franklin

"Lock yourself in a room; throw the key away; do something! Seek God and be found of Him. That is His promise: '*If you will seek for Me with all your heart and all your soul, you shall be found of Me*' (Deut. 4:29). When you do obtain that knowledge, maintain it, or else you will lose it."
- Art Katz

"Our age is without passion. Everyone knows a great deal, we all know which way we ought to go and all the different ways we can go, but nobody is really willing to move."
- Soren Kierkegaard

"But this had been a sin of passion, not of principle, nor even purpose."
- Nathaniel Hawthorne, in *The Scarlett Letter*

"If I find in myself a desire which no experience in this world can satisfy, then the most probable explanation is that I was made for another world."
- C.S. Lewis

"If I should neglect prayer but a single day, I should lose a great deal of the fire of faith."
- Martin Luther

"Ferdinand Foch said, 'The most powerful weapon on earth is the human soul on fire!' All the crafting in the world can't save a message that has no passion in it. If you can't get excited about a subject, don't preach on it."
- John Maxwell

"God always visits his people when they reach the point of desperation."
- Stephen Olford

"Put all your heart into what you do, or else put none of it in."
- C.H. Spurgeon

"Don't ask yourself what the world needs; ask yourself what makes you come alive. And then go and do that. Because what the world needs is people who have come alive."
- Howard Thurman

"The call of the Cross, therefore, is to enter into this passion of Christ. We must have upon us the print of the nails."
- Gordon Watt

"Passion and prejudice govern the world, only under the name of reason."

- John Wesley

"Tell me what you do with your time and money and I will tell you where your heart is."

- Francis Xavier

PAST – See HISTORY

PASTOR - See AUTHORITY; PREACHERS

PATIENCE

"I waited patiently for the LORD; and he inclined unto me, and heard my cry."

- Psalm 40:1

"Be still, and know that I am God: I will be exalted among the heathen, I will be exalted in the earth."

- Psalm 46:10

"In your patience possess ye your souls."

- Luke 21:19

"And not only so, but we glory in tribulations also: knowing that tribulation worketh patience; And patience, experience; and experience, hope: And hope maketh not ashamed; because the love of God is shed abroad in our hearts by the Holy Ghost which is given unto us."

- Romans 5:3-5

"Slow and steady wins the race."

- Aesop

"Patience is a most necessary qualification for business; many a man would rather you heard his story than granted his request."

- Lord Chesterfield

"Beware the fury of a patient man."
- John Dryden

"Adopt the pace of nature: her secret is patience."
- Ralph Waldo Emerson

"He that can have patience can have what he will."
- Benjamin Franklin

"Everything has its wonders, even darkness and silence, and I learn, whatever state I may be in, therin to be content."
- Helen Keller

"Men love to trust God (as they profess) for what they have in their hands, in possession, or what lies in an easy view; place their desires afar off, carry their accomplishment behind the clouds out of their sight, interpose difficulties and perplexities -- their hearts are instantly sick. They cannot wait for God; they do not trust Him, nor ever did. Would you have the presence of God with you? Learn to wait quietly for the salvation you expect from Him."
- John Owen

"Only those who have the patience to do simple things perfectly will acquire the skill to do difficult things easily."
- Johann Friedrich von Schiller

"All things come to him who waits - provided he knows what he is waiting for."
- Woodrow Wilson

"Patience is the virtue you admire in the driver behind you, but despise in the driver in front of you."
- American Proverb

"Patience is something you admire in the driver behind you and scorn in the one ahead."
- American Proverb

"One moment of patience may ward off great disaster. One moment of impatience may ruin a whole life."
- Chinese Proverb

"Beating a dead horse will not get you to the market any sooner."
- English Proverb

"Patience is the ability to count down before you blast off."
- Unknown

PATRIOTISM

"They say unto him, Caesar's. Then saith he unto them, Render therefore unto Caesar the things which are Caesar's; and unto God the things that are God's."
- Matthew 22:21

"Let every soul be subject unto the higher powers. For there is no power but of God: the powers that be are ordained of God. Whosoever therefore resisteth the power, resisteth the ordinance of God: and they that resist shall receive to themselves damnation.
For rulers are not a terror to good works, but to the evil. Wilt thou then not be afraid of the power? do that which is good, and thou shalt have praise of the same: For he is the minister of God to thee for good. But if thou do that which is evil, be afraid; for he beareth not the sword in vain: for he is the minister of God, a revenger to execute wrath upon him that doeth evil."
- Romans 13:1-4

"Honour all men. Love the brotherhood. Fear God. Honour the king."
- I Peter 2:17

"Our country is not the only thing to which we owe our allegiance. It is also owed to justice and to humanity. Patriotism consists not in waving the flag, but in striving that our country shall be righteous as well as strong."
- James Bryce

"My country, right or wrong," is a thing that no patriot would think of saying except in a desperate case. It is like saying, "My mother, drunk or sober."

- G. K. Chesterton

"Those who claim to be citizens of this world have never tried to celebrate Christmas in the Soviet Union."

- Winston Churchill

"I have heard something said about allegiance to the South: I know no South, no North, no East, no West, to which I owe any allegiance."

- Henry Clay

"There is nothing wrong with America that cannot be cured with what is right in America."

- William Jefferson Clinton

"If our country is worth dying for in time of war let us resolve that it is truly worth living for in time of peace."

- Hamilton Fish

"I only regret that I have but one life to lose for my country."

- Nathan Hale, just before
  his death by hanging

"I know not what course others may take, but as for me, give me liberty, or give me death!"

- Patrick Henry

"I like to see a man proud of the place in which he lives. I like to see a man live so that his place will be proud of him."

- Abraham Lincoln

"This nation, under God, shall have a new birth of freedom--and that government of the people, by the people, for the people, shall not perish from the earth."

- Abraham Lincoln

"It is a wonderful thing to die for one's country. It is a better thing to live nobly for one's country."
-     Jack Murphy

"My county may not be perfect, but neither is my family. I love my family. I love my country."
-     George S. Patton

"We love America because we love freedom. Freedom of ideas is civility. Freedom of business is capitalism. Freedom of thought is a clear conscience. America is a beacon for freedom."
-     Ronald Reagan

"The world cannot understand America because the world cannot understand its love of country. The world cannot comprehend how a diverse group of people gathered from the ends of the world can be unified in love of country. Yet it is not the country that is loved. Rather, it is the principles upon which this nation was founded that make it endeared. Americans love this country because this country loves Americans."
-     Ronald Reagan

PEACE

"The wolf shall also dwell with the lamb, and the leopard shall lie down with the kid; and the calf and the young lion and the fatling together; and a little child shall lead them."
-     Isaiah 11:6

"There is no peace, saith the LORD, unto the wicked."
-     Isaiah 48:22

"And suddenly there was with the angel a multitude of the heavenly host praising God, and saying
  Glory to God in the highest, and on earth peace, good will toward men."
-     Luke 2:13-14

"Blessed are the peacemakers: for they shall be called the children of God."
- Matthew 5:9

"If they want peace, nations should avoid the pin-pricks that precede cannon shots. "
- Napoleon Bonaparte

"The Pilgrim they laid in a large upper chamber, whose window opened toward the sun-rising; the name of the chamber was Peace, where he slept till break of day, and then he awoke and sang."
- John Bunyan, in
The Pilgrim's Progress

"With union grounded on falsehood and ordering us to speak and act lies, we will not have anything to do. Peace? A brutal lethargy is peaceable; the noisome is peaceable. We hope for a living peace, not a dead one!"
- Thomas Carlyle

"There are interests by the sacrifice of which peace is too dearly purchased. One should never be at peace to the shame of his own soul--to the violation of his integrity or of his allegiance to God."
- Edwin Hubbell Chapin

"Peace and justice are two sides of the same coin."
- Dwight D. Eisenhower

"We will have peace – even if we must fight for it!"
- Dwight D. Eisenhower

"I could not live in peace if I put the shadow of a willful sin between myself and God."
- George Eliot

"Even peace may be purchased at too high a price."
- Benjamin Franklin

"An eye for eye only ends up making the whole world blind."
- Mahatma Gandhi

"Peace with all nations, and the rights which that gives us with respect to all nations, are our object."
- Thomas Jefferson

"We shall never be able to effect physical disarmament until we have succeeded in effecting moral disarmament."
- Ramsay MacDonald

"You cannot shake hands with a clenched fist."
- Golda Meir

"Peace will come when the Arabs love their children more than they hate us."
- Golda Meir

"To be prepared for war is one of the most effective means of preserving peace."
- George Washington

"Lord, make Thyself always present to my mind, and let Thy love fill and rule my soul in all those places, companies and employments to which Thou callest me. Amen."
- John Wesley

PERFECTION

"Be ye therefore perfect, even as your Father which is in heaven is perfect."
- Matthew 5:48

"Jesus said unto him, If thou wilt be perfect, go and sell that thou hast, and give to the poor, and thou shalt have treasure in heaven: and come and follow me."
- Matthew 19:21

"But when that which is perfect is come, then that which is in part shall be done away."
-     I Corinthians 13:10

"This is the very perfection of a man, to find out his own imperfections."
-     Augustine of Hippo

"Aim at perfection in everything, though in most things it is unattainable. However, they who aim at it, and persevere, will come much nearer to it than those whose laziness and despondency make them give it up as unattainable."
-     Lord Chesterfield

"They say that nobody is perfect. Then they tell you practice makes perfect. I wish they'd make up their minds."
-     Winston Churchill

"Many things impossible to thought have been by need to full perfection brought."
-     John Dryden

"*Nobody's perfect.* This is the hypocrites' couch. This is the believers' bed of thorns."
-     Al Martin

"Trifles make perfection, and perfection is no trifle."
-     Michelangelo

"A perfectionist is never happy, for they pursue that which is humanly unattainable on this side of Eternity."
-     Jack Murphy

"Even Einstein's pencils have erasers!"
-     Will Rogers

"He who boasts of being perfect is perfect in folly. I never saw a perfect man. Every rose has its thorns, and every day its night. Even the sun shows spots, and the skies are darkened with clouds; and faults of some kind nestle in every bosom."
- Charles Spurgeon

"His house was perfect, whether you liked food, or sleep, or work, or story-telling, or singing, or just sitting and thinking, best, or a pleasant mixture of them all."
- J. R. R. Tolkien, in
The Lord of the Rings

"The most difficult part of attaining perfection is finding something to do for an encore."
- American Proverb

"Nobody's perfect – except on their resume."
- American Proverb

"Perfection is a journey, not a destination. Pursue perfection, even though you never arrive."
- English Proverb

"Beauty and personality are found in imperfections."
- Japanese Proverb

PERSECUTION

"Remember the word that I said unto you, The servant is not greater than his lord. If they have persecuted me, they will also persecute you; if they have kept my saying, they will keep yours also. But all these things will they do unto you for my name's sake, because they know not him that sent me."
- John 15:20-21

"They shall put you out of the synagogues: yea, the time cometh, that whosoever killeth you will think that he doeth God service."
- John 16:2

"But we have this treasure in earthen vessels, that the excellency of the power may be of God, and not of us. We are troubled on every side, yet not distressed; we are perplexed, but not in despair; Persecuted, but not forsaken; cast down, but not destroyed."
-    II Corinthians 4:7-9

"It has become a settled principle that nothing which is good and true can be destroyed by persecution, but that the effect ultimately is to establish more firmly, and to spread more widely, that which it was designed to overthrow. It has long since passed into a proverb that 'the blood of the martyrs is the seed of the church.'"
-    Albert Barnes

"The poorest being that crawls on earth, contending to save itself from injustice and oppression, is an object respectable in the eyes of God and man."
-    Edmund Burke

"In politics, as in religion, it is equally absurd to aim at making proselytes by fire and sword. Heresies in either can rarely be cured by persecution."
-    Alexander Hamilton

"Wherever you see persecution, there is more than a probability that truth lies on the persecuted side."
-    Hugh Latimer

"Of all tyrannies, a tyranny exercised for the good of its victims may be the most oppressive... those who torment us for our own good will torment us without end, for they do so with the approval of their own conscience."
-    C. S. Lewis

"Many people claim to have been 'persecuted' because they stood for 'truth' when in reality they were merely offended simply because others found them annoying."
-    Jack Murphy

"Whoever is right, the persecutor must be wrong."
- William Penn

"Galileo probably would have escaped persecution if his discoveries could have been disproved."
- Richard Whately

"It was strictly forbidden to preach to other prisoners, as it is in captive nations today. It was understood that whoever was caught doing this received a severe beating. A number of us decided to pay the price for the privilege of preaching, so we accepted their terms. It was a deal: we preached and they beat us. We were happy preaching; they were happy beating us - so everyone was happy."
- Richard Wurmbrand

"The monster, fanaticism, still exists, and whoever seeks after truth will run the risk of being persecuted."
- Voltaire

"When you are persecuted, it might help to understand why."
- English Proverb

PERSEVERANCE

"For a just man falleth seven times, and riseth up again."
- Proverbs 24:16

"But he that shall endure unto the end, the same shall be saved."
- Matthew 24:13

"No man is conquered until his heart is conquered."
- George Barlow

"The difference between perseverance and obstinacy is that one comes from a strong will, and the other from a strong won't."
- Henry Ward Beecher

"In the confrontation between the stream and the rock, the stream always wins, not through strength but by perseverance."
- H. Jackson Brown

"By gnawing through a dike, even a rat may drown a nation."
- Edmund Burke

"The block of granite, which was an obstacle in the pathway of the weak, becomes a stepping stone in the pathway of the strong."
- Thomas Carlyle

"By preserving over all obstacles and distractions, one may unfailingly arrive at his chosen goal or destination."
- Christopher Columbus

"Difficult things take a long time, impossible things a little longer."
- Thomas Edison

"It's not that I'm so smart, it's just that I stay with problems longer."
- Albert Einstein

"One with God is a majority."
- Billy Graham

"It is interesting to notice how some minds seem almost to create themselves, springing up under every disadvantage, and working their solitary but irresistible way through a thousand obstacles."
- Washington Irving

"When God gave Christ to this world, He gave the best He had, and He wants us to do the same."
- Dwight L. Moody

"Beautiful canyons are carved by the slow moving waters of determination."
- Jack Murphy

"Our adversary, the devil, is a very determined foe. He continues after every failure with terrible resolve. We must be vigilant and even more determined than he."
- Jack Murphy

"When you come to the end of your rope, tie a knot and hang on."
- Franklin D. Roosevelt

"Don't let the fear of striking out keep you from playing the game."
- Babe Ruth

"Much rain smoothes and polishes the marble."
- William Shakespeare

"The greatest oak was once a little nut who held its ground."
- American Proverb

"Everyone loses their first game of chess."
- English Proverb

"Fall seven times, stand up eight."
- Japanese Proverb

"There are no crown-wearers in heaven who were not cross-bearers here below."
- Unknown

"When the world says, '*Give up,*'
Hope whispers, '*Try it one more time.*'"
- Unknown

PLANS

"Without counsel purposes are disappointed: but in the multitude of counselors they are established."
- Proverbs 15:22

"For I know the thoughts that I think toward you, saith the LORD, thoughts of peace, and not of evil, to give you an expected end."
- Jeremiah 29:11

"Go to now, ye that say, To day or to morrow we will go into such a city, and continue there a year, and buy and sell, and get gain: Whereas ye know not what shall be on the morrow. For what is your life? It is even a vapour, that appeareth for a little time, and then vanisheth away. For that ye ought to say, If the Lord will, we shall live, and do this, or that. But now ye rejoice in your boastings: all such rejoicing is evil."
- James 4:13-16

"Set your course by the stars, not by the lights of every passing ship."
- Omar Bradley

"Don't plan without God. God seems to have a delightful way of upsetting the plans we have made, when we have not taken Him into account."
- Oswald Chambers

"Being busy does not always mean real work. The object of all work is production or accomplishment and to either of these ends there must be forethought, system, planning, intelligence, and honest purpose, as well as perspiration. Seeming to do is not doing."
- Thomas Edison

"It will not do to leave a live dragon out of your plans if you live near one."
- J. R. R. Tolkien

"If you fail to plan, you plan to fail."
- American Proverb

POLITICS

"Let every soul be subject unto the higher powers. For there is no power but of God: the powers that be are ordained of God. Whosoever therefore resisteth the power, resisteth the ordinance of God: and they that resist shall receive to themselves damnation.

For rulers are not a terror to good works, but to the evil. Wilt thou then not be afraid of the power? do that which is good, and thou shalt have praise of the same: For he is the minister of God to thee for good. But if thou do that which is evil, be afraid; for he beareth not the sword in vain: for he is the minister of God, a revenger to execute wrath upon him that doeth evil."

- Romans 13:1-4

"Honour all men. Love the brotherhood. Fear God. Honour the king."
- I Peter 2:17

"Some men change their party for the sake of their principles; others their principles for the sake of their party."
- Winston Churchill

"I never vote for anybody, I always vote against."
- W. C. Fields

"We'd all like to vote for the best man, but he's never a candidate."
- Frank Hubbard

"What is conservatism? Is it not the adherence to the old and tried against the new and untried?"
- Abraham Lincoln

"It is not in the nature of politics that the best men should be elected. The best men do not want to govern their fellowmen. Like Washington, they only do so after lengthy agonizing of the heart."
- George MacDonald

"A conservative looks to the good from the proven ideas of the past. A liberal looks toward the good that might come from change. A realist is cautious of the extremism of both."
- Jack Murphy

"We are all conservatives. We are all liberals. We remember the greatness of the past and aspire to the greatness that can be in our future. We are, after all, Americans."

- Jack Murphy

"Those who are too smart to engage in politics are punished by being governed by those who are dumber."

- Plato

"Politics is supposed to be the second oldest profession. I have come to realize that it bears a very close resemblance to the first."

- Ronald Reagan

"The best thing that I can say about this group of candidates is that only one of them can win."

- Will Rogers

"There are many men of principle in both parties in America, but there is no party of principle."

- Alexis de Tocqueville

"George Washington is the only president who didn't blame the previous administration for his troubles."

- Unknown

"A politician is a fellow who will lay down your life for his country."

- Unknown

POOR – See NEED

POPULARITY

"So the LORD was with Joshua; and his fame was noised throughout all the country."

- Joshua 6:27

"And when the queen of Sheba heard of the fame of Solomon concerning the name of the LORD, she came to prove him with hard questions."

- I Kings 10:1

"And the fame of David went out into all lands; and the LORD brought the fear of him upon all nations."

- I Chronicles 14:17

"But thou didst trust in thine own beauty, and playedst the harlot because of thy renown, and pouredst out thy fornications on every one that passed by; his it was."

- Ezekiel 16:15

"I do not seek unpopularity as a badge of honor, but sometimes it is the price of leadership and the cost of conviction."

- Tony Blair

"Popular opinion is the greatest lie of the world."

- Thomas Carlyle

"Popularity is like the brightness of a falling star, the fleeting splendor of a rainbow, the bubble that is sure to burst by its very inflation."

- Paul Chatfield

"O breath of public praise,
 Short liv'd and vain! oft gain'd without desert,
  As often lost, unmerited; composed
   But of extremes: Thou first beginn'st with love
    Enthusiastic, madness of affection; then
     (Bounding o'er moderation and o'er reason)
      Thou turn'st to hate, as causeless and as fierce."

- William Harvard

"Could the departed, whoever he may be, return in a week after his decease, he would almost invariably find himself at a higher or a tower point than he had formerly occupied on the scale of public appreciation."

- Nathaniel Hawthorne

"To his dog, every man is Napoleon; hence the constant popularity of dogs."

- Aldous Huxley

"Avoid popularity; it has many snares, and no real benefit."
- William Penn

"The Sunday morning service shows how popular your church is. The evening services show how popular your pastor is. Your private prayer time shows you how popular God is!"
- Leonard Ravenhill

"The most successful politician is he who says what everybody is thinking most often and in the loudest voice."
- Theodore Roosevelt

"A free society is one where it is safe to be unpopular."
- Adlai Stevenson

"A strict call for holiness will never make you popular anywhere except before the throne of God."
- A. W. Tozer

"How far would Moses have gone if he had taken a poll in Egypt?"
- Harry Truman

"God helps us seek popularity where it counts – at the court of God!"
- S. R. Zepp

POWER

"Let every soul be subject unto the higher powers. For there is no power but of God: the powers that be are ordained of God."
- Romans 13:1

"Even in war, moral power is to physical as three parts out of four."
- Napoleon Bonaparte

"Do not pray for tasks equal to your powers. Pray for powers equal to your tasks."
- Phillips Brooks

"Power corrupts the few, while weakness corrupts the many."
- Edmund Burke

"The worst thing that can be said of the most powerful is that they can take your life; but the same thing can be said of the most weak."
- Charles Coulton

"Sell not virtue to purchase wealth, nor liberty to purchase power."
- Benjamin Franklin

"An honest man can feel no pleasure in the exercise of power over his fellow citizens. Power is not alluring to pure minds. It must never be trusted without a check."
- Thomas Jefferson

"In the past, those who foolishly sought power by riding on the back of the tiger ended up inside."
- John F. Kennedy

"Nearly all men can stand adversity, but if you want to test a man's character, give him power."
- Abraham Lincoln

"If added power attends the united prayer of two or three, what mighty triumphs there will be when hundreds of thousands of consistent members of the Church are with one accord day by day making intercession for the extension of Christ's Kingdom."
- John R. Mott

"Yes, the sound of a dog's bark might suffice for some time. But sooner or later, someone will be willing to challenge the bark to check the power of the bite!"
- Jack Murphy

"Meekness: Having the power to do something while utilizing moral or spiritual discretion."
- Jack Murphy

"We can have no power from Christ unless we live in a persuasion that we have none of our own."

- John Owen

"We put the power in the people."

- William Penn

"You cannot have power until you have first known purity."

- Leonard Ravenhill

"Isn't it staggering when you think that one sermon on the day of Pentecost produced 3000 people? And we had some cities yesterday where 3000 sermons were preached and nobody was saved. And it doesn't even faze us."

- Leonard Ravenhill

"My biggest fear is that a backward leader will one day obtain nuclear capabilities and will not fear and respect the idea of mutually assured destruction."

- Ronald Reagan, when asked about his greatest fear following the collapse of the Soviet Union

"In a democratic nation, power must be linked with responsibility, and obliged to defend and justify itself within the framework of the general good."

- Franklin Roosevelt

"We have, I fear, confused power with greatness."

- Stewart Udall

"It's not the size of the dog that matters; it is the sound of his bark!"

- American Proverb

"Those that desire power while neglecting purity will receive neither power nor purity."

- Unknown

"Inner purity results in outer power."
- Unknown

"A minister who operates upon the power of his supposed 'umbrella of authority' is a tyrant."
- Unknown

PRAISE – See WORSHIP

PRAYER

"The effectual fervent prayer of a righteous man availeth much."
- James 5:16

"Oh brother, pray; in spite of Satan, pray; spend hours in prayer; rather neglect friends than not pray; rather fast, and lose breakfast, dinner, tea, and supper – and sleep too – than not pray. And we must not talk about prayer, we must pray in right earnest. The Lord is near. He comes softly while the virgins slumber."
- Andrew A. Bonar

"Is prayer your steering wheel or your spare tire?"
- Corrie Ten Boom

"No Man can do a great and enduring work of God, who is not a man of prayer, and no man can be a man of prayer who does not give much time to praying."
- E. M. Bounds

"The story of every great Christian achievement is the history of answered prayer."
- E. M. Bounds

"Prayer breaks all bars, dissolves all chains, opens all prisons, and widens all straits by which God's saints have been held."
- E. M. Bounds

"Talking to men for God is a great thing, but talking to God for men is greater still."
- E.M. Bounds

"Prayer can do anything that God can do."
- E.M. Bounds

"No erudition, no purity of diction, no width of mental outlook, no flowers of eloquence, no grace of person can atone for lack of fire. Prayer ascends by fire. Flame gives prayer access as well as wings, acceptance as well as energy. There is no incense without fire; no prayer without flame."
- E. M. Bounds

"Walking with God down the avenue of prayer we acquire something of His likeness, and unconsciously we become witnesses to others of His beauty and His grace."
- E. M. Bounds

"Prayer succeeds when all else fails."
- E.M. Bounds

"Pray hardest when it is hardest to pray."
- Charles H. Brent

"When thou prayest, rather let thy heart be without words, than thy words without a heart."
- John Bunyan

"Prayer, not works, is the acid test of devotion."
- Samuel Chadwick

"The one concern of the devil is to keep Christians from praying. He fears nothing from prayerless studies, prayerless work and prayerless religion. He laughs at our toil, mocks at our wisdom, but trembles when we pray."
- Samuel Chadwick

"We have to pray with our eyes on God, not on the difficulties."
- Oswald Chambers

"The battle of prayer is against two things in the earthlies: wandering thoughts, and lack of intimacy with God's character as revealed in His word. Neither can be cured at once, but they can be cured by discipline."
- Oswald Chambers

"And Satan trembles when he sees,
The weakest saint upon his knees."
- William Cowper

"The greatest blow sent Satan-ward is made by weeping warriors of prayer."
- Dick Eastman

"Of all the duties enjoined by Christianity none is more essential and yet more neglected than prayer. Most people consider the exercise a fatiguing ceremony, which they are justified in abridging as much as possible. Even those whose profession or fears lead them to pray, pray with such languor and wanderings of mind that their prayers, far from drawing down blessings, only increase their condemnation."
- François Fénelon

"You can do more than pray after you have prayed, but you cannot do more than pray until you have prayed."
- A. J. Gordon

"Lock yourself in a room; throw the key away; do something! Seek God and be found of Him. That is His promise: '*If you will seek for Me with all your heart and all your soul, you shall be found of Me*' (Deut. 4:29). When you do obtain that knowledge, maintain it, or else you will lose it."
- Art Katz

"Prayer is a silent surrendering of everything to God."
- Soren Kierkegaard

"I have so much to do that I shall spend my first hours in prayer."
- Martin Luther

"Let me burn out for God! After all, whatever God may appoint, prayer is the great thing. Oh, that I may be a man of prayer!"
- Henry Martyn

"God hears every one of your cries in the busy hour of the daytime and in the lonely watches of the night."
- Robert Murray M'Cheyne

"I ought to pray before seeing any one. Often when I sleep long, or meet with others early, it is eleven or twelve o'clock before I begin secret prayer. This is a wretched system. It is unscriptural. Christ arose before day and went into a solitary place. David says: 'Early will I seek thee', 'Thou shalt early hear my voice.' Family prayer loses much of its power and sweetness, and I can do no good to those who come to seek from me. The conscience feels guilty, the soul unfed, the lamp not trimmed. Then when in secret prayer the soul is often out of tune. I feel it is far better to begin with God-to see His face first, to get my soul near Him before it is near another."
- Robert Murray M'Cheyne

"Give yourselves to prayer and the ministry of the Word. If you do not pray, God will probably lay you aside from your ministry, as He did me, to teach you to pray."
- Robert Murray M'Cheyne

"The men that will change the colleges and seminaries here represented are the men that will spend the most time alone with God. It takes time for the fires to burn. It takes time for God to draw near and for us to know that He is there. It takes time to assimilate His truth. You ask me, How much time? I do not know. I know it means time enough to forget time."
- John Mott

"The Church has not yet touched the fringe of the possibilities of intercessory prayer. Her largest victories will be witnessed when individual Christians everywhere come to recognize their priesthood unto God and day by day give themselves unto prayer."
- John R. Mott

"If added power attends the united prayer of two or three, what mighty triumphs there will be when hundreds of thousands of consistent members of the Church are with one accord day by day making intercession for the extension of Christ's Kingdom."
- John R. Mott

"Let methods be changed, therefore, if necessary, that prayer may be given its true place. Let there be days set apart for intercession; let the original purpose of the monthly concert of prayer for missions be given a larger place; let missionary prayer cycles be used by families and by individual Christians; let the best literature on prayer be circulated among the members of the Church; let special sermons on the Subject of intercession be preached. By these and by all other practical means a larger, deeper, wider spirit of prayer should be cultivated in the churches."
- John R. Mott

"I live in the spirit of prayer; I pray as I walk, when I lie down and when I rise, and the answers are always coming."
- George Mueller

"Prayer is the power of the Church; and could I speak as loud as the trumpet which is to wake the dead, I would thus call upon the Church, in all branches and in all lands: 'Awake! awake! put on thy strength, 0 Zion! put on thy beautiful garments, O Jerusalem! Arise, shine, for thy light is come, and the glory of the Lord is risen upon thee.' Patriarchs, prophets, apostles. martyrs, reformers, were mighty in prayer."
- Nicholas Murray

"From the day of Pentecost, there has been not one great spiritual awakening in any land which has not begun in a union of prayer, though only two or three. No such outward, upward movement has continued after such prayer meetings declined."

- A. T. Pierson

"A prayerless Christian is like a bus driver trying alone to push his bus out of a ditch because he doesn't know Clark Kent is on board. If you knew, you would ask."

- John Piper

"The secret of praying is praying in secret."

- Leonard Ravenhill

"The only power that God will yield to is that of prayer."

- Leonard Ravenhill

"The Sunday morning service shows how popular your church is. The evening services show how popular your pastor is. Your private prayer time shows you how popular God is!"

- Leonard Ravenhill

"No man is greater than his prayer life. The pastor who is not praying is playing; the people who are not praying are straying. The pulpit can be a shop window to display one's talents; the prayer closet allows no showing off."

- Leonard Ravenhill

"Today, we are living in desperate times. Yet the Church is not so desperate before God in prayer."

- Chuck Smith

"A prayerless man is proud and independent, and any church that neglects corporate prayer is sadly no better. Only God's humble and needy children take the time to pray. Everyone else is just going through the motions and naively trusting in their own strength!"

- David Smithers

"He who knows how to overcome with God in prayer has heaven and earth at his disposal."
- C. H. Spurgeon

"A prayerless soul is a Christless soul. Prayer is the lisping of the believing infant, the shout of the fighting believer, the requiem of the dying saint falling asleep in Jesus. It is the breath, the watchword, the comfort, the strength, the honor of a Christian."
- Charles H. Spurgeon

"You can draw near to God even though you cannot say a word. A prayer may be crystallized in a tear. A tear is enough water to float a desire to God."
- Charles H. Spurgeon

"Whether we like it or not, asking is the rule of the Kingdom. If you may have everything by asking in His Name, and nothing without asking, I beg you to see how absolutely vital prayer is."
- C. H. Spurgeon

"If you don't desire to meet the Devil during the day, meet Jesus before dawn."
- C.T. Studd

"Brother, if you would enter that Province, you must go forward on your knees."
- J. Hudson Taylor

"Once a poor soul entered the school of prayer after his arrival in hell. He asked for relief from his agony; it was refused. He asked that a beggar warn his brothers; he was turned down. He was praying to Abraham, a man; he could not locate God. He dared not ask to get out; he plainly knew that he was beyond all hope. Prayerless on earth, unanswered in hell, he suffers on as the man who tried to learn to pray too late."
- Cameron V. Thompson

"When we become too glib in prayer we are most surely talking to ourselves."
-    A. W. Tozer

"How hard is it sometimes to get leave of hearts to seek God! Jesus Christ went more willingly to the cross than we do to the throne of grace."
-    Thomas Watson

"Whole days and WEEKS have I spent prostrate on the ground in silent or vocal prayer."
-    George Whitefield

"God is far more concerned with getting prayer back in the prayer closet than in the public schools."
-    David Wilkerson

"The day that you are publicly specific with your praying is the day that you will experience power."
-    David Wilkerson

"Satan laughs at our toiling, mocks at our wisdom, but trembles when we pray."
-    Unknown

"The secret of all failure is our failure in secret prayer."
-    Unknown

"The shortest distance between a problem and the solution is the distance between your knees and the floor."
-    Unknown

"Beware of prayerless tears and beware of tearless prayers."
-    Unknown

"Our prayers often resemble the mischievous tricks of town children, who knock at their neighbor's houses and then run away; we often knock at heaven's door and then run off into the spirit of the world. Instead of

waiting for entrance to be granted, we act as if we were afraid of having our prayers answered."
- Unknown

"Keep looking up...with your face down."
- Unknown

"Prayer, real prayer, is lethal to Satan's cause."
- Unknown

"Get on your knees and fight like a Christian!"
- Unknown

"The price of prayerlessness far exceeds the price of prayer."
- Unknown

PREACHERS

"God never saved any man for being a preacher, nor because he was an able preacher; but because he was a justified, sanctified man, and consequently faithful in his Master's work. Take heed, therefore, to ourselves first, that you he that which you persuade your hearers to be, and believe that which you persuade them to believe, and heartily entertain that Savior whom you offer to them. He that bade you love your neighbors as yourselves, did imply that you should love yourselves, and not hate and destroy yourselves and them."
- Richard Baxter

"Actors speak of things imaginary as if they were real, while you preachers too often speak of things real as if they were imaginary."
- Thomas Betterton

"What I'm calling for is a radically different way of thinking about our world. Instead of running from it, we need to rush into it. And instead of just hanging outside the fringes of our culture, we need to be right smack dab in the middle of it."
- Bob Briner

"Every man who seeks to be a pastor should spend time watching a shepherd as he tends his sheep. He should not leave that field until he has a revelation of the relationship between the sheep and their shepherd."
- John Bunyan

"You will develop more in the next 2 months by taking a sincere interest in 2 people than spending the next 2 years trying to get people interested in you."
- Dale Carnegie

"Instead of preaching the good news that sinners can be made righteous in Christ and escape the wrath to come, the gospel has degenerated into the pretext that we can be happy in Christ and escape the hassles of life."
- Ray Comfort

"Shame on you liberal theologians sending people to hell so you can keep a job!"
- Keith Daniel

"Is it possible that the church is in such a state, that if God looks for a man who he can show him self strong through and he finds none?""
- Keith Daniel

"It is God's way to let ministers try all their strength first, and then He Himself comes and subdues the hearts they cannot."
- Jonathan Edwards

"Ministers often preach about the Gospel instead of preaching the Gospel. They often preach about sinners instead of preaching to them."
- Charles Finney

"Make it an object of constant study, and of daily reflection and prayer, to learn how to deal with sinners so as to promote their conversion."
- Charles Finney

"Preach the gospel everyday, use words only when necessary."
- Francis of Assisi

"A good example is the best sermon."
-    Benjamin Franklin

"I don't want to preach GOOD; I want to preach GOD!"
-    G.A. Jarquin

"We are so ministerial-minded, and we want so to come into our ministries, and a lot of souls are made shipwreck by a premature coming into ministry when there had been no attention to the foundation of relationship with God and men."
-    Art Katz

"As Christian teachers and leaders we are to bring comfort for the afflicted and affliction to the comfortable."
-    Kimber Kauffman

"It is not our business to make the message acceptable, but to make it available. We are not to see that they like it, but that they get it."
-    Vance Havner

"The devil doesn't mind how many sermons we preach or prepare if it will keep us from preparing ourselves."
-    Vance Havner

"God is not looking for brilliant men, is not depending upon eloquent men, is not shut up to the use of talented men in sending His gospel out in the world. God is looking for broken men who have judged themselves in the light of the cross of Christ. When He wants anything done, He takes up men who have come to the end of themselves, whose confidence is not in themselves, but in God."
-    H.A. Ironside

"You must preach as a mother suckles her child."
-    Martin Luther

"A preacher must be both soldier and shepherd. He must nourish, defend, and teach; he must have teeth in his mouth, and be able to bite and fight."

      -    Martin Luther

"Give yourselves to prayer and the ministry of the Word. If you do not pray, God will probably lay you aside from your ministry, as He did me, to teach you to pray."

      -    Robert Murray M'Cheyne

"A preacher who preaches the truth uncompromisingly will be asked "does your preaching always have to be so pointy? Does it always have to be so sharp?" And of coarse the answer is no. He can blunt his message if he'd like and become just as dull as the average preacher."

      -    Jesse Morrell

"We must frankly face the fact that there is in this teaching a revolutionary element which could be dangerously subversive of our existing ways of thought. Let us admit that it is part of the fallen human nature of ecclesiastics, no less than of others in responsible positions, to desire always criteria of judgment which can be used without making too heavy demands upon the delicate faculty of spiritual discernment, clear-cut rules by which we may hope to be saved from making mistakes -- or rather, from being obviously and personally responsible for the mistakes. We are uncomfortable without definite principles by which we may guide our steps. We fear uncharted country, and the fanatics of all kinds who, upon the alleged authority of the Holy Spirit, summon us with strident cries in all directions simultaneously.
Only those who have never borne the heavy burden of pastoral responsibility will mock at the cautious spirit of the ecclesiastic."

      -    Leslie Newbigin

"None but He who made the world can make a minister."

      -    John Newton

"Too often I looked at being relevant, popular and powerful as ingredients of an effective ministry. The truth, however, is that these are not vocations but temptations."
- Henri Nouwen

"Finney preached and sometimes the whole congregation would get up and leave! That's good preaching."
- Leonard Ravenhill

"Isn't it staggering when you think that one sermon on the day of Pentecost produced 3000 people? And we had some cities yesterday where 3000 sermons were preached and nobody was saved. And it doesn't even faze us."
- Leonard Ravenhill

"If Jesus had preached the same message that ministers preach today, He would never have been crucified."
- Leonard Ravenhill

"If you look down into a well, if it be empty it will appear to be very deep, but if there be water in it you will see its brightness. I believe that many 'deep' preachers are simply so because they are like dry wells with nothing whatever in them, except decaying leaves, a few stones, and perhaps a dead cat or two. If there be living water in your preaching it may be very deep, but the light of truth will give clearness to it."
- C.H. Spurgeon

"The preacher who neglects to preach to himself has forgotten a very important part of his audience. We must first address our own soul. If we can move that by the words we may utter, we may hope to have some power with the souls of others."
- C.H. Spurgeon

"I have now concentrated all my prayers into one, and that one prayer is this, that I may die to self, and live wholly to him."
- C.H. Spurgeon

"A man says to me, 'Can you explain the seven trumpets of the Revelation?' No, but I can blow one in your ear, and warn you to escape from the wrath to come."

- C.H. Spurgeon

"Let this be to you the mark of true gospel preaching - where Christ is everything, and the creature is nothing; where it is salvation all of grace, through the work of the Holy Spirit applying to the soul the precious blood of Jesus."

- Charles H. Spurgeon

"I cannot agree with those who say that they have 'new truth' to teach. The two words seem to me to contradict each other; that which is new is not true. It is the old that is true, for truth is as old as God himself."

- Charles Spurgeon

"To be effective the preacher's message must be alive; it must alarm, arouse, challenge; it must be God's present voice to a particular people."

- A.W. Tozer

"When preachers do not call sin, sin, the people begin to wink at sin!"

- Dr. Micheal Useph

"Here is a different kind of 'gem from the pulpit'. For many years the most conservative of Anglican theological colleges in the UK was (and is?) Oakhill Theological College. Young men fulfilled their courses of study as preparation for ordination into the Anglican ministry. The chapel had a simple pulpit where the young students preached their apprentice sermons to each other. As a young would-be ordained I was once permitted to enter the pulpit and discovered an irregular brass plate set into the pulpit and visible only to someone as they stood to preach. On the brass plate were engraved the words

'Sir, we would see Jesus
John 12:21'

"I never heard or read of better advice given for preachers of any age."

- Unknown

"A man who spoke little English gave this description of a sermon he had heard: he said 'Big wind. Much lightening. Loud thunder. No rain!'"
- Unknown

"God does not call the qualified; He qualifies the called."
- Unknown

PREJUDICE

"But the LORD said unto Samuel, Look not on his countenance, or on the height of his stature; because I have refused him: for the LORD seeth not as man seeth; for man looketh on the outward appearance, but the LORD looketh on the heart."
- I Samuel 16:7

"Then Peter opened his mouth, and said, Of a truth I perceive that God is no respecter of persons: But in every nation he that feareth him, and worketh righteousness, is accepted with him."
- Acts 10:34-35

"There is neither Jew nor Greek, there is neither bond nor free, there is neither male nor female: for ye are all one in Christ Jesus."
- Galatians 3:28

"Prejudices are not complete evils. Prejudices based upon ignorance or uneducated predisposition should always be rejected. Prejudices that produce hate for any man should be despised. However, prejudices based upon principle should be highly regarded and never easily dismissed."
- Thomas Jefferson

"I have a dream that my four little children will one day live in a nation where they will not be judged by the color of their skin but by the content of their character."
- Martin Luther King, Jr.

"Whenever I hear anyone arguing for slavery, I feel a strong impulse to see it tried on him personally."
- Abraham Lincoln

"To prejudge other men's notions before we have looked into them is not to show their darkness but to put out our own eye."
- John Locke

"You cannot shake hands with a clenched fist."
- Golda Meir

"He who knows only his own side of the case knows little of that."
- John Stuart Mill

"It is a test of courage to be in the minority. It is a test of tolerance to be in the majority."
- Jack Murphy

"Some would destroy religion and traditional virtue for the sake of modern tolerance."
- Jack Murphy

"If you want to make beautiful music, you must play the black and the white notes together."
- Richard Nixon

"Prejudice, like the spider, makes everywhere its home. It has neither taste nor choice of place, and all that it requires is room. If the one prepares her food by poisoning it to her palate and her use, the other does the same. Prejudice may be denominated the spider of the mind."
- Thomas Paine

"Abraham Lincoln freed the black man. In many ways, Dr. King freed the white man. How did he accomplish this tremendous feat? Where others— white and black— preached hatred, he taught the principles of love and nonviolence. We can be so thankful that Dr. King raised his mighty eloquence for love and hope rather than for hostility and bitterness. He took the tension he found in our nation, a tension of

injustice, and channeled it for the good of America and all her people."
- Ronald Reagan

"We should all be prejudiced against stupidity and hatred of our fellow man."
- Will Rogers

"Some men, under the notion of weeding out prejudices, eradicate virtue, honesty, and religion."
- Jonathan Swift

"I have no color prejudices nor caste prejudices nor creed prejudices. All I care to know is that a man is a human being, and that is enough for me; he can't be any worse."
- Mark Twain

"Morality is simply the attitude we adopt towards people whom we personally dislike."
- Oscar Wilde

"Prejudice is a weed of the mind."
- American Proverb

"It is hypocrisy to only tolerate those who agree with you."
- American Proverb

"We are each burdened with prejudice; against the poor or the rich, the smart or the slow, the gaunt or the obese. It is natural to develop prejudices. It is noble to rise above them."
- Unknown

"God is color blind in regards to justice, mercy and love."
- Unknown

"Prejudice is a great timesaver. It enables you to form opinions without bothering to get facts."
- Unknown

PRESENCE OF GOD

"And the angel answering said unto him, I am Gabriel, that stand in the presence of God; and am sent to speak unto thee, and to shew thee these glad tidings."
- Luke 1:19

"Immediately therefore I sent to thee; and thou hast well done that thou art come. Now therefore are we all here present before God, to hear all things that are commanded thee of God."
- Acts 10:33

"Do not fear tomorrow. God is already there."
- Corrie ten Boom

"Hence that dread and amazement with which as Scripture uniformly relates holy men were struck and overwhelmed whenever they beheld the presence of God men are never duly touched and impressed with a conviction of their insignificance until they have contrasted themselves with the majesty of God."
- John Calvin

"Having the reality of God's presence is not dependent on our being in a particular circumstance or place, but is only dependent on our determination to keep the Lord before us continually."
- Oswald Chambers

"I throw myself down in my chamber, and I call in and invite God and his angels thither, and when they are there, I neglect God and his angels, for the noise of a fly, for the rattling of a coach, for the whining of a door."
- John Donne

"His center is everywhere, His circumference is nowhere."
- Henery Law

"Hell is not a place of torment because of the presence of fire and everlasting pain. It is a place of torment because it completely lacks the presence of God."

- Jack Murphy

"Security is not the absence of danger, but the presence of God, no matter what the danger."

- Unknown

"We act as though God's presence is here for a while and then gone. God is here always. His presence will never leave us nor forsake us."

- Unknown

PRESIDENTS – See POLITICS

PRIDE

"Pride goeth before destruction, and an haughty spirit before a fall."

- Proverbs 16:18

"'Tis pride, rank pride, and haughtiness of soul: I think the Romans call it stoicism."

- Joseph Addison

"I think half the troubles for which men go slouching in prayer to God are caused by their intolerable pride. Many of our cares are but a morbid way of looking at our privileges. We let our blessings get mouldy, and then call them curses."

- Henry Ward Beecher

"Some people are proud of their humility."

- Henry Ward Beecher

"As for environments, the kingliest being ever born in the flesh lay in a manger."

- Edwin Hubbell Chapin

"Pride, the first peer and president of hell."
- Daniel Defoe

"As soon as there was two there was pride."
- John Donne

"Pride eradicates all vices but itself."
- Ralph Waldo Emerson

"Pride that dines on vanity, sups on contempt."
- Benjamin Franklin

"Vanity and pride sustain so close an alliance as to be often mistaken for each other."
- William Gladstone

"Pride makes us artificial and humility makes us real."
- Thomas Merton

"You have nothing to be proud of. If you are ever used at all, bear in mind that it is God speaking in you, and not you yourself."
- Dwight L. Moody

"God sends no one away empty, except those who are full of themselves."
- Dwight L. Moody

"Sinful pride is the simple love of one's self."
- Jack Murphy

"Pride is both a virtue and a vice. Pride in the accomplishments of others is a virtue. Pride in one's self is a vice."
- Theodore Parker

"Charity feeds the poor, so does pride; charity builds an hospital, so does pride. In this they differ: charity gives her glory to God; pride takes her glory from man."
- Francis Quarles

"Pride is the common forerunner of a fall. It was the devil's sin, and the devil's ruin; and has been, ever since, the devil's stratagem, who, like an expert wrestler, usually gives a man a lift before he gives him a throw."
- Robert South

"John Bunyan had a great dread of spiritual pride; and once, after he had preached a very fine sermon, and his friends crowded round to shake him by the hand, while they expressed the utmost admiration of his eloquence, he interrupted them, saying: 'Ay! you need not remind me of that, for the devil told me of it before I was out of the pulpit!'"
- Robert South

"Jesus reserved his hardest words for the hidden sins of hypocrisy, pride, greed and legalism."
- Philip Yancey

"Pride is the original sin. It is the cause of Satan's fall, and it is the sin today that Satan still uses most."
- Unknown

PRIORITIES – See RESPONSIBILITY

PROPERTY

"The earth is the LORD's, and the fullness thereof; the world, and they that dwell therein."
- Psalm 24:1

"And if ye have not been faithful in that which is another man's, who shall give you that which is your own?"
- Luke 16:12

"By faith he [Abraham] sojourned in the land of promise, as in a strange country, dwelling in tabernacles with Isaac and Jacob, the heirs with him of the same promise: For he looked for a city which hath foundations, whose builder and maker is God."
- Hebrews 11:9-10

"The preservation of the means of knowledge among the lowest ranks is of more importance to the public than all the property of all the rich men in the country."

- John Adams

"So great moreover is the regard of the law for private property, that it will not authorize the least violation of it; no, not even for the general good of the whole community."

- Sir William Blackstone

"Thieves respect property. They merely wish the property to become their property that they may more perfectly respect it."

- G.K. Chesterton

"Property is intended to serve life, and no matter how much we surround it with rights and respect, it has no personal being. It is part of the earth man walks on. It is not man."

- Martin Luther King, Jr.

"Whenever there is a conflict between human rights and property rights, human rights must prevail."

- Abraham Lincoln

"The love of property and consciousness of right and wrong have conflicting places in our organization, which often makes a man's course seem crooked, his conduct a riddle."

- Abraham Lincoln

"Private property was the original source of freedom. It still is its main bulwark."

- Walter Lippmann

"Every man has a property in his own person. This nobody has a right to, but himself."

- John Locke

"So long as the great majority of men are not deprived of either property or honor, they are satisfied."
- Niccolo Machiavelli

"As a man is said to have a right to his property, he may be equally said to have a property in his rights."
- James Madison

"In a real estate man's eye, the most expensive part of the city is where he has a house to sell."
- Will Rogers

"The first man who, having enclosed a piece of ground, bethought himself of saying '*This is mine*,' and found people simple enough to believe him, was the real founder of civil society. From how many crimes, wars and murders, from how many horrors and misfortunes might not anyone have saved mankind, by pulling up the stakes, or filling up the ditch, and crying to his fellows, 'Beware of listening to this impostor; you are undone if you once forget that the fruits of the earth belong to us all, and the earth itself to nobody.'"
- Jean Jacques Rousseau

"As soon as the land of any country has all become private property, the landlords, like all other men, love to reap where they never sowed, and demand a rent even for its natural produce. "
- Adam Smith

"The dichotomy between personal liberties and property rights is a false one. Property does not have rights. People have rights."
- Potter Stewart

"No man's life, liberty or property are safe while the legislature is in session."
- Mark Twain

PROSPERITY

"No one would invest in a company that would show little or no return

for the investment. God is a wise investor in the affairs of this world.
Why do we ask him to make blind investments? God will only invest in
the man or woman who may endeavor to show a return."
- Tommy Barnett

"Watch lest prosperity destroy generosity."
- Henry Ward Beecher

"Economic advance is not the same thing as human progress."
- John Clapham,
- in *A Concise Economic History of Britain*

"Prosperity knits a man to the World. He feels that he is "finding his
place in it", while really it is finding its place in him. His increasing
reputation, his widening circle of acquaintances, his sense of importance,
the growing pressure of absorbing and agreeable work, build up in him a
sense of being really at home in earth which is just what we want."
- Demon Screwtape,
from C.S. Lewis'
The Screwtape Letters

"In general, mankind, since the improvement of cookery, eats twice as
much as nature requires."
- Benjamin Franklin

"We've got the most prosperous culture in human history and we've also
got the biggest spiritual hole in human history."
- Mark Victor Hansen

"Prosperity, in regard of our corrupt inclination to abuse the blessings of
Almighty God, doth prove a thing dangerous to the soul of man."
- Richard Hooker

"There is in every true woman's heart a spark of heavenly fire, which lies
dormant in the broad daylight of prosperity; but which kindles up, and
beams and blazes in the dark hour of adversity."
- Washington Irving

385

"Agriculture, manufactures, commerce and navigation, the four pillars of our prosperity, are the most thriving when left most free to individual enterprise."

- Thomas Jefferson

"Most of us are alcoholics when it comes to material things."

- Rich Nathan

"Luxury... corrupts at once rich and poor, the rich by possession and the poor by covetousness."

- Jean Jacques Rousseau,

"God's work, done in God's way, will never lack God's supplies."

- J. Hudson Taylor

"Prosperities can only be enjoyed by those who fear not at all to lose them."

- Jeremy Taylor

"Many are not able to suffer and endure prosperity; it is like the light of the sun to a weak eye,--glorious indeed in itself, but not proportioned to such an instrument."

- Jeremy Taylor

"More people are sidetracked by serving materialism than by anything else."

- Rick Warren

"But there are those who are conscious before God that they are rich. And, doubtless, some among you are of the number. You have more of the goods of this world than is needful either for yourself or your family. Let each consider for himself. Do your riches increase? Do not you understand that plain expression? Have you not more money, or more of money's worth, than you had ten or twenty years ago, or at this time last year?"

- John Wesley

"Riches and the things that are necessary in life are not evil in themselves. And all of us face cares and troubles in this life. The sin comes in the time and energy we spend in pursuing these things, at the expense of neglecting Christ."
- David Wilkerson

"The prosperity message is an American Gospel invented and spread by rich, American evangelists and pastors."
- David Wilkerson

"Beloved, do not listen to this false gospel. It is satanic. It comes from the heart of men who are light and frivolous, jokesters, greedy for more. Isaiah the prophet, in chapter 56 verse 11, has their number: 'Yea, they are greedy dogs which can never have enough, and they are shepherds that cannot understand: they all look to their own way, every one for his gain, from his quarter.'"
- David Wilkerson

"Men can bear all things except good days."
- Dutch Proverb

"Is the goal of my spiritual walk to bring myself (and family) more comfort in this world or is the goal conformity to Christ?"
- Unknown

PURITY

"Blessed are the pure in heart: for they shall see God."
- Matthew 5:8

"Unto the pure all things are pure: but unto them that are defiled and unbelieving is nothing pure; but even their mind and conscience is defiled."
- Titus 1:15

"Nevertheless I have somewhat against thee, because thou hast left thy first love. Remember therefore from whence thou art fallen, and repent, and do the first works; or else I will come unto thee quickly, and will remove thy candlestick out of his place, except thou repent."

- Revelation 2:4-5

"Purity of heart is the noblest inheritance, and love the fairest ornament, of woman."

- Matthias Claudius

"If a woman be herself pure and noble-hearted, she will come into every circle as a person does into a heated room, who carries with her the freshness of the woods where she has been walking."

- Francis P. Cobbe

"Purity lives and derives its life solely from the Spirit of God."

- Charles Caleb Coulton

"There dwelleth in the sinlessness of youth a sweet rebuke that vice may not endure."

- Emma Catherine Embury

"The smallest speck is seen on snow."

- John Gay

"The way to preserve the peace of the church is to preserve its purity."

- Matthew Henry

"God be thanked that there are some in the world to whose hearts the barnacles will not cling."

- Josiah Gilbert Holland

"As to the pure mind all things are pure, so to the poetic mind all things are poetical."

- Henry Wadsworth Longfellow

"A spirit pure as hers,
  Is always pure, even while it errs:
    As sunshine, broken in the rill,
      Though turned astray, is sunshine still."
                    -    Thomas Moore

"Purity is that beauty that is undefiled in the heart, mind and soul. While
the elements of this world will ravage this outer shell, the heart, mind and
soul still reflect the image and loveliness of God."
                    -    Jack Murphy

"The stream is always purer at its source."
                    -    Blaise Pascal

"You cannot have power until you have first known purity."
                    -    Leonard Ravenhill

"As pure in thought as angels are, to know her was to love her."
                    -    Samuel Rogers

"Come, night; come, Romeo;
  come, thou day in night;
    For thou wilt lie upon the wings of night
      Whiter than new snow upon a raven's back."
                    -    Juliet,
                         in William Shakespeare's *Romeo and Juliet*

"Her form was fresher than the morning rose
  When the dew wets its leaves; unstained and pure
    As is the lily, or the mountain snow."
                    -    James Thomson

"True purity of character is not reflected by what others think of thee. It
is reflected only when all is revealed at the Judgment. There, your
innermost thoughts and deeds are revealed. From those things no man
can hide or make excuses."
                    -    George Whitefield

"While our hearts are pure,
  Our lives are happy and our peace is sure."
                    -    William Winter

"Inner purity results in outer power"
                    -    Unknown

PURPOSE – See DEDICATION; PASSION; SERVICE

Q

QUESTIONS

"And the LORD God called unto Adam, and said unto him, Where art thou?"
- Genesis 3:9

"And Solomon told her all her questions: there was not any thing hid from the king, which he told her not."
- I Kings 10:3

"He that is first in his own cause seemeth just; but his neighbour cometh and questioneth him."
- I Kings 18:17

"He saith unto them, But whom say ye that I am?"
- Matthew 16:15

"Then said Jesus unto the twelve, Will ye also go away?"
- John 6:67

"A prudent question is one half of wisdom."
- Sir Francis Bacon

"A sudden, bold, and unexpected question doth many times surprise a man and lay him open."
- Sir Francis Bacon

"A woman questions the man who loves exactly as a judge questions a criminal. This being so, a flash of the eye, a mere word, an inflection of the voice or a moment's hesitation suffice to expose the fact, betrayal or crime he is attempting to conceal."

- Honore de Balzac

"Animals are such agreeable friends - they ask no questions, they pass no criticisms."

- George Eliot

"The uncreative mind can spot wrong answers, but it takes a very creative mind to spot wrong questions."

- Arthur Jay

"Questions show the mind's range, and answers, its subtlety."

- Joseph Joubert

"Certainty without respect for inquiry is uncertainty."

- Jack Murphy

"Beware of the biased questions of the press. Many of their questions are answered before they are even asked."

- Will Rogers

"To be or not to be that is the question. Whether it is nobler in the mind to suffer the stings and arrows of outrageous fortune, or take up arms against a sea of troubles, and by opposing them, end them."

- William Shakespeare,
  in *Hamlet*

"No question is so difficult to answer as that to which the answer is obvious."

- George Bernard Shaw

"You see things; and you say, 'Why'; But I dream things that never were; and I say, 'Why not?'"

- George Bernard Shaw

"It is foolish to ask questions that the wise cannot answer."
- Oscar Wilde

QUIETNESS

"Be still, and know that I am God."
- Psalm 46:10

"For thus saith the Lord God, the Holy One of Israel; In returning and rest shall ye be saved; in quietness and in confidence shall be your strength: and ye would not."
- Isaiah 30:15

"The heart that is to be filled to the brim with holy joy must be held still."
- George Seaton Bowes

"If we have not quiet in our minds, outward comfort will do no more for us than a golden slipper on a gouty foot."
- John Bunyan

"The grandest operations, both in nature and in grace, are the most silent and imperceptible. The shallow brook babbles in its passage, and is heard by every one; but the coming on of the seasons is silent and unseen. The storm rages and alarms, but its fury is soon exhausted, and its effects are partial and soon remedied; but the dew, though gentle and unheard, is immense in quantity, and the very life of large portions of the earth. And these are pictures of the operations of grace in the church and in the soul."
- Richard Cecil

"A gentleman makes no noise; a lady is serene."
- Ralph Waldo Emerson

"Stillness of person and steadiness of features are signal marks of good breeding. Vulgar persons can't sit still, or, at least, they must work their limbs or features."
- Oliver Wendell Holmes

"In quiet places, reason abounds."
- Adlai Stevenson

"Quiet minds cannot be perplexed or frightened but go on in fortune or misfortune at their own private pace, like a clock during a thunderstorm."
- Robert Louis Stevenson

"Many quiet people are only listening to the loud song in their heart."
- American Proverb

"It is better to keep quiet and be thought of as a fool than to open your mouth and remove all doubt."
- American Proverb

"A quiet conscious sleeps in thunder."
- English Proverb

"Can you keep your peace when the world around you falls apart? This is the mark of a resolute man."
- English Proverb

"Keep quiet and people will think that you are a philosopher."
- Latin Proverb

QUOTATIONS

"Thou shalt not bear false witness against thy neighbor."
- Exodus 20:16

"Behold, every one that useth proverbs shall use this proverb against thee, saying, As is the mother, so is her daughter."
- Ezekiel 16:44

"To appreciate and use correctly a valuable maxim requires a genius; a vital appropriating exercise of mind closely allied to that which first created it."
- William Alger

"I am of opinion that there is no proverb which is not true, because they are all sentences drawn from experience itself, the mother of all the sciences."

- Cervantes

"It is a good thing for an educated man to read books of quotations."

- Winston Churchill

"The wisdom of the wise, and the experience of the ages, may be preserved by quotations."

- Benjamin Disraeli

"Well done is better than well said."

- Benjamin Franklin

"The most valuable of all talents is that of never using two words when one will do."

- Thomas Jefferson

"Maxims are to the intellect what laws are to actions; they do not enlighten, but they guide and direct, and, although themselves blind, are protective."

- Joseph Joubert

"General notions are generally wrong."

- Mary Wortley Montagu

"Quotes are like the seeds that are planted deeply into the heart of a man. They can bear great fruit if properly nourished by the elements of sunlight, water and observation."

- Jack Murphy

"Wise men make proverbs, but fools misquote them."

- Will Rogers

"Actions speak louder than words."

- Theodore Roosevelt

"Copy from one, it's plagiarism; copy from two, it's research."
- Wilson Mizner

"Information is the oxygen of the modern age. It seeps through the walls topped by barbed wire; it wafts across the electrified borders."
- Ronald Reagan

"If a student submits a paper that is good enough to be published, maybe it has."
- Academic Proverb

"When in doubt, leave it out."
- English Proverb

"A half truth is a whole lie."
- Yiddish Proverb

R

RACE – See PREDJUDICE

READING

"And the Lord answered me, and said, Write the vision, and make it plain upon tables, that he may run that readeth it."
- Habakkuk 2:2

"And he arose and went: and, behold, a man of Ethiopia, an eunuch of great authority under Candace queen of the Ethiopians, who had the charge of all her treasure, and had come to Jerusalem for to worship, Was returning, and sitting in his chariot read Esaias the prophet. Then the Spirit said unto Philip, Go near, and join thyself to this chariot. And Philip ran thither to him, and heard him read the prophet Esaias, and said, Understandest thou what thou readest?"
- Acts 8:27-30

"Ye are our epistle written in our hearts, known and read of all men: Forasmuch as ye are manifestly declared to be the epistle of Christ ministered by us, written not with ink, but with the Spirit of the living God; not in tables of stone, but in fleshy tables of the heart."
- II Corinthians 3:2-3

"Till I come, give attendance to reading, to exhortation, to doctrine."
- I Timothy 4:13

"To choose a good book, look in an inquisitor's prohibited list."
- John Aikin

"Some books are to be tasted, others to be swallowed, and some few to be chewed and digested."
- Sir Francis Bacon

"Books are not made for furniture, but there is nothing else that so beautifully furnishes a house."
- Henry Ward Beecher

"No man can be called friendless who has God and the companionship of good books."
- Elizabeth Barrett Browning

"The worth of a book is to be measured by what you can carry away from it."
- James Bryce

"To read without reflecting is like eating without digesting."
- Edmund Burke

"God be thanked for books! they are the voices of the distant and the dead, and make us heirs of the spiritual life of past ages."
- William Ellery Channing

"The mere brute pleasure of reading - the sort of pleasure a cow must have in grazing."
- Lord Chesterfield

"There is a great deal of difference between an eager man who wants to read a book and a tired man who wants a book to read."
- G.K. Chesterton

"A man may as well expect to grow stronger by always eating as wiser by always reading."
- Jeremy Collier

"A good book has no ending."
- R. D. Cumming

"These are not books, lumps of lifeless paper, but *minds* alive on the shelves."
- Gilbert Highet

"You are the same today as you will be in five years, except for two things: the people you meet and the books you read."
- Charlie Jones

"Books serve to show a man that those original thoughts of his aren't very new after all."
- Abraham Lincoln

"A house without books is like a room without windows."
- Heinrich Mann

"A book is the only place in which you can examine a fragile thought without breaking it, or explore an explosive idea without fear it will go off in your face. It is one of the few havens remaining where a man's mind can get both provocation and privacy."
- Edward P. Morgan

"Never fear reading something that will challenge your convictions. Books will either strengthen your beliefs or cause you to consider other possibilities."
- Jack Murphy

"Always read something that will make you look good if you die in the middle of it."
- P.J. O'Rourke

"I divide all readers into two classes; those who read to remember and those who read to forget."
- William Lyon Phelps

"Reading is to the mind what exercise is to the body."
- Richard Steele

"The man who doesn't read has no advantage over the man who can't read."

> - Mark Twain

"Nothing is worth reading that does not require an alert mind."

> - Charles Dudley Warner

"Books are lighthouses erected in the great sea of time."

> - Edwin Percy Whipple

"Medicine for the soul."

> - Inscription over the door of the Library at Thebes

"He who lends a book is an idiot. He who returns the book is more of an idiot."

> - Arab Proverb

"A book is like a garden carried in the pocket."

> - Chinese Proverb

"To read a book for the first time is to make an acquaintance with a new friend; to read it for a second time is to meet an old one."

> - Chinese Proverb

"If 'eyes are the windows to the soul,' then books are the windows of the heart of an author."

> - Unknown

"A good book is rarely dusty."

> - Unknown

REPENTANCE

"Bring forth therefore fruits meet for repentance."

> - Matthew3:8

"For godly sorrow worketh repentance to salvation not to be repented of:
but the sorrow of the world worketh death."
-    II Corinthians 7:10

"The Lord is not slack concerning his promise, as some men count
slackness; but is longsuffering to us-ward, not willing that any should
perish, but that all should come to repentance."
-    II Peter 3:9

"Any concept of grace that makes us feel more comfortable sinning is not
biblical grace. God's grace never encourages us to live in sin, on the
contrary, it empowers us to say no to sin and yes to truth."
-    Randy Alcorn

"Suppose I should call out a sinner by name -- one of the sinners of this
congregation, a son of pious parents -- and should call up the father also.
I might say, Is this your son? Yes. What testimony can you bear about this
son of yours? I have endeavored to teach him all the ways of the Lord.
Son, what can you say? I know my duty. I have heard it a thousand times.
I know I ought to repent, but I never would.

Oh! if we understood this matter in all its bearings, it would fill every
bosom with consternation and grief. How would our bowels hum and
heave as a volcano! There would be one universal outcry of anguish and
terror at the awful guilt and fearful doom of such a sinner!"
-    Charles Finney

"We have a strange illusion that mere time cancels sin. But mere time
does nothing either to the fact or to the guilt of a sin."
-    C. S. Lewis

"Repentance is not saying 'I'm sorry!' It is not enough to merely be sorry
for your sins. It is loving God and despising your sins enough to stop
committing them."
-    Leonard Ravenhill

"A person repents when he comes to the place where he discovers that the will of God is the government of his life and the glory of God is the reason for his life. He only has repented who has changed his mind about his reason for being."

- Paris Reidhead

"Evangelical repentance is repentance of sin as sin: not of this sin nor of that, but of the whole mass. We repent of the sin of our nature as well as the sin of our practice. We bemoan sin within us and without us. We repent of sin itself as being an insult to God. Anything short of this is a mere surface repentance, and not a repentance which reaches to the bottom of the mischief. Repentance of the evil act, and not of the evil heart, is like men pumping water out of a leaky vessel, but forgetting to stop the leak. Some would dam up the stream, but leave the fountain still flowing; they would remove the eruption from the skin, but leave the disease in the flesh."

- Charles Spurgeon

"How else but through a broken heart may Lord Christ enter in?"

- Oscar Wilde

"The cross is the cost of my forgiveness."

- Unknown

REPUTATION

"Let not mercy and truth forsake thee: bind them about thy neck; write them upon the table of thine heart: So shalt thou find favour and good understanding in the sight of God and man."

- Proverbs 3:3-4

"Debate thy cause with thy neighbor himself; and discover not a secret to another: Lest he that heareth it put thee to shame, and thine infamy turn not away."

- Proverbs 25:9-10

"Let this mind be in you, which was also in Christ Jesus: Who, being in the form of God, thought it not robbery to be equal with God: But made

himself of no reputation, and took upon him the form of a servant, and was made in the likeness of men: And being found in fashion as a man, he humbled himself, and became obedient unto death, even the death of the cross. Wherefore God also hath highly exalted him, and given him a name which is above every name: That at the name of Jesus every knee should bow, of things in heaven, and things in earth, and things under the earth; And that every tongue should confess that Jesus Christ is Lord, to the glory of God the Father."
- Philippians 2:5-11

"Time never fails to bring every exalted reputation to a strict scrutiny."
- Fisher Ames

"A reputation for a thousand years may depend upon the conduct of a single moment."
- Ernest Bramah

"A good name is better than bags of gold."
- Cervantes

"An honest reputation is within the reach of all men; they obtain it by social virtues, and by doing their duty. This kind of reputation, it is true, is neither brilliant nor startling, but it is often the most useful for happiness."
- Charles Duclos

"What you seem to be, be really."
- Benjamin Franklin

"Glass, China, and Reputation, are easily crack'd, and never well mended."
- Benjamin Franklin

"A lost good name is ne'er retriev'd."
- John Gay

"A reputation once broken may possibly be repaired, but the world will always keep their eyes on the spot where the crack was."
- Joseph Hall

"How many people live on the reputation of the reputation they might have made!"

-    Oliver Wendell Holmes

"Many a man's reputation would not know his character if they met on the street."

-    Elbert Hubbard

"Those who desire but fail to destroy your character will turn their cravings upon the next best thing: your reputation. If they cannot make you into an evil person, they will at least try to make others think that you are an evil."

-    Jack Murphy

"Reputation is what men and women think of us; character is what God and angels know of us."

-    Thomas Paine

"The evil that men do lives after them. The good is oft interned with the bones. So let it be with Caesar!"

-    Mark Anthony,
  in Shakespeare's
  Julius Caesar

"If you can't get rid of the skeleton in your closet, you'd best teach it to dance."

-    George Bernard Shaw

"The way to gain a good reputation is to endeavor to be what you desire to appear."

-    Socrates

"He that tears away a man's good name tears his flesh from his bones, and, by letting him live, gives him only a cruel opportunity of feeling his misery, of burying his better part, and surviving himself."

-    Robert South

"Associate with men of good quality, if you esteem your own reputation; for it is better to be alone than in bad company."
-    George Washington

"Reputation is created in a moment. Character is developed over a lifetime. Reputation grows like a weed. Character is developed over a lifetime."
-    Bill Wilson

"Reputation and character are not the same. Reputation is often based upon gossip and perception. Character is based upon understanding."
-    Ray Zimmerman

"Only a fool bases their opinions upon the reputation of a man."
-    Chinese Proverb

"It is better to die with a good name than to live with a bad one."
-    English Proverb

"Your reputation may be tarnished, but your character can still be gold."
-    English Proverb

"Tell me who your friends are, and I will tell you who you are."
-    Spanish Proverb

RESPONSIBILITY

"The soul that sinneth, it shall die. The son shall not bear the iniquity of the father, neither shall the father bear the iniquity of the son: the righteousness of the righteous shall be upon him, and the wickedness of the wicked shall be upon him."
-    Ezekiel 18:20

"Then shall he answer them, saying, Verily I say unto you, Inasmuch as ye did it not to one of the least of these, ye did it not to me."
-    Matthew 25:45

"Jesus said unto them, If ye were blind, ye should have no sin: but now ye say, We see; therefore your sin remaineth."
- John 9:41

"So then every one of us shall give account of himself to God."
- Romans 14:12

"I have planted, Apollos watered; but God gave the increase. So then neither is he that planteth any thing, neither he that watereth; but God that giveth the increase."
- I Corinthians 3:6-7

"Work out your own salvation with fear and trembling."
- Philippians 2:12

"But if any provide not for his own, and especially for those of his own house, he hath denied the faith, and is worse than an infidel."
- I Timothy 5:8

"Responsibility: A detachable burden easily shifted to the shoulders of God, Fate, Fortune, Luck or one's neighbor."
- Ambrose Bierce

"Action springs not from thought, but from a readiness for responsibility."
- Dietrich Bonhoeffer

"The best years of your life are the ones in which you decide your problems are your own. You do not blame them on your mother, the ecology, or the president. You realize that you control your own destiny."
- Albert Ellis

"Set priorities with sooner being better than perfect."
- Lou Gerstner

"This generation of Christians is responsible for this generation of souls."
- Keith Green

"With every civil right there has to be a corresponding civil obligation."
- Edison Haines

"Responsibility is a tremendous engine in a free government."
- Thomas Jefferson

"In the long history of the world, only a few generations have been granted the role of defending freedom in its hour of maximum danger. I do not shrink from this responsibility-I welcome it."
- John F. Kennedy

"Freedom is not the right to do what we want, but what we ought."
- Abraham Lincoln

"You cannot escape the responsibility of tomorrow by evading it today."
- Abraham Lincoln

"You are not only responsible for what you say, but also for what you do not say."
- Martin Luther

"Responsibility educates."
- Wendell Phillips

"Most of us can read the writing on the wall; though, we just assume it's addressed to someone else."
- Mark Twain

"If you want children to keep their feet on the ground, put some responsibility on their shoulders."
- Abigail Van Buren

"Few things help an individual more than to place responsibility upon him, and to let him know that you trust him."
- Booker T. Washington

"If you mess up, 'fess up.'"
- American Proverb

"When you blame others, you give up your power to change."
- Japanese Proverb

"Creativity without implementation is irresponsibility. Ideas are nothing without execution."
- Unknown

REVIVAL

"Revivals begin with God's own people; the Holy Spirit touches their heart anew, and gives them new fervor and compassion, and zeal, new light and life, and when He has thus come to you, He next goes forth to the valley of dry bones...Oh, what responsibility this lays on the Church of God! If you grieve Him away from yourselves, or hinder His visit, then the poor perishing world suffers sorely!"
- Andrew A. Bonar

"So tremendous has been this sense of an awareness of God, that I have known men out in the fields, so overcome that they were prostrate upon the ground."
- Duncan Campbell

"The assembly were in tears while the Word was preached; some weeping sorrows and distress, others with joy and love, others with concern for the souls of their neighbors."
- Jonathan Edwards

"Revival is no more a miracle than a crop of wheat. Revival comes from heaven when heroic souls enter the conflict determined to win or die – or if need be, to win and die! 'The kingdom of heaven suffereth violence, and the violent take it by force."
- Charles Finney

"Revival is a renewed conviction of sin and repentance, followed by an intense desire to live in obedience to God. It is giving up one's will to God in deep humility."
- Charles Finney

"Nothing but a revival of religion can preserve such a Church from annihilation. A Church declining in this way cannot continue to exist without a revival. If it receives new members, they will, for the most part, be made up of ungodly persons. Without revivals there will not ordinarily be as many persons converted as will die off in a year. There have been Churches in this country where the members have died off, and, since there were no revivals to convert others in their place, the Church has 'run out,' and the organization has been dissolved."
- Charles Finney

"Revival comes from heaven when heroic souls enter the conflict determined to win or die-or if need be, to win and die! 'The kingdom of heaven suffereth violence, and the violent take it by force.'"
- Charles G. Finney

"You can do more than pray after you have prayed, but you cannot do more than pray until you have prayed."
- A. J. Gordon

"Sometimes your medicine bottle has on it, "Shake well before using." That is what God has to do with some of His people. He has to shake them well before they are ever usable."
- Vance Havner

"We sometimes talk about the price of revival, and we need to be very careful as to what we mean when we speak like this. We may place that price so high that we put revival right beyond the reach of the ordinary run of mortals. Maybe that is our way of attempting to justify God, that He has not yet, apparently, given the revival His people need. But that is a wrong done to God and a cruelty done to his church. There is without doubt a price to be paid for revival, but it is not of necessity the long nights of prayer or excruciating sacrifices, but of simply humbling pride to repent of sin."
- Roy Hession

"Before the great revival in Gallneukirchen broke out, Martin Boos spent hours and days and often nights in lonely agonies of intercession. Afterwards, when he preached, his words were as flame, and the hearts of the people as grass."

- D. M. McIntyre

"Revival cannot be organized, but we can set our sails to catch the wind from heaven when God chooses to blow upon His people once again."

- G. Campbell Morgan

"The evangelization of the world depends first of all upon a revival of prayer. Deeper than the need for men - aye, deep down at the bottom of our spiritless life, is the need for the forgotten secret of prevailing, world-wide prayer."

- Andrew Murray

"The coming revival must begin with a great revival of prayer. It is in the closet, with the door shut, that the sound of abundance of rain will first be heard. An increase of secret prayer with ministers will be the sure harbinger of blessing."

- Andrew Murray

"God always visits his people when they reach the point of desperation."

- Stephen Olford

"Revival is the inrush of the Spirit into the body that threatens to become a corpse."

- D. M. Panton

"From the day of Pentecost, there has been not one great spiritual awakening in any land which has not begun in a union of prayer, though only two or three. No such outward, upward movement has continued after such prayer meetings declined."

- A. T. Pierson

"The reason revival tarries, is because men do not."

- Leonard Ravenhill

"Some in the Church would not recognize a revival if they were sitting in the middle of it."
- Leonard Ravenhill

"The only reason we don't have revival is because we are willing to live without it!"
- Leonard Ravenhill

"Hannah prayed, *'Give me a child or I die!'* This dark generation must pray with the same audacity, *'Give me revival or we die!'*"
- Leonard Ravenhill

"God pity us that after years of writing, using mountains of paper and rivers of ink, exhausting flashy terminology about the biggest revival meetings in history, we are still faced with gross corruption in every nation, as well as with the most prayerless church age since Pentecost."
- Leonard Ravenhill

"In the Irish Revival of 1859, people became so weak that they could not get back to their homes. Men and women would fall by the wayside and would be found hours later pleading with God to save their souls. They felt that they were slipping into hell and that nothing else in life mattered but to get right with God... To them eternity meant everything. Nothing else was of any consequence. They felt that if God did not have mercy on them and save them, they were doomed for all time to come."
- Oswald J. Smith

"We need a Heaven-sent revival,
a burning fire from on high,
  A purifying passion and a
forsaking of our stubborn pride.
  We need a vision of eternity,
of Hell and the Judgement Day,
  A fervent love for our Savior,
that will gladly serve and obey.
  We need a Pentecostal purging
and a breaking deep within,
  A vision of God Almighty

and a river of tears for our nations sin.
   We need a Heaven-sent revival,
a burning fire set ablaze.
   Yet, we'll never see such glory,
until the Church begins to pray."
                              -    David Smithers

"A man can not lead others where he is not willing to go himself.
Therefore, beware of the prayerless church leader who no longer readily
admits his own need for more of the person and power of Jesus Christ.
Only a seeking, praying heart can truly encourage spiritual HUNGER in
others!"
                              -    David Smithers

"Oh, Brethren, it is sickening work to think of your cushioned seats, your
chants, your anthems, your choirs, your organs, your gowns, and your
bands, and I know not what besides, all made to be instruments of
religious luxury, if not of pious dissipation, while ye need far more to be
stirred up and incited to holy ardor for the propagation of the truth as it is
in Jesus."
                              -    Charles H. Spurgeon

"Revival is the people of God constrained, gripped, overmastered, and
overwhelmed by the love of Christ, so that they are feverishly restless to
win souls for Christ."
                              -    James A. Stewart

"Revival is the recognition of the ministry of insignificant members of the
body, and deliverance from idol worship of the more prominent members
who are in the limelight."
                              -    James A. Stewart

"Revival is the beauty of holiness adorning the saints.
Revival is torrents of living water flowing out of the individual believer.
Revival is the Church of God as a conquering army putting to rout the
hosts of hell.
Revival is Zion travailing in spiritual childbirth.
Revival is the heathen saying, "The Lord hath done great things for

them." (Psa. 126:2)

Revival is living the Christ life in the home.

Revival is the child of God desperately in love with his glorious Savior and Lord.

Revival is the people of God living in the power of an aggrieved, unquenched Spirit.

Revival is the saints of God agonizing on behalf of lost souls going to hell.

Revival is the assemblies of God manifesting the oneness of the membership in the mystical, supernatural body of Christ, delivered from denominational bigotry."

- James A. Stewart

"I contend that whatever does not raise the moral standard of the church or community has not been a revival from God."

- A. W. Tozer

"I weep when I see these videos that are sent to me from all over the country. Whole groups of bodies are jerking out of control, falling on the floor, laughing hysterically, staggering around like mindless drunkards. Anything that cannot be found in Scripture has to be rejected outright...and totally rejected."

- David Wilkerson

"Revival comes in spite of the evangelist."

- Ravi Zacharias

RIGHTEOUSNESS – See HOLINESS

ROMANCE

"And Jacob served seven years for Rachel; and they seemed unto him but a few days, for the love he had to her."

- Genesis 29:20

"Keep thy heart with all diligence; for out of it are the issues of life."

- Proverbs 4:23

"Let him kiss me with the kisses of his mouth: for thy love is better than wine."
- Song of Solomon 1:2

"My beloved is mine, and I am his."
- Song of Solomon 2:16

"Set me as a seal upon thine heart, as a seal upon thine arm: for love is strong as death; jealousy is cruel as the grave: the coals thereof are coals of fire, which hath a most vehement flame."
- Song of Solomon 8:6

"Many waters cannot quench love, neither can the floods drown it: if a man would give all the substance of his house for love, it would utterly be contemned."
- Song of Solomon 8:7

"It is with our passions as it is with fire and water, they are good servants, but bad masters."
- Aesop

"She had been forced into prudence in her youth, she learned romance as she grew older - the natural sequence of an unnatural beginning."
- Jane Austen

"Love cannot endure indifference. It needs to be wanted. Like a lamp, it needs to be fed out of the oil of another's heart, or its flame burns low."
- Henry Ward Beecher

"She walks in beauty,
Like the night of cloudless climes and starry skies;
And all that's best of dark and bright
Meet in her aspect and her eyes."
- Lord Byron

"Romance has been elegantly defined as the offspring of fiction and love."
- Benjamin Disraeli

"Love reckons hours for months, and days for years; and every little absence is an age."
- 　John Dryden

"A few hours ago I discharged my last duty as King and Emperor, and now that I have been succeeded by my brother, the Duke of York, my first words must be to declare my allegiance to him. This I do with all my heart. You all know the reasons which have impelled me to renounce the throne. But I want you to understand that in making up my mind I did not forget the country or the empire, which, as Prince of Wales and lately as King, I have for twenty-five years tried to serve. But you must believe me when I tell you that I have found it impossible to carry the heavy burden of responsibility and to discharge my duties as King as I would wish to do without the help and support of the woman I love."
- 　King Edward VIII
　　upon abdicating his throne in order to marry
　　American Wallis Simpson

"Gravitation is not responsible for people falling in love. How on earth are you ever going to explain in terms of chemistry and physics so important a biological phenomenon as first love?"
- 　Albert Einstein

"Immature love says: 'I love you because I need you.'
Mature love says: 'I need you because I love you.'"
- 　Erich Fromm

"Love is that condition in which the happiness of another person is essential to your own."
- 　Robert Heinlein

"I think we dream so we dont have to be apart so long. If we're in each others dreams, we can be together all the time."
- 　Thomas Hobbes

"And what's romance? Usually, a nice little tale where you have everything as you like it, where rain never wets your jacket and gnats never bite your nose, and it's always daisy-time."

- D. H. Lawrence

"In the arithmetic of love, one plus one equals everything, and two minus one equals nothing."

- Mignon McLaughlin

"Romance is that burning desire and unquenchable fire to be one with another. It is Adam longing for his rib and his rib longing to return to Adam."

- Jack Murphy

"So dear I love him that with him,
All deaths I could endure.
Without him, live no life."

- Juliet, in Shakespeare's *Romeo and Juliet*

"Love seems the swiftest, but it is the slowest of all growths. No man or woman really knows what perfect love is until they have been married a quarter of a century."

- Mark Twain

"He must have a truly romantic nature, for he weeps when there is nothing at all to weep about."

- Oscar Wilde

"A romantic heart is forever young."

- Greek Proverb

S

SACRIFICE (See DEDICATION)

SADNESS

"Wherefore the king said unto me, Why is thy countenance sad, seeing thou art not sick? this is nothing else but sorrow of heart. Then I was very sore afraid, And said unto the king, Let the king live for ever: why should not my countenance be sad, when the city, the place of my fathers' sepulchres, lieth waste, and the gates thereof are consumed with fire?"
- Nehemiah 2:2-3

"The sacrifices of God are a broken spirit: a broken and a contrite heart, O God, thou wilt not despise."
- Psalm 51:17

"He is despised and rejected of men; a man of sorrows, and acquainted with grief: and we hid as it were our faces from him; he was despised, and we esteemed him not."
- Isaiah 53:3

"For godly sorrow worketh repentance to salvation not to be repented of: but the sorrow of the world worketh death."
- II Corinthians 7:10

"Religion prescribes to every miserable man the means of bettering his condition; nay, it shows him that the bearing of his afflictions as he ought to do, will naturally end in the removal of them."
- Joseph Addison

"Sorrow makes men sincere. Sorrow is Mount Sinai. If one will, one may go up and talk with God, face to face."
- Henry Ward Beecher

"We may learn from children how large a part of our grievances is imaginary. But the pain is just as real."
- Christian Nevell Bovee

"Of all tales 'tis the saddest – and more sad, Because it makes us smile."
- Lord Byron

"Sorrow is knowledge; they who know thee most must mourn the deepest over the fatal truth; the tree of knowledge is not that of life."
- Lord Byron

"It is those who make the least display of their sorrow who mourn the deepest."
- Edwin Hubbell Chapin

"The sorrow for the dead is the only sorrow from which we refuse to be divorced. Every other wound we seek to heal, every other affliction to forget; but this wound we consider it a duty to keep open, this affliction we cherish and brood over in solitude."
- Washington Irving

"To ease another's heartache is to forget one's own."
- Abraham Lincoln

"A feeling of sadness and longing,
 That is not akin to pain,
  And resembles sorrow only
   As the mist resembles the rain."
- Henry Wadsworth Longfellow

"Believe me, every man has his secret sorrows which the world knows not; and oftentimes we call a man cold when he is only sad."
- Henry Wadsworth Longfellow

"Dim sadness did not spare that time celestial visages; yet, mixed with pity, violated not their bliss."
- John Milton

"Earth hath no sorrow that heaven cannot heal."
- Thomas Moore

"I have hurt more than any man should ever hurt. I have pained more than any man should ever be pained. And I have still also offended, hurt and pained others. Yet Christ has hurt even more. He has pained even more. And yet He still understands our faults and forgives our offenses. This is incomprehensible grace!"
- Jack Murphy

"Personal sorrows and failures help us to empathize with others."
- Jack Murphy

"They praise my rustling show, and never see my heart is breaking for a little love."
- Christina Rossetti

"Those things which were hard to bear are sweet to remember."
- Seneca

"Any mind that is capable of a real sorrow is capable of good."
- Harriet Beecher Stowe

"It takes your enemy and your friend, working together, to hurt you to the heart: the one to slander you and the other to get the news to you."
- Mark Twain

"There can be no rainbow without a cloud and a storm."
- John Vincent

"'Tis impious in a good man to be sad."
- Edward Young

"It is not your outlook but your 'uplook' that counts!"
-     Christian Proverb

SALVATION

"The LORD is my strength and song, and he is become my salvation: he is my God, and I will prepare him an habitation; my father's God, and I will exalt him."
-     Exodus 15:2

"Behold, God is my salvation; I will trust, and not be afraid: for the LORD JEHOVAH is my strength and my song; he also is become my salvation. Therefore with joy shall ye draw water out of the wells of salvation."
-     Isaiah 12:2-3

"And take the helmet of salvation, and the sword of the Spirit, which is the word of God."
-     Ephesians 6:17

"Wherefore, my beloved, as ye have always obeyed, not as in my presence only, but now much more in my absence, work out your own salvation with fear and trembling."
-     Philippians 2:12

"I commit my soul to the mercy of God, through our Lord and Saviour Jesus Christ, and exhort my dear children humbly to try to guide themselves by the teachings of the New Testament."
-     Last Will and Testament of
      Charles Dickens

"It is time that we all understood this subject fully, and appreciated all its bearings. It is no doubt true, that however moral our children may be, they are more guilty than any other sinners under heaven, if they live in sin, and will not yield to the light under which they live. We may be perhaps congratulating ourselves on their fair morality; but if we saw their case in all its real bearings, our souls would groan with agony -- our bowels would be all liquid with anguish -- our very hearts within us would

heave as if volcanic fires were kindled there -- so deep a sense should we
have of their fearful guilt and of the awful doom they incur in denying the
Lord that bought them and setting at naught a known salvation. Oh! if we
ever pray, we should pour out our prayers for our offspring as if nothing
could ever satisfy us or stay our importunity, but the blessings of a full
salvation realized in their souls."

- Charles Finney

"But what an mortal man do to secure his own salvation? Mortal man can
do just what God bids him do. He can repent and believe. He can arise
and follow Christ as Matthew did."

- Washington Gladden

"Salvation is a helmet, not a nightcap."

- Vance Havner

"I have noticed even people who claim everything is predestined, and that
we can do nothing to change it, look before they cross the road."

- Stephen Hawking

"None shall be saved by Christ but those only who work out their own
salvation while God is working in them by His truth and His Holy Spirit.
We cannot do without God; and God will not do without us."

- Matthew Henry

"The very blood of God Himself was the price of your salvation. It was
willingly purchased by His love for you and me."

- Jack Murphy

"The condition of salvation is that kind of belief in Jesus Christ which
authenticates itself in repentance for the past and in an amendment of life
for the future."

- Louis Noble

"If I was to ask you tonight if you were saved? Do you say 'Yes, I am
saved.' When? 'Oh so and so preached, I got baptized and...' Are you
saved?
What are you saved from, hell?

Are you saved from bitterness?
Are you saved from lust?
Are you saved from cheating?
Are you saved from lying?
Are you saved from bad manners?
Are you saved from rebellion against your parents?
Come on, what are you saved from?"

-   Leonard Ravenhill

"I commend my soul into the hands of God, my Creator, hoping and assuredly believing, through the only merits of Jesus Christ my Saviour, to be made partaker of life everlasting."

-   Last Will and Testament of William Shakespeare

"What hinders that you should be a child of God? Is not salvation free? Is not the invitation to it flung out to you on every page of the New Testament? Is not Christ offered to you in all His offices? and are you not welcome to all His benefits if you want them? Is not the Holy Spirit promised to them that ask Him? Nothing can hinder you from being a Christian, but your own worldly, selfish, proud, obstinate, unworthy, and self-righteous heart."

-   Ichabod Spencer

"Reply implicitly upon the old, old gospel. You need no other nets when you fish for men; those your Master has given you are strong enough to hold the little ones. Spread these nets and no others, and you need not fear the fulfillment of His word, 'I will make you fishers of men.'"

-   Charles H. Spurgeon

"Salvation is free…but it didn't come cheap."

-   Christian Proverb

SCIENCE

"Then the LORD answered Job out of the whirlwind, and said, 'Who is this that darkeneth counsel by words without knowledge? Gird up now thy loins like a man; for I will demand of thee, and answer thou me.

Where wast thou when I laid the foundations of the earth? declare, if thou hast understanding.'"
-   Job 38:1-4

"And I gave my heart to seek and search out by wisdom concerning all things that are done under heaven: this sore travail hath God given to the sons of man to be exercised therewith."
-   Ecclesiastes 1:13

"Now when Jesus was born in Bethlehem of Judaea in the days of Herod the king, behold, there came wise men from the east to Jerusalem, Saying, 'Where is he that is born King of the Jews? for we have seen his star in the east, and are come to worship him.'"
-   Matthew 2:1-2

"O Timothy, keep that which is committed to thy trust, avoiding profane and vain babblings, and oppositions of science falsely so called."
-   I Timothy 6:20

"We have grasped the mystery of the atom and rejected the sermon on the mount."
-   Omar Bradley

"No one should approach the temple of science with the soul of a money changer."
-   Thomas Browne

"Through all God's works there runs a beautiful harmony. The remotest truth in His universe is linked to that which lies nearest the throne."
-   Edwin Hubbell Chapin

"Science is a wonderful thing if one does not have to earn one's living at it."
-   Albert Einstein

"Science can only ascertain what *is*, but not what *should be*, and outside of its domain value judgments of all kinds remain necessary."
-   Albert Einstein

"Science without religion is lame, religion without science is blind."
-    Albert Einstein

"Science does not know its debt to imagination."
-    Ralph Waldo Emerson

"My worldly faculties are slipping away day by day. Happy it is for all of us that the true good does not lie in them. As they ebb, may they leave us as little children trusting in the Father of Mercies and accepting His unspeakable gift. I bow before Him who is Lord of all."
-    Michael Faraday

"Equipped with his five senses, man explores the universe around him and calls the adventure Science."
-    Edwin Hubble

"The man of science has learned to believe in justification, not by faith, but by verification."
-    Thomas Huxley

"When we try to pick out anything by itself, we find it is tied to everything else in the universe."
-    John Muir

"Science often builds a house of concrete upon the movable sands of theory. God, however, built the Laws of Nature and Science out of nothing. As the supreme Author of such laws, He is neither confined nor restricted by them."
-    Jack Murphy

"Many men will stand before God in Judgment and argue that science just made more sense. Nevertheless, God will remind them that Nature reflected His glory, which these men attributed to pure chance."
-    Jack Murphy

"Skepticism is a virtue in all things – including matters of religion and doctrine. It is acceptable in everything except our intimacy with God. No man would dare look God in the eye and ask Him to 'prove' His

existence or reasoning. No one could prove that God exists except for
God. No one is so wise as to question the rationale for His creation.
Our faith in God must be large enough to realize that:

1. He created the Natural Laws; and,
2. He Himself is not confined to them; and,
3. Man cannot understand His ways, for they are 'higher than ours.'
   We can merely observe."

> \- Jack Murphy

"I do not know what I may appear to the world; but to myself I seem to
have been only like a boy playing on the seashore, and diverting myself in
now and then finding of a smoother pebble or a prettier shell than
ordinary, whilst the great ocean of truth lay all undiscovered before me."

> \- Sir Isaac Newton

"Science is built up of facts, as a house is built of stones; but an
accumulation of facts is no more a science than a heap of stones is a
house."

> \- Henri Poincaré

"Science is the great antidote to the poison of enthusiasm and
superstition."

> \- Adam Smith

"A man gazing at the stars is proverbially at the mercy of the clouds in the
night."

> \- Alexander Smith

"Research is what I'm doing when I don't know what I'm doing."

> \- Wernher Von Braun

"We can lick gravity, but sometimes the paperwork is overwhelming."

> \- Wernher Von Braun

"Science is not the enemy of religion; rather, science is the enemy of
superstition."

> \- English Proverb

"Only one thing is certain – that is, nothing is certain. If this statement is true, it is also false."

- Greek Proverb

"In the beginning, God created 'Atom and Eve.' He created 'Atom' because we are all made of atoms. He created 'Eve' because we are all on the eve of eternity."

- Unknown

"Scientists have theorized both the beginning and ending of the universe. They have theorized the entire evolution of the Earth. They have theorized the existence of unlimited parallel universes. Yet they still can't figure out why there are males and females. And they still can't figure out where all of this dark matter is."

- Unknown

SECRETS

"The secret things belong unto the Lord our God: but those things which are revealed belong unto us and to our children for ever, that we may do all the words of this law."

- Deuteronomy 29:29

"A talebearer revealeth secrets: but he that is of a faithful spirit concealeth the matter."

- Proverbs 11:13

"For nothing is secret, that shall not be made manifest; neither any thing hid, that shall not be known and come abroad."

- Luke 8:17

"For the king knoweth of these things, before whom also I speak freely: for I am persuaded that none of these things are hidden from him; for this thing was not done in a corner."

- Acts 26:26

"In the day when God shall judge the secrets of men by Jesus Christ according to my gospel."

-     Romans 2:16

"There are some occasions when a man must tell half his secret, in order to conceal the rest."

-     Lord Chesterfield

"None are so fond of secrets as those who do not mean to keep them."

-     Charles Caleb Colton

"I find she loves him because she hides it. Love teaches cunning even to innocence; and when he gets possession, his first work is to dig deep within a heart, and there lie hid, and like a miser in the dark, feast alone."

-     John Dryden

"Three may keep a secret, if two of them are dead."

-     Benjamin Franklin

"To whom you betray your secret you sell your liberty."

-     Benjamin Franklin

"To keep your secret is wisdom; but to expect others to keep it is folly."

-     Oliver Wendell Holmes

"Thou hast betrayed thy secret as a bird betrays her nest, by striving to conceal it."

-     Henry Wadsworth Longfellow

"A gossip will shout a secret using a still, small voice."

-     Jack Murphy

"Beware of those who always search for skeletons in the closet. They will find them even if the closet is clean."

-     Jack Murphy

"You can tell the political leanings of the media by their willingness to publish dirt on one politician and their ability to keep such dirt a secret regarding another."

- Jack Murphy

"It is wise not to seek a secret; and honest, not to reveal one."

- William Penn

"If you can't get rid of the skeleton in your closet, you'd best teach it to dance."

- George Bernard Shaw

"Secrecy is the chastity of friendship."

- Jeremy Taylor

"A woman can keep only one secret – the secret of her age."

- Voltaire

"A gossip with a secret is like a contagious disease that longs to infect anyone who will listen."

- American Proverb

"Hide from those who ask, *'Can you keep a secret?'*"

- American Proverb

"Beware of 'sanctified gossip.' It usually begins with, 'And please pray for so-and-so because of...'"

- Christian Proverb

"A fool is apt to tell what secrets they know from the vanity of having been entrusted."

- English Proverb

"Every family hides skeletons in the closet."

- English Proverb

"A secret known to two is no longer a secret."

- French Proverb

SERMONS

"And seeing the multitudes, he went up into a mountain: and when he was set, his disciples came unto him: And he opened his mouth, and taught them…"
- Matthew 5:1-2

"In England we see people lulled sleep with solid and elaborate discourses of piety, who would be warmed and transported out of themselves by the bellowing and distortions of enthusiasm."
- Joseph Addison

"Preach the Gospel always. If necessary, use words."
- Augustine of Hippo

"Every sermon must have a solid rest in Scripture, and the pointedness which comes of a clear subject, and the conviction which belongs to well-thought argument, and the warmth that proceeds from earnest appeal."
- Phillips Brooks

"Jesus chose this method of extending the knowledge of Himself throughout the world; He taught His truth to a few men, and then He said, "Now go and tell that truth to other men."
- Phillips Brooks

"That is not the best sermon which makes the hearers go away talking to one another, and praising the speaker, but which makes them go away thoughtful and serious, and hastening to be alone."
- Gilbert Burnet

"The world looks at ministers out of the pulpit to know what they mean when in it."
- David Cecil

"Oh, the unspeakable littleness of a soul which, intrusted with Christianity, speaking in God's name to immortal beings, with infinite excitements to the most enlarged, fervent love, sinks down into narrow self-regard, and is chiefly solicitous of his own honor."
- William Ellery Channing

"When I compare the clamorous preaching and passionate declamation too common in the Christian world with the composed dignity, the deliberate wisdom, the freedom from all extravagance, which characterized Jesus, I can imagine no greater contrast; and I am sure that the fiery zealot is no representative of Christianity."
- William Ellery Channing

"The minister should preach as if he felt that although the congregation own the church, and have bought the pews, they have not bought him. His soul is worth no more than any other man's, but it is all he has, and he cannot be expected to sell it for a salary. The terms are by no means equal. If a parishioner does not like the preaching, he can go elsewhere and get another pew, but the preacher cannot get another soul."
- Edwin Hubbell Chapin

"In pulpit eloquence, the grand difficulty lies here--to give the subject all the dignity it so fully deserves, without attaching any importance to ourselves. The Christian messenger cannot think too highly of his prince, nor too humbly of himself."
- Charles Caleb Coulton

"Would I describe a preacher,
    I would express him simple, grave, sincere;
    In doctrine uncorrupt; in language plain,
        And plain in manner; decent, solemn, chaste,
        And natural in gesture; much impress'd
            Himself, as conscious of his awful charge,
            And anxious mainly that the flock he feeds
            May feel it too; affectionate in look,
            And tender in address, as well becomes
            A messenger of grace to guilty men."
- William Cowper

"He that negotiates between God and man,
  As God's ambassador, the grand concerns
    Of judgment and of mercy, should beware
      Of lightness in his speech."
                    -    William Cowper

"God preaches, a noted clergyman,
  And the sermon is never long;
    So instead of getting to heaven at last,
      I'm going all along."
                    -    Emily Dickenson

"The province of the soul is large enough to fill up every cranny of your time, and leave you much to answer for if one wretch be damned by your neglect."
                    -    John Dryden

"Alas for the unhappy man that is called to stand in the pulpit, and not give the bread of life."
                    -    Ralph Waldo Emerson

"Be short in all religious exercises. Better leave the people longing than loathing."
                    -    Nathaniel Emmons

"I would have every minister of the gospel address his audience with the zeal of a friend, with the generous energy of a father, and with the exuberant affection of a mother."
                    -    François Fénelon

"It was said of one who preached very well and lived very ill, '*that when he was out of the pulpit it was pity he should ever go into it*,' and '*when he was in the pulpit, it was pity he should ever come out of it.*'"
                    -    Thomas Fuller

"This I quarreled at, that he went far from his text to come close to me, and so was faulty himself in telling me of my faults."
                    -    Thomas Fuller

"There are but few talents requisite to become a popular preacher; for the people are easily pleased if they perceive any endeavors in the orator to please them. The meanest qualifications will work this effect if the preacher sincerely sets about it."

- Oliver Goldsmith

"You can preach a better sermon with your life than with your lips."

- Oliver Goldsmith

"A minister, without boldness, is like a smooth file, a knife without an edge, a sentinel that is afraid to let off his gun. If men will be bold in sin, ministers must be bold to reprove."

- William Gurnall

"Settle in your mind, that no sermon is worth much in which the Lord is not the principal speaker. There may be poetry, refinement, historic truth, moral truth, pathos, and all the charms of rhetoric; but all will be lost, for the purposes of preaching, if the word of the Lord is not the staple of the discourse."

- John Hall

"To get, then, the mind of Christ, and to declare it, is the primary end of the teaching offices of the church. The living body of sympathetic men, saturated with the truth and feeling of the Book, must bring it into contact with other men, through that marvelous organ, the human voice, and with such aid as comes from the subtle sympathy that pervades assemblies of human beings."

- John Hall

"Gospel ministers should not only be like dials on watches, or mile-stones upon the road, but like clocks and larums, to sound the alarm to sinners. Aaron wore bells as well as pomegranates, and the prophets were commanded to lift up their voice like a trumpet. A sleeping sentinel may be the loss of the city."

- Joseph Hall

"His words had power because they accorded with his thoughts; and his thoughts had reality and depth because they harmonized with the life he had always lived. It was not mere breath that this preacher uttered; they were the words of life, because a life of good deeds and holy love was melted into them. Pearls, pure and rich, had been dissolved into the precious draught."

> \- Nathaniel Hawthorne,
> in *The Scarlett Letter*

"A preacher should have the skill to teach the unlearned simply roundly, and plainly; for teaching is of more importance than exhorting."

> \- Martin Luther

"Let all your preaching be in the most simple and plainest manner; look not to the prince, but to the plain, simple, gross, unlearned people, of which cloth the prince also himself is made. If I, in my preaching, should have regard to Philip Melancthon and other learned doctors, then should I do but little good. I preach in the simplest manner to the unskillful, and that giveth content to all. Hebrew, Greek and Latin I spare until we learned ones come together."

> \- Martin Luther

"Some plague the people with too long sermons; for the faculty of listening is a tender thing, and soon becomes weary and satiated."

> \- Martin Luther

"Some men still preach when they have nothing to say."

> \- Jack Murphy

"The Christian ministry is the worst of all trades, but the best of all professions."

> \- Sir Isaac Newton

"If the truth were known, many sermons are prepared and preached with more regard for the sermon than the souls of the hearers."

> \- George Pentecost

"Isn't it staggering when you think that one sermon on the day of Pentecost produced 3000 people? And we had some cities yesterday where 3000 sermons were preached and nobody was saved. And it doesn't even faze us."
- Leonard Ravenhill

"Do you know what the last words of Jesus to the church in Revelation were? 'Repent!'"
- Leonard Ravenhill

"A true shepherd leads the way. He does not merely point the way."
- Leonard Ravenhill

"If you are prepared to scold your congregation as Jesus did with the moneychangers, just remember that *Jesus wept before he whipped.* He wept as he approached Jerusalem saying, "*O Jerusalem, Jerusalem!*" No man of God has any business preaching unless he weeps over his words."
- Leonard Ravenhill

"Tell men that God is love; that right is right, and wrong, wrong; let them cease to admire philanthropy, and begin to love men; cease to pant for heaven, and begin to love God; then the spirit of liberty begins."
- Frederick William Robertson

"Preachers say, 'Do as I say, not as I do.' But if a physician had the same disease upon him that I have, and he should bid me do one thing and he do quite another, could I believe him?"
- John Seldon

"That is not the best sermon which makes the hearers go away talking to one another and praising the speaker, but which makes them go away thoughtful and serious, and hastening to be alone."
- William Shakespeare

"Beware of preachers who believe the best and believe the worst. They usually are preaching to themselves and forget everything in between."
- Mark Twain

"You cannot preach what you do not know;
  You cannot lead where you do not go."
- American Proverb

"Beware of preachers who turn the pulpit into a gossip fence."
- American Proverb

"You are the only sermon many will ever see."
- Christian Proverb

"Nature is God's eternal sermon for mankind."
- English Proverb

"Do as I say and not as I do."
- English Proverb

SERVICE

"And Hazael said, But what, is thy servant a dog, that he should do this great thing? And Elisha answered, The Lord hath shewed me that thou shalt be king over Syria."
- II Kings 8:13

"But when he saw the multitudes, he was moved with compassion on them, because they fainted, and were scattered abroad, as sheep having no shepherd."
- Matthew 9:36

"But it shall not be so among you: but whosoever will be great among you, let him be your minister; And whosoever will be chief among you, let him be your servant: Even as the Son of man came not to be ministered unto, but to minister, and to give his life a ransom for many."
- Matthew 20:26-28

"His lord said unto him, Well done, thou good and faithful servant: thou hast been faithful over a few things, I will make thee ruler over many things: enter thou into the joy of thy lord."
- Matthew 25:21

"If I can stop one heart from breaking,
I shall not live in vain;
If I can ease one life the aching,
Or cool one pain,
Or help one fainting robin
Up to his nest again,
I shall not live in vain."

- Emily Dickinson

"He is no fool who gives that which he cannot keep to gain what he cannot lose."

- Jim Elliot

"Nothing disciplines the inordinate desires of the flesh like service, and nothing transforms the desires of the flesh like serving in secret. The flesh whines against service but it screams against hidden service. It strains and pulls for honor and recognition."

- Richard Foster

"How wonderful it is that nobody needs to wait a single moment before starting to improve the world."

- Anne Frank

"Sometimes your medicine bottle has on it, "Shake well before using." That is what God has to do with some of His people. He has to shake them well before they are ever usable."

- Vance Havner

"If you want to be the first among your brothers and sisters, then you have to be a bond-slave, not only to Christ, but to your brothers and sisters."

- Stephen Kaung

"The Church exists for nothing else but to draw men into Christ, to make them little Christs. If they are not doing that, all the cathedrals, clergy, missions, sermons, even the Bible itself, are simply a waste of time. God became Man for no other purpose."

- C.S. Lewis

"The true gospel is a call to self sacrifice not self fulfillment."
-    John MacArthur

"Every wise workman takes his tools away from the work from time to time that they may be ground and sharpened; so does the only-wise Jehovah take his ministers oftentimes away into darkness and loneliness and trouble, that he may sharpen and prepare them for harder work in his service."
-    Robert Murray M'Cheyne

"A servant of God has but one Master."
-    George Muller

"This is the true joy of life: the being used up for a purpose recognized by yourself as a mighty one; being a force of nature instead of a feverish, selfish little clot of ailments and grievances, complaining that the world will not devote itself to making you happy."
-    George Bernard Shaw

"It appears that too many Christians want to enjoy the thrill of feeling right but are not willing to endure the inconvenience of being right."
-    A. W. Tozer

"There is no work better than another to please God; to pour water, to wash dishes, to be a cobbler, or an apostle, all is one; to wash dishes and to preach is all one to please God."
-    William Tyndale

"If I have no love for others, no desire to serve others and I'm only concerned about my needs, I should question whether Christ is really in my life."
-    Rick Warren

"The consideration that human happiness and moral duty are inseparably connected will always continue to prompt me to promote the progress of the former by inculcating the practice of the latter."
-    George Washington

"The most fruitful and elevating influence I have ever seemed to meet has been my impression of obligation to God."
- Daniel Webster

"You can never have a perfect day without doing something for someone who will never be able to repay you."
- John Wooden

"Maturity begins to grow when you can sense your concern for others outweighing your concern for yourself."
- Unknown

SEX

"Let thy fountain be blessed: and rejoice with the wife of thy youth."
- Proverbs 5:18

"Flee fornication. Every sin that a man doeth is without the body; but he that committeth fornication sinneth against his own body. What? Know ye not that your body is the temple of the Holy Ghost which is in you, which ye have of God, and ye are not your own? For ye are bought with a price: therefore glorify God in your body, and in your spirit, which are God's."
- I Corinthians 6:18-20

"This I say then, Walk in the Spirit, and ye shall not fulfill the lust of the flesh."
- Galatians 5:16

"Marriage is honourable in all, and the bed undefiled: but whoremongers and adulterers God will judge."
- Hebrews 13:4

"Nuptial love maketh mankind; friendly love perfecteth it; but wanton love corrupteth and embaseth it."
- Sir Francis Bacon

"If venereal delight and the power of propagating the species were permitted only to the virtuous, it would make the world very good."
- James Boswell

"A moment of passionate intimacy often results in over 18 years of extremely agonizing responsibility."
- Jack Murphy

"Many people have sex in a vain search for intimacy. Sex is not intimacy, nor is it supposed to be the commencement of intimacy. Sex is supposed to be the pinnacle of intimacy. Sex is greatest when experienced by two people who love one another enough to withhold their bodies until after a lasting covenant is established. Sex outside of marriage is simply a cheap means of lustful gratification."
- Jack Murphy

"No man, after having contracted a venereal disease, and no unmarried girl, after having become pregnant, fondly thinks back to the experience as 'the best half hour' of their life."
- George Phillips

"Sex might feel good at the time, but the regret can be painful for years to come."
- George Phillips

"As to marriage or celibacy, let a man take which course he will. Either way, he will be sure to repent."
- Socrates

"Lie back…and think of England."
- Lady Alice Hillingdon, attributed

"Sex is like pizza. When it's good – it's extremely good. When it's bad – it's still good."
- Unknown

SIN

"My son, if sinners entice thee, consent thou not."
- Proverbs 1:10

"And the publican, standing afar off, would not lift up so much as his eyes unto heaven, but smote upon his breast, saying, God be merciful to me a sinner."
- Luke 18:13

"For the wages of sin is death; but the gift of God is eternal life through Jesus Christ our Lord."
- Romans 6:23

"Once she has committed sin, there is nothing left for the Protestant woman, whereas the Catholic Church, hope of forgiveness makes a woman sublime."
- Honore de Balzac

"Sin is never at a stay; if we do not retreat from it, we shall advance in it; and the farther on we go, the more we have to come back."
- Isaac Barrow

"Many Christians are unthinkably horrified when a real sinner is suddenly discovered among the righteous. So we remain alone with our sin, living in lies and hypocrisy...He who is alone with his sins is utterly alone."
- Dietrich Bonhoeffer

"What sin is so sweet or profitable, that is worth burning in hell for—or worth being shut out of heaven for?"
- Thomas Brooks

"There are sins of omission as well as those of commission."
- Dorothee DeLuzy

"The greatest hindrance to effective prayer is sin. Satan's greatest goal is to keep us from our knees."

- Dick Eastman

"I could not live in peace if I put the shadow of a wilful sin between myself and God."

- George Eliot

"Sin is not hurtful because it is forbidden, but it is forbidden because it is hurtful."

- Benjamin Franklin

"He that falls into sin is a man; that grieves at it, is a saint; that boasts of it, is a devil."

- Thomas Fuller

"We are sinful not merely because we have eaten of the tree of knowledge, but also because we have not eaten of the tree of life."

- Frank Kafka

"The poor man and woman of the gospel have made peace with their flawed existence. They are aware of their lack of wholeness, their brokenness, the simple fact that they don't have it all together. While they do not excuse their sin, they are humbly aware that sin is precisely what has caused them to throw themselves at the mercy of the Father. They do not pretend to be anything but what they are: sinners saved by grace."

- Brennan Manning

"First we practice sin, then defend it, then boast of it."

- Thomas Manton

"We are too Christian really to enjoy sinning, and too fond of sinning really to enjoy Christianity."

- Peter Marshall

"In the epic war between sin and holiness, the side that you join will determine your eternal status."

- Jack Murphy

"The power of sin? Adam and Eve ate the fruit and men and women are still dying."
- Jack Murphy

"Sin carries with it a certain moral myopia...it distorts our ability to detect its presence."
- John Ortberg

"If thou wouldst conquer thy weakness, thou must never gratify it. No man is compelled to evil: his consent only makes it his. It is no sin to be tempted, but to be overcome."
- William Penn

"There are only two kinds of persons: those dead in sin and those dead to sin."
- Leonard Ravenhill

"Cast out thy Jonah--every sleeping and secure sin that brings a tempest upon thy ship, vexation to thy spirit."
- Friedrich Reynolds

"In Exodus chapter four, God told Moses to place his hand in his bosom and then take it out. It became leprous as snow. God was revealing to Moses that sinfulness is a part of our nature. Next, the Lord told Moses to put it in and take it out, and it was clean. Only God can clean us from our sin."
- David Wilkerson

"I felt a physical pain for every man and woman who passed by. It was like a knife in my heart, so burning was the question of whether or not her or she was saved. If a member of the congregation sinned I would weep for hours. The longing for the salvation of all souls has remained in my heart."
- Richard Wurmbrand

"Woe to those who lose their blush of sin! When a person becomes indifferent to sin, it displays the cold, callousness of a sinful heart."
- Unknown

"The cost of your sins is more than you can pay. The gift of your God is more than you can imagine."
- Unknown

SINCERITY

"Therefore let us keep the feast, not with old leaven, neither with the leaven of malice and wickedness; but with the unleavened bread of sincerity and truth."
- I Corinthians 5:8

"For we are not as many, which corrupt the word of God: but as of sincerity, but as of God, in the sight of God speak we in Christ."
- II Corinthians 2:17

"Loss of sincerity is loss of vital power."
- Christian Nestell Bovee

"I should say sincerity, a deep, great, genuine sincerity, is the first characteristic of all men in any way heroic."
- Thomas Carlyle

"Never apologize for showing feeling. My friend, remember that when you do so you apologize for truth."
- Benjamin Disraeli

"Sincerity is always subject to proof."
- John F. Kennedy

"Nothing in all the world is more dangerous than sincere ignorance and conscientious stupidity."
- Martin Luther King, Jr.

"I can only say that I have acted upon my best convictions, without selfishness or malice, and that by the help of God I shall continue to do so."
- Abraham Lincoln

"Sincerity is word or action without pretense. It is the status of not speaking or acting out of selfish motives regarding reputation or personal and public benefit. It is acting out of truth."

- Jack Murphy

"Many pastors criticize me for taking the Gospel so seriously. But do they really think that on Judgment Day, Christ will chastise me, saying, *'Leonard, you took Me too seriously'*?"

- Leonard Ravenhill

"Your doctrine can be as straight as a gun barrel—and just as empty!"

- Leonard Ravenhill

"The Church used to be a lifeboat rescuing the perishing. Now she is a cruise ship recruiting the promising."

- Leonard Ravenhill

"Sincerity is an openness of heart; we find it in very few people; what we usually see is only an artful dissimulation to win the confidence of others."

- François Rochefoucauld

"God takes away the world, so that the heart may cleave more to Him in sincerity."

- Thomas Watson

"Many tragedies were caused by sincerity. Save your sincerity for only those things that you know to be true."

- Chinese Proverb

"It is possible to be both sincere and sincerely wrong."

- Unknown

"It is dangerous to be publicly sincere if you are wrong. Sincerity is not an excuse for sin or stupidity."

- Unknown

SLANDER – See FALSE WITNESS

SMOKING

"Smoking killed more people in 1945 than both atomic bombs. We see multitudes of activists protesting the instantaneous deaths caused by splitting the atom, yet none who dare to protest those who slowly kill themselves and destroy the environment through the act of smoking. In fact, some of the same folks who are marching for legalized marijuana are also out marching against the atom bomb. Do they not realize the hypocrisy of such activism?"
- Jack Murphy

"To cease smoking is the easiest thing I ever did. I ought to know because I've done it a thousand times."
- Mark Twain

"Smoking is betraying your lungs and your health for momentary relaxation."
- Chinese Proverb

"A cigarette is a pipe with a fire at one end and a fool at the other."
- Irish Proverb

"Dying is the most common way people stop smoking."
- Poster found in Hospital

"Smoking areas in restaurants are like peeing areas in swimming pools."
- Sign in a restaurant in Dallas, Texas

"Smoking is a form of government-protected suicide that is greatly promoted by Hollywood."
- Unknown

"A cigarette is a pipe with a fire at one end and a fool at the other."
- Unknown

"Smoking is industry assisted suicide."
- Unknown

SOCIALISM

"And all that believed were together, and had all things common; And sold their possessions and goods, and parted them to all men, as every man had need."
- Acts 2:44-45

"Neither was there any among them that lacked: for as many as were possessors of lands or houses sold them, and brought the prices of the things that were sold, and laid them down at the apostles' feet: and distribution was made unto every man according as he had need."
- Acts 4:34-35

"While it remained unsold, did it not remain your own? And after it was sold, was it not at your disposal?"
- Acts 5:4

"And in those days, when the number of the disciples was multiplied, there arose a murmuring of the Grecians against the Hebrews, because their widows were neglected in the daily ministration."
- Acts 6:1

"A socialist nation that gives the people the opportunity to decide whether or not they want to be socialists is actually a democracy."
- George H. W. Bush

"Socialism is a philosophy of failure, the creed of ignorance, and the gospel of envy, its inherent virtue is the equal sharing of misery."
- Winston Churchill

"The inherent vice of capitalism is the unequal sharing of blessings; the inherent virtue of socialism is the equal sharing of miseries."
- Winston Churchill

"I believe that for the past twenty years there has been a creeping socialism spreading in the United States."
- Dwight D. Eisenhower

"I believe that communism would be defeated if the people living under communist rule could truly see how much the American government cares for the people."

-   Dwight D. Eisenhower

"From each according to his ability, to each according to his need."

-   Karl Marx

"Socialism: nothing more than the theory that the slave is always more virtuous than his master."

-   Henry Louis Mencken

"Some mistakenly teach that the early Church practiced a form of socialism. The distinct difference was that those who desired to share their belongings did so *willingly*. It was not the result of compulsion, obligation, law or a governmental decree. The difference comes down to this: a free will. Freedom is the essence of Christianity. Remember, '*Where the Spirit of the Lord is, there is liberty.*'"

-   Jack Murphy

"Socialism is the government mandating equality in a world where not everyone is equal. It ignores the fact that some are more gifted in certain areas than others, but requires that no man can enjoy the fruit of his gifts or labors. It is a practice that requires everyone to work for the government."

-   Jack Murphy

"As with the Christian religion, the worst advertisement for Socialism is often its adherents."

-   George Orwell

"How do you tell a Communist? Well, it's someone who reads Marx and Lenin. And how do you tell an anti-Communist? It's someone who *understands* Marx and Lenin."

-   Ronald Reagan

"Socialism is a 100% tax rate on income in a nation that forces you to rent and buy from the government. It is the belief that the government knows more about what is best for your children."
- Ronald Reagan

"The problem is that, under socialism, no one can choose to be a socialist. It is the law of the land. A contrary opinion is often punished by death."
- Ronald Reagan

"Democracy and socialism have nothing in common but one word, equality. But notice the difference: while democracy seeks equality in liberty, socialism seeks equality in restraint and servitude."
- Alexis de Tocqueville

"Under capitalism man exploits man; under socialism the reverse is true."
- Polish Proverb

SPEECH

"He that loveth pureness of heart, for the grace of his lips the king shall be his friend."
- Proverbs 22:11

"For a dream cometh through the multitude of business; and a fool's voice is known by multitude of words."
- Ecclesiastes 5:3

"For out of the abundance of the heart the mouth speaketh."
- Matthew 12:34

"But I say unto you, that every idle word that men shall speak, they shall give account thereof in the day of judgment. For by thy words thou shalt be justified, and by thy words thou shalt be condemned."
- Matthew 12:36-37

"Let your speech be always with grace, seasoned with salt, that ye may know how ye ought to answer every man."
- Colossians 4:6

"A thing is not necessarily true because badly uttered, nor false because spoken magnificently."
- Augustine

"Speak when you are angry and you will make the best speech you will ever regret."
- Ambrose Bierce

"Don't speak too much when you counsel sir. Get to the point and pray. Let God do it!"
- Keith Daniel

"One of the lessons of history is that nothing is often a good thing to do and always a clever thing to say."
- Will Durant

"Half the world is composed of people who have something to say and can't, and the other half who have nothing to say and keep on saying it."
- Robert Frost

"Don't use words too big for the subject. Don't say "infinitely" when you mean "very"; otherwise you'll have no word left when you want to talk about something really infinite."
- C.S. Lewis

"Speak properly, and in as few words as you can, but always plainly; for the end of speech is not ostentation, but to be understood."
- William Penn

"Wise men talk because they have something to say; fools, because they have to say something."
- Plato

"Never miss a good chance to shut up."
- Will Rogers

"Grasp the subject. The words will follow."
- Cato the Elder

"Learn to say no. It will be of more use to you than to be able to read Latin."

- Charles Spurgeon

"The bitterest tears shed over graves are for words left unsaid and deeds left undone."

- Harriet Beecher Stowe

"Where there have been mighty deeds, there need be no multitude of words to tell of them. Many words are required only where the deeds have been too feeble to speak for themselves."

- A.W. Tozer

"The difference between the right word and the almost right word is the difference between lightning and the lightning bug."

- Mark Twain

"Woman, God wouldn't care a bit if you would bury that talent."

- John Wesley,
  when informed by a hot-headed woman that "speaking her mind" was her "talent"

"The trouble with talking too fast is you may say something you haven't thought of yet."

- American Proverb

"Speech has three important uses--it expresses thought, conceals thought, and takes the place of thought."

- German Proverb

"When you have spoken the word, it reigns over you. When it is unspoken you reign over it."

- Persian Proverb

"When you are arguing with a fool, make sure he isn't doing the same thing."

- Spanish Proverb

"Don't speak unless you can improve on the silence."
- Spanish Proverb

"Great minds talk about ideas. Average minds talk about things. Small minds talk about other people."
- Unknown

SPORTS

"Know ye not that they which run in a race run all, but one receiveth the prize? So run, that ye may obtain."
- I Corinthians 9:24

"For bodily exercise profiteth unto some value: but godliness is profitable unto all things, having promise of the life that now is, and of that which is to come."
- I Timothy 4:8

"He may well win the race that runs by himself."
- Benjamin Franklin

"Tell them to go in there with all they've got and win just one for the Gipper."
- George Gipp

"You're never as good as everyone tells you when you win, and you're never as bad as they say when you lose."
- Lou Holtz

"We are inclined that if we watch a football game or baseball game, we have taken part in it."
- John F. Kennedy

"We didn't lose the game; we just ran out of time."
- Vince Lombardi

"If winning isn't everything, why do they keep score?"
- Vince Lombardi

"The joy of hunting and fishing is often experienced even in the presence of no animals. It is the time when many men learn to appreciate both the beauty of nature and lessons of patience."

- Jack Murphy

"Serious sport has nothing to do with fair play. It is bound up with hatred, jealousy, boastfulness, disregard of all rules and sadistic pleasure in witnessing violence. In other words, it is war minus the shooting."

- George Orwell

"Thus so wretched is man that he would weary even without any cause for weariness...and so frivolous is he that, though full of a thousand reasons for weariness, the least thing, such as playing billiards or hitting a ball, is sufficient enough to amuse him."

- Blaise Pascal

"May the Americans always remain uninterested in (international) football, cricket or rugby. The rest of the world needs something for which we can claim dominance."

- Narottam Puri

"Men think better while fishing. I've long believed that peace could be better negotiated in a lake or stream than in the diplomatic halls of an international summit."

- Ronald Reagan

"Even if you're on the right track, you'll still get run over if you just sit there."

- Will Rogers

"Don't let the fear of striking out keep you from stepping up to the plate."

- Babe Ruth

"It is a noteworthy fact that kicking and beating have played so considerable a part in the habits which necessity has imposed on mankind in past ages that the only way of preventing civilized men from beating and kicking their wives is to organize games in which they can kick and beat balls."

- George Bernard Shaw

"I figure practice puts your brains in your muscles."

- Sam Snead

"Most games are lost, not won."

- Casey Stengel

"Adversity causes some men to break; others to break records."

- William Arthur Ward

"I always turn to the sports section first. The sports page records people's accomplishments; the front page has nothing but man's failures."

- Earl Warren

"It's not winning or losing that matters, but how you played the game."

- American Proverb

"A winner never quits and a quitter never wins."

- American Proverb

"'Almost' only counts in Horseshoes, hand grenades and nuclear war."

- American Proverb

"The more you sweat in practice, the less you bleed in battle."

- Russian Proverb

"Fishing is a stick and a string with a fly at one end and a fool at the other."

- Unknown

STRENGTH

"And Moses was an hundred and twenty years old when he died: his eye was not dim, nor his natural force abated."
- Deuteronomy 34:7

"Then he said unto them, Go your way, eat the fat, and drink the sweet, and send portions unto them for whom nothing is prepared: for this day is holy unto our LORD: neither be ye sorry; for the joy of the LORD is your strength."
- Nehemiah 8:10

"They go from strength to strength, every one of them in Zion appeareth before God."
- Psalm 84:7

"For their redeemer is mighty; he shall plead their cause with thee."
- Proverbs 23:11

"And if one prevail against him, two shall withstand him; and a three-fold cord is not quickly broken."
- Ecclesiastes 4:12

""Fear thou not; for I am with thee: be not dismayed; for I am thy God: I will strengthen thee; yea, I will help thee; yea, I will uphold thee with the right hand of my righteousness."
- Isaiah 41:10

"And he said unto me, My grace is sufficient for thee: for my strength is made perfect in weakness. Most gladly therefore will I rather glory in my infirmities, that the power of Christ may rest upon me."
- II Corinthians 12:9

"If God sends us on strong paths, we are provided strong shoes."
- Corrie ten Boom

"Almost always are greatest strengths are also are at the root of our greatest weaknesses."
-    Marcus Buckingham

"Rudeness is the weak man's imitation of strength."
-    Edmund Burke

"Don't expect to build up the weak by pulling down the strong."
-    Calvin Coolidge

"We confide in our strength, without boasting of it; we respect that of others, without fearing it."
-    Thomas Jefferson

"Know your strengths and know your limits. When you have got an elephant by the hind legs and he is trying to run away, it's best to let him run."
-    Abraham Lincoln

"[God desires] not that He may say to them, 'Look how mighty I am, and go down upon your knees and worship', for power alone was never yet worthy of prayer; but that He may say thus: 'Look, my children, you will never be strong but with my strength. I have no other to give you. And that you can get only by trusting in me. I can not give it you any other way. There is no other way.'"
-    George Macdonald

"What does not destroy me, makes me strong."
-    Friedrich Nietzsche

"Never grow a wishbone, daughter, where your backbone ought to be."
-    Clementine Paddleford

"No nation was ever conquered because they were too strong and well prepared."
-    Ronald Reagan

"Speak softly, but carry a big stick."
- Theodore Roosevelt

"There are two ways of exerting one's strength: one is pushing down, the other is pulling up."
- Booker T. Washington

"It is a strength to know your weaknesses."
- American Proverb

SUCCESS

"Only be thou strong and very courageous, that thou mayest observe to do according to all the law, which Moses my servant commanded thee: turn not from it to the right hand or to the left, that thou mayest prosper withersoever thou goest. This book of the law shall not depart out of thy mouth; but thou shalt meditate therein day and night, that thou mayest observe to do according to all that is written therein: for then thou shalt make thy way prosperous, and then thou shalt have good success."
- Joshua 1:7-8

"For promotion cometh neither from the east, nor from the west, nor from the south."
- Psalm 75:6

"I returned, and saw under the sun, that the race is not to the swift, nor the battle to the strong, neither yet bread to the wise, nor yet riches to men of understanding, nor yet favour to men of skill; but time and chance happeneth to them all."
- Ecclesiastes 9:11

"There is no comparison between that which is lost by not succeeding, and that which is lost by not trying."
- Sir Francis Bacon

"A minute's success pays for the failure of years."
- Robert Browning

"Better have failed in the high aim, as I,
  Than vulgarly in the low aim succeed
    As, God be thanked! I do not."
                        -    Robert Browning

"Anything that can go wrong, will – at the worst possible moment."
                        -    John W. Campbell
                             ("Finagle's Law" or "Finagle's corollary to
                             Murphy's Law")

"The real secret of success is enthusiasm."
                        -    Walter Chrysler

"Success is going from failure to failure without a loss of enthusiasm."
                        -    Winston Churchill

"To judge by the event is an error all commit: for in every instance
courage, if crowned with success, is heroism; if clouded by defeat,
temerity. When Nelson fought his battle in the Sound, it was the result
alone that decided whether he was to kiss a hand at court or a rod at a
court-martial."
                        -    Charles Caleb Colton

"To know a man, observe how he wins his object, rather than how he
loses it; for when we fail, our pride supports us,--when we succeed, it
betrays us."
                        -    Charles Caleb Colton

"Success is counted sweetest
  By those who ne'er succeed."
                        -    Emily Dickinson

"Success is the child of audacity."
                        -    Benjamin Disraeli

"Work only on things that will make a great deal of difference if you
succeed."
                        -    Peter Drucker

"Be nice to people on your way up because you might meet 'em on your way down."

- Jimmy Durante

"Success is ten percent inspiration and ninety percent perspiration."

- Thomas Edison

"Success is achieved simply by working past anxiety, boredom, discouragement and near-success."

- Thomas Edison

"Everything comes to him who hustles while he waits."

- Thomas Edison

"If A is success in life, then A equals X + Y + Z. Work is X, Y is play, and Z is keeping your mouth shut."

- Albert Einstein

"Whether you think you can do a thing or not, you're right."

- Henry Ford

"In success, remain kind."

- Thomas Jefferson, to his daughter

"Your success and happiness lie in you."

- Helen Keller

"Success is not a matter of mastering subtle, sophisticated theory, but rather of embracing common sense with uncommon levels of discipline and persistence."

- Patrick Lencioni

"If there's more than one way to do a job, and one of those ways will result in disaster, then somebody will do it that way."

- Major Edward Murphy
  ("Murphy's Law")

"Success is not measured in houses, cars or land. It is measured by what you bring before God. Can you truly stand before God with clean hands and a pure heart? Did you raise a family in the ways of the Lord? Can someone stand in Eternity and point to you as the instrument that tuned their ears to Heaven?

- Jack Murphy

"Success without honor is an unseasoned dish; it will satisfy your hunger, but it won't taste good."

- Joe Paterno

"The difference between a successful person and others is not a lack of strength, not a lack of knowledge, but a lack of will."

- Norman Vincent Peale

"Success is measured by your adversity. The lions rush to attack bulls; they do not attack butterflies. Don't claim success after merely swatting flies. Strive to conquer something greater."

- Will Rogers

"Success does not consist in never making blunders, but in never making the same one the second time."

- Henry Wheeler Shaw

"Who shoots at the midday Sun, though he be sure, he shall never hit the mark; yet as sure as his is, he shall shoot higher than who aims but at a bush."

- Sir Philip Sidney

"People seldom see the halting and painful steps by which the most insignificant success is achieved."

- Anne Sullivan

"No one can be successful in pleasing everyone."

- Publilius Syrus

"Success usually comes to those who are too busy to look for it."

- Henry David Thoreau

"If life gives you lemons, squeeze them and make lemonade."
- American Proverb

"The secret to success is to start from scratch and to keep on scratching."
- American Proverb

"Although *the battle is the Lord's*, David still tossed the stone."
- Hebrew Proverb

"Fear less, hope more; whine less, breathe more; talk less, say more; hate less, love more; and all good things are yours."
- Swedish proverb

SUFFERING – See TRIALS & TRIBULATIONS

SUICIDE

"Thou shalt not kill."
- Exodus 20:13

"And Samson took hold of the two middle pillars upon which the house stood, and on which it was borne up, of the one with his right hand, and of the other with his left. And Samson said, Let me die with the Philistines. And he bowed himself with all his might; and the house fell upon the lords, and upon all the people that were therein. So the dead which he slew at his death were more than they which he slew in his life."
- Judges 16:29-30

"Then Judas, which had betrayed him, when he saw that he was condemned, repented himself, and brought again the thirty pieces of silver to the chief priests and elders, Saying, I have sinned in that I have betrayed the innocent blood. And they said, What is that to us? see thou to that. And he cast down the pieces of silver in the temple, and departed, and went and hanged himself."
- Matthew 27:3-5

"Know ye not that ye are the temple of God, and that the Spirit of God dwelleth in you? If any man defile the temple of God, him shall God destroy; for the temple of God is holy, which temple ye are."
-      I Corinthians 3:16-17

"And as it is appointed unto men once to die, but after this the judgment."
-      Hebrews 9:27

"And in those days shall men seek death, and shall not find it; and shall desire to die, and death shall flee from them."
-      Revelation 9:6

"To die in order to avoid the pains of poverty, love, or anything that is disagreeable, is not the part of a brave man, but of a coward."
-      Aristotle

"We must not pluck death from the Maker's hand."
-      Philip James Bailey

"True heroism consists in being superior to the ills of life in whatever shape they may challenge him to combat."
-      Napoleon Bonaparte

"Suicide is not to fear death, but yet to be afraid of life. It is a brave act of valour to contemn death; but when life is more terrible than death, it is then the truest valour to dare to live; and herein religion hath taught us a noble example, for all the valiant acts of Curtius, Scarvola, or Codrus, do not parallel or match that one of Job."
-      Sir Thomas Browne

"Many live because they are afraid to die as die because they are afraid to live."
-      Charles Caleb Colton

"'Tis more brave to live than to die."
-      Edward George Lytton

"Suicide is the exit of cowards who fear the burdens of life far more than they fear the unfathomable terrors of the Day of Judgment."
- Jack Murphy

"The coward sneaks to death; the brave live on."
- George Sewell

"To be or not to be – that is the question:
Whether 'tis nobler in the mind to suffer
The slings and arrows of outrageous fortune
Or to take arms against a sea of troubles
And by opposing end them."
- William Shakespeare

"I have no problem with suicide bombing – as long as no one else gets hurt."
- Unknown

T

TAXES

"They say unto him, Caesar's. Then saith he unto them, Render therefore unto Caesar the things which are Caesar's; and unto God the things that are God's."
- Matthew 22:21

"For imposing Taxes on us without our Consent.... We therefore...solemnly publish and declare, That these United Colonies are, and of Right ought to be Free and Independent States."
- The Declaration of Independence

"Taxation with representation ain't so hot either."
- Gerald Barzan

"Over-taxation cost England her colonies of North America."
- Edmund Burke

"Taxation is the Democrats' great cure for having spent too much."
- Ronald Reagan

"Our new Constitution is now established, and has an appearance that promises permanency; but in this world nothing can be said to be certain, except death and taxes."
- Benjamin Franklin

"Idleness and pride tax with a heavier hand than kings and parliaments."
- Benjamin Franklin

"I'm proud to pay taxes in the United States; the only thing is, I could be just as proud for half the money."
- Arthur Godfrey

"Be wary of strong drink. It can make you shoot at tax collectors... and miss."
- Robert Heinlein

"Kings ought to shear, not skin their sheep."
- Robert Herrick

"Taxation has evolved from simply providing the means to protect, defend and administer the government of the United States into a system that takes from those who have in order to give to those who have not. This form of 'Robin Hood' taxation has been the battle cry of Democrats since FDR. Ironically, it was also the cry of socialists and communists. It was the philosophical experiment of Marx, Lenin and Stalin. Yet it stifled opportunity and production and plundered and penalized success. Is it no wonder that it has failed in every form? Why, then, is it still the marching orders of the Democratic Party? Do they wonder why many Americans equate the Democratic Party's 'tax and spend' philosophy with socialism?"
- Jack Murphy

"Patriotism says, '*Ask not what your country can do for you...*' Modern socialism says, '*Take from those who work and give it to those who can't or won't and then blame everything on the rich.*'"
- Jack Murphy

"A fair system of taxation would cause all men to pay a similar percentage of their income or spending. Our current system targets those who work hard and earn more to pay for the services and items of those who work little or earn nothing. Yet somehow this is 'fair' to the Democrats."
- Jack Murphy

"Paying taxes is like investing in a large company for which the greatest dividend is paid to those who invested the least."
- Jack Murphy

"The greatest exodus from the Democratic Party into the Republican Party happens either during prayer or when paying taxes. Both lead to a philosophical epiphany of sorts."

- Jack Murphy

"That in which every man is interested, is every man's duty to support; and any burden which falls equally on all men, and from which every man is to receive an equal benefit, is consistent with the most perfect ideas of liberty."

- Thomas Paine

"The taxpayer - that's someone who works for the federal government but doesn't have to take the civil service examination."

- Ronald Reagan

"The modern Democratic Party needs to change their name to 'Tax Collectors of America.'"

- Ronald Reagan

"The government's view of the economy could be summed up in a few short phrases: If it moves, tax it. If it keeps moving, regulate it. And if it stops moving, subsidize it."

- Ronald Reagan

"The income tax has made more liars out of the American people than golf has."

- Will Rogers

"Taxes, after all, are dues that we pay for the privileges of membership in an organized society."

- Franklin D. Roosevelt

"What is the difference between a taxidermist and a tax collector? The taxidermist takes only your skin."

- Mark Twain

"Did you ever notice that when you put the words 'The' and 'IRS' together, it spells 'THEIRS?'"

- American Proverb

"Two types of people complain about taxes: Men and Women."

- American Proverb

"It now takes more intelligence to file your taxes than it does to earn your income!"

- American Proverb

"A fine is a tax for doing something wrong. A tax is a fine for doing something right."

- English Proverb

"Taxes: Of life's two certainties, the only one for which you can get an automatic extension."

- Unknown

TEACHING

"But ask now the beasts, any they shall teach thee; and the fowls of the air, and they shall tell thee:
  Or speak to the earth, and it shall teach thee: and the fishes of the sea shall declare unto thee."

- Job 12:7-8

"Train up a child in the way he should go: and when he is old, he will not depart from it."

- Proverbs 22:6

"Woe unto you, scribes and Pharisees, hypocrites! for ye compass sea and land to make one proselyte, and when he is made, ye make him twofold more the child of hell than yourselves."

- Matthew 23:15

"And he gave some ... teachers; For the perfecting of the saints, for the work of the ministry, for the edifying of the body of Christ: Till we all come in the unity of the faith, and of the knowledge of the Son of God, unto a perfect man, unto the measure of the stature of the fullness of Christ."

-   Ephesians 4:11-13

"A teacher affects eternity; he can never tell where his influence stops."

-   Henry Brooks Adams

"If you cannot teach me to fly, teach me to dream, write and sing about flying."

-   Sir J. M. Barrie

"You cannot teach old dogs new tricks."

-   Joseph Chamberlain

"Teachers have powers at their disposal with which Prime Ministers and Presidents have never been invested."

-   Winston Churchill

"The school is the factory of humanity. The teacher builds only until the pupil is inspired to take over."

-   John Amos Comenius

"You teach me baseball and I'll teach you relativity. . . . No we must not. You will learn about relativity faster than I learn baseball."

-   Albert Einstein

""Whoever said, '*He who can, does. He who cannot, teaches.*' Obviously didn't understand Theoretical Physics."

-   Jack Murphy

"You can take a horse to water, but you can't force it to drink. You can drag a child to school, but you can't force him to learn. Motivating kids can be as difficult as breaking a horse."

-   Ray Everett

"A good schoolmaster minces his precepts for children to swallow, hanging clogs on the nimbleness of his own soul, that his scholars may go along with him."

- Thomas Fuller

"You cannot teach a man anything.; you can only help him to find it for himself."

- Galilei Galileo

"Good teaching is one-fourth preparation and three-fourths theater."

- Gail Godwin

"Prosperity is a great teacher; adversity a greater."

- William Hazlitt

"One good father is worth 100 schoolmasters."

- George Herbert

"A teacher must believe in the value and interest of his subject as a doctor believes in health."

- Gilbert Highest

"Have you ever been at sea in a dense fog, when it seemed as if a tangible white darkness shut you in and the great ship, tense and anxious, groped her way toward the shore with plummet and sounding-line, and you waited with beating heart for something to happen? I was like that ship before my education began, only I was without compass or sounding line, and no way of knowing how near the harbor was. 'Light! Give me light!' was the wordless cry of my soul, and the light of love shone on me in that very hour."

- Helen Keller

"Modern cynics and skeptics... see no harm in paying those to whom they entrust the minds of their children a smaller wage than is paid to those to whom they entrust the care of their plumbing."

- John F. Kennedy

"Experience is the worst teacher; it gives the test before presenting the lesson."
- Vernon Law

"Give me four years to teach the children, and the seed I have sown will never be uprooted."
- Vladimir Lenin

"The basic proposal of the new education is to be that dunces and idlers must not be made to feel inferior to intelligent and industrious pupils. Children who are fit to proceed may be artificially kept back, because the others would get a trauma by being left behind. The bright pupil thus remains democratically fettered to his own age group throughout his school career, and a boy who would be capable of tackling Aeschylus or Dante sits listening to his coeval's attempts to spell out A CAT SAT ON A MAT.

We may reasonably hope for the virtual abolition of education when 'I'm as good as you' has fully had its way. All incentives to learn and all penalties for not learning will vanish. The few who might want to learn will be prevented; who are they to overtop their fellows? And anyway, the teachers -- or should I say nurses? -- will be far too busy reassuring the dunces and patting them on the back to waste any time on real teaching. We shall no longer have to plan and toil to spread imperturbable conceit and incurable ignorance among men."
- C. S. Lewis

"A preacher must be both soldier and shepherd. He must nourish, defend, and teach; he must have teeth in his mouth, and be able to bite and fight."
- Martin Luther

"Count it one of the highest virtues upon earth to educate faithfully the children of others, which so few, and scarcely any, do by their own."
- Martin Luther

"A teacher who is attempting to teach without inspiring the pupil with a desire to learn is hammering on cold iron."
- Horace Mann

"The fruit of teaching often goes unseen for at least twenty years."
- Jack Murphy

"A teacher who can inspire a student to raise his grade from a 35 to a 68 is far greater than a teacher who inspires a student to lift his grade from a 69 to a 71. Unfortunately, the state will only recognize the latter."
- Jack Murphy

"Even Einstein had a teacher."
- Jack Murphy

"Socrates taught Plato. Plato taught Aristotle. Aristotle taught Alexander. Alexander conquered the world."
- Jack Murphy

"The secret of teaching is to appear to have known all your life what you learned this afternoon."
- Will Rogers

"He who can, does. He who cannot, teaches."
- George Bernard Shaw

"Good teachers are costly, but bad teachers cost more."
- Bob Talbert

"The mediocre teacher tells. The good teacher explains. The superior teacher demonstrates. The great teacher inspires."
- William Arthur Ward

"People don't care how much you know until they know how much you care."
- American Proverb

"You are not teaching lessons; You are teaching children."
- American Proverb

"You can't teach what you do not know. You can't lead where you do not go."
- English Proverb

"Teach a child how to think, not what to think."
- English Proverb

"He who dares to teach must never cease to learn."
- Jewish Proverb

"By learning you will teach, by teaching you will learn."
- Latin Proverb

"Teaching is the profession that teaches all other professions."
- Unknown

"The difference between genius and stupidity is that genius has its limits."
- Unknown

TECHNOLOGY

"And he made in Jerusalem engines, invented by cunning men, to be on the towers and upon the bulwarks, to shoot arrows and great stones withal. And his name spread far abroad; for he was marvellously helped, till he was strong."
- 2 Chronicles 26:15

"But thou, O Daniel, shut up the words, and seal the book, even to the time of the end: many shall run to and fro, and knowledge shall be increased."
- Daniel 12:4

"I do not fear computers. I fear the lack of them."
- Isaac Asimov

"The saddest aspect of life right now is that science gathers knowledge faster than society gathers wisdom."
- Isaac Asimov

"The factory of the future will have only two employees, a man and a dog. The man will be there to feed the dog. The dog will be there to keep the man from touching the equipment."
- Warren G. Bennis

"Ours is a world of nuclear giants and ethical infants. If we continue to develop our technology without wisdom or prudence, our servant may prove to be our executioner."
- General Omar Bradley

"Basic research is what I'm doing when I don't know what I'm doing."
- Werner von Braun

"Concern for man and his fate must always form the chief interest of all technical endeavors. Never forget this in the midst of your diagrams and equations."
- Albert Einstein

"The greatest task before civilization at present is to make machines what they ought to be, the slaves, instead of the masters of men."
- Havelock Ellis

"Gutenberg made everybody a reader. Xerox makes everybody a publisher."
- Marshall McLuhan

"Is technology a means of advancement or an attempt by man to reverse the curse placed on man in the Garden of Eden? Is it an attempt to simply avoid working by the sweat of our brows? Are they merely supplements for our laziness?"
- Jonathan Moody

"One day, someone will look at our most expensive and advanced computers and wonder how on Earth we ever survived. Ironically, we say the same thing about the computers, cell phones and televisions that we used just ten years ago. What is 'cutting edge' today will be archaic in less than a decade."
- Jack Murphy

472

"Our generation has advanced to the point where 'Star Trek' looks completely uninventive."
-   Jack Murphy

"Television is like McDonalds. You can eat healthy things or satisfying things. At McDonalds, you can eat yogurt or artery clogging fries and burgers. But who really goes to McDonalds for the yogurt?"
-   Jack Murphy

"Lo! Men have become the tools of their tools."
-   Henry David Thoreau

"The cure for crime is found in the high chair – not the electric chair."
-   American Proverb

"Technology is wonderful. It has allowed men to sell water and air."
-   Spanish Proverb

"Technology can educate or it can spawn idiocy in its users. In the case of the television, it can do both."
-   Unknown

"The electric light cured blindness. Edison prevented millions of vision problems through his invention. Without the incandescent bulb, mankind would still be straining to read by candlelight."
-   Unknown

TEENAGERS

"And Saul said to David, Thou art not able to go against this Philistine to fight with him: for thou art but a youth, and he a man of war from his youth.
Thy servant slew both the lion and the bear: and this uncircumcised Philistine shall be as one of them, seeing he hath defied the armies of the living God. David said moreover, The LORD that delivered me out of the paw of the lion, and out of the paw of the bear, he will deliver me out of the hand of this Philistine."
-   I Samuel 17:33,37

"For thou writest bitter things against me, and makest me to possess the iniquities of my youth."
- Job 13:26

"Remember now thy Creator in the days of thy youth, while the evil days come not, nor the years draw nigh, when thou shalt say, 'I have no pleasure in them.'"
- Ecclesiastes 12:1

"Let no man despise thy youth; but be thou an example of the believers, in word, in conversation, in charity, in spirit, in faith, in purity."
- I Timothy 4:12

"Flee also youthful lusts: but follow righteousness, faith, charity, peace, with them that call on the Lord out of a pure heart."
- II Timothy 2:22

"Never lend your car to anyone to whom you have given birth."
- Erma Bombeck

"There is nothing wrong with a young man that twenty years cannot cure."
- Benjamin Franklin

"Two things are extremely painful to mothers: Bringing a child into the world and sending a child out into the world."
- Jack Murphy

"It has been proposed that young men suspend their education between the ages of 13 and 24. During this period, many young men often have their minds set upon one thing --- and it isn't education."
- Will Rogers

"I never expected to see the day when girls would get sunburned in the places they do now."
- Will Rogers

"When I was a boy of fourteen, my father was so ignorant I could hardly stand to have the old man around. But when I got to be twenty-one, I was astonished at how much he had learned in seven years."
- Mark Twain

"Do you know why teenagers are so stupid? When they need advice, who do they go to? Other teenagers! They don't go to those who have already experienced the problems and issues that they are currently facing. They turn to the inexperienced advice of one another. And they wonder why they keep doing stupid things?"
- Bill Wilson

"Adolescence is a period of rapid changes. Between the ages of 12 and 17, for example, a parent ages as much as 20 years."
- American Proverb

"My son, learn from my mistakes and the mistakes of others. It is much better than making all of these mistakes yourself."
- American Proverb

"Some children who are sent into the brave new world will quickly return with dirty laundry for their mother."
- English Proverb

"A teenage boy has a wolf in his belly and brain.
- German Proverb

"Little children, headache; big children, heartache."
- Italian Proverb

"Small children disturb your sleep, big children your life."
- Jewish Proverb

"Too many of today's teens have straight teeth and crooked morals."
- Unknown

"When buying a used car, punch the buttons on the radio. If all the stations are rock and roll, there's a good chance the transmission is shot."
- Unknown

"When my child was 7, I dreaded the day when he would leave home. When he was 17, I welcomed those thoughts with silent adulation. When he was 27, I counted the days when I would see him again."
- Unknown

"It is better to teach your kids the 'facts of life' before they learn it from firsthand experience."
- Unknown

"It's difficult to decide whether growing pains are something teenagers have - or are."
- Unknown

TEMPER

"He that is slow to wrath is of great understanding: but he that is hasty of spirit exalteth folly."
- Proverbs 14:29

"He that is slow to anger is better than the mighty; and he that ruleth his spirit than he that taketh a city."
- Proverbs 16:32

"For a bishop must be blameless, as the steward of God; not selfwilled, not soon angry, not given to wine, no striker, not given to filthy lucre."
- Titus 1:7

"Temperament is the thermometer of character."
- Honore de Balzac

"If we desire to live securely, comfortably, and quietly, that by all honest means we should endeavor to purchase the good will of all men, and provoke no man's enmity needlessly; since any man's love may be useful, and every man's hatred is dangerous."
- Isaac Barrow

"By indulging this fretful temper, you alienate those on whose affection much of your comfort depends."
- Hugh Blair

"Such is the active power of good temperament! Great sweetness of temper neutralizes such vast amounts of acid."
- Ralph Waldo Emerson

"Hot heads and cold hearts never solved anything."
- Billy Graham

"He is happy whose circumstances suit his temper but he is more excellent who can suit his temper to any circumstances."
- David Hume

"A tart temper never mellows with age; and a sharp tongue is the only edged tool that grows keener with constant use."
- Washington Irving

"A temper is the spoiled attitude of a selfish child revealed in a grown man."
- Jack Murphy

"When angry, count to ten. When very angry, count sheep and get some sleep."
- American Proverb

"With 'gentleness' in his own character, 'comfort' in his house, and 'good temper' in his wife, the earthly felicity of man is complete."
- German Proverb

"A temper is a reflection of a selfish heart."
- Yiddish Proverb

TEMPTATION

"And lead us not into temptation, but deliver us from evil: For thine is the kingdom, and the power, and the glory, forever. Amen."
- Matthew 6:13

"But he turned, and said unto Peter, Get thee behind me, Satan: thou art an offence unto me: for thou savourest not the things that be of God, but those that be of men."
- Matthew 16:23

"For what shall it profit a man, if he shall gain the whole world, and lose his own soul?"
- Mark 8:36

"There hath no temptation taken you but such as is common to man: but God is faithful, who will not suffer you to be tempted above that ye are able; but will with the temptation also make a way to escape, that ye may be able to bear it."
- I Corinthians 10:13

"Blessed is the man that endureth temptation: for when he is tried, he shall receive the crown of life, which the Lord hath promised to them that love him."
- James 1:12

"Submit yourselves therefore to God. Resist the devil, and he will flee from you."
- James 4:7

"Every temptation is an opportunity of our getting nearer to God."
- John Quincy Adams

"Temptations, when we meet them at first, are as the lion that reared upon Samson; but if we overcome them, the next time we see them we shall find a nest of honey within them."
- John Bunyan

"A beautiful woman, if poor, should use double circumspection; for her beauty will tempt others, her poverty herself."
- Charles Caleb Colton

"Faith's most severe tests come not when we see nothing, but when we see a stunning array of evidence that seems to prove our faith vain."
- Elizabeth Elliot

"On this earth all is temptation. Crosses tempt us by irritating our pride, and prosperity by flattering it. Our life is a continual combat, but one in which Jesus Christ fights for us. We must pass on unmoved, while temptations rage around us, as the traveler, overtaken by a storm, simply wraps his cloak more closely about him, and pushes on more vigorously toward his destined home."
- François Fénelon

"The realization of God's presence is the one sovereign remedy against temptation."
- François Fénelon

"Many a dangerous temptation comes to us in fine gay colours, that are but skin-deep."
- Matthew Henry

"Do not bite at the bait of pleasure till you know there is no hook beneath it."
- Thomas Jefferson

"In so far as you approach temptation to a man, you do him an injury; and if he is overcome, you share his guilt."
- Samuel Johnson

"If passion drives you, let reason hold the reins."
- Benjamin Franklin

"The Devil has a great advantage against us inasmuch as he has a strong bastion and bulwark against us in our own flesh and blood."
- Martin Luther

"Satan is a master fisherman. He tirelessly fishes for the souls of men. Instead of using nets, he uses bait. He draws from his endless tackle box to find the temptation that will finally achieve your bite. God, on the other hand, uses no bait. He provides only Himself. Is your love for Him greater than any bait of this world? Can you truly say *'Take the whole world but give me Jesus?'*"
- Jack Murphy

"Temptation will come in many forms but with one purpose – to steal your song of worship to God."
- Jack Murphy

"Augustine teaches us that there is in each man a Serpent, an Eve, and an Adam. Our senses and natural propensities are the Serpent; the excitable desire is the Eve; and reason is the Adam. Our nature tempts us perpetually; criminal desire is often excited; but sin is not completed till reason consents."
- Blaise Pascal

"The time for reasoning is before we have approached near enough to the forbidden fruit to look at it and admire."
- Margaret Percival

"It is opportunity that makes the thief."
- Seneca

"It is one thing to be tempted, another thing to fall."
- William Shakespeare

"Some temptations come to the industrious, but all temptations attack the idle."

- Charles H. Spurgeon

"Many men enjoy the quick taste of temptation, but they despise the aftertaste."

- Unknown

"If your faith can't be tested, it can't be trusted."

- Unknown

"Since God will not allow you to be tempted beyond what you can withstand, it is reasonable to conclude that such trials of your faith will be determined by the caliber of man that God believes you are. How you face those trials will show you what kind of man you are."

- Unknown

TESTIMONY

"Thou shalt not bear false witness against thy neighbour."

- Exodus 20:16

"One witness shall not rise up against a man for any iniquity, or for any sin, in any sin that he sinneth: at the mouth of two witnesses, or at the mouth of three witnesses, shall the matter be established."

- Deuteronomy 19:15

"I, John, who also am your brother, and companion in tribulation, and in the kingdom and patience of Jesus Christ, was in the isle that is called Patmos, for the word of God, and for the testimony of Jesus Christ."

- Revelation 1:9

"And they overcame him by the blood of the Lamb, and by the word of their testimony; and they loved not their lives unto the death."

- Revelation 12:11

"I am not struck so much by the diversity of testimony as by the many-sidedness of truth."
-    Stanley Baldwin

"Remember the sufferings of Christ, the storms that were weathered...the crown that came from those sufferings which gave new radiance to the faith... All saints give testimony to the truth that without real effort, no one ever wins the crown."
-    Thomas Beckett

"No testimony is sufficient to establish a miracle, unless the testimony be of such a kind, that its falsehood would be more miraculous than the fact which it endeavors to establish."
-    David Hume

"Testimony is like an arrow shot from a long bow; the force of it depends on the strength of the hand that draws it. Argument is like an arrow from a crossbow, which has equal force though shot by a child."
-    Samuel Johnson

"Seek not the favor of the multitude; it is seldom got by honest and lawful means. But seek the testimony of few; and number not voices, but weigh them."
-    Immanuel Kant

"Live your life in such a manner that your testimony will hold the weight of truth."
-    Jack Murphy

"At the end of Revelation there is again that solemn insistence on the personal testimony, and even more solemn warning to those who would impugn it."
-    Alfred Noyes

"The principle that certain sins should not receive the Church's testimony of forgiveness was probably no novelty at all, but had been applied in various churches; perhaps, however, with no strict consistency."
-    Robert Rainy

"His word was his bond."
- American Proverb

TESTS

"Then said the LORD unto Moses, Behold, I will rain bread from heaven for you; and the people shall go out and gather a certain rate every day, that I may prove them, whether they will walk in my law, or no."
- Exodus 16:4

"For the ear trieth words, as the mouth tasteth meat."
- Job 34:3

"The fining pot is for silver, and the furnace for gold: but the LORD trieth the hearts."
- Proverbs 17:3

"Prove everything. Hold on to that which is good."
- I Thessalonians 5:21

"Here is the test to find whether your mission on earth is finished. If you're alive, it isn't."
- Richard Bach

"Examinations are formidable even to the best prepared, for the greatest fool may ask more than the wisest man can answer."
- Charles Caleb Coulton

"Not everything that counts can be counted and not everything that can be counted counts."
- Albert Einstein

"The test of a first-rate intelligence is the ability to hold two opposed ideas in the mind at the same time, and still retain the ability to function."
- F. Scott Fitzgerald

"The greatest test of courage on earth is to bear defeat without losing heart."

- Robert Green Ingersoll

"Do not rely completely on any other human being, however dear. We meet all life's greatest tests alone."

- Agnes Macphail

"American's high schools and colleges have created a population of information memorizers. They memorize the information to achieve a passing grade, and it is quickly forgotten. The problems of life are not answered by A, B, C, D, or 'None of the Above.'"

- Jack Murphy

"The only meaningful test in school is the IQ test. Everything else amounts to what a person happens to have remembered on a given day in time."

- Jack Murphy

"The purpose of the test is not to promote, but to reveal areas of failure. A good teacher and a good student must recognize error and work to correct it."

- Jack Murphy

"Anyone can confirm how little the grading that results from examinations corresponds to the final useful work of people in life."

- Jean Piaget

"What we want is to see the child in pursuit of knowledge and not knowledge in pursuit of the child."

- George Bernard Shaw

"Do not test the depth of a river with both feet."

- African Proverb

"As long as there are tests, there will always be prayer in public schools."

- American Proverb

"Education ceases to be learning when the 3 R's are read, remember, and regurgitate."
- American Proverb

"Einstein failed many school tests, but his genius goes beyond question."
- Jewish Proverb

"The test of a man's character is how he faces adversity."
- Unknown

THEOLOGY

"Then the LORD answered Job out of the whirlwind, and said,
Who is this that darkeneth counsel by words without knowledge?
Gird up now thy loins like a man; for I will demand of thee, and answer thou me.
Where wast thou when I laid the foundations of the earth? declare, if thou hast understanding."
- Job 38:1-4

"For who hath known the mind of the Lord? or who hath been his counsellor?"
- Romans 11:34

"All my theology is reduced to this narrow compass – 'Jesus Christ came into the world to save sinners.'"
- Archibald Alexander

"Theology is but our ideas of truth classified and arranged."
- Henry Ward Beecher

"The theological systems of men and schools of men are determined always by the character of their ideal of Christ, the central fact of the Christian system."
- Josiah Holland

"Let us put theology out of religion. Theology attempts to send the worst to heaven, the best to hell."
- Robert Green Ingersoll

"Medicine makes people ill, mathematics makes them sad, and theology makes them sinful."
- Martin Luther

"Theology is the study of God. Why then do seminarians study denominational doctrine? The study of God can only be fulfilled in a Bible and a prayer closet."
- Jack Murphy

"Comparative theology testifies that Jesus Christ, who is not less truly the incarnation of the Christian's theology than of the Christian's God, is indeed the desire of the nations, but not their product, their invention, or their discovery."
- George Pepper

"Theology is better learned praying in a lonely field than reading in a crowded classroom."
- Will Rogers

"A man must have a stout digestion to feed upon some men's theology; no sap, no sweetness, no life, but all stern accuracy, and fleshless definition. Proclaimed without tenderness, and argued without affection, the gospel from such men rather resembles a missile from a catapult than bread from a Father's hand."
- Charles H. Spurgeon

"The best theology is rather a divine life than a divine knowledge."
- Jeremy Taylor

"The devil is a better theologian than any of us and is a devil still."
- A.W. Tozer

"Your life teaches theology to the world around you. You are the only Jesus some people will ever see."
- 	Christian Proverb

"Theology attempts to translate the unfathomable knowledge of God into plain words. It would be easier to contain the entire Universe within a thimble than to use scientific method to describe the mind of God."
- 	Unknown

THOUGHT

"Search me, O God, and know my heart: try me, and know my thoughts: And see if there be any wicked way in me, and lead me in the way everlasting."
- 	Psalm 139:23-24

"The thoughts of the wicked are an abomination to the LORD: but the words of the pure are pleasant words."
- 	Proverbs 15:26

"For as he thinketh in his heart, so is he."
- 	Proverbs 23:7

"Finally, brethren, whatsoever things are true, whatsoever things are honest, whatsoever things are just, whatsoever things are pure, whatsoever things are lovely, whatsoever things are of good report; if there be any virtue, and if there be any praise, think on these things."
- 	Philippians 4:8

"Set your affection on things above, not on things on the earth."
- 	Colossians 3:2

"For the word of God is quick, and powerful, and sharper than any two-edged sword, piercing even to the dividing asunder of soul and spirit, and of the joints and marrow, and is a discerner of the thoughts and intents of the heart."
- 	Hebrews 4:12

"Let thy chief fort and place of defense be a mind free from passions. A stronger place and better fortified than this, hath no man."
- Marcus Antoninus Aurelius

"A man would do well to carry a pencil in his pocket, and write down the thoughts of the moment. Those that come unsought for are commonly the most valuable, and should be secured, because they seldom return."
- Sir Francis Bacon

"Not a single path
  Of thought I tread, but that it leads to God."
- Phillip James Bailey

"Farewell, vain world; my soul can bid Adieu. My Savior taught me to abandon you. Your charms may gratify a sensual mind, but cannot please a soul for God Designed. Oh! How amazing it is that people can talk so much about men's power and goodness, when if God did not hold us back every moment, we should be devils incarnate!"
- David Brainerd

"The world can be divided into 3 parts: those who make things happen, those who watch things happen and those who don't know what's happening."
- Bill Bright

"There is a boundary to men's passions when they act from feelings; but none when they are under the influence of imagination."
- Edmund Burke

"Reading without reflecting is like eating without digesting."
- Edmund Burke

"A thinking man is the worst enemy the Prince of Darkness can have; every time such a one announces himself, I doubt not there runs a shudder through the nether empire; and new emissaries are trained with new tactics, to, if possible, entrap him, and hoodwink and handcuff him."
- Thomas Carlyle

"The empires of the future are the empires of the mind."
- Winston Churchill

"Nurture your mind with great thoughts; to believe in the heroic makes heroes."
- Benjamin Disraeli

"The world we have created is a product of our thinking; it cannot be changed without changing our thinking."
- Albert Einstein

"As a Christian, I am responsible for the furniture of my mind."
- Frank E. Gaebelein

"I'll put that in my thinking cap."
- John Fletcher

"One thing that separates man from other animals is that man can, on occasion, ponder his thoughts."
- Jack Murphy

"Two Laws that govern my life: The law of cognition: I am what I think. The law of exposure: My mind will think most about what it is most exposed to."
- John Ortberg

"Research has shown that one's thought life influences every aspect of one's being. Whether we are filled with confidence or fear depends on the kind of thoughts that habitually occupy our minds."
- John Ortberg

"He who thinks by the inch and talks by the yard deserves to be kicked by the foot."
- American Proverb

"If you understand everything, you must be misinformed."
- Japanese proverb

"Our job is not to make up anybody's mind, but to open minds and to make the agony of the decision-making so intense you can escape only by thinking."

- Unknown

TIME

"To everything there is a season, and a time to every purpose under the heaven:

A time to be born, and a time to die; a time to plant, and a time to pluck up that which is planted;

A time to kill, and a time to heal; a time to break down, and a time to build up;

A time to weep, and a time to laugh; a time to mourn, and a time to dance;

A time to cast away stones, and a time to gather stones together; a time to embrace, and a time to refrain from embracing;

A time to get, and a time to lose; a time to keep, and a time to cast away;

A time to rend, and a time to sew; a time to keep silence, and a time to speak;

A time to love, and a time to hate; a time of war, and a time of peace."

- Ecclesiastes 3:1-8

"He hath made everything beautiful in his time."

- Ecclesiastes 3:11

"Declaring the end from the beginning, and from ancient times the things that are not yet done, saying, My counsel shall stand, and I will do all my pleasure."

- Isaiah 46:10

"For he saith, I have heard thee in a time accepted, and in the day of salvation have I succoured thee: behold, now is the accepted time; behold now is the day of salvation."

- II Corinthians 6:2

"But, beloved, be not ignorant of this one thing, that one day is with the Lord as a thousand years, and a thousand years as one day."
- II Peter 3:8

"The hours of a wise man are lengthened by his ideas, as those of a fool are by his passions. The time of the one is long, because he does not know what to do with it; so is that of the other, because he distinguishes every moment of it with useful or amusing thoughts--or, in other words, because the one is always wishing it away, and the other always enjoying it."
- Joseph Addison

"The bad news is time flies. The good news is you're the pilot."
- Michael Althsuler

"Men talk of killing time, while it is actually time that quietly kills them."
- Dion Boucicault

"It was the best of times, it was the worst of times..."
- Charles Dickens,
in *A Tale of Two Cities*

"Time is precious; but truth is more precious than time."
- Benjamin Disraeli

"Practice the 'First 5 Minutes.' The first 5 minutes occurring between people sets the tone for everything that is to follow. For example, a public speaker is given very few moments to convince his audience that he really does have something worthwhile to say. This simple principle relates to family members as well. The first 5 minutes of the morning might determine how a mother will interact with her children on that day. It concerns the sheer power of words."
- James Dobson

"Resolve never to do anything which you would be afraid to do if it were the last hour of your life."
- Jonathan Edwards

"All of my kingdom and crowns for but a moment of time!"
- Queen Elizabeth I,
attributed to her deathbed

"Time is given us that we may take care for eternity; and eternity will not be too long to regret the loss of our time if we have misspent it."
- François Fénelon

"Does thou love life? Then do not squander time; for that's the stuff life is made of."
- Benjamin Franklin

"Fish and visitors stink after three days."
- Benjamin Franklin

"Never put off for tomorrow what you can do today."
- Benjamin Franklin

"Set priorities with sooner being better than perfect."
- Lou Gerstner

"Statistics show that roughly 100 out of every 100 people die at some time during their lives. The question is how they spent that time before death."
- Keith Green

"The Future is something which everyone reaches at the rate of sixty minutes an hour, whatever he does, whoever he is."
- C. S. Lewis

"The 4 Laws of Unseized Time:
1) Unseized time flows toward my weakness.
2) Unseized time comes under the influence of dominant people in my world.
3) Unseized time surrenders to the demands of all emergencies.
4) Unseized time gets invested in things that gain public acclamation."

- Gordon MacDonald

"Time never stands still on this side of Eternity."
- Jack Murphy

"The whole of human history and the totality of its timeline – from Creation to Armageddon – are not even a drop in the bucket when compared to this vast thing called *Eternity*. Your ultimate state in Eternity is dependent upon what you did with this little thing called 'Life.'"
- Jack Murphy

"Einstein, in his *Theory of Relativity*, argued that time is not a constant. It can speed up and slow down relative to perspective. Proof of this can be experienced by witnessing how quickly time flies on the honeymoon and how slowly it crawls when spending time with your mother-in-law."
- Jack Murphy

"If you are fortunate enough to have a job, do it with all your heart. But remember that although it is a vital part of your life, it is only a part, and although you may rise to great heights, somebody else will one day take your place at the work bench or at the boardroom table. Nobody will ever take your place as the father of the child you are now cradling in your arms. You may well work for the best part of half a century, but the time you have been given to pass on the things that matter to your child is so very limited. There will be many demands on your time, and you will not always be able to give your children the time they ask. But so far as is possible, count the days. Try not to miss one of them."
- Rob Parsons

"God only allows us so many opportunities with our children to read a story, go fishing, play catch, and say our prayers together. Try not to miss one of them. The office can wait. It will still be there after the children are gone."
- Rob Parsons

"In the end, time will give way to eternity."
- Leonard Ravenhill

"At any point in all of eternity, we can say, *'This is only the beginning.'*"
- Leonard Ravenhill

"There is no refund for wasted time."
- Will Rogers

"Increase the proportion of your time on the few things that produce the most benefit."
- Andy Stanley

"Folks it getting late and its getting serious."
- David Wilkerson

"Tell me what you do with your time and money and I will tell you where your heart is."
- Frances Xavier

"The art of being a good guest is knowing when to leave."
- American Proverb

"Time goes very slowly on the last day of school, as the last seconds of the day tick away like an eternity. That is…unless you are bringing home a report card full of failing grades. No matter how much you wish that time would slow down, it flies to the point of a blur until you meet your parents' indignation."
- American Proverb

"For some, life is but a fleeting moment. For others, life is 120 years. But to all, it is too short."
- English Proverb

"Four things come not back: the spoken word, the spent arrow, time past, the neglected opportunity."
- Irish Proverb

"Carpe Diem." (Latin for "Seize the Day")
- U.S. Marine Corp

"You either run the day or the day runs you."
- Unknown

"The Law of Diminishing Intent--Time kills all good intentions that are not acted upon quickly."
- Unknown

"Time heals all wounds."
- Unknown

"It has been said that 'Time heals all wounds.' This is true...except for our eternal wounds. Sin separates mankind for all eternity from God. No matter of time will ever heal that separation."
- Unknown

"Live each moment as if it were your last."
- Unknown

"The past, present and future. To God, they are but epilogue."
- Unknown

TITHING – See GIVING

TOLERANCE

"The religion that fosters intolerance needs another Christ to die for it."
- Henry Ward Beecher

"Toleration is good for all, or it is good for none."
- Edmund Burke

"I have seen gross intolerance shown in support of tolerance."
- Samuel Taylor Coleridge

"As no roads are so rough as those that have just been mended, so no sinners are so intolerant as those that have just turned saints."
- Charles Caleb Colton

"Do not mistake my suggestions for prejudice nor my patience for tolerance, nor my tolerance for acceptance."
- Benjamin Franklin

"They who boast of their tolerance merely give others leave to be as careless about religion as they are themselves. A walrus might as well pride itself on its endurance of cold."
- A. W. Hare

"The highest result of education is tolerance."
- Helen Keller

"The first weapon of the wicked is to shout, '*Intolerance!*'"
- Jack Murphy

"It is easy to tolerate those you agree with. It is difficult to tolerate those with whom you disagree. But it is sinful to tolerate wicked behavior in the name of 'tolerance.'"
- Jack Murphy

"To be broad-minded' is just another way of saying a fellow's too lazy to form an opinion."
- Will Rogers

"It is easy to be tolerant of the principles of other people if you have none of your own."
- Herbert Samuel

"Let us all resolve, first, to attain the grace of silence; second, to deem all fault-finding that does no good a sin, and to resolve, when we are ourselves happy, not to poison the atmosphere for our neighbors by calling upon them to remark every painful and disagreeable feature in their daily life, third, to practice the grace and virtue of praise."
- Harriet Beecher Stowe

"The law tolerates no lawbreaker."
- English Proverb

"Live and let live."
- Scottish Proverb

"Tolerate others as God tolerates you. But, like God, do not make excuses for sin."

- Spanish Proverb

"Tolerance does not mark the progress of a religion. It is the fatal sign of its decline."

- Unknown

TRAVEL

"I have been a stranger in a strange land."

- Exodus 2:22

"Now Jacob's well was there. Jesus therefore, being wearied with his journey, sat thus on the well: and it was about the sixth hour."

- John 4:6

"By faith Abraham, when he was called to go out into a place which he should after receive for an inheritance, obeyed; and he went out, not knowing whither he went.

By faith he sojourned in the land of promise, as in a strange country, dwelling in tabernacles with Isaac and Jacob, the heirs with him of the same promise:

For he looked for a city which hath foundations, whose builder and maker is God."

- Hebrews 11:8-12

"These all died in faith, not having received the promises, but having seen them afar off, and were persuaded of them, and embraced them, and confessed that they were strangers and pilgrims on the earth."

- Hebrews 11:13

"As a child, I wanted to go to *Rock City* on Lookout Mountain in Chattanooga and 'see seven states.' Instead, I went to the moon and saw the entire world in one moment. This desire for discovery is one and the same. You know, I still want to see *Rock City*."

- Buzz Aldrin

"Some places are not worth conquering."
- Aristotle

"The World is a book, and those who do not travel read only a page."
- St. Augustine

"He that travels into a country before he has some entrance into the language, goeth to school and not to travel."
- Sir Francis Bacon

"The most important trip you may take in life is meeting people halfway."
- Henry Boye

"Half the fun of the travel is the esthetic of lostness."
- Ray Bradbury

"Some of the citizens of London who want to see the world have not even truly seen the wonders of London yet."
- Winston Churchill

"Those who visit foreign nations, but who associate only with their own countrymen, change their climate, but not their customs; they see new meridians, but the same men; and with heads as empty as their pockets, return home with traveled bodies, but untraveled minds."
- Charles Caleb Colton

"Every traveler has a home of his own, and he learns to appreciate it the more from his wandering."
- Charles Dickens

"Like all great travelers, I have seen more than I remember, and remember more than I have seen."
- Benjamin Disraeli

"I think that travel comes from some deep urge to see the world, like the urge that brings up a worm in an Irish bog to see the moon when it is full."
- Lord Dunsany

"I love to travel,
  But hate to arrive."

>   -   Albert Einstein

"Do not go where the path may lead, go instead where there is no path and leave a trail."

>   -   Ralph Waldo Emerson

"The world is bigger than the horizon. It is a shame that many only discover its wonders by reading National Geographic."

>   -   Ernest Hemingway

"Two roads diverged in a wood, and I--
  I took the one less traveled by,
    And that has made all the difference."

>   -   Robert Frost

"One travels more usefully when alone, because he reflects more."

>   -   Thomas Jefferson

"It is not down in any map; true places never are."

>   -   Herman Melville

"It is good to travel. But if you reject the food, ignore the customs, fear the religion and avoid the people, you might better stay home."

>   -   James Michener

"I'd like to see for myself that the world is round rather than simply know that it is so from my books."

>   -   L. M. Montgomery

"The easiest way to realize how much you love America? Travel abroad. Even if you enjoy seeing the sights, you will quickly realize how glad you are to live in this country!"

>   -   Jack Murphy

"Every honeymoon should begin traveling abroad. There is something about getting lost in a foreign land that makes a couple appreciate the loneliness of one another."
- Will Rogers

"Travel and change of place impart new vigor to the mind."
- Seneca

"I dislike feeling at home when I am abroad."
- George Bernard Shaw

"I travel not to go anywhere, but to go. I travel for travel's sake. The great affair is to move."
- Robert Louis Stevenson

"Not all those who wander are lost."
- J. R. R. Tolkien

"I have found out that there ain't no surer way to find out whether you like people or hate them than to travel with them."
- Mark Twain

"Travel is fatal to prejudice, bigotry, and narrow-mindedness, and many of our people need it sorely on these accounts. Broad, wholesome, charitable views of men and things cannot be acquired by vegetating in one little corner of the earth all one's lifetime."
- Mark Twain

"When preparing to travel, lay out all your clothes and all your money. Then take half the clothes and twice the money."
- American Proverb

"I thought that Venice and Paris were beautiful – until I visited them for a week. I realized that traveling by boat, although romantic, becomes tiresome very quickly – especially in a cold rain."
- English Proverb

"I traveled abroad in search of cultures and only then truly discovered myself."

- Unknown

"Most travel is best of all in the anticipation or the remembering; the reality has more to do with losing your luggage."

- Unknown

TRIALS & TRIBULATIONS

"But he knoweth the way that I take: when he hath tried me, I shall come forth as gold."

- Job 33:10

"My brethren, count it all joy when ye fall into divers temptations; Knowing this, that the trying of your faith worketh patience."

- James 1:2-3

"By His trials, God means to purify us, to take away all our self-confidence, and our trust in each other, and bring us into implicit, humble trust in Himself."

- Horace Bushnell

"As the musician straineth his strings, and yet he breaketh none of them, but maketh thereby a sweeter melody and better concord; so God, through affliction makes His own better unto the fruition and enjoying of the life to come."

- Daniel Cawdrey

"Never was there a man of deep piety, who has not been brought into extremities--who has not been put into fire--who has been taught to say, 'Though He slay me, yet will I trust in Him.'"

- Richard Cecil

"Cease from disquietude,
Fret not, this is unto thee
a preparation time;
Thou must be made in likeness
unto Him thou wouldest serve.
Wait, the diamond must be cut
ere from its tiny facets
Flash the glory of the sun's pure ray.
Rain must descend,
Else from yon dull grey bulb
springeth no sweet perfumed flower.
Be silent upon God,
thy time for service has not come;
Patience,
this waiting trial is by Him who loves thee sent;
Be still...
...He knoweth all, thou knowest that His will is best."
- Oswald Chambers

"Under the shadow of earthly disappointment, all unconscious to ourselves, our Divine Redeemer is walking by our side."
- Edward Hubbell Chapin

"It is the easiest thing in the world for us to obey God when He commands us to do what we like, and to trust Him when the path is all sunshine. The real victory of faith is to trust God in the dark, and through the dark. Let us be assured of this, that if the lesson and the rod are of His appointing, and that His all-wise love has engineered the deep tunnel of trial on the heavenward road. He will never desert us during the discipline. The vital thing for us is not to deny and desert Him."
- Theodore Ledyard Cuyler

"Sanctified afflictions are spiritual promotions."
- Matthew Henry

"We can decide to let our trials crush us, or we can convert them to new forces of good."
- Helen Keller

"God whispers to us in our pleasures, speaks to us in our conscious but shouts to us in our pains. Suffering is God's megaphone in a deaf world."
-     C.S. Lewis

"If I profess with the loudest voice and clearest exposition every portion of the truth of God except precisely that little point which the world and the devil are at that moment attacking, I am not confessing Christ, however boldly I may be professing Christ. Where the battle rages, there the loyalty of the soldier is proved; and to be steady on all the battlefield besides, is mere flight and disgrace if he flinches at that point."
-     Martin Luther

"A dark hour makes Jesus bright."
-     Robert Murray M'Cheyne

"It is necessary that our sharpest trials should sometimes spring from our dearest comforts, else we should be in danger of forgetting ourselves and setting up our rest here."
-     John Newton

"The secret formula of the saints: When I am in the cellar of affliction, I look for the Lord's choicest wines."
-     Samuel Rutherford

"Trials teach us what we are; they dig up the soil, and let us see what we are made of."
-     Charles Spurgeon

"Many men owe the grandeur of their lives to their tremendous difficulties."
-     Charles Spurgeon

"Great hearts can only be made by great troubles. Great faith must have great trials."
-     Charles Spurgeon

"Give me the comforts of God, and I can well bear the taunts of men. Let me lay my head on the bosom of Jesus, and I fear no distraction of care and trouble. If my God will ever give me the light of his smile, and grant his benediction - it is enough."
-     Charles Spurgeon

"Nothing is intolerable that is necessary. Now God hath bound thy trouble upon thee by His special providence, and with a design to try thee, and with purposes to reward and crown thee. These cords thou canst not break, and therefore lie thou down gently, and suffer the hand of God to do what He pleases."
-     Jeremy Taylor

"As I look back over fifty years of ministry, I recall innumerable tests, trials and times of crushing pain. But through it all, the Lord has proven faithful, loving, and totally true to all his promises."
-     David Wilkerson

"A gem cannot be polished without friction,
nor a man perfected without trials."
-     Chinese Proverb

"Great faith is birthed through great trials."
-     English Proverb

"God tries you with a little, to see what you'd do with a lot."
-     Jewish Proverb

"The Lord gets his best soldiers out of the highlands of affliction."
-     Unknown

TRUST – See FAITH

TRUTH

"Lord, who shall abide in thy tabernacle? who shall dwell in thy holy hill?
  He that walketh uprightly, and worketh righteousness, and speaketh the truth in his heart." - Psalm 15:1-2

"Then said Jesus to those Jews which believed on him, If ye continue in my word, then are ye my disciples indeed; And ye shall know the truth, and the truth shall make you free."
- John 8:32

"I am the way, the truth and the life. No man comes to the father but by me."
- John 14:6

"Thy word is truth."
- John 17:17

"What is truth?"
- Pilate, in John 18:38

"Truth sits often upon the lips of dying men."
- Matthew Arnold

"Let those," he very beautifully says to the Manichæans, "burn with hatred against you, who do not know how much pains it costs to find the truth, how hard it is to guard against error;—but I, who after so great and long wavering came to know the truth, must bear myself towards you with the same patience which my fellow-believers showed towards me while I was wandering in blind madness in your opinions."
- Augustine

"If you believe what you like in the Gospel, and reject what you don't like, it is not the Gospel you believe, but yourself."
- Augustine

"There were some things that were true and some things that were trite; but what was true was trite, and what was not trite was not true."
- Arthur James Balfour

"Whatever is only almost true is quite false, and among the most dangerous of errors, because being so near truth, it is the more likely to lead astray."
- Henry Ward Beecher

"Think truly, and thy thoughts
Shall the world's famine feed.
Speak truly, and each word of thine
Shall be a fruitful seed.
Live truly, and thy life shall be
A great and noble creed."
- Horatio Bonar

"Truth is mighty and will prevail."
- Thomas Brooks

"Truth gets well if she is run over by a locomotive, while error dies of lockjaw if she scratches her finger."
- William Cullen Bryant

"Old truths are always new to us, if they come with the smell of heaven upon them."
- John Bunyan

"Falsehood and delusion are allowed in no case whatever; but, as in the exercise of all the virtues, there is an economy of truth. It is a sort of temperance, by which a man speaks truth with measure, that he may speak it the longer."
- Sir Edmund Burke

"Blessed be the God's voice; for it is true, and falsehoods have to cease before it!"
- Thomas Carlyle

"Truth rises above falsehood as oil rises above water."
- Cervantes

"Truth, of course, must of necessity be stranger than fiction; for we have made fiction to suit ourselves."
- G. K. Chesterton

"Truth is incontrovertible; malice may attack it and ignorance may deride it; but, in the end; there it is."
- Winston Churchill

"The greatest friend of truth is time; her greatest enemy is prejudice; and her constant companion is humility."
- Charles Caleb Colton

"The search for truth implies a duty. One must not conceal any part of what one has recognized to be true."
- Albert Einstein

"Truth is beautiful, without doubt; but so are lies."
- Ralph Waldo Emerson

"Half a truth is often a great lie."
- Benjamin Franklin

"All truths are easy to understand once they are discovered; the point is to discover them."
- Galileo Galilei

"Religious truth is captive in a small number of little manuscripts which guard the common treasures, instead of expanding them. Let us break the seal which binds these holy things; let us give wings to truth that it may fly with the Word, no longer prepared at vast expense, but multitudes everlastingly by a machine which never wearies to every soul which enters life."
- Johann Gutenberg

"Truth is not only stranger than fiction, it is more interesting."
- William Randolph Hearst

"We are apt to shut our eyes against a painful truth… For my part, I am willing to know the whole truth; to know the worst; and to provide for it."
- Patrick Henry

"Should I keep back my opinions at such a time, through fear of giving offense, I should consider myself as guilty of treason towards my country, and of an act of disloyalty toward the Majesty of Heaven, which I revere above all earthly kings."

- Patrick Henry

"Make the lie big, make it simple, keep saying it, and eventually they will believe it."

- Adolf Hitler

"Great truths that are stumbling blocks to the natural man are nevertheless the very foundations upon which the confidence of the spiritual man is built."

- Harry B. Ironside

"It is error alone which needs the support of government. Truth can stand by itself."

- Thomas Jefferson

"It does not require many words to speak the truth."

- Chief Joseph

"The powers of the air are only obliged to recognize one thing; authenticity, reality, truth. They see through the appearances and they yawn."

- Art Katz

"A lie told often enough becomes the truth."

- Vladimir Lenin

"It matters enormously if I alienate anyone from the truth."

- C.S. Lewis

"A wooden key is not so beautiful as a golden one, but if it can open the door when the golden one cannot, it is more useful."

- Martin Luther

"For the great majority of mankind are satisfied with appearances, as though they were realities, and are often more influenced by the things that seem than by those that are."
- Niccolo Machiavelli

"A preacher who preaches the truth uncompromisingly will be asked "does your preaching always have to be so pointy? Does it always have to be so sharp?" And of coarse the answer is no. He can blunt his message if he'd like and become just as dull as the average preacher."
- Jesse Morrell

"The process [of mass-media deception] has to be conscious, or it would not be carried out with sufficient precision, but it also has to be unconscious, or it would bring with it a feeling of falsity and hence of guilt.... To tell deliberate lies while genuinely believing in them, to forget any fact that has become inconvenient, and then, when it becomes necessary again, to draw it back from oblivion for just so long as it is needed, to deny the existence of objective reality and all the while to take account of the reality which one denies all this is indispensably necessary."
- George Orwell

"We have entered an era in which men stand behind the pulpit and smugly call the truths of the Word of God to be theories, opinions or parables!"
- Leonard Ravenhill

"We have the truth and we need not be afraid to say so."
- J.C. Ryle

"As scarce as truth is, the supply has always been in excess of the demand."
- Henry Wheeler Shaw

"To tell the truth will shame the devil."
- Jonathan Swift

"Always tell the truth. That way you don't have to remember what you said."

- Mark Twain

"Love truth, but pardon error that is done in sincerity."

- Voltaire

"Never take a bone away from a hungry dog. Give him a lamb chop and he will drop the bone. The Truth tastes better than a lie."

- David Wilkerson

"When people who are honestly mistaken learn the truth, they will either cease being mistaken, or cease being honest!"

- Unknown

U

UGLINESS

"For he shall grow up before him as a tender plant, and as a root out of a dry ground: he hath no form nor comeliness; and when we shall see him, there is no beauty that we should desire him."
- Isaiah 53:2

"Nothing is irredeemably ugly but sin."
- Honore de Balzac

"Though ugliness be the opposite of beauty, it is not the opposite to proportion and fitness; for it is possible that a thing may be very ugly with any proportions, and with a perfect fitness for any use."
- Sir Edmund Burke

"An ugly face and the want of exterior beauty generally increases the interior beauty."
- Paul Chatfield

"Both beauty and ugliness are equally to be dreaded; the one as a dangerous gift, the other as a melancholy affliction."
- Eliza Cook

"Better an ugly face than an ugly mind."
- James Ellis

"Beauty, like supreme dominion
Is but supported by opinion."
- Benjamin Franklin

"Ugliness without tact is horrible."
- Nathaniel Hawthorne

"I do not know if she was virtuous, but she was ugly, and with a woman that is half the battle."
- Heinrich Heine

"Beauty in things exists merely in the mind which contemplates them."
- David Hume

"Beauty is only skin deep – but ugliness can go to the bone."
- Dorothy Parker

"No living thing is truly ugly. It is only ugly to those without an imagination and to those who are easily influenced by the petty whims of persuasion."
- Will Rogers

"Absolute and entire ugliness is rare."
- John Ruskin

"Absolute ugliness is admitted as rarely as perfect beauty; but degrees of it more or less distinct are associated with whatever has the nature of death and sin, just as beauty is associated with what has the nature of virtue and of life."
- John Ruskin

"Beauty is bought by judgement of the eye,
Not utter'd by base sale of chapmen's tongues."
- William Shakespeare

"There is a sort of charm in ugliness, if the person has some redeeming qualities and is only ugly enough."
- Henry Wheeler Shaw

"Nobody's sweetheart is ugly."
-      Jean Joseph Vade

"Beauty is in the eye of the beholder."
-      English Proverb

"Ugliness, after virtue, is the best guardian of a young woman."
-      French Proverb

UNBELIEF – See FAITH

UNDERSTANDING

"Through thy precepts I get understanding: therefore I hate every false way."
-      Psalm 119:104

"Trust in the LORD with all thine heart; and lean not unto thine own understanding."
-      Proverbs 3:5

"Wisdom is the principal thing; therefore get wisdom: and with all thy getting get understanding."
-      Proverbs 4:7

"The fear of the LORD is the beginning of wisdom: and the knowledge of the holy is understanding."
-      Proverbs 9:10

"And I gave my heart to know wisdom, and to know madness and folly: I perceived that this also is vexation of spirit."
-      Ecclesiastes 1:17

"Though I speak with the tongues of men and of angels, and have not charity, I am become as sounding brass, or a tinkling cymbal.
    And though I have the gift of prophecy, and understand all mysteries, and all knowledge; and though I have all faith, so that I could remove mountains, and have not charity, I am nothing." - I Corinthians 13:1-2

"Who is a wise man and endued with knowledge among you? let him shew out of a good conversation his works with meekness of wisdom."
- James 3:13

"And we know that the Son of God is come, and hath given us an understanding, that we may know him that is true, and we are in him that is true, even in his Son Jesus Christ. This is the true God, and eternal life."
- I John 5:20

"Understanding is the reward of faith. Therefore seek not to understand that thou mayest believe, but believe, that thou mayest understand."
- Augustine of Hippo

"The eye of the understanding is like the eye of the sense; for as you may see great objects through small crannies or holes, so you may see great axioms of nature through small and contemptible instances."
- Sir Francis Bacon

"Humility is the light of the understanding."
- John Bunyan

"If you cannot explain it simply – even to a child – you just don't understand it well enough."
- Albert Einstein

"Men and melons are hard to understand."
- Benjamin Franklin

"Fully to understand a grand and beautiful thought requires, perhaps, as much time as to conceive it."
- Joseph Joubert

"Knowing is seeing. Until we ourselves see it with our own eyes, and perceive it by our own understandings, we are as much in the dark and as void of knowledge as before, let us believe any learned author as much as we will."
- John Locke

"The power of perception is that which we call the understanding."
-   John Locke

"Those who have read of everything are though to understand everything too; but it is not always so--reading furnishes the mind only with materials of knowledge; it is thinking that makes what is read ours. We are of the ruminating kind, and it is not enough to cram ourselves with a great load of collections; unless we chew them over again, they will not give us strength and nourishment."
-   John Locke

"A matter that becomes clear ceases to concern us."
-   Friedrich Nietzsche

"No law or ordinance is mightier than understanding."
-   Plato

"Women have the understanding of the heart, which is better than that of the head."
-   Samuel Rogers

"It is not the eye, that sees the beauty of the heaven, nor the ear, that hears the sweetness of music or the glad tidings of a prosperous accident, but the soul, that perceives all the relishes of sensual and intellectual perfections; and the more noble and excellent the soul is, the greater and more savory are its perceptions."
-   Jeremy Taylor

"The superior man understands what is right; the inferior man understands what will sell."
-   Chinese Proverb

"We can sometimes study what we do not understand, but it is impossible completely to understand what we do not study."
-   English Proverb

"It is difficult to expect a man who is warm to understand a man who is cold."

- Russian Proverb

"People don't care how much you know until they know how much you care."

- Unknown

"You cannot teach what you do not know; You cannot lead where you do not go."

- Unknown

UNITY

"Behold, how good and how pleasant it is for brethren to dwell together in unity!"

- Psalm 133:1

"Two are better than one; because they have a good reward for their labour.

For if they fall, the one will lift up his fellow: but woe to him that is alone when he falleth; for he hath not another to help him up.

Again, if two lie together, then they have heat: but how can one be warm alone?

And if one prevail against him, two shall withstand him; and a threefold cord is not quickly broken."

- Ecclesiastes 4:9-12

"He that is not with me is against me: and he that gathereth not with me scattereth."

- Luke 11:23

"And when the day of Pentecost was fully come, they were all with one accord in one place."

- Acts 2:1

"Endeavouring to keep the unity of the Spirit in the bond of peace."

- Ephesians 4:3

"God plans all perfect combinations."
-    David Brainard

"When bad men combine, the good must associate; else they will fall, one by one, an unpitied sacrifice in a contemptible struggle."
-    Sir Edmund Burke

"Men's hearts ought not to be set against one another, but set with one another, and all against evil only."
-    Thomas Carlyle

"The Constitution in all its provisions looks to an indestructible union disposed of indestructible States."
-    Salmon Portland Chase

"There is no more sure tie between friends than when they are united in their objects and wishes."
-    Marcus Tullius Cicero

"Then join hand in hand, brave Americans all!
United we stand, but divided we fall."
-    John Dickinson

"Every kind of peaceful cooperation among men is primarily based on mutual trust and only secondarily on institutions such as courts of justice and police."
-    Albert Einstein

"When our two lives grew like two buds that kiss
At lightest thrill from the bee's swinging chime,
Because the one so near the other is."
-    George Eliot

"We must all hang together, or assuredly we shall all hang separately."
-    Benjamin Franklin
upon signing the
Declaration of Independence

"Divide and command, a wise maxim;
  Unite and guide, a better."
            -   Johann Wolfgang von Goethe

"Our Union is river, lake, ocean, and sky:
  Man breaks not the medal, when God cuts the die!
    Though darkened with sulfur,
     though cloven with steel,
      The blue arch will brighten, the waters will heal!"
            -   Oliver Wendell Holmes

"Alone we can do so little; together we can do so much."
            -   Helen Keller

"And so, my fellow Americans: ask not what your country can do for you-
-ask what you can do for your country. My fellow citizens of the world:
ask not what America will do for you, but what together we can do for the
freedom of man."
            -   John F. Kennedy

"I know that there is one God in heaven, the Father of all humanity, and
heaven is therefore one. I know that there is one sun in the sky, which
gives light to all the world. As there is unity in God, and unity in the light,
so is there unity in the principles of freedom. Wherever it is broken,
wherever a shadow is cast upon the sunny rays of the sun of liberty, there
is always danger of free principles everywhere in the world."
            -   Louis Kossuth

"Two souls with but a single thought,
  Two hearts that beat as one."
            -   Mary Anne Lacy Lovell

"The union of lakes--the union of lands--
  The union of States none can sever--
    The union of hearts--the union of hands--
     And the flag of our Union forever!"
            -   George Pope Morris

"The multitude which does not reduce itself to unity is confusion exemplified."
- Blaise Pascal

"By union the smallest states thrive, by discord the greatest are destroyed."
- Sallust

"If you have an apple and I have an apple and we exchange apples then you and I will still each have one apple. But if you have an idea and I have an idea and we exchange these ideas, then each of us will have two ideas."
- George Bernard Shaw

"Liberty and Union, now and forever, one and inseparable."
- Daniel Webster

"Beware of a dividing spirit; shun whatever has the least aspect that way. Therefore say not 'I am of Paul, or of Apollos:' the very thing which occasioned the schism at Corinth. Say not "This is my preacher, the best preacher in the land; give me him and take all the rest..." Do not run down any preacher. Do not exalt any one above the rest, lest you hurt both him and the cause of God. On the other hand, do not bear hard upon any by reason of some incoherence, or inaccuracy of expression; no nor for some mistakes, were there really such...We are to bear with those we cannot amend, and to be content with offering them to God. This is true resignation. And since he has borne our infirmities we may well bear those of each other for his sake."
- John Wesley

"In the essentials -- unity, in the non-essentials -- freedom, in all things -- love."
- John Wesley

"We should not only use the brains we have, but all that we can borrow. There is no safety in numbers, unless we are united by purpose."
- Woodrow Wilson

USEFULNESS

"For we are his workmanship, created in Christ Jesus unto good works, which God hath before ordained that we should walk in them."
- Ephesians 2:10

"If a man therefore purge himself from these, he shall be a vessel unto honour, sanctified, and meet for the master's use, and prepared unto every good work."
- II Timothy 2:21

"I beseech thee for my son Onesimus, whom I have begotten in my bonds: Which in time past was to thee unprofitable, but now profitable to thee and to me."
- Philemon 1:10

"For the earth which drinketh in the rain that cometh oft upon it, and bringeth forth herbs meet for them by whom it is dressed, receiveth blessing from God."
- Hebrews 6:7

"We often despise what is most useful to us."
- Aesop

"Nothing in this world is so good as usefulness. It binds your fellow-creatures to you, and you to them; it tends to the improvement of your own character; and it gives you a real importance in society, much beyond what any artificial station can bestow."
- Sir Benjamin Brodie

"Live for something. Do good, and leave behind you a monument of virtue that the storm of time can never destroy. Write your name in kindness, love, and mercy, on the hearts of thousands you come in contact with year by year; you will never be forgotten. No, your name, your deeds, will be as legible on the hearts you leave behind as the stars on the brow of evening. Good deeds will shine as the stars of heaven."
- Thomas Chalmers

"Thousands of men breathe, move, and live; pass off the stage of life and are heard of no more. Why? They did not a particle of good in the world; and none were blest by them, none could point to them as the instrument of their redemption; not a line they wrote, not a word they spoke, could be recalled, and so they perished--their light went out in darkness, and they were not remembered more than the insects of yesterday. Will you thus live and die, O man immortal? Live for something."

-     Thomas Chalmers

"When the air balloon was first discovered, someone flippantly asked Dr. Franklin what was the use of it. The doctor answered this question by asking another: 'What is the use of a new-born infant? It may become a man.'"

-     Charles Caleb Colton

"How often do we sigh for opportunities of doing good, whilst we neglect the openings of Providence in little things, which would frequently lead to the accomplishment of most important usefulness! Dr. Johnson used to say, "He who waits to do a great deal of good at once will never do any." Good is done by degrees. However small in proportion the benefits which follow individual attempts to do good, a great deal may thus be accomplished by perseverance, even in the midst of discouragements and disappointments."

-     George Crabbe

"No one is useless in this world who lightens the burdens of another."
-     Charles Dickens

"Have I done aught of value to my fellow-men? Then have I done much for myself."

-     Johann Kaspar Lavater

"A rooster, having found a pearl, said that a grain of corn would be of more value to him."

-     Pierre Leroux

"It is a sin to complain but fail to do correct an offense."
-     Will Rogers

"A life spent in making mistakes is not only more honorable but more useful than a life spent doing nothing."
- George Bernard Shaw

"If you have a good day, think about what made it so good. If you have a bad day, think about what might have made it so bad. Such information might be helpful in the future. Who knows? You might want to have a another day like it in the future."
- Bill Wilson

"A pint of sweat will save a gallon of blood."
- George Patton

"Give a man a fish, and you have fed him for a day. Teach a man to fish, and you have fed him for a lifetime."
- American Proverb

"A cloak is not made for a single shower of rain."
- Italian Proverb

V

VALUE

"And David said, Nay; but I will surely buy it of thee at a price: neither will I offer burnt offerings unto the LORD my God of that which doth cost me nothing. So David bought the threshing floor and the oxen for fifty shekels of silver."

- II Samuel 24:24

"For a day in thy courts is better than a thousand. I had rather be a doorkeeper in the house of my God, than to dwell in the tents of wickedness."

- Psalm 84:10

"Treasures of wickedness profit nothing: but righteousness delivereth from death."

- Proverbs 10:2

"Again, the kingdom of heaven is like a merchant looking for fine pearls. When he found one of great value, he went away and sold everything he had and bought it."

- Matthew 13:45-46

"For what is a man profited, if he shall gain the whole world, and lose his own soul? or what shall a man give in exchange for his soul?"

- Matthew 16:26

"Are not five sparrows sold for two farthings, and not one of them is forgotten before God?

But even the very hairs of your head are all numbered. Fear not therefore: ye are of more value than many sparrows."

- Luke 12:6-7

"And these thinks, brethren, I have in a figure transferred to myself and to Apollos for your sakes; that ye might learn in us not to think of men above that which is written, that no one of you be puffed up for one against another."

- I Corinthians 4:6

"The ultimate value of life depends upon awareness, and the power of contemplation rather than upon mere survival."

- Aristotle

"A nickel ain't worth a dime anymore."

- Yogi Berra

"For anything worth having one must pay the price; and the price is always work, patience, love, self-sacrifice."

- John Burroughs

"Our American values are not luxuries but necessities, not the salt in our bread, but the bread itself. Our common vision of a free and just society is our greatest source of cohesion at home and strength abroad, greater than the bounty of our material blessings."

- Jimmy Carter

"That which costs little is less valued."

- Cervantes

"A bird in the hand is worth two in the bush."

- Cervantes

"Heavenly God, teach us that wealth is not elegance, that profusion is not magnificence, that splendor is not beauty."

- Benjamin Disraeli

"Not everything that can be counted counts, and not everything that counts can be counted."
- Albert Einstein

"Strive not to be a success, but rather to be of value."
- Albert Einstein

"The value of a man resides in what he gives and not in what he is capable of receiving."
- Albert Einstein

"I conceive that the great part of the miseries of mankind are brought upon them by false estimates they have made of the value of things."
- Benjamin Franklin

"A penny saved is a penny earned."
- Benjamin Franklin

"True worth is as inevitably discovered by the facial expression, as its opposite is sure to be clearly represented there. The human face is nature's tablet, the truth is certainly written thereon."
- Johann Kaspar Lavater

"An ounce of enterprise is worth a pound of privilege."
- Frederic Marvin

"Those on the left no longer value values."
- John McCain

"What we obtain too cheap, we esteem too lightly; it is dearness only that gives everything its value."
- Thomas Paine

"We ought not to treat living creatures like shoes or household belongings, which when worn with use we throw away."
- Plutarch

"Authors, like coins, grow dear as they grow old;
  It is the rust we value, not the gold."
                    -    Alexander Pope

"It is easy enough to be prudent,
  When nothing tempts you to stray;
    When without or within no voice of sin
      Is luring your soul away;
        But it's only a negative virtue
          Until it is tried by fire,
            And the life that is worth the honor of earth,
              Is the one that resists desire."
                    -    Ella Wheeler Wilcox

"A cynic is a man who knows the price of everything and the value of
nothing."
                    -    Oscar Wilde

"Price is what you pay. Value is what you get."
                    -    Spanish Proverb

"Many can estimate value while few are willing to pay the price."
                    -    Unknown

VANITY

"Behold, thou hast made my days as an handbreadth; and mine age is as
nothing before thee: verily every man at his best state is altogether vanity."
                    -    Psalm 39:5

"Surely men of low degree are vanity, and men of high degree are a lie: to
be laid in the balance, they are altogether lighter than vanity."
                    -    Psalm 62:9

"Vanity of vanities, declares the Preacher. All is vanity."
                    -    Ecclesiastes 1:2

"I have seen all the works that are done under the sun; and, behold, all is vanity and vexation of spirit."

- Ecclesiastes 1:14

"Vanity, I am sensible, is my cardinal vice and cardinal folly; and I am in continual danger, when in company, of being led an *ignis fatuus* chase by it."

- John Adams

"Vanity is the natural weakness of an ambitious man, which exposes him to the secret scorn and derision of those he converses with, and ruins the character he is so industrious to advance by it."

- Joseph Addison

"Never expect justice from a vain man; if he has the negative magnanimity not to disparage you, it is the most you can expect."

- Washington Allston

"All men are selfish, but the vain man is in love with himself. He admires, like the lover his adored one, everything which to others is indifferent."

- Berthold Auerbach

"Vain-glorious men are the scorn of the wise, the admiration of fools, the idols of paradise, and the slaves of their own vaunts."

- Sir Francis Bacon

"A man's own vanity is a swindler that never lacks for a dupe."

- Honore de Balzac

"I would much rather fight pride than vanity, because pride has a stand-up way of fighting. You know where it is. It throws its black shadow on you, and you are not at a loss where to strike. But vanity is that delusive, that insectiferous, that multiplied feeling, and men that fight vanities are like men that fight midges and butterflies. It is easier to chase them than to hit them."

- Henry Ward Beecher

"There is nothing which vanity does not desecrate."
- Henry Ward Beecher

"When a man has no longer any conception of excellence above his own, his voyage is done, he is dead,--dead in trespasses and sin of blear-eyed vanity. He is dead while he yet lives."
- Henry Ward Beecher

"Pride makes us esteem ourselves; vanity makes us desire the esteem of others."
- Hugh Blair

"What labor and pains worldlings take to obtain the vain things of this life -- to obtain the poor things of this world, which are but shadows and dreams, and mere nothings! Pambus wept when he saw a harlot dressed with much care and cost -- partly to see one take so much pains to go to hell; and partly because he had not been so careful to please God, as she had been to please her sluttish lovers. Ah, Christians!
what great reason have you to sit down and weep bitterly -- that worldlings take so much pains to make
themselves miserable -- and that you have taken no more pains to get more of Christ into your hearts!"
- Thomas Brooks

"It beareth the name of Vanity Fair, because the town where it is kept is 'lighter than vanity.'"
- John Bunyan

"Greater mischief happens often from folly, meanness, and vanity than from the greater sins of avarice and ambition."
- Sir Edmund Burke

"Guard against that vanity which courts a compliment, or is fed by it."
- Thomas Chalmers

"Vanity is a strong temptation to lying; it makes people magnify their merit, over flourish their family, and tell strange stories of their interest and acquaintance."
- Jeremy Collier

"Vanity finds in self-love so powerful an ally that it storms, as it were, by a *coup de main*, the citadel of our heads, where, having blinded the two watchmen, it readily descends into the heart."
- Charles Caleb Colton

"Since the well-known victory over the hare by the tortoise the descendants of the tortoise think themselves miracles of speed."
- Marie Von Ebner

"Those who live on vanity must not unreasonably expect to die of mortification."
- Alice Ellis

"The youth who, like a woman, loves to adorn his person, has renounced all claim to wisdom and to glory; glory is due to those only who dare to associate with pain, and have trampled pleasure under their feet."
- François Fénelon

"Most people dislike vanity in others, whatever share they have of it themselves; but I give it fair quarter, wherever I meet with it, being persuaded that it is often productive of good to the possessor, and to others who are within his sphere of action: and therefore, in many cases, it would not be altogether absurd if a man were to thank God for his vanity among the other comforts of life."
- Benjamin Franklin

"People who are wrapped up in themselves make small packages."
- Benjamin Franklin

"Pride that dines on vanity, sups on contempt."
- Benjamin Franklin

"I give vanity fair quarter, wherever I meet with it, being persuaded that it is often productive of good to the possessor, and to others who are within his sphere of action; and therefore, in many cases, it would not be altogether absurd if a man were to thank God for his vanity, among the other comforts of life."
- Benjamin Franklin

"People who are very vain are usually equally susceptible. Their lives and decisions are directed by the esteem of others."
- Edward George Lytton

"There is nothing so agonizing to the fine skin of vanity as the application of a rough truth."
- Edward George Lytton

"Vanity, indeed, is the very antidote to conceit; for while the former makes us all nerve to the opinion of others, the latter is perfectly satisfied with its opinion of itself."
- Edward George Lytton

"Vanity, like pride, will attempt to exhibit humility."
- Jack Murphy

"We are so presumptuous that we wish to be known to all the world, even to those who come after us; and we are so vain that the esteem of five or six persons immediately around us is enough to amuse and satisfy us."
- Blaise Pascal

"To be a man's own fool is bad enough; but the vain man is everybody's."
- William Penn

"Every man's vanity ought to be his greatest shame; and every man's folly ought to be his greatest secret."
- Frances Quarles

"Pride does not wish to owe and vanity does not wish to pay."
- François Rochefoucauld

"If most married women possessed as much prudence as they do vanity, we should find many husbands far happier."
-    Will Rogers

"There is no limit to the vanity of this world. Each spoke in the wheel thinks the whole strength of the wheel depends upon it."
-    Henry Wheeler Shaw

"Vanity is the foundation of the most ridiculous and contemptible vices-- the vices of affectation and common lying."
-    Adam Smith

"There are no grades of vanity, there are only grades of ability in concealing it."
-    Mark Twain

"The cure for vanity is found in the Golden Rule – to love others before one's self."
-    George Washington

"Every one at the bottom of his heart cherishes vanity; even the toad thinks himself good-looking."
-    Woodrow Wilson

"The surest cure for vanity is loneliness."
-    Thomas Wolfe

"Beauty's sister is vanity, and its daughter lust."
-    English Proverb

VICE – See SIN

VICTORY

"And he said, It is not the voice of them that shout for victory, neither is it the voice of them that cry for being overcome: but the noise of them that sing do I hear."
-    Exodus 32:18

"For the LORD your God is he that goeth with you, to fight for you against your enemies, to save you."

- Deuteronomy 20:4

"For he did put his life in his hand, and slew the Philistine, and the LORD wrought a great salvation for all Israel: thou sawest it, and didst rejoice: wherefore then wilt thou sin against innocent blood, to slay David without a cause?"

- I Samuel 19:5

"For I will not trust in my bow, neither shall my sword save me.
  But thou hast saved us from our enemies, and hast put them to shame that hated us."

- Psalm 44:6-7

"But thanks be to God, which giveth us the victory through our Lord Jesus Christ."

- I Corinthians 15:57

"For whatsoever is born of God overcometh the world: and this is the victory that overcometh the world, even our faith."

- I John 5:4

"The best policy is to declare victory and leave."

- George Aiken

"We won.
  But if
    We have such another victory, we are undone."

- Sir Francis Bacon

"The day will dawn when Europe will believe only in the man who tramples her underfoot."

- Honore de Balzac

"Victories that are easy are cheap. The only victories worth having are those which come as the result of hard fighting."

- Henry Ward Beecher

"He who fears being conquered is sure of defeat."
- Napoleon Bonaparte

"It is the right of war for conquerors to treat those whom they have conquered according to their pleasure."
- Julius Caesar

"History is written by the victors."
- Winston Churchill

"Hannibal knew better how to conquer than how to profit by the conquest; and Napoleon was more skilful in taking positions than in maintaining them. As to reverses, no general can presume to say that he may not be defeated; but he can, and ought to say, that he will not be surprised."
- Charles Caleb Colton

"They conquer who believe they can."
- John Dryden

"You must either conquer and rule or serve and lose, suffer or triumph, be the anvil or the hammer."
- Johann Wolfgang von Goethe

"It's not the mountain we conquer but ourselves."
- Sir Edmund Hillary

"To the victors belong the spoils of war."
- Andrew Jackson

"Conquer only when attacked."
- Thomas Jefferson

"Victory and defeat are each of the same price."
- Thomas Jefferson

"Wars may be fought with weapons, but they are won by men."
- George Patton

"Who overcomes
  By force, hath overcome but half his foe."
                    -    John Milton

"The more acquisitions the government makes abroad, the more taxes the people have to pay at home."
                    -    Thomas Paine

"To conquer is only half the victory. To rule is the other half – and far more difficult."
                    -    George Patton

"Conquer – or be conquered."
                    -    George Patton

"We conquered France, but felt our captive's charms,
  Her arts victorious triumph'd o'er our arms."
                    -    Alexander Pope

"Victory has a hundred fathers, but defeat is an orphan."
                    -    Will Rogers

"It is more difficult to look upon victory than upon battle."
                    -    Sir Walter Scott

"With dying hand, above his head,
  He shook the fragment of his blade,
    And shouted "Victory!--
     Charge, Chester, charge! on Stanley, on!"
      Were the last words of Marmion."
                    -    Sir Walter Scott

"I came, saw, and overcame."
                    -    William Shakespeare

"To whom God will, there be the victory."
                    -    William Shakespeare

"All the territorial possessions of all the political establishments in the earth--including America, of course-- consist of pilferings from other people's wash. No tribe, howsoever insignificant, and no nation, howsoever mighty occupies a foot of land that was not stolen at one time or other."
-    Mark Twain

"There is nothing so dreadful as a great victory--except a great defeat."
-    Arthur Wellesley

"The smile of God is victory."
-    John Whittier

"Just a victory in battle is won only through the shedding of blood, so a victory over sin is won only through the shedding of tears through prayer."
-    David Wilkerson

"It must be a peace without victory. . . . Victory would mean peace forced upon the loser; a victor's terms imposed upon the vanquished. It would be accepted in humiliation, under duress, at an intolerable sacrifice, and would leave a sting, a resentment, a bitter memory upon which terms of peace would rest, not permanently, but only as upon quicksand. Only a peace between equals can last: only a peace, the very principle of which is equality, and a common participation in a common benefit."
-    Woodrow Wilson

"In chess and in battle, victory goes to the player who makes the next-to-last mistake."
-    Russian Proverb

"An admission of guilt is a victory over error."
-    Spanish Proverb

VISION

"Where there is no vision, the people perish."
-    Proverbs 29:18

"I have also spoken by the prophets, and I have multiplied visions, and used similitudes, by the ministry of the prophets."
- Hosea 12:10

"Now faith is the substance of things hoped for, the evidence of things not seen."
- Hebrews 11:1

"Concerning perfect blessed ness which consists in a vision of God."
- Thomas Aquinas

"Faith is to believe what you do not yet see; the reward for this faith is to see what you believe."
- Augustine of Hippo

"The empires of the future are empires of the mind."
- Winston Churchill

"The people's prayer, the glad diviner's theme!
The young men's vision, and the old men's dream."
- John Dryden

"One may miss the mark by aiming too high as too low."
- Thomas Fuller

"The vision must be followed by the venture. It is not enough to stare up the steps - we must step up the stairs."
- Vance Havner

"It is a terrible thing to see and have no vision. It is far worse than being blind."
- Helen Keller

"It is a dream, sweet child! a waking dream,
A blissful certainty, a vision bright,
Of that rare happiness, which even on earth
Heaven gives to those it loves."
- Henry Wadsworth Longfellow

"Every present moment will one day become a vision of the past. Endeavor to make those visions happy ones."
- Jack Murphy

"If I have seen further, it is by standing upon the shoulders of giants."
- Sir Isaac Newton

"Do not follow where the path my lead. Go instead where there is no path and leave a trail."
- George Bernard Shaw

"Vision is the art of seeing things invisible."
- Jonathan Swift

"No man that does not see visions will ever realize any high hope or undertake any high enterprise."
- Woodrow Wilson

"Fond man! the vision of a moment made!
  Dream of a dream! and shadow of a shade!"
- Edward Young

"The whole world steps aside for the man who knows where he is going."
- American Proverb

"Vision without action is a daydream. Action with without vision is a nightmare."
- Japanese Proverb

"Even before the slaughter, the shepherd always tries to persuade the sheep that their interests and his own are the same."
- Italian Proverb

"When the horse is dead, get off."
- Spanish Proverb

VOTING

"Take you wise men, and understanding, and known among your tribes, and I will make them rulers over you."
-     Deuteronomy 1:13

"Now at that feast the governor was wont to release unto the people a prisoner, whom they would."
-     Matthew 27:15

"Then the twelve called the multitude of the disciples unto them, and said, It is not reason that we should leave the word of God, and serve tables.
   Wherefore, brethren, look ye out among you seven men of honest report, full of the Holy Ghost and wisdom, whom we may appoint over this business.
   But we will give ourselves continually to prayer, and to the ministry of the word.
   And the saying pleased the whole multitude: and they chose Stephen, a man full of faith and of the Holy Ghost, and Philip, and Prochorus, and Nicanor, and Timon, and Parmenas, and Nicolas a proselyte of Antioch."
-     Acts 6:2-5

"Elections are won by men and women chiefly because most people vote against somebody rather than for somebody."
-     Franklin Pierce Adams

"Vote early and vote often."
-     Al Capone

"No country can find eternal peace and comfort where the vote of Judas Iscariot is as good as the vote of the Saviour of mankind."
-     Thomas Carlyle

"One man should have one vote. This is the foundation of democracy."
-     John Cartwright

"Your every voter, as surely as your chief magistrate, under the same high sanction, though in a different sphere, exercises a public trust."
-      Grover Cleveland

"Those who stay away from the election think that one vote will do no good: 'Tis but one step more to think one vote will do no harm."
-      Ralph Waldo Emerson

"If we could but weigh in place of counting votes."
-      Alexander Everett

"The only thing worse than not voting is an uneducated vote."
-      Ray Everett

"Those who complain about both candidates vote for apathy."
-      Benjamin Franklin

"A straw vote only shows which way the hot air blows."
-      O. Henry

"The freeman casting, with unpurchased hand,
  The vote that shakes the turrets of the land."
-      Oliver Wendell Holmes

"You can milk a cow the wrong way once and still be a farmer, but vote the wrong way on a water tower and you can be in trouble."
-      John F. Kennedy

"To make democracy work, we must be a notion of participants, not simply observers. One who does not vote has no right to complain."
-      Louis L'Amour

"Ballots are the rightful and peaceful successors to bullets."
-      Abraham Lincoln

"It may be conjectured that it is cheaper in the long run to lift men up than to hold them down, and that the ballot in their hands is less dangerous to society than a sense of wrong is in their heads."

- James Russell Lowell

"If we can not trust a freeman with his right to keep and bear arms, then how can we trust him with the right to vote. Surely the right of a freeman to vote has a much greater effect on our collective lives than does any individual's firearm. If one argues that the effect of any one freeman's vote is minimal, then why allow it in the first place? To be armed is to secure one's right to representation."

- Thomas Mincher

"Those who do not choose to exercise their right to voice – which is what their vote truly is – should not choose to use their voice to later complain about those in office."

- Jack Murphy

"Elections are often won by the greater of two evils simply because some men refused to vote for the other. Their decision not to vote secured the victory for the greater evil."

- Jack Murphy

"Bad officials are elected by good citizens who do not vote."

- George Jean Nathan

"An election does not reveal the candidate who is best suited for a job. Rather, it reveals the candidate who has best won the esteem of majority."

- Will Rogers

"Let us never forget that government is ourselves and not an alien power over us. The ultimate rulers of our democracy are not a President and senators and congressmen and government officials, but the voters of this country."

- Franklin D. Roosevelt

"I will not accept if nominated, and will not serve if elected."

- General William Sherman

"When voting, think of needs of your fellow man before yourselves."
-     George Washington

"Sink or swim, live or die, survive or perish, I give my hand and heart to this vote."
-     Daniel Webster

"Slavery is but half abolished, emancipation is but half completed, while millions of freeman with votes in their hands are left without education."
-     Robert Charles Winthrop

"Vote for the man who promises least. He'll be the least disappointing."
-     French Proverb

"It is the man who counts the votes who holds the most power over a nation."
-     Italian Proverb

"I would not vote for the mayor. It's not just because he didn't invite me to dinner, but because on my way into town from the airport there were such enormous potholes."
-     Spanish Proverb

W

WAITING – See PATIENCE

WAR

"So David triumphed over the Philistine with a sling and a stone; without a sword in his hand he struck down the Philistine and killed him."
- I Samuel 17:50

"He teacheth my hands to war, so that a bow of steel is broken by mine arms."
- Psalm 18:34

"A thousand shall fall at thy side, and ten thousand at thy right hand; but it shall not come nigh thee."
- Psalm 91:7

"A time to love, and a time to hate; a time of war, and a time of peace."
- Ecclesiastes 3:8

"There is no man that hath power over the spirit to retain the spirit; neither hath he power in the day of death: and there is no discharge in that war; neither shall wickedness deliver those that are given to it."
- Ecclesiastes 8:8

"I returned, and saw under the sun, that the race is not to the swift, nor the battle to the strong, neither yet bread to the wise, nor yet riches to men of understanding, nor yet favour to men of skill; but time and chance happeneth to them all." - Ecclesiastes 9:11

"And ye shall hear of wars and rumours of wars: see that ye be not troubled: for all these things must come to pass, but the end is not yet."
- Matthew 24:6

"Fight the good fight of faith, lay hold on eternal life, whereupon thou art also called, and hast professed a good profession before many witnesses."
- I Timothy 6:12

"And he gathered them together into a place called in the Hebrew tongue Armageddon."
- Revelation 16:16

"In war, truth is the first casualty."
- Aeschylus of Eleusis

"A just fear of an imminent danger, though there be no blow given, is a lawful cause of war."
- Sir Francis Bacon

"The release of atom power has changed everything except our way of thinking...the solution to this problem lies in the heart of mankind. If only I had known, I should have become a watchmaker."
- Albert Einstein

"I don't know how man will fight World War III, but I do know how they will fight World War IV; with sticks and stones."
- Albert Einstein

"Every gun that is made, every warship launched, every rocket fired signifies in the final sense, a theft from those who hunger and are not fed, those who are cold and are not clothed. This world in arms is not spending money alone. It is spending the sweat of its laborers, the genius of its scientists, the hopes of its children. This is not a way of life at all in any true sense. Under the clouds of war, it is humanity hanging on a cross of iron."
- Dwight D. Eisenhower

"There is nothing that war has ever achieved that we could not better achieve without it."
- Havelock Ellis

"A war against oppression, slavery and tyranny is to fight on the side of God."
- George W. Bush

"All wars are civil wars, because all men are brothers."
- François Fénelon

"Every creature lives in a state of war by nature."
- Thomas Hobbes

"A day of battle is a day of harvest for the devil."
- William Hooke

"You're an old-timer if you can remember when setting the world on fire was a figure of speech."
- Robert Franklin Jones, concerning the atom bomb

"Mankind must put an end to war, or war will put an end to mankind."
- John F. Kennedy

"War will exist until that distant day when the conscientious objector enjoys the same reputation and prestige that the warrior does today."
- John F. Kennedy

"What a cruel thing is war: to separate and destroy families and friends, and mar the purest joys and happiness God has granted us in this world; to fill our hearts with hatred instead of love for our neighbors, and to devastate the fair face of this beautiful world."
- Robert E. Lee

"Dear Madam,

I have been shown in the files of the War Department a statement of the Adjutant General of Massachusetts that you are the mother of five sons who have died gloriously on the field of battle.
I feel how weak and fruitless must be any word of mine which should attempt to beguile you from the grief of a loss so overwhelming. But I cannot refrain from tendering you the consolation that may be found in the thanks of the Republic they died to save.
I pray that our Heavenly Father may assuage the anguish of your bereavement, and leave you only the cherished memory of the loved and lost, and the solemn pride that must be yours to have laid so costly a sacrifice upon the altar of freedom.

Yours, very sincerely and respectfully,
    A. Lincoln"

-     Letter from Abraham Lincoln to Mrs. Bixby, upon learning of the deaths of her children

"I'm fed up to the ears with old men dreaming up wars for young men to die in."

-     George McGovern

"The Egyptians could run to Egypt, the Syrians into Syria. The only place we could run was into the sea, and before we did that we might as well fight."

-     Golda Meir

"War is an ugly thing, but not the ugliest of things. The decayed and degraded state of moral and patriotic feeling which thinks that nothing is worth war is much worse. The person who has nothing for which he is willing to fight, nothing which is more important than his own personal safety, is a miserable creature and has no chance of being free unless made and kept so by the exertions of better men than himself."

-     John Stewart Mill

"Oddly enough, the goal of war is usually to secure the peace."
- Jack Murphy

"Pacifists want someone else to fight for their right to publicly oppose war."
- Jack Murphy

"War does not always determine who is right. But it always determines who is left."
- George Patton

"The object of war is not to die for your country but to make the other bastard die for his."
- George Patton

"Only the dead have seen the end of war."
- Plato

"I couldn't help but say to Mr. Gorbachev, just think how easy his task and mine might be in these meetings that we held if suddenly there was a threat to this world from another planet. We'd find out once and for all that we really are all human beings here on this earth together."
- Ronald Reagan

"You can't say civilization don't advance, however, for in every war they kill you in a new way."
- Will Rogers

"Yesterday, December 7, 1941 – a date which will live in infamy – the United States was suddenly and deliberately attacked by naval and air forces of the Empire of Japan."
- Franklin D. Roosevelt

"A just war is in the long run far better for a man's soul than the most prosperous peace."
- Theodore Roosevelt

"We live in a great and free country only because our forefathers were willing to wage war rather than accept the peace that spells destruction."
- Theodore Roosevelt

"To you men who, in your turn, have come together to spend and be be spent in the endless crusade against wrong; to you who face the future resolute and confident; to you who strive in a spirit of brotherhood for the betterment of our nation; to you who gird yourselves for this great new fight in the never-ending warfare for the good of mankind, I say in closing what I said in that speech in closing: 'We stand at Armageddon and we battle for the Lord.'"
- Theodore Roosevelt

"The great respect that I have for your leadership, Mr. President, in this little-understood, unfamiliar war, the first war of the 21st century--it is not well-known, it was not well-understood; it is complex for people to comprehend. And I know with certainty that, over time, the contributions you've made will be recorded by history."
- Donald Rumsfeld

"Patriots always talk of dying for their country and never of killing for their country."
- Bertrand Russell

"Sometime they'll give a war and nobody will come."
- Carl Sandburg

"War is Hell."
- General William Sherman

"Every attempt to make war easy and safe will result in humiliation and disaster."
- General William Sherman

"The death of one man is a tragedy. The death of millions is a statistic."
- Joseph Stalin

"A professional soldier understands that war means killing people, war means maiming people, war means families left without fathers and mothers. All you have to do is hold your first dying soldier in your arms, and have that terribly futile feeling that his life is flowing out and you can't do anything about it. Then you understand the horror of war. Any soldier worth his salt should should be antiwar. And still, there are things worth fighting for."

- Norman Schwarzkopf

"I disapprove of what you say, but I will fight to the death for your right to say it."

- Voltaire

"It is forbidden to kill; therefore all murderers are punished unless they kill to the sound of trumpets and applause."

- Voltaire

"It is said that God is always on the side of the heaviest battalions."

- Voltaire

"The power of making war often prevents it, and in our case would give efficacy to our desire of peace."

- George Washington

"To be prepared for war is one of the most effective means of preserving peace."

- George Washington

"My first wish is to see this plague of mankind, war, banished from the earth."

- George Washington

"If we don't end war, war will end us."

- H. G. Wells

"I can predict with absolute certainty that within another generation there will be another world war if the nations of the world do not concert the method by which to prevent it."
- Woodrow Wilson, at the end of WWI

"A great war leaves the country with three armies - an army of cripples, an army of mourners, and an army of thieves."
- German Proverb

"There are no atheists in foxholes."
- Unknown

"Everyone's a pacifist between wars. It's like being a vegetarian between meals."
- Unknown

"Why do we kill people who are killing people to show that killing people is wrong?"
- Unknown

WEAKNESS

"Have mercy upon me, O LORD; for I am weak: O LORD, heal me; for my bones are vexed."
- Psalm 6:2

"But they that wait upon the LORD shall renew their strength; they shall mount up with wings as eagles; they shall run, and not be weary; and they shall walk, and not faint."
- Isaiah 40:31

"Beat your plowshares into swords and your pruninghooks into spears: let the weak say, I am strong."
- Joel 3:10

"Watch and pray, that ye enter not into temptation: the spirit indeed is willing, but the flesh is weak."
- Matthew 26:41

"Because the foolishness of God is wiser than men; and the weakness of God is stronger than men."
- I Corinthians 1:25

"And he said unto me, My grace is sufficient for thee: for my strength is made perfect in weakness. Most gladly therefore will I rather glory in my infirmities, that the power of Christ may rest upon me."
- II Corinthians 12:9

"Therefore I take pleasure in infirmities, in reproaches, in necessities, in persecutions, in distresses for Christ's sake: for when I am weak, then am I strong."
- II Corinthians 12:10

"For though he was crucified through weakness, yet he liveth by the power of God. For we also are weak in him, but we shall live with him by the power of God toward you."
- II Corinthians 13:4

"Quenched the violence of fire, escaped the edge of the sword, out of weakness were made strong, waxed valiant in fight, turned to flight the armies of the aliens."
- Hebrews 11:34

"Guard thy heart on this weak side, where most our nature fails."
- Joseph Addison

"The cord breaketh at last by the weakest pull."
- Sir Francis Bacon

"The strength of man sinks in the hour of trial; but there doth live a Power that to the battle girdeth the weak."
- Joanna Baillie

"There are some weaknesses that are peculiar and distinctive to generous characters, as freckles are to a fair skin."
- Christian Nestell Bovee

"Weakness ineffectually seeks to disguise itself,--like a drunken man trying to show how sober he is."
- Christian Nestell Bovee

"Rudeness is the weak man's imitation of strength."
- Sir Edmund Burke

"History does not long entrust the care of freedom to the weak or the timid."
- Dwight D. Eisenhower

"Some of our weaknesses are born in us, others are the result of education; it is a question which of the two gives us most trouble."
- Johann Wolfgang von Goethe

"We are not so easily guided by our most prominent weaknesses as by those of which we are least aware."
- Sir Arthur Helps

"How many weak shoulders have craved heavy burdens!"
- Joseph Joubert

"Weaknesses, so called, are often nothing more nor less than vice in disguise!"
- Johann Kaspar Lavater

"You cannot strengthen the weak by weakening the strong."
- Abraham Lincoln

"I have never quite understood the relationship between beauty and weakness, womanly sweetness and womanly silliness; to my mind, indeed, that woman being the most beautiful who is the most capable, while weakness and silliness can never by any chance be other than unlovely."
- Lynn Linton

"There are two kinds of weakness, that which breaks and that which bends."
- James Russell Lowell

"It is not because men's desires are strong that they act ill; it is because their consciences are weak. There is no natural connection between strong impulses and a weak conscience."
- John Stuart Mill

"Women are generally regarded as the weaker of the sexes in terms of physical strength and emotional stability, but the stronger of the two in terms of everything else."
- Jack Murphy

"Some weak people are so sensible of their weakness as to be able to make a good use of it."
- François Rochefoucauld

"Many take pleasure in spreading abroad the weakness of an exalted character."
- Sir Richard Steele

"Although men are accused of not knowing their own weakness, yet perhaps few know their own strength. It is in men as in soils, where sometimes there is a vein of gold which the owner knows not of."
- Jonathan Swift

"It is weak to be unaware of your strength."
- Unknown

WEIGHT

"When thou sittest to eat with a ruler, consider diligently what is before thee:
  And put a knife to thy throat, if thou be a man given to appetite."
- Proverbs 23:1-2

"For the drunkard and the glutton shall come to poverty: and drowsiness shall clothe a man with rags."
- Proverbs 23:21

"Know ye not that ye are the temple of God, and that the Spirit of God dwelleth in you?
  If any man defile the temple of God, him shall God destroy; for the temple of God is holy, which temple ye are."
- I Corinthians 3:16-17

"Do you not know that your body is a temple of the Holy Spirit, who is in you, whom you have received from God?"
- I Corinthians 6:19

"One should eat to live, not live to eat."
- Marcus Tullius Cicero

"Gluttony is an emotional escape, a sign something is eating us."
- Peter DeVries

"You have to exercise for a week to work off the thigh fat from a single Snickers."
- Albert Einstein

"In general, mankind, since the improvement of cookery, eats twice as much as nature requires."
- Benjamin Franklin

"We never repent of having eaten too little."
- Thomas Jefferson

"Govern well thy appetite, lest Sin
Surprise thee, and her black attendant, Death."
- John Milton

"A diet is the penalty we pay for exceeding the feed limit."
- Jack Murphy

"You cannot escape your waist size. Even in the weightlessness of space, you must still fit your stomach inside your spacesuit."
- Jack Murphy

"The biggest seller is cookbooks and the second is diet books – how not to eat what you've just learned how to cook."
- Andy Rooney

"No diet will remove all the fat from your body because the brain is entirely fat. Without a brain, you might look good, but all you could do is run for public office."
- George Bernard Shaw

"To promise not to do a thing is the surest way in the world to make a body want to go and do that very thing."
- Mark Twain

"It is a hard matter, my fellow citizens, to argue with the belly, since it has no ears."
- Plutarch

"My doctor told me to stop having intimate dinners for four. Unless there are three other people."
- Orson Welles

"A balanced diet is a cookie in each hand."
- American Proverb

"Dieting is not a piece of cake."
- American Proverb

"Only in America would books on dieting and weight loss become bestsellers. I suppose that this is a testament to our blessings and our misuse of those blessings."
- American Proverb

"Don't dig your grave with your own knife and fork."
- English Proverb

"Ewes not fat, ewes just fluffy."
- English Proverb

"Rich, fatty foods are like destiny. They too, shape our ends."
-    Spanish Proverb

"Your stomach shouldn't be a waist basket."
-    Unknown

"Inside some of us is a thin person struggling to get out, but they can usually be sedated with a few pieces of chocolate cake."
-    Unknown

"People are so worried about what they eat between Christmas and the New Year, but they really should be worried about what they eat between the New Year and Christmas."
-    Unknown

"I've been on a diet for two weeks and all I've lost is fourteen days."
-    Unknown

"You know it's time to diet when you push away from the table and the table moves."
-    Unknown

"I'm in shape. Round is a shape... isn't it?"
-    Unknown

"A waist is a terrible thing to mind."
-    Unknown

WELFARE

"When thou cuttest down thine harvest in thy field, and hast forgot a sheaf in the field, thou shalt not go again to fetch it: it shall be for the stranger, for the fatherless, and for the widow: that the LORD thy God may bless thee in all the work of thine hands.

When thou beatest thine olive tree, thou shalt not go over the boughs again: it shall be for the stranger, for the fatherless, and for the widow.

When thou gatherest the grapes of thy vineyard, thou shalt not glean it afterward: it shall be for the stranger, for the fatherless, and for the widow.

And thou shalt remember that thou wast a bondman in the land of Egypt: therefore I command thee to do this thing."

> - Deuteronomy 24:19-22

"And the king said unto Araunah, Nay; but I will surely buy it of thee at a price: neither will I offer burnt offerings unto the LORD my God of that which doth cost me nothing. So David bought the threshingfloor and the oxen for fifty shekels of silver."

> - II Samuel 24:24

"For even when we were with you, this we commanded you, that if any would not work, neither should he eat."

> - II Thessalonians 3:10

"But if any provide not for his own, and especially for those of his own house, he hath denied the faith, and is worse than an infidel."

> - I Timothy 5:8

"The cure for poverty is not in the State continuously handing out food, money, healthcare or even jobs to those who are poor and have not earned it; rather, it comes from the State doing all that it can to provide an opportunity for all people to help themselves out of the curses of public assistance."

> - Martin Luther King, Jr.

"If pigs could vote, the man with the slop bucket would be elected swineherd every time, no matter how much slaughtering he did on the side."

> - Orson Scott Card

"The budget should be balanced, the Treasury should be refilled, public debt should be reduced, the arrogance of officialdom should be tempered and controlled, and the assistance to foreign lands should be curtailed lest

Rome become bankrupt. People must again learn to work, instead of living on public assistance."
-    Marcus Tullius Cicero

"Welfare was initially meant to help the nation out of a time of crisis. It evolved into the use of public funds to buy votes. It turned socialists into Democrats and hard working citizens into wards of the State."
-    Greg Gutfeld

"The best way to put more money in people's wallets is to leave it there in the first place."
-    Edwin Feulner

"Repeal that [welfare] law, and you will soon see a change in their manners. ... Six days shalt thou labor, though one of the old commandments long treated as out of date, will again be looked upon as a respectable precept; industry will increase, and with it plenty among the lower people; their circumstances will mend, and more will be done for their happiness by inuring them to provide for themselves, than could be done by dividing all your estates among them."
-    Benjamin Franklin

"He can have no right to the benefits of Society, who will not pay his Club towards the Support of it."
-    Benjamin Franklin

"A government that is big enough to give you all you want is big enough to take it all away."
-    Barry Goldwater

"And here we encounter the seeds of government disaster and collapse -- the kind that wrecked ancient Rome and every other civilization that allowed a sociopolitical monster called the welfare state to exist."
-    Barry Goldwater

"Parties who want milk should not seat themselves on a stool in the middle of a field in hope that the cow will back up to them."
-    Elbert Hubbard

"The democracy will cease to exist when you take away from those who are willing to work and give to those who would not."
- Thomas Jefferson

"Congress has not unlimited powers to provide for the general welfare, but only those specifically enumerated."
- Thomas Jefferson

"Ask not what your country can do for you – ask what you can do for your country."
- John F. Kennedy

"Never do for someone what they can and should do for themselves."
- Abraham Lincoln

"Will the magistrate provide by an express Law, that such an one shall not become poor or sick? Laws provide, as much as is possible, that the goods and health of subjects be not injured by the fraud and violence of others; they do not guard them from the negligence or ill-husbandry of the possessors themselves."
- John Locke

"I cannot undertake to lay my finger on that article of the Constitution which granted a right to Congress of expending, on the objects of benevolence, the money of their constituents."
- James Madison

"Alms only help those who despise their use. We must learn to hate any dependence on what is given to us – and strive to reach a point where we are no longer a drain on the welfare of others."
- Jack Murphy

"Welfare brings out the most awful forms of greed, laziness and a criminal mindset in the poor and the most revolting desire to control votes by those politicians who hand it out promising more."
- Jack Murphy

"Charity begins at home."
-    Ovid

"Welfare's purpose should be to eliminate, as far as possible, the need for its own existence."
-    Ronald Reagan

"We should measure welfare's success by how many people leave welfare, not by how many are added."
-    Ronald Reagan

"I think that the best possible social welfare program is a job."
-    Ronald Reagan

"We are sure living in a peculiar time. You can get more for not working than you will for working, more for not raising corn than raising it and more for not raising a hog than for raising it. The government is taking our tax dollars to pay for inactivity."
-    Will Rogers

"Welfare is the consumption of wealth without producing it."
-    George Bernard Shaw

"There is great danger that our people will lose our independence of thought and action which is the cause of much of our greatness, and sink into the helplessness of the Frenchman or German who expects his government to feed him when hungry, clothe him when naked, to prescribe when his child may be born and when he may die, and, in time, to regulate every act of humanity from the cradle to the tomb, including the manner in which he may seek future admission to paradise."
-    Mark Twain

"There is a class of colored people who make a business of keeping the troubles, the wrongs, and the hardships of the Negro race before the public. Some of these people do not want the Negro to lose his grievances, because they do not want to lose their jobs. There is a certain class of race-problem solvers who don't want the patient to get well."
-    Booker T. Washington

"Give a man a fish and you have fed him for a day. Teach a man to fish; and you have fed him for a lifetime."
-    American Proverb

"A man who reaches for a handout should be embarrassed lest he become accustomed to it."
-    Spanish Proverb

"Government is created to protect the poor from the lust of the rich, and to protect the rich from the lust of the poor."
-    Unknown

"They have gun control in Cuba. They have a massive public welfare system in Cuba. They even have universal health care in Cuba. But why do you suppose that they still want to come here?"
-    Unknown

WISDOM

"Wisdom is the principal thing; therefore get wisdom: and with all thy getting get understanding."
-    Proverbs 4:7

"For in much wisdom is much grief: and he that increaseth knowledge increaseth sorrow."
-    Ecclesiastes 1:18

"It is better to hear the rebuke of the wise, than for a man to hear the song of fools."
-    Ecclesiastes 7:5

"The words of the wise are as goads, and as nails fastened by the masters of assemblies, which are given from one shepherd."
-    Ecclesiastes 12:11

"The price of wisdom is above rubies."
-    Job 28:18

"Great men are not always wise: neither do the aged understand judgment."
- Job 32:9

"Behold, I send you forth as sheep in the midst of wolves: be ye therefore wise as serpents, and harmless as doves."
- Matthew 10:16

"For unto whomsoever much is given, of him shall be much required: and to whom men have committed much, of him they will ask the more."
- Luke 12:48

"And the load commended the unjust steward, because he had done wisely: for the children of this world are in their generation wiser than the children of light."
- Luke 16:8

"For your obedience is come abroad unto all men. I am glad therefore on your behalf: but yet I would have you wise unto that which is good, and simple concerning evil."
- Romans 6:9

"Socrates was pronounced by the Oracle of Delphos to be the wisest man in Greece, which he would turn from himself ironically, saying there could be nothing in him to verify the oracle, except this, that he was not wise and knew it, and others were not wise and knew it not."
- Sir Francis Bacon

"There is this difference between happiness and wisdom: he that thinks himself the happiest man is really so; but he that thinks himself the wisest is generally the greatest fool."
- Sir Francis Bacon

"Thank God, men that art greatly guilty are never wise. A truly wise man would know the benefits of integrity."
- Edmund Burke

"Great is wisdom; infinite is the value of wisdom. It cannot be exaggerated; it is the highest achievement of man."
- Thomas Carlyle

"Wisdom is not a product of schooling but of the life-long attempt to acquire it."
- Albert Einstein

"Wise men learn more from fools than fools from the wise."
- Cato the Elder

"Every moment instructs, and every object; for wisdom is infused into every form. It has been poured into us as blood; it convulsed us as pain; it slid into us as pleasure; it enveloped us in dull, melancholy days, or in days of cheerful labor; we did not guess its essence until after long time."
- Ralph Waldo Emerson

"Professors teach facts. Experience teaches probability. Only God teaches wisdom."
- Ralph Waldo Emerson

"These are the signs of a wise man: to reprove nobody, to praise nobody, to blame nobody, nor even to speak of himself or his own merits."
- Epictetus

"Tim was so learned, that he could name his new horse in nine Languages. But he was so ignorant, that he actually bought a cow to ride on."
- Benjamin Franklin

"The wisdom of the wise, and the experience of ages, may be preserved by quotations."
- Benjamin Disraeli

"The heart is wiser than the intellect."
- Josiah Holland

"Teach a man to read and write, and you have put into his hands the two great keys of the treasure-box of wisdom."
-      Thomas Huxley

"I don't think much of a man who is not wiser today than he was yesterday."
-      Abraham Lincoln

"If the young were wise, the devil couldn't do anything to them, but since they aren't wise, they need us who are old."
-      Martin Luther

"Though wisdom wake, suspicion sleeps
   At wisdom's gate, and to simplicity
      Resigns her charge, while goodness thinks no ill
         Where no ill seems."
-      John Milton

"Wisdom is not the characteristic of the man who knows everything. It is the characteristic of a man who knows what to do with those things of which he is certain."
-      Jack Murphy

"Wisdom is knowledge multiplied by experience added to the awareness of ignorance divided by discretion."
-      Jack Murphy

"A man should never be ashamed to own he has been in the wrong, which is but saying, in other words, that he is wiser today than he was yesterday."
-      Alexander Pope

"Be wise of the world, but not worldly wise."
-      Francis Quarles

"Seek wisdom where it may be found. Seek it in the knowledge of God, the holy, the just and the merciful God, as revealed to us in the gospel; of Him who is just, and yet the justifier of them that believe in Jesus."

- Henry Raikes

"The fool doth think he is wise, but the wise man knows himself to be a fool."

- William Shakespeare

"A man cannot learn to be wise any more than he can learn to be handsome."

- Henry Wheeler Shaw

"The doorstep to the temple of wisdom is a knowledge of our own ignorance."

- Charles H. Spurgeon

"The sublimity of wisdom is to do those things living which are to be desired when dying."

- Jeremy Taylor

"People who count their chickens before they are hatched, act very wisely. It is better to count the total eggs and then subtract the ones remaining after the rest have hatched, because chickens run about so absurdly that it is impossible to count them accurately."

- Oscar Wilde

"Live and learn."

- American Proverb

"Wisdom is learning that truth sooner rather than later."

- American Proverb

"Knowledge speaks, but wisdom listens."

- English Proverb

"You can tell whether a man is intelligent by his answers. You can tell whether a man is wise by his questions."
-     Greek Proverb

"As clever as he was, even Einstein slept in the doghouse, divorced and then married his own cousin."
-     Jewish Proverb

"Wisdom is simply knowing what to do next."
-     Spanish Proverb

WOMEN

"And the LORD God said, It is not good that the man should be alone; I will make him an help meet for him."
-     Genesis 2:18

"And Adam gave names to all cattle, and to the fowl of the air, and to every beast of the field; but for Adam there was not found an help meet for him.
And the LORD God caused a deep sleep to fall upon Adam, and he slept: and he took one of his ribs, and closed up the flesh instead thereof;
And the rib, which the LORD God had taken from man, made he a woman, and brought her unto the man.
And Adam said, This is now bone of my bones, and flesh of my flesh: she shall be called Woman, because she was taken out of Man.
Therefore shall a man leave his father and his mother, and shall cleave unto his wife: and they shall be one flesh."
-     Genesis 2:20-24

"It is better to dwell in a corner of the housetop, than with a brawling woman in a wide house."
-     Proverbs 21:9

"Favour is deceitful, and beauty is vain: but a woman that feareth the LORD, she shall be praised."
-     Proverbs 31:30

"And it shall come to pass afterward, that I will pour out my spirit upon all flesh; and your sons and your daughters shall prophesy, your old men shall dream dreams, your young men shall see visions:

And also upon the servants and upon the handmaids in those days will I pour out my spirit."

- Joel 2:28-29

"In like manner also, that women adorn themselves in modest apparel, with shamefacedness and sobriety; not with broided hair, or gold, or pearls, or costly array;

But (which becometh women professing godliness) with good works."

- I Timothy 2:9

"The aged women likewise, that they be in behaviour as becometh holiness, not false accusers, not given to much wine, teachers of good things;

That they may teach the young women to be sober, to love their husbands, to love their children,

To be discreet, chaste, keepers at home, good, obedient to their own husbands, that the word of God be not blasphemed."

- Titus 2:3-5

"When women are the advisers, the lords of creation don't take the advice till they have persuaded themselves that it is just what they intended to do; then they act upon it, and if it succeeds, they give the weaker vessel half the credit of it; if it fails, they generously give her the whole."

- Louisa May Alcott

"Woman is stronger by virtue of her feelings than man by virtue of his power."

- Honore de Balzac

"If there be any one whose power is in beauty, in purity, in goodness, it is a woman."

- Henry Ward Beecher

"A beautiful woman appeals to the eye; a good woman appeals to the heart. One is a jewel; the other, a treasure."
- Napoleon Bonaparte

"Next to God, we are indebted to women, first for life itself, and then for making it worth having."
- Christian Nestell Bovee

"A woman is not made to be the admiration of all, but the happiness of one."
- Sir Edmund Burke

"Somewhere out in this audience may even be someone who will one day follow in my footsteps, and preside over the White House as the President's spouse. I wish him well!"
- Barbara Bush

"The very first
  Of human life must spring from woman's breast:
  Your first small words are taught you from her lips;
  Your first tears quench'd by her, and your last sighs
    Too often breath'd out in a woman's hearing,
      When men have shrunk from the ignoble care
      Of watching the last hour of him who led them."
- Lord Byron

"I've seen your stormy seas and stormy women,
  And I pity husbands rather more than seamen."
- Lord Byron

"There said once a clerk in two verse,
  What is better than Gold? Jasper.
    What is better than Jasper? Wisdom.
    And what is better than Wisdom? Woman.
    And what is bettre than a good Woman?
                              Nothing."
- Geoffrey Chaucer

"Heaven has no rage like love to hatred turned;
  Nor hell a fury like a woman scorned."
                    -    William Congreve

"Women made us lose paradise, but how frequently we find it again in their arms."
                    -    J. De Finod

"If thou wouldest please the ladies, thou must endeavor to make them pleased with themselves."
                    -    Thomas Fuller

"A young man rarely gets a better vision of himself than that which is reflected from a true woman's eyes; for God himself sits behind them."
                    -    Josiah Holland

"Behind every great man is a woman."
                    -    Elbert Hubbard

"There is in every true woman's heart a spark of heavenly fire, which beams and blazes in the dark hours of adversity."
                    -    Washington Irving

"Women are afraid of mice and of murder, and of very little in between."
                    -    Mignon McLaughlin

"A jealous husband only worries about a particular Other Man; a jealous wife distrusts her whole species."
                    -    Mignon McLaughlin

"No matter how happily a woman may be married, it always pleases her to discover that there is a nice man who wishes that she were not."
                    -    Henry Louis Mencken

"O fairest of creation! last and best
  Of all God's works! creature in whom excell'd
    Whatever can to sight or thought form'd
      Holy, divine, good, amiable, or sweet!"
              -   John Milton

"The average woman would rather have beauty than brains, because the average man can see better than he can think."
              -   Lucy M. Montgomery

"I have found that many men who would forbid women to teach are often those who thought very highly of their mother's instruction. It seems that they have simply forgotten the education that they received upon their mother's lap."
              -   Jack Murphy

"Woman is at best a contradiction still."
              -   Alexander Pope

"Whoever said, *'Frailty, thy name is woman'* does not realize the patience needed to live with a man for several years nor the strength necessary to give birth to a child. A woman's true name is *'Courage.'"*
              -   Will Rogers

"Frailty, thy name is woman."
              -   William Shakespeare

"Can you imagine a world without men? No crime and lots of happy fat women."
              -   Mark Twain

"My mother was the most beautiful woman I ever saw. All I am I owe to my mother. I attribute all my success in life to the moral, intellectual and physical education I received from her."
              -   George Washington

"A man's face is his autobiography. A woman's face is her work of fiction."
-    Oscar Wilde

"Women get the last word in every argument. Anything a man says after that is the beginning of a new argument."
-    American Proverb

"Behind every great man is a woman – rolling her eyes."
-    American Proverb

"Whatever women do they must do twice as well as men to be thought half as good. Luckily, this is not difficult."
-    Canadian Proverb

"Women are a masterpiece."
-    Chinese Proverb

"A woman can say more in a sigh than a man can say in a sermon."
-    English Proverb

"Women always worry about the things that men forget; men always worry about the things women remember."
-    Spanish Proverb

"God created man before woman. So what? You always make a rough draft before the final masterpiece."
-    Unknown

"It is common to see a smart man with a dumb woman. It is rare to see a smart woman with a dumb man."
-    Unknown

WORDS

"And God said, Let there be light: and there was light."
-    Genesis 1:3

"And thou shalt speak unto him, and put words in his mouth: and I will be with thy mouth, and with his mouth, and will teach you what ye shall do."

- Exodus 4:15

"And thou shalt take no gift: for the gift blindeth the wise, and perverteth the words of the righteous."

- Exodus 23:8

"Who is this that darkeneth counsel by words without knowledge?"

- Job 38:2

"Pleasant words are as an honeycomb, sweet to the soul, and health to the bones."

- Proverb 16:24

"Be not rash with thy mouth, and let not thine heart be hasty to utter any thing before God; for God is in heaven, and thou upon earth: therefore let thy words be few."

- Ecclesiastes 5:2

"In the beginning was the Word, and the Word was with God, and the Word was God."

- John 1:1

"But he said, I am not mad, most noble Festus said; but speak forth the words of truth and soberness."

- Acts 26:25

"Let no man deceive you with vain words: for because of these things cometh the wrath of God upon the children of disobedience."

- Ephesians 5:6

"We have too many high sounding words, and too few actions that correspond with them."

- Abigail Adams

"Men believe that their reason governs their words; but it often happens the words have power to react on reason."
- Sir Francis Bacon

"Words, when written, crystallize history; their very structure gives permanence to the unchangeable past."
- Sir Francis Bacon

"There are words which cut like steel."
- Honore de Balzac

"One picture is worth ten thousand words."
- Frederick Barnard

"One half the troubles in this life can be traced to saying yes too quickly and not saying no soon enough."
- Josh Billings

"The word "impossible" is not in my dictionary."
- Napoleon Bonaparte

"The pen is mightier than the sword."
- Edward Bulwer Lytton

"Rudeness is the weak man's imitation of strength."
- Edmund Burke

"Swallowing angry words is better than having to eat them later."
- Winston Churchill

"It depends on what the meaning of the word 'is' is."
- William Jefferson Clinton

"One of the lessons of history is that nothing is often a good thing to do and always a clever thing to say."
- Will Durant

"If A is success in life, then A equals X + Y + Z. Work is X, Y is play, and Z is keeping your mouth shut."
- Albert Einstein

"Words are also actions, and actions are a kind of words."
- Ralph Waldo Emerson

"Watch how much of our speech is aimed at justifying our actions. We find it almost impossible to act and allow the act to speak for itself. No, we must explain it, justify it, demonstrate the righteousness of it. Why do we feel this compulsion to set the record straight? Because of pride and fear, because our reputations are at stake."
- Richard Foster

"I want to write, but more than that, I want to bring out all kinds of things that lie buried deep in my heart."
- Anne Frank

"Well done is better than well said."
- Benjamin Franklin

"Three may keep a secret, if two of them are dead."
- Benjamin Franklin

"He that speaks much, is much mistaken."
- Benjamin Franklin

"Silence is not always a Sign of Wisdom, but Babbling is ever a folly."
- Benjamin Franklin

"Sticks and stones can break your bones, but names hurt worse of all."
- Benjamin Franklin

"Half the world is composed of people who have something to say and can't, and the other half who have nothing to say and keep on saying it."
- Robert Frost

"A holy mind cannot repeat a vile thing, let alone be the creator of a vile suggestion."
- John G. Lake

"Don't use words too big for the subject. Don't say "infinitely" when you mean "very"; otherwise you'll have no word left when you want to talk about something really infinite."
- C.S. Lewis

"We should have a great many fewer disputes in the world if words were taken for what they are, the signs of our ideas only, and not for things themselves."
- John Locke

"If one cannot state a matter clearly enough so that even an intelligent twelve year old can understand it, one should remain within the cloistered walls of the university and laboratory until one gets a better grasp of one's subject matter."
- Margaret Mead

"A picture may be worth a thousand words, but a single word spoken at the right moment may be worth a thousand images."
- Jack Murphy

"Human conversation is largely an endless attempt to convince others that we are more assertive or clever or generous or successful than they might think if we did not carefully educate them."
- John Ortberg

"Kind words do not cost much. They never blister the tongue or lips. They make other people good-natured. They also produce their own image on men's souls, and a beautiful image it is."
- Blaise Pascal

"Speak properly, and in as few words as you can, but always plainly; for the end of speech is not ostentation, but to be understood."
- William Penn

"On a single winged word hath hung the destiny of nations."
- Wendell Phillips

"As it is the mark of great minds to say many things in a few words, so it is that of little minds to use many words to say nothing."
- François Rochefoucauld

"Never miss a good chance to shut up."
- Will Rogers

"Beware of smooth talkers. Many fools are endowed with the gift of gab."
- Will Rogers

"These words are razors to my wounded heart."
- William Shakespeare

"The trouble with her is that she lacks the power of conversation but not the power of speech."
- George Bernard Shaw

"The bitterest tears shed over graves are for words left unsaid and deeds left undone."
- Harriet Beecher Stowe

"Learn to say no. It will be of more use to you than to be able to read Latin."
- Charles Spurgeon

"I sometimes hold it half a sin
 To put in words the grief I feel;
  For words, like Nature, half reveal
   And half conceal the Soul within."
- Lord Alfred Tennyson

"It usually takes me more than three weeks to prepare a good impromptu speech."
- Mark Twain

"I disapprove of what you say, but I will defend to the death your right to say it."
- Voltaire

"A hotheaded woman told John Wesley, 'My talent is to speak my mind.' Replied Mr. Wesley, 'Woman, God wouldn't care a bit if you would bury that talent.'"
- John Wesley

"For of all sad words of tongue or pen,
  The saddest are these: 'It might have been!'"
- John Whittier

"I'm all in favor of keeping dangerous weapons out of the hands of fools. Let's start with typewriters."
- Frank Lloyd Wright

"It is better to be silent and thought a fool than to open your mouth and remove all doubt."
- Unknown

"The word 'no' is the most difficult to say, to hear and to understand in the English language."
- American Proverb

"The trouble with talking too fast is you may say something you haven't thought of yet."
- American Proverb

"Great minds talk about ideas; Average minds talk about things; Small minds talk about other people."
- English Proverb

"Four things come not back: the spoken word, the spent arrow, time past, the neglected opportunity."
- Irish Proverb

"Don't speak unless you can improve on the silence."
- Spanish Proverb

"After all is said and done, a lot more is said than done."
- Unknown

"Handle them carefully, for words have more power than atom bombs."
- Unknown

WORK

"In the sweat of thy face shalt thou eat bread, till thou return unto the ground; for out of it wast thou taken: for dust thou art, and unto dust shalt thou return."
- Genesis 3:19

"Thou shalt surely give him, and thine, and thine heart shall not be grieved when thou givest unto him: because that for this thing the Lord thy God shall bless thee in all thy works, and in all that thou puttest thine hand unto."
- Deuteronomy 15:10

"Remember now thy Creator in the days of thy youth, while the evil days come not, nor the years draw nigh, when thou shalt say, I have no pleasure in them;
While the sun, or the light, or the moon, or the stars, be not darkened, nor the clouds return after the rain:
In the day when the keepers of the house shall tremble, and the strong men shall bow themselves, and the grinders cease because they are few, and those that look out of the windows be darkened."
- Ecclesiastes 12:1-3

"For we are his workmanship, created in Christ Jesus unto good works, which God hath before ordained that we should walk in them."
- Ephesians 2:10

"For even when we were with you, this we commanded you, that if any would not work, neither should he eat."
- II Thessalonians 3:10

"Standardizing the end prevents a manager from having to standardize the means.'"
- Marcus Buckingham

"Never despair, but if you do, work on in despair."
- Edmund Burke

"We make a living by what we get; we make a life by what we give."
- Winston Churchill

"God sells us all things at the price of labor."
- Leonardo da Vinci

"Work only on things that will make a great deal of difference if you succeed."
- Peter Drucker

"Efficiency is doing things right. Effectiveness is doing the right things."
- Peter Drucker

"As a cure for worrying, work is better than whiskey."
- Thomas A. Edison

"Work should be for all of us a word as honorable and appealing as patriotism."
- Dwight D. Eisenhower

"A man is relieved and happy when he has put his heart into his work and done his best."
- Ralph Waldo Emerson

"Chop your own wood, and it will warm you twice."
- Henry Ford

"Work as if you were to live a hundred years; Pray as if you were to die tomorrow."
- Benjamin Franklin

"By working faithfully eight hours a day, you may get to be a boss and work twelve hours a day."
- Robert Frost

"I find that the harder I work, the more luck I seem to have. Perhaps this is not in fact luck?"
- Thomas Jefferson

"Never do for someone what they can and should do for themselves."
- Abraham Lincoln

"God set the example: Work then rest. Too often in today's world, it is the other way around."
- Jack Murphy

"Far away the best prize that life offers is the chance to work hard at work worth doing."
- Theodore Roosevelt

"If you do not wish for His kingdom do not pray for it. But if you do you must do more than pray for it, you must work for it."
- John Ruskin

"Labor was the first price, the original purchase-money that was paid for all things. It was not by gold or by silver, but by labor, that all wealth of the world was originally purchased."
- Adam Smith

"Respect results with the least possible effort. Never substitute effort for accomplishment. Disassociate effort and reward."
- Fred Smith

"There is no necessary correlation between how busy you are and how productive you are."
- Andy Stanley

"Poverty is the child of laziness."
- Voltaire

"Creativity without implementation is irresponsibility. Ideas are nothing without execution."
- Unknown

"Anyone who can walk to the welfare office can walk to work."
- American Proverb

"If you have time to lean, you have time to clean."
- American Proverb

"No success at work can make up for failure at home."
- English Proverb

"There are two kinds of people: those who work and those who take the credit. Try to be in the first group; there is less competition there."
- Indian Proverb

"A farmer on his legs is higher than a gentleman on his knees."
- Latin Proverb

"If you are fat, then work harder."
- Spanish Proverb

WORKS – See ACTION

WORLDLINESS

"Nevertheless the people refused to obey the voice of Samuel; and they said, Nay; but we will have a king over us;
That we also may be like all the nations; and that our king may judge us, and go out before us, and fight our battles." - I Samuel 8:19-20

"For ye are yet carnal: for whereas there is among you envying, and strife, and divisions, are ye not carnal, and walk as men?"

- I Corinthians 3:3

"Wherefore henceforth know we no man after the flesh: yea, though we have known Christ after the flesh, yet now henceforth know we him no more."

- II Corinthians 5:16

"Teaching us that, denying ungodliness and worldly lusts, we should live soberly, righteously, and godly, in this present world."

- Titus 2:12

"O miserable man, what a deformed monster has sin made you! God made you 'little lower than the angels'; sin has made you little better than devils, a monster that has his head and his heart where his feet should be, and his feet kicking against heaven, and everything out of place. The world that was formed to serve you, is come to rule you- the deceitful harlot has bewitched you with her enchantments, and made you bow down and serve her."

- Joseph Alliene

"They best pass over the world who trip over it quickly; for it is but a bog. If we stop, we sink."

- Elizabeth I

"Buying, possessing, accumulating--this is not worldliness. But doing this in the love of it, with no love of God paramount--doing it so that thoughts of eternity and God are an intrusion--doing it so that one's spirit is secularized in the process; this is worldliness."

- Robert Herrick

"Christians should live in the world, but not be filled with it. A ship lives in the water; but if the water gets into the ship, she goes to the bottom. So Christians may live in the world; but if the world gets into them, they sink."

- D. L. Moody

"We must assess our thoughts and beliefs and reckon whether they are moving us closer to conformity to Christ or farther away from it."
-    John Ortberg

"It has been well said that there is a sin of other-worldliness no less than a sin of worldliness, and Christendom has had a large measure of the former sin as well as of the latter. People have been taught so much about preparing for heaven that they sometimes become very indifferent workers on earth, and in anticipating the joys of the future world have overlooked the infinite possibilities for good in the world that now is."
-    William James Potter

"Set not your heart upon the world, since God hath not made it your portion. He will destroy it by fire anyway."
-    Samuel Rutherford

"O my God! close my eyes, that I may see Thee; separate me from the world, that I may enjoy Thy company."
-    Christian Scriver

"As the love of the heavens makes us heavenly, the love of virtue virtuous, so doth the love of the world make one become worldly."
-    Philip Sidney

"An unholy church! It is useless to the world, and of no esteem among men. It is an abomination, hell's laughter, heaven's abhorrence. The worst evils which have ever come upon the world have been brought upon her by an unholy church."
-    C.H. Spurgeon

"Worldliness is what any particular culture does to make sin look normal and righteousness look strange."
-    David Wells

"Get rid of this bunkum about the 'carnal Christian'. Forget it! If you're carnal, you're not saved."
-    Leonard Ravenhill

"The magnetic needle always points to the North, and hence it is that the sailing vessel does not lose her direction. So long as the heart of man is directed towards God, he cannot be lost in the ocean of worldliness."
-     Unknown

WORRY – See ANXIETY

WORSHIP

"They have turned aside quickly out of the way which I commanded them: they have made them a molten calf, and have worshipped it, and have sacrificed thereunto, and said, These be thy gods, O Israel, which have brought thee up out of the land of Egypt."
-     Exodus 32:8

"For thou shalt worship no other god: for the LORD, whose name is Jealous, is a jealous God."
-     Exodus 34:14

"Give unto the LORD the glory due unto his name: bring an offering, and come before him: worship the LORD in the beauty of holiness."
-     I Chronicles 16:29

"Who shall ascend into the hill of the LORD? Or who shall stand in his holy place?
He that hath clean hands, and a pure heart; who hath not lifted up his soul unto vanity, nor sworn deceitfully."
-     Psalm 24:3-4

"O come, let us worship and bow down: let us kneel before the LORD our maker."
-     Psalm 95:6

"If it be so, our God whom we serve is able to deliver us from the burning fiery furnace, and he will deliver us out of thine hand, O king.
But if not, be it known unto thee, O king, that we will not serve thy gods, nor worship the golden image which thou hast set up."
-     Daniel 3:17-18

"But in vain they do worship me, teaching for doctrines the commandments of men."
- Matthew 15:9

"God is a Spirit: and they that worship him must worship him in spirit and in truth."
- John 4:24

"For as I passed by, and beheld your devotions, I found an altar with this inscription, TO THE UNKNOWN GOD. Whom therefore ye ignorantly worship, him declare I unto you."
- Acts 17:23

"I never knew how to worship until I knew how to love."
- Henry Ward Beecher

"It is for the sake of man, not of God, that worship and prayers are required; not that God may be rendered more glorious, but that man may be made better,--that he may be confirmed in a proper sense of his dependent state, and acquire those pious and virtuous dispositions in which his highest improvement consists."
- Hugh Blair

"Worship renews the spirit as sleep renews the body."
- Richard Clarke Cabot

"When we believe that we should be satisfied rather than God glorified in our worship, then we put God below ourselves as though He had been made for us rather than that we had been made for Him."
- Stephen Charnock

"Without the heart it is not worship; it is a stage play; an acting a part without being that person really...a hypocrite. We may truly be said to worship God-though we lack perfection; but we cannot be said to worship Him if we lack sincerity."
- Stephen Charnock

"It is only when men begin to worship that they begin to grow wise. Man cannot understand his abilities until he realizes how dependent he is upon the mercies of the Lord."

- Calvin Coolidge

"They will pay $15 for a Christian concert to hear a Christian singer and for free they won't come into the presence of God and call upon the name of the Lord."

- Jim Cymbala

"Worship is the honour and adoration which are rendered to God by reason of what he is in himself, and what he is for those who render it."

- J. N. Darby

"And what greater calamity can fall upon a nation than the loss of worship."

- Ralph Waldo Emerson

"A striking feature of worship in the Bible is that people gathered in what we would call "holy expectancy". They believed they would actually hear the voice of God. It was not surprising to them that the building in which they met shook with the power of God."

- Richard Foster

"They that worship God merely from fear, Would worship the devil too, if he appear."

- Thomas Fuller

"It is not truly worship if for this hour they worship, and the next they blaspheme."

- Samuel Garth

"The only music minister to whom the Lord will say, "Well done, thy good and faithful servant," is the one whose life proves what their lyrics are saying, and to whom music is the least important part of their life. Glorifying the only worthy One has to be a minister's most important goal!"

- Keith Green

"Remember that God will not be mocked; that it is the heart of the worshiper which He regards. We are never safe till we love Him with our whole heart whom we pretend to worship."

- Joseph Henshaw

"Worship requires only a man and God."

- Thomas Jefferson

"The end we ought to propose to ourselves is to become, in this life, the most perfect worshippers of God we can possibly be, as we hope to be through all eternity""

- Brother Lawrence

"The most valuable thing the Psalms do for me is to express the same delight in God which made David dance."

- C. S. Lewis

"It is in the process of being worshipped that God communicates His presence to men."

- C. S. Lewis

"A man can no more diminish God's glory by refusing to worship Him than a lunatic can put out the sun by scribbling the word, 'darkness' on the walls of his cell."

- C. S. Lewis

"The men that will change the colleges and seminaries here represented are the men that will spend the most time alone with God. It takes time for the fires to burn. It takes time for God to draw near and for us to know that He is there. It takes time to assimilate His truth. You ask me, How much time? I do not know. I know it means time enough to forget time."

- John Mott

"Prayer is preoccupation with our needs.
 Praise is preoccupation with God's blessings.
 Worship is preoccupation with God."

- Leonard Ravenhill

"Singing is not worship! Music is not worship! Worship is the act of pure sacrifice in which you surrender your heart, your soul, your mind, your time, your talents, your strengths, your weaknesses, your voice, your silence, your happiness, your anguish and your tears upon an invisible altar for a God that you desperately long to see!"

- Leonard Ravenhill

"In the end, worship can never be a performance, something you're pretending or putting on."

- Matt Redman

"God's goal is not to make sure you're happy. Life is not about your being comfortable, happy, successful and pain free. It is about becoming the man God has called you to be. Life is not about you. It's about God. He doesn't exist to make us happy. We exist to bring Him glory."

- Chuck Swindoll

"To worship is to quicken the conscience by the holiness of God
To feed the mind with the truth of God
To purge the imagination by the beauty of God
To open the heart to the love of God
To devote the will to the purpose of God."

- William Temple

"Christians don't tell lies they just go to church and sing them."

- A.W. Tozer

"If I go to hell, you'll have one lamb in hell. If I go to hell, you'll have one man there singing your praises. If I go to hell, you'll have one man that won't keep his mouth shut. Gonna run all around that dark place tellin' how good God is and how wonderful is the blood of the Lamb."

- A.W. Tozer
(spoken in prayer)

"God gave us music that we might be able to pray without using words."

- Unknown

WRITING – See WORDS

X Y Z

YEARNING

"Oh that I might have my request: and that God would grant me the thing that I long for."
- Job 6:8

"For the wicked boasteth of his heart's desire, and blesseth the covetous, whom the LORD abhorreth."
- Psalm 10:3

"Delight thyself also in the LORD: and he shall give thee the desires of thine heart."
- Psalm 37:4

"As the hart panteth after the water brooks, so panteth my soul after thee, O God."
- Psalm 42:1

"O God, thou art my God; early will I seek thee: my soul thirsteth for thee, my flesh longeth for thee in a dry and thirsty land, where no water is."
- Psalm 63:1

"My soul longeth, yea, even fainteth for the courts of the LORD: my heart and my flesh crieth out for the living God."
- Psalm 84:2

"Be careful what you wish for. You may get it and regret it."
-    Aesop

"I distrust those people who know so well what God wants them to do, because I notice it always coincides with their own desires."
-    Susan B. Anthony

"Your persistent longing is your persistent voice. But when love grows cold, the heart grows silent. Burning love is the outcry of the heart! If you are filled with longing all the time, you will keep crying out, and if your love perseveres, your cry will be heard without fail."
-    Augustine of Hippo

"Subdue your appetites, my dears, and you've conquered human nature."
-    Charles Dickens

"It is easier to suppress the first desire than to satisfy all that follow it."
-    Benjamin Franklin

"Almost every one has a predominant inclination, to which his other desires and affections submit, and which governs him, though perhaps with some intervals, though the whole course of his life."
-    David Hume

"Every desire bears its death in its very gratification. Curiosity languishes under repeated stimulants, and novelties cease to excite and surprise, until at length we cannot wonder even at a miracle."
-    Washington Irving

"I seldom think about my limitations, and they never make me sad. Perhaps there is just a touch of yearning at times; but it is vague, like a breeze among flowers."
-    Helen Keller

"Your yearning is your compass for life. It will either lead you to safety and greatness or evil and hopelessness. One wrong turn now can lead to the pit of despair."
-    George MacDonald

"Govern well thy appetite, lest Sin
Surprise thee, and her black attendant Death."
- John Milton

"Every girl yearns for marriage and motherhood. Afterward, they each wonder, *"What was I thinking?"*
- Lucy M. Montgomery

"When yearning, remember consequence."
- Jack Murphy

"There are two tragedies in life. One is not to get your heart's desire. The other is to get it."
- George Bernard Shaw

"Forbidden fruit tastes the sweetest. It does also separate man from God."
- English Proverb

"Our cravings are a difficult and necessary thing to conquer."
- English Proverb

"The yearnings of youth, when caught, become the regrets of manhood."
- Italian Proverb

"A man is what he yearns for."
- Spanish Proverb

YOUTH

"And Saul said to David, Thou art not able to go against this Philistine to fight with him: for thou art but a youth, and he a man of war from his youth.
 And David said unto Saul, Thy servant kept his father's sheep, and there came a lion, and a bear, and took a lamb out of the flock:
 And I went out after him, and smote him, and delivered it out of his mouth: and when he arose against me, I caught him by his beard, and smote him, and slew him.

Thy servant slew both the lion and the bear: and this uncircumcised Philistine shall be as one of them, seeing he hath defied the armies of the living God."
- I Samuel 17:33-36

"Remember not the sins of my youth, nor my transgressions: according to thy mercy remember thou me for thy goodness' sake, O LORD."
- Psalm 25:7

"Who satisfieth thy mouth with good things; so that thy youth is renewed like the eagle's."
- Psalm 103:5

"Remember now thy Creator in the days of thy youth, while the evil days come not, nor the years draw nigh, when thou shalt say, I have no pleasure in them."
- Ecclesiastes 12:1

"Even the youths shall faint and be weary, and the young men shall utterly fall."
- Isaiah 40:30

"Let no man despise thy youth; but be thou an example of the believers, in word, in conversation, in charity, in spirit, in faith, in purity."
- I Timothy 4:12

"Flee also youthful lusts: but follow righteousness, faith, charity, peace, with them that call on the Lord out of a pure heart."
- II Timothy 2:22

"Nobody understands anyone 18, including those who are 18."
- Jim Bishop

"At 20 years of age the will reigns; at 30 the wit; at 40 the judgment."
- Benjamin Franklin

"Nothing can be so amusingly arrogant as a young man who has just discovered an old idea and thinks it is his own."
- Sydney Harris

"Forty is the old age of youth; fifty the youth of old age."
- Victor Hugo

"Youth today are different than any other youth in history. Because of the media, they know more about sex, deviance, violence and mature topics than their parents and grandparents did at the age of 40. Yet they have never been more 'protected' than they are now. Fifty years ago, we treated a youth as a young adult when they were teens. Today, we treat 16, 17 and 18 year olds as though they were still children. Why? Our best wishes tell us to. Yet the youth of today enjoy the best of two worlds: They dabble in the vices of adulthood while still enjoying the label of childhood. They want to eat of the Tree of the Knowledge of Good and Evil while continuing to dwell in the Garden of Eden. We must teach them that a single bite from the Tree of errant knowledge merits banishment from the Garden of Childhood."
- C. S. Lewis

"You are as young as your faith, as old as your doubt; as young as your self-confidence, as old as your fear; as young as your hope, as old as your despair."
- Douglas MacArthur

"When I was a school girl, I longed to turn 21. When I was 21, I feared to turn 30. When I was 50, I longed to be 30. Now that I approach 70, I dream of being 21."
- Lucy M. Montgomery

"You never know what peace is until you walk on the shores or in the fields or along the winding red roads of Prince Edward Island in a summer twilight when the dew is falling and the old stars are peeping out and the sea keeps its mighty tryst with the little land it loves. You find your soul then. You realize that youth is not a vanished thing but something that dwells forever in the heart."
- Lucy M. Montgomery

"Wisdom begins when a youth realizes that his youthful days are numbered and that, if God allows, he will soon become a man."
- Jack Murphy

"Some old men, continually praise the time of their youth. In fact, you would almost think that there were no fools in their days, but unluckily they themselves are left as an example."
- Alexander Pope

"A man is a young as he thinks he is. I have met old men who were 20 and young men who were 50."
- Will Rogers

"I was in Church one Sunday listening to an extraordinarily long sermon on how short life will be. The preacher ended his message with, '*And remember always that life is short.*' One youngster said, '*Thank God!*'"
- Will Rogers

"We cannot always build the future for our youth, but we can build our youth for the future."
- Franklin D. Roosevelt

"Some men can live up to their loftiest ideals without ever going higher than a basement."
- Theodore Roosevelt

"Youth is a wonderful thing. What a crime to waste it on children."
- George Bernard Shaw

"There is no greater tragedy than wasted youth. Occasionally, you hear a man lament of lost opportunities to chase the vices of youth. More often, you hear of old men who lament having caught, during their youth, that vicious wind."
- Jeremy Taylor

"Don't be afraid of growing up. Just remember that wrinkles should merely indicate where smiles have been."
- Mark Twain

"When I was young, I had dreams. When I became old, those dreams gave way to regrets."
- Mark Twain

"The greatest lesson learned in youth is that life is short. Unfortunately, it is difficult to teach this to a youth who thinks that he will live forever."
- Mark Twain

"The deepest definition of youth is life as yet untouched by tragedy."
- Alfred North Whitehead

"You know why teenagers are so stupid? When they have a problem, who do they turn to for advice? Other teenagers! How stupid is that? If they really wanted help, they would turn to those who successfully graduated from their teenage years."
- Bill Wilson

"Before you go and criticize the younger generation, just remember who raised them."
- American Proverb

"Growing old is mandatory; growing up is optional."
- American Proverb

"If youth only knew: if age only could."
- English Proverb

"We are young only once. After that we need some other excuse."
- Italian Proverb

"Everyone is the age of their heart."
- Spanish Proverb

"You don't realize how to take advantage of your youthfulness until you are no longer youthful."
- Unknown

ZEAL

"For the zeal of thine house hath eaten me up; and the reproaches of them that reproached thee are fallen upon me."
- Psalm 69:9

"A wise man feareth, and departeth from evil; but the fool rageth, and is confident."
- Proverbs 14:16

"For I bear them record that they have a zeal of God, but not according to knowledge."
- Romans 10:2

"But it is good to be zealously affected always in a good thing, and not only when I am present with you."
- Galatians 4:18

"As many as I love, I rebuke and chasten: be zealous therefore, and repent."
- Revelation 3:19

"There are zealots for slavery as well as zealots for freedom."
- William Henry Burleigh

"Experience shows that success is due less to ability than to zeal. The winner is he who gives himself to his work, body and soul."
- Charles Buxton

"Zeal without humility is like a ship without a rudder, liable to be stranded at any moment."
- Owen Feltham

"Zeal without knowledge is fire without light."
- Thomas Fuller

"Zeal, unless it be rightly guided, when it endeavors the most busily to please God, forceth upon Him those unseasonable offices which please Him not."
- Richard Hooker

"A wild fire, even on a cold night, will be remembered for what it destroyed rather than who it warmed."
- Jack Murphy

"Zeal without knowledge is like an expedition to a man in the dark."
- Sir Isaac Newton

"Not the zeal alone of those who seek Him proves God, but the blindness of those who seek Him not."
- Blaise Pascal

"It is a coal from God's altar must kindle our fire; and without fire, true fire, no acceptable sacrifice."
- William Penn

"Many poets and painters hide deficient skill behind an excess of zeal."
- Alexander Pope

"Zeal without reason becomes fanaticism. Jesus was not a fanatic. Yes, His love was blind to all the possible dangers of His mission. This love ignores personal safety, disregards the odds against it, drops "sacrifice" from its vocabulary, requires no crutches, ignores all danger, is intolerant of sin, but not fanatical."
- Leonard Ravenhill

"We need a baptism of holy zeal to get us back to holy indignation that the money grabbers are back in the temple, and that God's heart is hurting."
- Leonard Ravenhill

"I am not sure that it can be proved that Nero fiddled while Rome burned. It can be proved that the Church is fiddling while the world is burning! The one reason that we do not have revival today is that we are content to live without it."

- Leonard Ravenhill

"There is nothing more dangerous than zeal in the hand of a well-meaning fool."

- Will Rogers

"Had I but serv'd my God with half the zeal I serv'd my king, he would not in mine age Have left me naked to mine enemies."

- William Shakespeare

"Do not pursue truth unless it is useful truth."

- Sydney Smith

"No zeal is spiritual that is not also charitable."

- Thomas Sprat

"Violent zeal for truth has a hundred to one odds to be either petulancy, ambition, or pride."

- Jonathan Swift

"Zeal is fit for wise men, but flourishes chiefly among fools."

- John Tillotson

"Zeal in the heart of a fool is like a gun in the hand of a blind man."

- Mark Twain

"God approves the depth, but not the tumult, of the soul."

- William Wordsworth

"Blind zeal can only do harm."

- German Proverb

INDEX

Alliene, Joseph
  -WORLDLINESS
Allston, Washington
  -IDOLATRY, VANITY
Althsuler, Michael
  -ACCOMPLISHMENT, TIME
Ames, Fisher
  -BIBLE, REPUTATION
Amiel, Henri-Frederic
  -ERROR
Anthony, Susan B.
  -YEARNING
Antonak, Chris
  -AGE
Aquinas, Thomas
  -LAW, VISION
Ariosto, Ludovico
  -INDIVIDUALITY
Aristotle
  -DEMOCRACY, FALSE TEACHING, LAW, SUICIDE,TEACHING, TRAVEL,
    VALUE
Arnold, Matthew
  -CREATIVITY, CULTURE, GOOD, JOURNALISM, TRUTH
Arnold, Edwin (Sir)
  -FUTURE
Arnold, Thomas
  -KNOWLEDGE
Asimov, Isaac
  -DEATH, TECHNOLOGY
Assisi, Francis (of)
  -ACCOMPLISHMENT, PREACHERS,
Auerbach, Berthold
  -DEATH, GENTLENESS, MUSIC, VANITY
Aughey, James
  -COMPLAINTS, DEATH
Augustine of Hippo
  -FUTURE, MIRACLES, PASSION, PERFECTION, SERMONS, SPEECH,
    TEMPTATION, TRAVEL, TRUTH, UNDERSTANDING, VISION,
    YEARNING
Aurelius Antoninus, Marcus
  -ACCOMPLISHMENT, ANGER, ART, BEAUTY, EDUCATION, THOUGHT,
Austen, Jane
  -KNOWLEDGE, ROMANCE
Authur, K
  -CHRISTIANITY
Ayala, Emmanuel
  -LIFE

Babcock, Maltbie Davenport
-FUTURE
Babinet, Jacques
-FOOLISHNESS
Bach, Johann Sebastian
-MUSIC
Bach, Richard
-TESTS
Bacon, Francis (Sir)
-ADVICE, ALCOHOL, ANGER, ATHEISM, BOLDNESS, BOOKS,
CERTAINTY, CLEANLINESS, COUNSEL, DEATH, EDUCATION, FALSE
TEACHING, FEAR, GOD, GOOD, GREATNESS, HYPOCRISY,
IMAGINATION, JOBS, KNOWLEDGE, MARRIAGE, MONEY,
OPPORTUNITY, QUESTIONS, READING, SEX, SUCCESS, THOUGHT,
TRAVEL, UNDERSTANDING, VANITY, VICTORY, WAR, WEAKNESS,
WISDOM, WORDS,
Bailey, Philip James
-GOD, MIRACLES, SUICIDE, THOUGHT
Baillie, Joanna
-WEAKNESS
Baker, Richard
-MUSIC
Baker, Wes
-CHRISTIANITY, DISCIPLESHIP
Baldwin, Faith
-CHANGE
Baldwin, James
-CHILDREN, EDUCATION,
Baldwin, Stanley
-TESTIMONY
Balfour, Arthur James
-TRUTH
Balzac, Honore de
-CERTAINTY, CRUELTY, FAMILY, FEAR, FOOLISHNESS, JEALOUSY, JOBS,
LAUGHTER, MARRIAGE, NATURE, NEED, QUESTIONS, SIN, TEMPER,
UGLINESS, VANITY, VICTORY, WOMEN, WORDS
Banks, Harry
-ABILITY
Barclay, William
-ENCOURAGEMENT
Barlow, George
-PERSEVERANCE
Barna, George
-LEADERSHIP
Barnard, Frederick
-WORDS
Barnett, Tommy
-PROSPERITY

Bierce, Ambrose
  -ANGER, FOOD, RESPONSIBILITY, SPEECH
Bigelow, John
  -GOVERNMENT
Billings, Josh
  -JEALOUSY, WORDS
Bishop, Jim
  -YOUTH
Blackstone, William (Sir)
  -JUSTICE, PROPERTY
Blair, Hugh
  -COMPASSION, ORGANIZATION, TEMPER, VANITY, WORSHIP
Blair, Tony
  -AMERICA, EDUCATION, LEADERSHIP, POPULARITY
Blake, William
  -ENEMIES, GREATNESS, INDIVIDUALITY, MERCY
Bok, Edward William
  -ACCOMPLISHMENT
Bombeck, Erma
  -CHILDREN, COURAGE, FAMILY, HOLIDAYS, TEENAGERS
Bonaparte, Napoleon
  -ABILITY, CHRIST, CRIME, ENEMIES, FIGHTING, GREATNESS,
      JOURNALISM, OPTIMISM v. PESSIMISM, ORGANIZATION, PEACE,
      POPULARITY, POWER, SUICIDE, VICTORY, WOMEN, WORDS
Bonar, Andrew A.
  -NEGLECT, PRAYER, REVIVAL
Bonar, Horatius
  -FAITH, FORGIVENESS, TRUTH
Bonheoffer, Dietrich
  -DISCIPLESHIP, GRACE, HYPOCRISY, RESPONSIBILITY, SIN
Bono
  -ART
Bono, Edward de
  -ARGUMENTS
Boom, Corrie ten
  -ABILITY, ANXIETY, FEAR, FUTURE, GIFTS, PRAYER, PRESENCE OF GOD,
      STRENGTH
Booth, Catherine
  -CHURCH
Booth, William
  -CHRIST, DISCIPLINE, EVANGELISM
Boswell, James
  -SEX
Boucicault, Dion
  -TIME
Bounds, E. M.
  -ACCOUNTABILITY, EVANGELISM, METHODS, OPPORTUNITY, PRAYER

Browning, Elizabeth Barrett
- READING
Browning, Robert
- AGE, MUSIC, SUCCESS
Bryan, William Jennings
- EVOLUTION, HONESTY
Bryant, William Cullen
- NEWS, TRUTH
Bryce, James
- PATRIOTISM, READING
Buckingham, Marcus
- STRENGTH, WORK
Bulwer-Lytton, Edward
- JOURNALISM, LAW, MONEY, MUSIC, SUICIDE, VANITY, WORDS
Bunyan, John
- FUTURE, HEAVEN & HELL, HYPOCRISY, INTELLIGENCE, NAMES,
     PEACE, PRAYER, PREACHERS, PRIDE, QUIETNESS, TEMPTATION,
     TRUTH, UNDERSTANDING, VANITY
Burke, Edmund (Sir)
- ABUSE, ACTION, BROKENESS, CAUSE, CHARACTER, COMPLAINTS,
     CONDEMNATION, CRIME, CRITICISM, DEDICATION,
     DEMOCRACY, ECONOMICS, EDUCATION, EVIL, FACTS, FAVOR,
     FEAR, FUTURE, GOD, GOVERNMENT, GREATNESS, HISTORY,
     HYPOCRISY, JUSTICE, LAW, LIBERTY, ORGANIZATION, PACIFISM,
     PERSECUTION, PERSEVERENCE, POWER, READING, STRENGTH,
     TAXES, THOUGHT, TOLERANCE, TRUTH, UGLINESS, UNITY,
     VANITY, WEAKNESS, WISDOM, WOMEN, WORDS, WORK
Burke, Leo
- CHILDREN
Burleigh, William Henry
- METHODS, ZEAL
Burnet, Gilbert
- SERMONS
Burnham, George
- ACCOMPLISHMENT
Burns, James Drummond
- LAST WORDS
Burroughs, John
- VALUE
Burton, Henry
- KINDNESS
Burton, Lady
- KNOWLEDGE
Bush, Barbara
- WOMEN
Bush, George H. W.
- SOCIALISM

Bush, George W.
- AMERICA, EVIL, MILITARY, WAR
Bushnell, Horace
- TRIALS & TRIBULATIONS
Buxton, Charles
- EDUCATION, ZEAL
Byron, George Gordon (Lord)
- APPEARANCE, CHRIST, COURAGE, DEATH, KNOWLEDGE, MUSIC,
    ROMANCE, SADNESS, WOMEN

Cabell, James
- OPTIMISM v. PESSIMISM
Cabot, Richard Clarke
- WORSHIP
Caesar, Julius
- VICTORY
Calhoun, John
- GOVERNMENT
Callaghan, James
- ADVICE
Calvin, John
- IDOLATRY, JOY, PRESENCE OF GOD
Campbell, Duncan
- HOLINESS, NEED, REVIVAL
Campbell, Joe
- PASSION
Campbell, John W.
- SUCCESS
Camus, Albert
- BOOKS, EVIL
Capone, Al
- VOTING
Card, Michael
- BETRAYAL
Card, Orson Scott
- WELFARE
Carey, George
- CONVERSION
Carey, William
- ACTION, DEDICATION, FRIENDSHIP, LONELINESS
Cargill, Donald
- CONVERSION
Carlyle, Thomas
- BOREDOM, CULTURE, EDUCATION, FAME, GOVERNMENT, LYING,
    MUSIC, OPPORTUNITY, PEACE, PERSEVERENCE, POPULARITY,
    SINCERITY, THOUGHT, TRUTH, UNITY, VOTING, WISDOM

Cowper, William
  - COMPASSION, FOOLISHNESS, FORGIVENESS, MUSIC, NATURE, PRAYER, SERMONS
Crabbe, George
  - USEFULNESS
Craggs, James
  - EPITAPHS
Cramer, Clayton
  - IMMIGRATION
Crashaw, Richard
  - MIRACLES
Crisp, Quentin
  - LANGUAGE
Cromwell, Oliver
  - OPPORTUNITY
Cross, John Walker
  - CULTURE,
Cumming, R. D.
  - READING
Cummings, William
  - ATHEISM
Curtis, Herber Doust
  - GOD
Cushing, Richard
  - APPEARANCE
Cuyler, Theodore Ledyard
  - TRIALS & TRIBULATIONS
Cymbala, Jim
  - PASSION, WORSHIP

D'Avenant, Sir William
  - MERCY
Da Vinci, Leonardo
  - ARGUMENTS, WORK
Daniel, Keith
  - COUNSEL, PREACHERS, SPEECH
Dante
  - FAME, PAIN
Darby, J. N.
  - WORSHIP
Darrow, Clarence
  - IGNORANCE, LAUGHTER
Darwin, Charles
  - EVOLUTION
Davis, Jefferson
  - INDEPENDENCE
De Balzac, Honore – See Balzac, Honore de
De Bono, Edward – See Bono, Edward de

De Finod, J.
-EXPERIENCE, MARRIAGE, WOMEN
Defoe, Daniel
-PRIDE
De La Rochefoucauld, François Duc
-ABILITY, BETRAYAL, EVIL, FAME, FOOLISHNESS, FORGIVENESS,
JEALOUSY, MONEY, SINCERITY, SMOKING, VANITY, WEAKNESS,
WORDS
DeLuzy, Dorothee
-FORGIVENESS, SIN
DeMoss, Nancy Leigh
-CHURCH, IMMORALITY
DeVries, Peter
-WEIGHT
Deitz, Steven
-BETRAYAL
Delius, Frederick
-MUSIC
Descartes, Rene
-ABILITY
Dickens, Charles
-AGE, BURDENS, CARE, CLEANLINESS, CLOTHING, CRUELTY,
CYNICISM, FORGIVENESS, FUN, HAPPINESS, HOLIDAYS,
LAUGHTER, SALVATION, TIME, TRAVEL, USEFULNESS, YEARNING
Dickinson, John
-UNITY
Dickinson, Emily
-BOOKS, SERMONS, SERVICE, SUCCESS
Dickson, Paul
-CERTAINTY
Diller, Phyllis
-AGE
Dinesen, Isaac
-HEALING & HEALTH
Disney, Walt
-ENTERTAINMENT
Disraeli, Benjamin
-CHRISTIANITY, CRITICISM, ECONOMICS, EDUCATION, EXPERIENCE,
FEAR, FOOLISHNESS, GREATNESS, IGNORANCE, KINDNESS,
KNOWLEDGE, MUSIC, OPPORTUNITY, QUOTATIONS, ROMANCE,
SINCERITY, SUCCESS, THOUGHTS, TIME, TRAVEL, VALUE
Ditka, Mike
-ACTION
Dobson, James
-TIME
Donne, John
-EQUALITY, PRESENCE OF GOD, PRIDE

Douglas, Charles
   -FAVOR
Douglas, William Orville
   -FREE SPEECH
Dow, Lorenzo
   -FAVOR
Dowd, Maureen
   -ACTION
Doyle, Arthur Conan (Sir)
   -KNOWLEDGE
Drake, Tom
   -MATERIALISM
Drew, Elizabeth
   -BOOKS
Drucker, Peter
   -FUTURE, SUCCESS, WORK
Dryden, John
   -MERCY, MUSIC, PATIENCE, PERFECTION, ROMANCE, SECRETS,
      SERMONS, VICTORY, VISION
DuBois, W. E. B.
   -LIBERTY
Duclos, Charles
   -REPUTATION
Duewel, Wesley L.
   -ACTION
Dunsany, Lord (Edward Plunkett)
   -TRAVEL
Durant, Will
   -GOVERNMENT, SPEECH, WORDS
Durante, Jimmy
   -SUCCESS
Durrell, Lawrence
   -JEALOUSY

Earhart, Amelia
   -ADVERSITY, DEDICATION
Eastman, Dick
   -PRAYER, SIN
Ebner-Eschenbach, Marie von
   -FORGIVENESS
Edelman, Marion Wright
   -ACTION, CHILDREN, DEDICATION
Edison, Thomas
   -AMBITION, BOREDOM, CRITICAL THINKING, DEDICATION,
      EDUCATION, FAILURE, INTELLIGENCE, MEMORY, OPPORTUNITY,
      PERSEVERANCE, PLANS, RESPONSIBILITY, SUCCESS, TECHNOLOGY,
      WORK

Edward VIII, King
-CHILDREN, LOVE, ROMANCE
Edwards, Jonathan
-LIFE, PREACHERS, REVIVAL, TIME
Edwards, Michael
-ACCOUNTABILITY
Edwards, Tryon
-EVIL
Einstein, Albert
-ANGER, ATHEISM, AUTHORITY, BEAUTY, CARELESSNESS, CLOTHING,
    COMPASSION, CREATIVITY, CRITICAL THINKING, EDUCATION,
    EQUALITY, EVIL, FACTS, FAME, FIGHTING, FUTURE, GOD,
    HAPPINESS, HEALING & HEALTH, IMAGINATION, INTELLIGENCE,
    LAW, MIRACLES, OPTIMISM v. PESSIMISM, PERSEVERANCE,
    ROMANCE, SCIENCE, SUCCESS, TEACHING, TECHNOLOGY, TESTS,
    THOUGHT, TRAVEL, TRUTH, UNDERSTANDING, UNITY, VALUE,
    WAR, WEIGHT, WISDOM, WORDS
Eisenhower, Dwight D.
-AMERICA, ARGUMENTS, BURDENS, CHANGE, EQUALITY, JUSTICE,
    MILITARY, PACIFISM, PEACE, SOCIALISM, WAR, WEAKNESS, WORK
Eldridge, Paul
-CRIME
Eliot, George
-ANIMALS, CRUELTY, GOSSIP, HATE, JEALOUSY, JOY, MERCY, PEACE,
    QUESTIONS, SIN, UNITY
Eliot, T. S.
-LONELINESS, MUSIC
Elizabeth I (Queen)
-DOCTRINE, LAST WORDS, TIME, WORLDLINESS
Elliot, Elizabeth
-TEMPTATION
Elliot, Jim
-ALTRUISM, DEDICATION, EVANGELISM, GIVING, LIFE, SERVICE
Ellis, Albert
-RESPONSIBILITY
Ellis, Alice
-VANITY
Ellis, Havelock
-BEAUTY, TECHNOLOGY, WAR
Ellis, James
-LAZINESS, UGLINESS
Ellis, W. T.
-HOLIDAYS
Embury, Emma Catherine
-PURITY
Emerson, Ralph Waldo
-CAUSE, CONCENTRATION, CRIME, CYNICISM, DARKNESS,
    ENTERTAINMENT, EQUALITY, FAME, FEAR, FUN, FUTURE,

INDIVIDUALITY, INTELLIGENCE, JOY, KINDNESS, LANGUAGE,
LAZINESS, MIRACLES, OPINION, PATIENCE, PRIDE, QUIETNESS,
SCIENCE, SERMONS, TEMPER, TRAVEL, TRUTH, VOTING, WISDOM,
WORDS, WORK, WORSHIP

Epictetus
-WISDOM
Eramus, Desiderius Gerhard
-EXPERIENCE
Erskine, Thomas (Lord)
-JOBS
Esar, Evan
-FAMILY
Euripides
-FOOLISHNESS
Evans, Bergen
-DEMOCRACY
Evans, Robert C.
-FAITH
Evans, White
-AMERICA
Everett, Alexander
-VOTING
Everett, Carol
-ABORTION
Everett, Edward
-BOOKS, BOREDOM, BURDENS, EDUCATION, FAME, , OPTIMISM v.
        PESSIMISM, PACIFISM
Everett, Ray Gene
-ANXIETY, LAZINESS, LONELINESS, TEACHING, VOTING,

Faber, Frederick William
-KINDNESS
Fairbanks, Douglas (Sr.)
-LAST WORDS
Faraday, Michael
-SCIENCE
Farreli, Michael
-COURAGE
Feherty, David
-FAILURE
Feltham, Owen
-ZEAL
Fénelon, François
-CARE, DEDICATION, GOD, PRAYER, SERMONS, TEMPTATION, TIME,
        VANITY, WAR
Feulner, Edwin
-WELFARE

Fielding, Henry
-MODESTY, MONEY
Fields, W. C.
-LAST WORDS, POLITICS
Finney, Charles G.
-BACKSLIDING, CHURCH, CONVERSION, EVANGELISM, JUDGMENT,
    NEED, PASSION, PREACHERS, REPENTENCE, REVIVAL, SALVATION
Finod, J. de – SEE De Finod, J.
Fish, Hamilton
-PATRIOTISM
Fitzgerald, F. Scott
-FAMILY, TESTS
Flavel, John
-LAW
Fletcher, John
-COMPASSION, THOUGHT
Foch, Ferdinand (Marshall)
-EVANGELISM, MILITARY, PASSION,
Forbes, B.C.
-BUSINESS
Ford, Henry
-ABILITY, ADVERSITY, AGE, BUSINESS, CRITICAL THINKING,
    DEDICATION, JUSTICE, SUCCESS, WORK
Foster, Richard
-ACTION, DISCIPLESHIP, DISCIPLINE, GOD, HUMILITY, MIRACLES,
    SERVICE, WORDS, WORSHIP
Fox, George
-HOLINESS
France, Anatole
-EDUCATION
Francis (of Assisi)
-ACCOMPLISHMENT, PREACHERS
Francis de Salas
-GENTLENESS
Frank, Anne
-CHILDREN, COURAGE, HAPPINESS, KINDNESS, LAZINESS, NATURE,
    SERVICE, WORDS
Franke, Emil
-DEMOCRACY
Franklin, Benjamin
-ACCOMPLISHMENT, ACTION, ADVICE, AGE, AMERICA, ANGER,
    APPEARANCE, BEAUTY, BIBLE, BUSINESS, CARELESSNESS,
    CRITICISM, ECONOMICS, EDUCATION, ENEMIES, EPITAPHS,
    ETERNITY, EXPERIENCE, FAILURE, FOOLISHNESS, FRIENDSHIP,
    FUTURE, GAMBLING, GOD, GOSSIP, GREATNESS, HOPE, HUMILITY,
    HYPOCRISY, KINDNESS, LAST WORDS, LAW, LAZINESS, LIBERTY,
    LIFE, LUST, MARRIAGE, MATERIALISM, MIRACLES, MONEY, NAMES,
    NEGLECT, ORGANIZATION, PASSION, PATIENCE, PEACE, POWER,

PREACHERS, PRIDE, PROSPERITY, QUOTATIONS, REPUTATION,
SECRETS, SIN, SPORTS, TAXES, TEENAGERS, TEMPTATION, TIME,
TOLERANCE, TRUTH, UGLINESS, UNDERSTANDING, UNITY,
VALUE, VANITY, VOTING, WEIGHT, WELFARE, WISDOM, WORDS,
WORK, YEARNING, YOUTH

Fraser, J. O.
  -EVANGELISM
Frederick the Great
  -LAST WORDS
Freeman, Beatrice and Ira
  -FOOD
French, Marilyn
  -CHILDREN
Freud, Anna
  -CREATIVITY
Friedman, Milton
  -LAZINESS
Fromm, Erich
  -NEED, ROMANCE
Frost, Robert
  -AGE, EDUCATION, FOOD, JUSTICE, LIBERALS, LIFE, SPEECH, TRAVEL,
    WORDS, WORK
Froude, James Anthony
  -EXPERIENCE
Fulbright, William
  -DEMOCRACY
Fuller, Thomas
  -CHILDREN, COUNSEL, DARKNESS, FAILURE, FAME, HOPE, HYPOCRISY,
    MARRIAGE, SERMONS, SIN, TEACHING, VISION, WOMEN, WORSHIP,
    ZEAL

Gaebelein, Frank E.
  -THOUGHT
Galilei, Galileo
  -GOD, NATURE, TEACHING, TRUTH
Gallagher, Robert
  -CHANGE
Gandhi, Mahatma
  -CHRIST, PEACE
Garfield, James
  -LAST WORDS, LYING
Garrick, David
  -EPITAPHS
Garth, Samuel (Sir)
  -WORSHIP
Gay, John
  -FALSE WITNESS, IGNORANCE, PURITY, REPUTATION

Geddie, John
   -DEDICATION, EVANGELISM
Gedge, Peter
   -EPITAPHS
Gerstner, Lou
   -RESPONSIBILITY, TIME
Getty, J. Paul
   -BUSINESS
Gibbs, Nancy
   -MIRACLES
Gipp, George
   -SPORTS
Gildersleeve, Virginia
   -ABILITY
Giles, Henry
   -INDIVIDUALITY
Gladden, Washington
   -SALVATION
Gladstone, William
   -EDUCATION, FAME, GOVERNMENT, INDIVIDUALITY, JUSTICE, PRIDE
Glasgow, Ellen
   -MEN
Glenconner, Pamela
   -CHILDREN
Godfrey, Arthur
   -TAXES
Godwin, Gail
   -TEACHING
Goethe, Johann Wolfgang von
   -BEAUTY, BOLDNESS, COMPLAINTS, COUNSEL, CREATIVITY, CULTURE,
      DECISIONS, ENCORUAGEMENT, FOOLISHNESS, GOVERNMENT,
      HOPE, IGNORANCE, INDIVIDUALITY, LANGUAGE, LAUGHTER,
      METHODS, NEED, UNITY, VICTORY, WEAKNESS
Goldsmith, Oliver
   -ECONOMICS, LAW, SERMONS
Goldwater, Barry
   -WELFARE
Goodrich, Samuel
   -ABUSE
Gordon, A. J.
   -PRAYER, REVIVAL
Gracian, Baltasar
   -FOOLISHNESS
Graham, Billy
   -CHARACTER, CHRIST, HUMOR, PERSEVERANCE, TEMPER

Graham, Katherine
   -FUN

Gramsci, Antonio
- OPTIMISM v. PESSIMISM
Graves, Richard
- COMPLAINTS
Gray, Albert
- DEDICATION, FAILURE
Gray, Thomas
- IGNORANCE
Green, Keith
- CHRISTIANITY, JUDGMENT, MUSIC, RESPONSIBILITY, TIME, WORSHIP
Greenley, Jan
- CONDEMNATION
Greentree, Isaac
- EPITAPHS
Griffith, John
- CHURCH
Grotius, Hugo
- LAST WORDS
Gurnall, William
- DEDICATION, FEAR, SERMONS
Gutenberg, Johann
- TECHNOLOGY, TRUTH
Guyon, Jeanne
- COURAGE, DISCIPLESHIP

Haines, Edison
- RESPONSIBILTY
Hale, Matthew (Sir)
- CLOTHING
Hale, Nathan
- LAST WORDS, PATRIOTISM
Hall, John
- SERMONS
Hall, Joseph
- CARE, ECONOMICS, FALSE WITNESS, FOOLISHNESS, NEGLECT,
    REPUTATION, SERMONS
Hall, Robert
- FAITH, FALSE TEACHING
Halliburton, Thomas
- ECONOMICS, IGNORANCE
Ham, Mordecai
- NEED,
Hammarskjold, Dag
- CREATIVITY, LONELINESS

Hansen, Mark Victor
- PROSPERITY

Hare, A. W. and J.C.
-EVIL, FOOLISHNESS, GOD, INDEPENDENCE, LANGUAGE, TOLERANCE
Harris, Sydney
-AGE, YOUTH
Harris, William
-GOD
Harvard, William
-FALSE TEACHING, LUST, POPULARITY
Harvey, William
-EPITAPHS
Hastings, Selina (Countess)
-LAST WORDS
Hauerwas, Stanley
-ATHEISM
Havner, Vance
-BROKENESS, CHURCH, EVANGELISM, HEAVEN & HELL, HOLINESS,
NEGLECT, PREACHERS, REVIVAL, SALVATION, SERVICE, VISION
Hawking, Stephen
-SALVATION
Hawthorne, Nathaniel
-EVIL, HAPPINESS, HYPOCRISY, PASSION, POPULARITY, SERMONS,
UGLINESS
Hazlitt, William
-LYING, TEACHING
Hearst, William Randolph
-NEWS, TRUTH
Heasley, Jacquelyn K.
-MERCY
Heinlein, Robert A.
-FOOLISHNESS, ROMANCE, TAXES
Heine, Heinrich
-BOOKS, FORGIVENESS, LAST WORDS, MUSIC, PAIN, UGLINESS
Helps, Arthur (Sir)
-WEAKNESS
Hemingway, Ernest
-TRAVEL
Hendricks, Howard
-CONCENTRATION
Henry, King (IV)
-FOOD
Henry, Matthew
-DISCIPLESHIP, GOD, GRACE, LIFE, LUST, NEWS, PAIN, PURITY,
SALVATION, TEMPTATION, TRIALS & TRIBULATIONS
Henry, Patrick
-CAUSE, CHRISTIANITY, EXPERIENCE, HISTORY, LIBERTY, PACIFISM,
PATRIOTISM, TRUTH
Henshaw, Joseph
-WORSHIP

Herbert, George
- CARE, FOOLISHNESS, TEACHING
Herford, Oliver
- MUSIC
Herrick, Robert
- TAXES, WORLDLINESS
Hession, Roy
- BROKENESS, REVIVAL
Highet, Gilbert
- READING
Hill, Napoleon
- CONCENTRATION, DECISIONS
Hillary, Edmund (Sir)
- ENTERTAINMENT, VICTORY,
Hillingdon, Alice (Lady)
- SEX
Hitler, Adolph
- ART, GOVERNMENT, LIES, LYING, TRUTH
Hoadley, Benjamin
- FORGIVENESS
Hobbes, Thomas
- LAST WORDS, LUST, ROMANCE, WAR
Hoffer, Eric
- CERTAINTY, FACTS, IGNORANCE
Holland, Josiah
- INDIVIDUALITY, PURITY, TESTS, WISDOM, WOMEN
Holmes, Oliver Wendell
- AGE, APOLOGY, JUSTICE, LANGUAGE, MUSIC, QUIETNESS,
     REPUTATION, SECRETS, UNITY, VOTING
Holtz, Lou
- ABILITY, SPORTS
Hooke, William
- WAR
Hooker, Richard
- ZEAL, LAW, PROSPERITY
Hoover, Herbert
- AGE, AMERICA, CHILDREN
Hope, Anthony
- INTELLIGENCE
Hope, Bob
- AGE, ENTERTAINMENT
Hopkins, Mark
- DECISIONS
Howard, Harlan
- MUSIC
Howe, Edgar Watson
- CRIME, GOSSIP, HYPOCRISY, MONEY

Hubbard, Elbert
  -REPUTATION, WELFARE, WOMEN
Hubbard, Frank
  -BUSINESS, MEN, POLITICS
Hubble, Edwin
  -SCIENCE
Hugo, Victor
  -AGE, DEATH, MUSIC, YOUTH
Humboldt, Alexander
  -CULTURE, EQUALITY
Hume, David
  -CULTURE, FALSE TEACHING, TEMPER, TESTIMONY, UGLINESS,
    YEARNING
Hunt, Josh
  -ACTION
Huss, John
  -DEDICATION, JOY
Huxley, Aldous
  -ORGANIZATION, POPULARITY
Huxley, Thomas
  -INDIVIDUALISM, SCIENCE, WISDOM

Inge, Dean
  -GAMBLING
Inge, William
  -LIBERALISM
Ingersoll, Robert Green
  -TESTS, THEOLOGY
Ironside, H. A.
  -PREACHERS, TRUTH
Irving, Washington
  -CHANGE, EVIL, IMAGINATION, PERSEVERANCE, PROSPERITY,
    SADNESS, TEMPER, WOMEN, YEARNING

Jackson, Andrew
  -VICTORY
Jackson, Thomas "Stonewall"
  -LAST WORDS
Jameson, Anna Brownell
  -FORGIVENESS
Jarquin, G. A.
  -FALSE WITNESS, HOLINESS, PREACHERS
Jarry, Alfred
  -GOD
Jay, Arthur
  -QUESTIONS

Jay, John
  -GOD
Jefferson, Thomas
  -ADVICE, AGE, ANXIETY, ARGUMENTS, BIBLE, BOOKS, CHRIST,
     DEMOCRACY, EDUCATION, EPITAPHS, EQUALITY, EXPERIENCE,
     FUTURE, GAMBLING, GOVERNMENT, HONESTY, HUMOR,
     IGNORANCE, INDEPENDENCE, JOURNALISM, LAST WORDS,
     LIBERTY, MERCY, MONEY, NATURE, OPINION, PEACE, POWER,
     PREJUDICE, PROSPERITY, QUOTATIONS, RESPONSIBILITY,
     STRENGTH, SUCCESS, TEMPTATION, TRAVEL, TRUTH, VICTORY,
     WEIGHT, WELFARE, WORK, WORSHIP
Jerome, Jerome K.
  -ALCOHOL
Johnson, Ben
  -FAME
Johnson, Harry G.
  -MEN
Johnson, Lyndon B.
  -CRIME, JOURNALISM, LEADERSHIP
Johnson, Samuel
  -COMPLAINTS, CRIME, EQUALITY, LANGUAGE, NEGLECT,
     TEMPTATION, TESTIMONY
Jones, Bob
  -FAITHFULNESS
Jones, Clarence W.
  -DEDICATION, HUMILITY
Jones, E. Stanley
  -CONVERSION
Jones, Franklin
  -ATHEISM, WAR
Jones, John Paul
  -ABILITY
Jortin, John
  -FAVOR
Joseph, Chief
  -TRUTH
Joubert, Joseph
  -INTELLIGENCE, QUESTIONS, QUOTATIONS, UNDERSTANDING,
     WEAKNESS
Jud, Gerald
  -CHURCH

Kafka, Frank
  -SIN
Kant, Immanuel
  -TESTIMONY

Landor, Walter Savage
-ERROR, GREATNESS
Lanier, Sydney
-MUSIC
Larson, Doug
-AGE
Latimer, Hugh
-PERSECUTION
Lavater, Johann Kaspar
-BOLDNESS, CLOTHING, FOOLISHNESS, FORGIVENESS, USEFULNESS, VALUE, WEAKNESS
Law, Henery
-PRESENCE OF GOD
Law, William
-MERCY
Lawrence, Brother
-KNOWLEDGE, LIES, WORSHIP
Lawrence, D. H.
-ROMANCE
Lazarus, Emma
-IMMIGRATION
Leavell, Don
-GOSSIP
Leighton, Robert
-FORGIVENESS, HUMILITY
Lencioni, Patrick
-DISCIPLINE, SUCCESS
Lenin, Vladimir
-TEACHING, TRUTH
Leroux, Pierre
-USEFULNESS
Levant, Oscar
-MUSIC
Levine, Michael
-CHILDREN
Levy, Martin
-AGE
Lewis, C.S.
-ACTION, ARGUMENTS, ATHEISM, BROKENESS, CHRIST, CHRISTIANITY, CHURCH, DISCIPLESHIP, ETERNITY, GOD, HEAVEN & HELL, LIFE, MATERIALISM, MERCY, MIRACLES, PAIN, PASSION, PERSECUTION, PROSPERITY, REPENTENCE, SERVICE, SPEECH, TEACHING, TIME, TRIALS & TRIBULATIONS, TRUTH, WORDS, WORSHIP, YOUTH
Lincoln, Abraham
-AMERICA, ANIMALS, APPEARANCE, ARGUMENTS, BIBLE, BOOKS, BUSINESS, CRITICISM, CRITICAL THINKING, DEMOCRACY, ENEMIES, EQUALITY, FAITH, FRIENDSHIP, GOD, GOVERNMENT,

HAPPINESS, HONESTY, HYPOCRISY, JUSTICE, LAW, LIBERTY, LIES,
LYING, MERCY, NAMES, PATRIOTISM, POLITICS, POWER,
PREJUDICE, PROPERTY, READING, RESPONSIBILITY, SADNESS,
SINCERITY, STRENGTH, VOTING, WAR, WEAKNESS, WELFARE,
WISDOM, WORK

Linton, Lynn
- WEAKNESS

Lippman, Walter
- CRITICAL THINKING, LEADERSHIP, PROPERTY

Livingstone, David
- EVANGELISM

Livy, Titus
- EXPERIENCE

Locke, John
- EDUCATION, EVIL, GENTLENESS, LANGUAGE, NAMES, PAIN,
PREJUDICE, PROPERTY, UNDERSTANDING, WELFARE, WORDS

Logan, John A.
- MUSIC

Lombardi, Vince
- DEDICATION, SPORTS

Long, Huey P.
- LAST WORDS

Longfellow, Henry Wadsworth
- CRITICISM, DISAPPOINTMENT, ENEMIES, EQUALITY, LAZINESS,
MUSIC, PURITY, SADNESS, SECRETS, VISION

Longworth, Alice Roosevelt
- EGO

Louis XIII (King)
- CRUELTY

Lovell, Mary Anne Lacy
- UNITY

Lowell, Amy
- BOOKS

Lowell, James
- CREATIVITY, DEMOCRACY, EXPERIENCE, VOTING, WEAKNESS

Lucado, Max
- CHANGE

Luce, Clare Booth
- GOOD

Luther, Martin
- ACTION, ANXIETY, BETRAYAL, BURDENS, CHURCH, CULTURE,
DISCIPLESHIP, ENEMIES, FAITH, FEAR, GOD, GRACE, LAW, NATURE,
NEED, OBEDIENCE, PASSION, PRAYER, PREACHERS,
RESPONSIBILITY, SERMONS, TEACHING, TEMPTATION,
THEOLOGY, TRIALS & TRIBULATIONS, TRUTH, WISDOM

Lyman, Abbott
- ANGER

Lytton, Edward George
   -JOURNALISM, LAW, MONEY, MUSIC, SUICIDE, VANITY, WORDS

MacArthur, Douglas
   -AGE, ANXIETY, PACIFICISM, YOUTH
MacArthur, John
   -OBEDIENCE, SERVICE
Macauley, Thomas
   -CHARACTER
MacDonald, David
   -BIBLE
MacDonald, George
   -FEAR, INDEPENDENCE, OBEDIENCE, POLITICS, STRENGTH, YEARNING
MacDonald, Gordon
   -CHARACTER, TIME
Machiavelli, Niccolo
   -ELECTIONS, GOVERNMENT, LAW, LIBERTY, PROPERTY, TRUTH
Maclaren, Alexander
   -LOVE
Macphail, Agnes
   -TESTS
Madison, James
   -ABUSE, EDUCATION, KNOWLEDGE, PROPERTY, WELFARE
Mahood, J. W.
   -NEED
Manilius, Anicius
   -DEATH
Mann, Horace
   -GIVING, TEACHING
Manning, Brennan
   -FAITH, SIN
Manton, Thomas
   -SIN
Marshall, Peter
   -FAITH, SIN
Martial, Marcus
   -FAME
Martin, Al
   -PERFECTION
Martyn, Henry
   -ACTION, PRAYER
Marvin, Frederic
   -VALUE
Marx, Karl
   -SOCIALISM
Matthews, William F.
   -DISAPPOINTMENT

Maxwell, John
 -ATHEISM, DISCIPLESHIP, EVANGELISM, PASSION
McGarvie, Grace
 -ABORTION
M'Cheyne, Robert Murray
 -ABILITY, FEAR, MERCY, PRAYER, PREACHERS, SERVICE, TRIALS
McCain, John
 -CHANGE, VALUES
McCracken, Mary
 -CHILDREN
McIntyre, D. M.
 -REVIVAL
McLaren, Brian
 -BIBLE, CULTURE, JUDGMENT
McLaughlin, Mignon
 -APOLOGY, MONEY, ROMANCE, WOMEN
McLuhan, Marshall
 -TECHNOLOGY
McManus, Erwin
 -DECISIONS, HYPOCRISY, LIFE
Mead, Margaret
 -WORDS
Meader, Oscar
 -EPITAPHS
Meir, Golda
 -MEN, PEACE, PREJUDICE, WAR
Melville, Herman
 -ALTRUISM, TRAVEL
Mendez, Carl
 -ABILITY
Mencken, Henry Louis
 -CYNICISM, FREE SPEECH, SOCIALISM, WOMEN
Mercier, Alfred
 -FUTURE
Merrill, William P.
 -MUSIC
Michelangelo
 -ART, PERFECTION
Mill, John Stuart
 -ACCOUNTABILITY, CAUSE, COURAGE, IMMORALITY, INDIVIDUALITY,
    LIBERTY, OPINION, PACIFISM, PREJUDICE, WAR, WEAKNESS
Miller, Dennis
 -ALCOHOL
Milton, John
 -APOLOGY, DARKNESS, GOOD, INDIVIDUALITY, LAW, LIBERTY, NEWS,
    SADNESS, VICTORY, WEIGHT, WISDOM, WOMEN, YEARNING
Mincher, Thomas
 -VOTING

OPTIMISM v. PESSIMISM, ORGANIZATION, PACIFISM, PAIN,
PATRIOTISM, PERFECTION, PERSECUTION, PERSEVERANCE,
POLITICS, POWER, PREJUDICE, PRESENCE OF GOD, PRIDE, PURITY,
QUOTATIONS, READING, REPUTATION, ROMANCE, SADNESS,
SALVATION, SCIENCE, SECRETS, SERMONS, SEX, SIN, SINCERITY,
SOCIALISM, SPORTS, SUCCESS, SUICIDE, TAXES,TEACHING,
TEENAGERS, TEMPER, TEMPTATION, TESTIMONY, TESTS,
THEOLOGY, THOUGHTS, TIME, TOLERANCE, VANITY, VISION,
VOTING, WAR, WOMEN, WEIGHT, WELFARE, WISDOM, WOMEN,
WORDS, YOUTH, ZEAL

Murray, Andrew
-FAITH, LOVE, NEED, REVIVAL
Murray, Nicholas
-PRAYER

Nash, Ogden
-GOD
Nathan, George Jean
-CRITICAL THINKING, VOTING
Nathan, Rich
-PROSPERITY
Nee, Watchman
-DISCIPLESHIP, HOLINESS, OBEDIENCE
Nelson, Horatio (Lord)
-FAME, LAST WORDS
Nettleton, Asahel
-EVANGELISM
Newbigin, Leslie
-PREACHERS
Newton, Isaac (Sir)
-GOD, NATURE, SCIENCE, SERMONS, TRIALS & TRIBULATIONS, VISION,
ZEAL
Newton, John
-ANXIETY, BURDENS, CHANGE, EXPERIENCE, PREACHERS
Nietzsche, Fredrich
-ATHEISM, CARELESSNESS, CHURCH, FAITHFULNESS, GOD, HOPE,
STRENGTH, UNDERSTANDING
Nixon, Richard
-PREJUDICE
Noble, Louis
-SALVATION
Nohria, Nitin
-ABILITY
Noonan, Peggy
-AMERICA
Nouwen, Henri
-CHRISTIANITY, PREACHERS

Noyes, Alfred
   -TESTIMONY

O'Rourke, P. J.
   -READING
Olford, Stephen
   -PASSION, REVIVAL
Onassis, Jacqueline Kennedy
   -CHILDREN
Ortberg, John
   -CHRISTIANITY, FAITH, HOLINESS, HUMILITY, SIN, THOUGHT,
      WORDS, WORLDLINESS
Orwell, George
   -EQUALITY, GOVERNMENT, LANGUAGE, LYING, PACIFISM, SOCIALISM,
      SPORTS, TRUTH
Osler, William (Sir)
   -EXPERIENCE
Ovid (Publius Ovidius Naso)
   -EVIL, FORGIVENESS, MARRIAGE, WELFARE
Owen, John
   -FAITH, OBEDIENCE, PATIENCE, POWER

Pace, Peter (Gen)
   -LAW
Paddleford, Clementine
   -STRENGTH
Paine, Thomas
   -ARGUMENTS, COURAGE, PREJUDICE, REPUTATION, TAXES, VALUE,
      VICTORY
Panton, D. M.
   -REVIVAL
Parker, Dorothy
   -BEAUTY, UGLINESS
Parker, Theodore
   -AMERICA, DEMOCRACY, DISAPPOINTMENT, PRIDE
Parr, Ellen
   -BOREDOM
Parsons, Rob
   -FAMILY, TIME
Pascal, Blaise
   -CERTAINTY, FEAR, HAPPINESS, KNOWLEDGE, LONELINESS, METHODS,
      PURITY, SPORTS, TEMPTATION, UNITY, VANITY, WORDS, ZEAL
Pasteur, Louis
   -CHILDREN
Paterno, Joe
   -ACCOMPLISHMENT, SUCCESS

Patton, George S. (Gen)
  -COURAGE, DEDICATION, INTELLIGENCE, LEADERSHIP, MEN,
    MILITARY, NAMES, PACIFISM, PATRIOTISM, USEFULNESS, VICTORY,
    WAR
Pavese, Cesare
  -MEMORY
Peale, Norman Vincent
  -DEDICATION, SUCCESS
Peck, Clay
  -CHRIST
Penn, William
  -DISAPPOINTMENT, ECONOMICS, EVIL, FALSE WITNESS, JEALOUSY,
    KINDNESS, LUST, NEGLECT, PERSECUTION, POPULARITY, POWER,
    SECRETS, SIN, SPEECH, VANITY, WORDS, ZEAL
Pentecost, George
  -SERMONS
Pepper, George
  -THEOLOGY
Pepper, Claude
  -DEMOCRACY
Percival, Margaret
  -TEMPTATION
Peter, Lawrence J.
  -MIRACLES
Peterson, Eugene
  -DISCIPLESHIP, LOVE, MONEY
Phelps, William Lyon
  -READING
Philby, Harold
  -BETRAYAL
Phillips, George
  -SEX
Phillips, Wendell
  -BOREDOM, GOD, RESPONSIBILITY, WORDS
Piaget, Jean
  -TESTS
Picasso, Pablo
  -ART, CHILDREN
Pierce, Bob
  -HOLINESS
Pierson, A. T.
  -PRAYER, REVIVAL
Pink, A. W.
  -DEDICATION
Piper, John
  -PRAYER

Rand, Ayn
- ACCOMPLISHMENT
Ravenhill, Leonard
- BOREDOM, CHRISTIANITY, CHURCH, DEATH, DEDICATION,
    DISCIPLESHIP, ENTERTAINMENT, EPITAPHS, EVANGELISM, FAITH,
    GOSSIP, HEAVEN & HELL, HISTORY, HOLINESS, JUDGMENT, LIFE,
    LUST, MONEY, MUSIC, NEGLECT, OBENDIENCE, OPINION,
    OPPORTUNITY, ORGANIZATION, POPULARITY, POWER, PRAYER,
    PREACHERS, PURITY, REPENTANCE, REVIVAL, SALVATION,
    SERMONS, SIN, SINCERITY, TIME, TRUTH, WORLDLINESS,
    WORSHIP, ZEAL
Reagan, Ronald
- ABORTION, ACCOUNTABILITY, AGE, AUTHORITY, COURAGE,
    CRUELTY, ECONOMICS, ELECTIONS, EVOLUTION, GOVERNMENT,
    IMMORALITY, LIBERALISM, LIBERTY, NATURE, OPTIMISM v.
    PESSIMISM, PATRIOTISM, POLITICS, POWER, PREJUDICE,
    QUOTATIONS, SOCIALISM, SPORTS, STRENGTH, TAXES, WAR,
    WELFARE
Redman, Matt
- WORSHIP
Reidhead, Paris
- OBEDIENCE, REPENTANCE
Reynolds, Friedrich
- SIN
Richter, Jean Paul Friedrich
- FORGIVENESS
Rieux, Madame de
- MARRIAGE
Riordan, Daniel J.
- OPTIMISM v. PESSIMISM
Roberts, Evan
- DEDICATION, NEED
Rochefoucauld, François - SEE De La Rochefoucauld, François Duc
Rodges, James
- LAST WORDS
Rohn, Jim
- DISCIPLINE, FRIENDSHIP
Rogers, Samuel
- PURITY, UNDERSTANDING
Rogers, Will
- ALCOHOL, ANGER, ANIMALS, BUSINESS, CRIME, CRITICISM,
    ECONOMICS, EXPERIENCE, FUN, GOVERNMENT, HUMOR,
    IGNORANCE, INTELLIGENCE, JOURNALISM, LANGUAGES,
    LIBERALISM, LYING, MONEY, NAMES, NEWS, OPINION, OPTIMISM v.
    PESSIMISM, ORGANIZATIONS, PAIN, PERFECTION, POLITICS,
    PREJUDICE, PROPERTY, QUESTIONS, QUOTATIONS, SPEECH,
    SPORTS, SUCCESS, TAX, TEACHING, TEENAGERS, THEOLOGY,
    TIME, TOLERANCE, TRAVEL, UGLINESS, USEFULNESS, VANITY,

VICTORY, VOTING, WAR, WELFARE, WOMEN, WORDS, YOUTH, ZEAL

Roland, Jeanne-Marie
- LIBERTY

Rooney, Andy
- WEIGHT

Roosevelt, Eleanor
- ANGER, BEAUTY, BETRAYAL, COMPLAINTS, DARKNESS, FAVOR, HAPPINESS, INTELLIGENCE

Roosevelt, Franklin Delano
- DEMOCRACY, ECONOMICS, ELECTIONS, FEAR, FREE SPEECH, OPINIONS, PERSEVERANCE, POWER, TAXES, VOTING, WAR, YOUTH

Roosevelt, Theodore
- ALTRUISM, BOLDNESS, CRITICISM, CYNICISM, DEDICATION, DEMOCRACY, EDUCATION, ELECTIONS, FAILURE, FAME, FIGHTING, FREE SPEECH, HOPE, IMMIGRATION, LAW, NATURE, POPULARITY, QUOTATIONS, STRENGTH, WAR, WORK, YOUTH

Rosenbaum, George
- FOOD

Rossetti, Christina
- SADNESS

Rossetti, Dante Gabriel
- ATHEISM

Rousseau, Jean Jacque
- CHRIST, EDUCATION, EVIL, FAME, LAST WORDS, PROPERTY, PROSPERITY

Roux, Joseph
- FALSE WITNESS

Rowland, Helen
- MEN

Royden, A. M.
- ETERNITY

Rumsfeld, Donald
- CERTAINTY, PACIFISM, WAR

Runyon, Damon
- FAITH

Ruskin, John
- HONESTY, IDOLATRY, UGLINESS, WORK

Russel, Bertrude Arthur
- CERTAINTY, CRITICAL THINKING, EVOLUTION, WAR

Ruth, Babe
- PRESEVERANCE, SPORTS

Rutherford, Samuel
- ENCOURAGEMENT, MIRACLES, TRIALS & TRIBULATIONS, WORLDLINESS

Ryle, J. C.
- CHRISTIANITY, FEAR, TRUTH

Sewell, George
  -SUICIDE
Shakespeare, William
  -CHILDREN, COMPASSION, DECISIONS, EPITAPHS, EVIL, EXPERIENCE,
    FALSE TEACHING, IDOLATRY, NAMES, NEGLECT, PERSEVERANCE,
    PURITY, QUESTIONS, REPUTATION, ROMANCE, SALVATION,
    SERMONS, SUICIDE, TEMPTATION, UGLINESS, VICTORY, WISDOM,
    WOMEN, WORDS, ZEAL
Shaw, Henry Wheeler
  -FUN, KNOWLEDGE, LAZINESS, METHODS, MONEY, OPINION, SUCCESS,
    TRUTH, UGLINESS, VANITY, WISDOM
Shaw, George Bernard
  -BUSINESS, CYNICISM, DEMOCRACY, ECONOMICS, EVIL, FAMILY, FEAR,
    FIGHTING, GAMBLING, GOVERNMENT, HONESTY, HUMOR,
    IDOLATRY, IMAGINATION, INTELLIGENCE, JOBS, LANGUAGE,
    LUST, MILITARY, NEWS, QUESTIONS, REPUTATION, SECRETS,
    SERVICE, SPORTS, TEACHING, TESTS, TOLERANCE, UNITY,
    USEFULNESS, VISION, WEIGHT, WELFARE, WORDS, YEARNING,
    YOUTH
Shawcross, Hartley
  -IMMORALITY
Sherman, William (General)
  -ELECTIONS, VOTING, WAR
Sidney, Philip (Sir)
  -SUCCESS, WORLDLINESS
Simone, John
  -CHANGE, CULTURE
Simpson, Alexander
  -FAITH
Singh, Sadhu Sundar
  -BURDENS, CHRISTIANITY, GOD
Skaggs, Ricky
  -CHURCH
Smiles, Samuel
  -AGE, BURDENS, FAILURE, HOPE, INDIVIDUALITY, JOBS, METHODS,
    YOUTH
Smiley, Sarah Frances
  -FEAR
Smith, Adam
  -FUTURE, PROPERTY, SCIENCE, VANITY, WORK
Smith, Alfred
  -DEMOCRACY
Smith, Chuck
  -PRAYER
Smith, Dodie
  -FAMILY
Smith, Fred
  -ACCOMPLISHMENT, CHANGE, DEMOCRACY, WORK

Smith, Hannah Whitall
   -FAITH, GOD, HUMILITY, MONEY
Smith, Oswald J.
   -EVANGELISM, REVIVAL
Smith, Sydney
   -ARGUMENTS, FOOLISHNESS, MUSIC, ZEAL
Smithers, David
   -NEED, PRAYER, REVIVAL
Snead, Sam
   -SPORTS
Snyder, Howard A.
   -NEED
Socrates
   -CHRIST, EQUALITY, IGNORANCE, REPUTATION, SEX, TEACHING,
      WISDOM
South, Robert
   -COMPASSION, IDOLATRY, PRIDE, REPUTATION
Sparks, T. Austin
   -CHURCH
Speer, Robert E.
   -OBEDIENCE, PRAYER
Spencer, Ichabod
   -DECISIONS, SALVATION
Sprat, Thomas
   -ZEAL
Spurgeon, Charles H.
   -ALTRUISM, APPEARANCE, BIBLE, CHRISTIANITY, DEDICATION,
      DISCIPLINE, ECONOMICS, EVANGELISM, FACTS, FAITH, GIVING,
      GOD, GOODNESS, HOLINESS, IMAGINATION, KINDNESS,
      KNOWLEDGE, PASSION, PERFECTION, PRAYER, PREACHERS,
      REPENTANCE, REVIVAL, SALVATION, SPEECH, TEMPTATION,
      THEOLOGY, TRIALS & TRIBULATIONS, WISDOM, WORDS,
      WORLDLINESS
St. John, Henry
   -LAW
Stachura, Mike
   -CHURCH, COMPASSION
Staël, Anne Louis Germaine de (Madame)
   -MEN
Stalin, Josef
   -GOVERNMENT, MEMORY, TAXES, WAR
Stanley, Andy
   -DEDICATION, TIME, WORK
Steele, Richard
   -READING, WEAKNESS
Stengel, Casey
   -SPORTS

Sterne, Lawrence
  -CLOTHING, MERCY
Stevenson, Adlai
  -ADVICE, CARELESSNESS, GOVERNMENT, JOURNALISM, KNOWLEDGE,
    LIBERTY, POPULARITY, QUIETNESS
Stevenson, Robert Louis
  -FUN, QUIETNESS, TRAVEL
Stewart, James A.
  -REVIVAL
Stewart, Potter
  -ABORTION, PROPERTY
Stillingfleet, Benjamin
  -IDOLATRY
Stine, Brad
  -AMERICA
Stokowski, Leopold
  -MUSIC
Stone, Elizabeth
  -CHILDREN
Stott, John R. W.
  -EVANGELISM
Stowe, Harriet Beecher
  -DEMOCRACY, SADNESS, SPEECH, TOLERANCE, WORDS
Stravinsky, Igor
  -ENTERTAINMENT
Stroebel, Lee
  -CHRIST
Stuart, Edwin
  -BUSINESS
Studd, Charles T.
  -COMPASSION, DEATH, DEDICATION, EVANGELISM, FAMILY, PRAYER
Sullivan, Anne
  -CHILDREN, SUCCESS
Sunday, Billy
  -CONVERSION,
Swedenborg, Emanuel
  -INTELLIGENCE
Swetchine, Anne Sophie
  -INDIVIDUALITY
Swift, Jonathan
  -ARGUMENTS, BOLDNESS, CONDEMNATION, CRITICISM, ENEMIES,
    FALSE TEACHING, FALSE WITNESS, GOVERNMENT, HATE, JUSTICE,
    LAUGHTER, LAW, MODESTY, PREJUDICE, TRUTH, VISION,
    WEAKNESS, ZEAL
Swindoll, Chuck
  -HAPPINESS, LIFE, WORSHIP
Syrus, Publilius
  -SUCCESS

Tolkien, J. R. R.
- COUNSEL, PERFECTION, PLANS, TRAVEL
Tozer, A.W.
- CHRIST, CHURCH, CONVERSION, DEDICATION, DISCIPLESHIP, FAITH,
    GOD, HOLINESS, LYING, MERCY, NEED, POPULARITY, PRAYER,
    PREACHERS, REVIVAL, SERVICE, SPEECH, THEOLOGY, WORSHIP
Trueblood, Elton
- CULTURE
Truman, Harry S
- ADVICE, FREE SPEECH, HUMILITY, LEADERSHIP, OPTIMISM v.
    PESSIMISM, POPULARITY,
Twain, Mark
- AGE, AMBITION, ANXIETY, BIBLE, BOOKS, CHILDREN, CHRIST,
    CLOTHING, CRITICISM, EDUCATION, ENTERTAINMENT,
    EVOLUTION, FACTS, FEAR, GOVERNMENT, GREATNESS, HEALING
    & HEALTH, HUMOR, IMAGINATION, INTELLIGENCE, JEALOUSY,
    JOURNALISM, JOY, KINDNESS, LANGUAGE, MEMORY, NAMES,
    NEED, NEWS, OPPORTUNITY, OPTIMISM v. PESSIMISM, PACIFISM,
    PAIN, PREJUDICE, PROPERTY, READING, RESPONSIBILITY,
    ROMANCE, SADNESS, SERMONS, SMOKING, SPEECH, TAXES,
    TEENAGERS, TRAVEL, TRUTH, VANITY, VICTORY, WEIGHT,
    WELFARE, WOMEN, WORDS, YOUTH, ZEAL
Tyndale, William
- SERVICE
Tyndall, Jonathan
- CONDEMNATION, FACTS

Udall, Stewart
- POWER
Useph, Michael
- PREACHERS

Vade, Jean Joseph
- UGLINESS
Vall, Claude du
- EPITAPHS
Van Buren, Abigail
- RESPONSIBILITY
Vaughn, Bill
- CHILDREN
Vidal, Gore
- ELECTIONS
Villa, Francisco "Pancho"
- LAST WORDS
Vincent, John
- SADNESS

Vinci, Leonardo da
  -ARGUMENTS, WORK
Voltaire
  -ANIMALS, CARE, EQUALITY, FOOD, GOOD, GOVERNMENT,
    INTELLIGENCE, LAST WORDS, PRESECUTION, SECRETS, TRUTH,
    WAR, WORDS, WORK
Von Braun, Wernher
  -SCIENCE, TECHNOLOGY
Von Ebner, Marie
  -VANITY
Von Goethe, Johann Wolfgang
  -BEAUTY, BOLDNESS, COMPLAINTS, COUNSEL, CREATIVITY,
    DECISIONS, ENCOURAGEMENT, FOOLISHNESS, GOVERNMENT,
    HOPE, IGNORANCE, INDIVIDUALITY, LANGUAGE, LAUGHTER,
    METHODS, NEED, UNITY, VICTORY, WEAKNESS

Wadsworth, Charles
  -AGE
Wagner, C. Peter
  -HOLINESS
Ward, William Arthur
  -CRITICISM, IMMORALITY, SPORTS, TEACHING
Warner, Charles Dudley
  -READING
Warner, Harold
  -CHRISTIANITY
Warren, Earl
  -JOURNALISM, JUSTICE, SPORTS
Warren, Rick
  -CHARACTER, ETERNITY, LIFE, MATERIALISM, PROSPERITY, SERVICE
Washington, Booker T.
  -ALTRUISM, FACTS, HATE, KINDNESS, RESPONSIBILITY, STRENGTH,
    WELFARE
Washington, George
  -ANXIETY, EPITAPHS, FAITH, FRIENDSHIP, GAMBLING, GOD,
    GOVERNMENT, HONESTY, LAWS, MERCY, MILITARY, NEGLECT,
    ORGANIZATION, PACIFISM, PEACE, POLITICS, REPUTATION,
    SERVICE, VANITY, VOTING, WAR, WOMEN
Watson, Thomas
  -ABILITY, COMPLAINTS, ETERNITY, FAITH, HEALING & HEALTH,
    KNOWLEDGE, MONEY, PRAYER, SINCERITY
Watt, Gordon
  -CHRISTIANITY, LIFE, PASSION
Watts, Isaac
  -GOD
Watterson, Bill
  -ART, CHILDREN

Wayland, Francis
   -ACCOMPLISHMENT
Webster, Daniel
   -ACCOUNTABILITY, AMERICA, APPEARANCE, AUTHORITY,
      CREATIVITY, GOOD, GOVERNMENT, INDEPENDENCE,
      INTELLIGENCE, JUDGMENT, SERVICE, UNITY, VOTE
Webster, Noah
   -LANGUAGE
Weil, Simone
   -CULTURE
Welles, Orson
   -WEIGHT
Wellesley, Arthur (Duke of Wellington)
   -VICTORY
Wells, David
   -WORLDLINESS
Wells, H. G.
   -WAR
Wesley, John
   -APPEARANCE, CHURCH, CLEANLINESS, ETERNITY, GOD, GOOD,
      INDIVIDUALITY, JUDGMENT, LOVE, MONEY, NEGLECT, PASSION,
      PEACE, PROSPERITY, SPEECH, UNITY, WORDS
West, Mae
   -ERROR
Whately, Richard
   -PERSECUTION
Whipple, Edwin Percy
   -NAMES, READING
White, E. B.
   -DEMOCRACY
White, William
   -ENCOURAGEMENT
Whitefield, George
   -DOCTRINE, HOLINESS, PRAYER, PURITY
Whitehead, Alfred North
   -AGE, YOUTH
Whitman, Walt
   -AGE, BUSINESS, DEMOCRACY, FRIENDSHIP, GIVING, GREATNESS,
      MIRACLES
Whittier, John
   -VICTORY, WORDS
Wigglesworth, Smith
   -BIBLE, FAITH
Wilburn, Steve
   -CHURCH
Wilcox, Ella Wheeler
   -VALUE

Wilde, Oscar
- BEAUTY, CHRIST, CYNICISM, EXPERIENCE, FAITHFULNESS,
    FORGIVENESS, GOSSIP, HUMOR, LAST WORDS, LAUGHTER,
    MARRIAGE, MEMORY, MEN, OPTIMISM v. PESSIMISM, PREJUDICE,
    QUESTIONS, REPENTANCE, ROMANCE, VALUE, WISDOM, WOMEN
Wilkerson, David
- BROKENESS, JUDGMENT, JUSTICE, LAW, MIRACLES, MONEY, PRAYER,
    PROSPERITY, REVIVAL, SIN, TIME, TRIALS & TRIBULATIONS,
    TRUTH, VICTORY
Williams, Tennessee
- BETRAYAL
Wilmot, James (Earl)
- CHILDREN
Wilson, Bill
- NAMES, REPUTATION, TEENAGERS, USEFULNESS, YOUTH
Wilson, Harold
- CHANGE, OPTIMISM v. PESSIMISM
Wilson, Woodrow
- AMERICA, CHANGE, DEMOCRACY, ECONOMICS, ENEMIES,
    INTELLIGENCE, OPTIMISM v. PESSIMISM, PACIFISM, PATIENCE,
    UNITY, VANITY, VICTORY, VISION, WAR
Winchell, Walter
- DEMOCRACY, GOSSIP
Winter, William
- PURITY
Witherspoon, John
- FEAR
Winthrop, Robert Charles
- VOTING
Wittgenstein, Ludwig
- LAST WORDS
Wolcott, John
- CARE
Wolfe, Thomas
- LIBERALISM, VANITY
Wooden, John
- ABILITY, SERVICE
Woods, C. Stacey
- CHURCH
Wordsworth, William
- GOOD, ZEAL
Wren, Christopher (Sir)
- EPITAPHS
Wright, Frank Lloyd
- ENTERTAINMENT, WORDS
Wurmbrand, Richard
- PERSECUTION, SIN

Wurtz, Robert
　-CHURCH
Wycliffe, John
　-BIBLE

Xavier, Frances (St.)
　-CHILDREN, PASSION, TIME

Yancey, Phillip
　-BIBLE, GRACE, HYPOCRISY, LOVE, PRIDE
Yeats, William Butler
　-JOY
Yohannan, K. P.
　-GIFTS
Young, Edward
　-ENCOURAGEMENT, SADNESS, VISION

Zacharias, Ravi
　-COMPASSION, REVIVAL
Zayas, Jose
　-ACTION
Zepp, S. R.
　-FAVOR, POPULARITY
Zigler, Zig
　-ABILITY
Zimmerman, Ray
　-REPUTATION
Zwemer, Samuel M.
　-EVANGELISM, NEED

MODERN PROVERBS